The Beverage Testing Institute's
Buying Guide
to Spirits

Other Publications from the Beverage Testing Institute
and Sterling Publishing Co., Inc.

Buying Guide to Imported Wines

Buying Guide to the Wines of North America

Buying Guide to Inexpensive Wines

Buying Guide to Beer

The Beverage Testing Institute's
Buying Guide
to Spirits

Edited By Alan S. Dikty

Sterling Publishing Co., Inc.
New York

Dedication

To my mother

Julian May Dikty

The family tradition continues.

Library of Congress Cataloging-in-Publication Data Available

10 9 8 7 6 5 4 3 2 1

Published by Sterling Publishing Company, Inc.
387 Park Avenue South, New York, N.Y. 10016
© 1999 by the Beverage Testing Institute
Distributed in Canada by Sterling Publishing
$^{c}/o$ Canadian Manda Group, One Atlantic Avenue, Suite 105
Toronto, Ontario, Canada M6K 3E7
Distributed in Great Britain and Europe by Cassell PLC
Wellington House, 125 Strand, London WC2R 0BB, England
Distributed in Australia by Capricorn Link (Australia) Pty Ltd.
P.O. Box 6651, Baulkham Hills, Business Centre, NSW 2153, Australia

Sterling ISBN 0-8069-2865-4

Acknowledgements

I'd like to thank, in no particular order, the following people who helped me, generously giving of their time and knowledge: Rick Cooper, Craig Goldwyn, Charles Laverick and Marc Dornan of the Beverage Testing Institute; Jim Krejcie of Applied Beverage Technologies; Bill Owens of the *American Brewer*; Michael Jackson; Joe Danno of the late and much missed Bucket 'o Suds; and Mark Gruber, wine and spirits instructor at Northwestern University and Romano Bros. Beverages.

Table of Contents

The Beverage Testing Institute's
Buying Guide
to Spirits

Foreword

From the shimmering, pre-dinner Martini, to the post-prandial grappa in hand-blown glass, consumers, bartenders and restaurateurs are showcasing the "water of life." The aromas and flavors of spirits, and their origins, are so diverse that they can be bewildering.

Today's new interest in them required a new primer. This is it: a timely distillation of the essential information, from an enthusiastic and diligent student of drinks, both offbeat and classic, combined with concise tasting notes from a panel of neutral judges.

Alan Dikty is a drinks industry insider, writer, and editor who has never lost his sense of excitement about the world of alcohols. We meet regularly to drink, dine, and talk. Whenever I see him, he has some new spiritous manifestation for me to experience. If I come bearing a gift, it had better be alcoholic or gastronomic—and unusual. Now he explains the universe of distillates with clarity, crispness, and deftly executed dashes of color.

Michael Jackson

London, 1999

*Author of The World Guide to Whisky and
Michael Jackson's Malt Whisky Companion*

"If I had a thousand sons, the first human principle I would teach them should be, to forswear thin potations."
– **William Shakespeare (Falstaff, Henry IV, Part 2)**

Introduction

The purpose of this book is to provide the interested reader and distilled beverage consumer with a basic understanding of the history and production of spirits, along with tasting panel ratings and tasting notes for a substantial cross-section of commercial brands of spirits. The Beverage Testing Institute of Chicago, Illinois, has provided the ratings and tasting notes. BTI, which rates spirits, wines, and beers, is the world's largest and oldest independent beverage testing service. It does not accept advertising from companies that submit their products for analysis. The results of the panel judgings are published in various periodicals, including its own monthly journal *Tastings*, and online at http://www.tastings.com.

BTI tasting panels consist of select trained beverage industry professionals and BTI personnel. Beverage samples are tasted "blind" in a controlled clinical environment. Spirits are judged on the basis of appearance, color, aroma, character, and palate.

What Are Spirits?

Alcohol, in its basic meaning, is a hydroxyl compound such as ethanol or methanol. Fermentation is the process by which an organic substance (usually a sugar) is converted by a single-celled microorganism such as yeast into alcohol. A spirit is distilled alcohol. Spirits distillation is the process of heating a fermented liquid, evaporating off the alcohol as vapor, and then condensing it back into liquid form.

How Are Spirits Made?

Spirits can be made from any organic substance that can be fermented to create alcohol. Most alcoholic beverages are made by fermenting fruit- or grain-based solutions. A still extracts alcohol from a fermented liquid by boiling it and then condensing the alcohol vapors, which evaporate from the boiling liquid at a lower temperature than water. For example, an 8% alcohol by volume (ABV) wine or beer distills into a 20% ABV distillate when it is run through a typical simple pot still. The alcohol content can be further increased by additional redistillations that further concentrate the alcohol and reduce the total volume of liquid.

The first and most basic type of still is the *pot still*, which is an enclosed vessel (the kettle or "pot") that narrows into a tube at the top to collect alcohol vapor that evaporates when the fermented contents are boiled. The tube bends downward off the top of the pot and runs through a bath of cold water. This causes the alcohol vapor to condense back into liquid and drain into a container at the end of the tube. Most pot stills are made from copper. They are considered "inefficient" in that they carry over a percentage of water and chemical compound vapors along with the alcohol vapor. This "inefficiency" can be considered an advantage when producing spirits such as brandy and whiskey that have distinctive flavors.

The *column* or *continuous still* has two enclosed copper or stainless steel columns. The fermented liquid is slowly fed down into the top of the first column while steam is sent up from the bottom. The rising steam strips the alcohol from the descending liquid and carries it over into the second column where it is recirculated and concentrated to the desired percentage of alcohol. Column stills are more "efficient" than pot stills in that they extract a higher concentration of alcohol. They are favored for neutral-flavored spirits such as vodka and white rum and also for industrial alcohol.

How Are Spirits Measured?

Spirits are measured by alcohol content. Different scales are used in different countries. Most countries use alcohol by volume (ABV), also known as the Gay-Lussac system, which expresses alcohol content as a percentage of the total liquid volume of the beverage. A 40% ABV spirit contains 40% alcohol. In the United States, the *proof* scale of measurement is used, with the proof of a spirit being double the ABV. Thus a 40% ABV spirit is 80° proof. A degree symbol is customarily used when expressing proof.

How Are Spirits Classified?

Generally speaking, spirits are classified by the fermented material that they are distilled from. Whiskies, Vodka, Gin and most types of Schnapps are made by distilling a kind of beer made from grain. Brandy is made from fermented grape juice, and Fruit Brandy is made from other fruits. Rum and Cane Spirits derive from fermented sugar cane juice or molasses. Tequila and Mezcal come from the fermented pulp of the agave plant. Fortified wines are hybrid beverages in that they are a blend of fermented wine and distilled spirits (usually Brandy).

About BTI

The Beverage Testing Institute (BTI) was founded in 1981, with a mission to create fair and reliable reviews. This led to the institute publishing a well-respected magazine, *International Wine Review*, from 1984 through 1990. Subsequently, the results of BTI tastings were featured first in *Wine & Spirits* magazine, and then in *Wine Enthusiast* magazine as an independently produced buying guide. Other publications, including the *Chicago Tribune* and the *Washington Post*, have showcased BTI reviews over the years.

In 1994, BTI began to review beer and spirits in addition to wine. Today, we are the largest full-time beverage review body in the world. In 1999 BTI will review more than 10,000 wines, beers, and spirits. We produce a bimonthly publication, *Tastings, The Journal*, which carries up-to-the-minute reviews and insight from the world of wine, beer, and spirits. *Tastings, The Journal* is supported by our website, Tastings.com, which carries a database of over 30,000 of our recent reviews, hundreds of articles, links to all things gustatory, including thousands of winery, distillery, and brewery listings and hundreds of links and reviews linked to retailers around the country so that you don't have to pull your hair out looking for that hard to find spirit. Additionally, Tastings.com features the Insiders Club, a subscription service that alerts consumers to highly rated products from upcoming issues of *Tastings, The Journal*. This puts you ahead of the crowd, before those products sell out. To subscribe, or to get more information about either *Tastings, The Journal* or the Insiders Club at Tastings.com, please email us at journal@tastings.com; write to us at Beverage Testing Institute, 310 South Peoria Street, Suite 504A, Chicago, IL 60607, or phone us at 312-226-7857.

In addition to these endeavors, BTI produces a range of books. These include *Buying Guide to the Wines of North America, Buying Guide to Imported Wines, Buying Guide to Inexpensive Wines from Around the World, Buying Guide to Beer,* and *Buying Guide to Spirits*. They are all published by Sterling Publishers. Other publications that currently carry our reviews and musings include *Restaurant Hospitality* magazine, *All About Beer* magazine, Epicurious—the website of *Bon Appetit* and *Gourmet* magazines, AOL at keyword "Drinks," and FooFoo.com, to name a few.

BTI employs eight people on a full-time basis. The BTI staff, in no particular order, is: Craig Goldwyn-web guy/guru, Jon Winsell-operations/man of databases, Richard Cooper-marketing/man of cigars, Charles Laverick-wine/outdoorsman, Marc Dornan-wine/beer/resident alien, Catherine Fallis-Journal/woman of words, Debra Bernstein-whip cracker/chef, Rochelle Calhoun-teamster/Latin dance instructor and Señor Alan Dikty-man of letters/spirits. As a group, we spend lots of time listening to Johnny Cash.

How BTI Reviews Are Created

My name is Charles Laverick. I am responsible for wine, beer, and spirits reviews at the Beverage Testing Institute, but I don't do it alone, and that is the difference between a BTI review and a review from a critic who is working alone. My colleague, Marc Dornan, sits in on nearly all reviewing sessions, as does an invited guest panelist chosen specifically for expertise in a given region. This panel of three convenes on a daily basis at 9:30 a.m. to conduct our spirits reviews, and uses a proprietary methodology that insures that BTI reviews are both consistent and meaningful.

The Quality Question

There are two widely used scales in the product-testing universe. These are the qualitative assessment scale and the consumer acceptance scale. While a consumer scale asks the taster whether or not they like a particular product and if so to what degree, a qualitative scale is focused on a given product's quality vis-à-vis its peers (i.e., Qualitative: "In the world of Bourbon is this a world-class product?" Consumer: "Do you personally care for Bourbon or the flavors of this Bourbon in particular?").

Other critics don't fit neatly into either category, but tend to put a great deal of weight on their personal spirits preferences, regardless of style. After some experimentation, we have come to the conclusion that a strict qualitative scale does the job better, as it more accurately reflects the consumer's understanding of the 100-point scale to which our reviews are ultimately translated. A 90 score signifies an excellent spirit in the wider context of the spirits of the world. Do consumers, or even professionals, like the flavors caused by aging whiskey in Sherry casks? Currants in Vodka? Oak-aged Tequila? We think these questions are best left to marketing professionals. Instead, a BTI panelist will look at any style of spirit as valid. We are not engaged in an endless quest for heavy whiskies with lots of oak or any other uniform spirits style. We believe diversity should be celebrated and endeavor not to set out on any stylistic crusades or frame qualitative decisions along purely stylistic guidelines. A BTI panelist will set aside any personal prejudices about particular spirit styles (Islay Scotch whiskies, flavored Vodkas, pot still Rums, etc.) and judge spirits solely on their own merits. Using this challenging set of criteria necessitates a small, well-trained cadre of tasting professionals.

Three's Company

While a consumer approach requires a broad base of panelists to get an accurate sample size, a qualitative approach requires a small number of professionals who specialize in whatever spirit or region that is being addressed, and have demonstrated expertise as such. A BTI panel will most always contain exactly three panelists. Why three? Relying on a single taster carries with it a certain risk. After all everyone has a bad day. However, panels have their faults as well. Chief among them is the "law of averages." Two panelists give a product low marks while two give a product high marks—the net result? The data "averages" to describe a middle-of-the-road product, what none of the four originally thought. Borrowing an approach from the Australian show system, we use a panel of three. This eliminates the inherent problem of averaging; helping to guarantee that what we print is what we meant to say. That's not to say that we won't on occasion have an extra individual in the room. We make a point of being transparent, welcome qualified visitors, and are happy to have them "audit" a session. Additionally, new panelists, or those without depth of experience in the category du jour will always "audit" the tasting (meaning their scores won't count) until such time as they are deemed ready. In order to achieve and maintain the desired level of consistency, the panel of three contains our two in-house tasting directors and one specifically invited expert for the "guest slot." This allows us to review very large categories, with most panelists seeing the majority, if not all, of the spirits in that category. Finally, all panelists undergo a rigorous warm-up exercise that is not only educational but allows each individual to determine whether or not they are "up to snuff" for the day's tasting. If there is the slightest doubt, that panelist is replaced by one of the other trained in-house tasters.

A Banded Approach

The scoring system that our panelists use is quite narrow, and hence testings are easily repeatable. A score is given only after a thorough, objective assessment is made of a spirit's qualities. We have devised a system based on the bands in the 100-point scale, which are widely recognized and roughly correspond to a five-star style system. These bands are:

96-100	Superlative
90-95	Exceptional
85-89	Highly Recommended
80-84	Recommended
<80	Not Recommended

But those 100 point scores come later; when we are tasting we use a different scale in each of two rounds. After a thorough assessment of a spirit's characteristics, a panelist is asked to place it in one of four quality bands.

Round One

1 - A spirit that one would not recommend in the wider context of today's global spirits market (<80 points)
2 - A spirit of sound commercial quality, though not overly exciting (80-84)
3 - A very good spirit showing style and character, yet probably not of the highest merit (85-89)
4 - A spirit that may be at the highest quality levels (potentially 90+)

Those spirits that receive at least two scores of 4 are sent to the "merit round" whose scale is as follows:

Round Two

3 - A very good spirit, yet upon comparison with examples of the highest quality, not of the highest merit (88-89 points)
4 - A truly excellent spirit, of style and distinction (90-92)
5 - An outstanding spirit, though not quite one of the world's finest (93-95)
6 - A world-class spirit, providing one of the world's great spirits experiences (96-100)

This banded approach allows our tasters to think in broad terms of general quality without getting mixed up in the minutiae of adding up points for ageability, color, or aftertaste. Just like the consumer, we are addressing the spirit in question only in its totality. Further, individual tasters do not have to concern themselves with what constitutes the differences between an 88 or an 86 or a 90 and a 91. Finally, one of the chief advantages of this system is the large percentage of spirits tasted more than once. To witness, spirits scoring over the critical 90-point barrier are without exception tasted twice, a virtual guarantee that a spirit rated as such will be deserving of the accolades. Also, after the first round, all spirits that show a wide disparity in scoring between panelists (controversial) are re-tasted at a later date under first round parameters, as are many low-scoring spirits.

A Novel Permutation

Final scores are reached using a novel mapping process that does not average the three scores but instead uses the mode, a statistic much closer to what the panelists, as a group, are really saying. If, for instance, a spirit in the first round receives three scores of "3," the computer places it in the upper center of the (85-89) band and it is given a final score of 88 points. Should the third score be a 4 or a 2, the spirit in question would be given an 89 or an 86, respectively. The third score is used to move the final score up or down within the same band. Again, permutations that are controversial will be re-tasted. While the need to further narrow down scores within bands is a topic of some debate in the industry, we have taken the position that it is still in the consumer's interest to do so for the top four recommended bands: 80-84, 85-89, 90-95, and 96-100. Spirits falling in the lowest band (<80) are simply noted as not recommended (NR) and no further breakdown is attempted. We realize that there are many conflicting views about the 100-point scale, but feel that we have devised the fairest system for using the scale, one that has become a standard.

Description Is Key

In our continued attempt to lead the consumer "beyond the scores," we have been putting ever-greater emphasis on our descriptive evaluations. In order to continue this process, and also to insure thorough and consistent assessments, we use a comprehensive evaluation form in our tasting room. These forms translate directly to the final "tasting notes," which we try to print with every recommended spirit. (In instances where space doesn't permit this, all notes can be found on our website, www.tastings.com.) This form places an emphasis on objective structural information from color through intensity of finish. It covers several vital parameters and is amended with a final qualitative comment. This insures that all of our tasting notes are consistent in style, yet readable, while accurately conveying stylistic information to the consumer.

In order to make this descriptive information as consistent as possible (not to mention our qualitative assessments) we continue to rely heavily on our state-of-the-art tasting facility in Chicago. This room was specially designed to minimize external factors, and maximize our panelists concentration. Tasting at the same time of day, blind, under the same conditions, our panel continually works under ideal conditions. Hand in hand with our scorecard, we have specially designed tasting aids in order to standardize our tasting vocabularies. To this end we have even gone to the length of installing a state-of-the-art natural lighting system, paired with a standardized color palate for ever-greater consistency.

If all this sounds fanatical, it's because we are fanatical. Our institute is unique in the world of spirits. We provide the world's only full-time professional reviewing service. This is not a contest, and couldn't be further from your typical "set 'em up and knock 'em down" spirits fair. We take what we do seriously and train rigorously; both out of respect for producers and with an eye to providing the most trustworthy reviews a consumer can find.

one

✌

Brandy,
Eau de Vie,
and Grappa

✌

*"No, Sir, claret is the liquor for boys; port for men;
but he who aspires to be a hero must drink brandy."*

– **Samuel Johnson**

An Overview and History

The word Brandy comes from the Dutch word *brandewijn* ("burnt wine"), which is how the straightforward Dutch traders who introduced it to northern Europe from southern France and Spain in the 16th century described wine that had been "burnt," or boiled, in order to distill it.

The origins of Brandy can be traced back to the expanding Moslem Mediterranean states in the 7th and 8th centuries. Arab alchemists experimented with distilling grapes and other fruits in order to make medicinal spirits. Their knowledge and techniques soon spread beyond the borders of Islam, with grape Brandy production appearing in Spain and probably Ireland (via missionary monks) by the end of the 8th century.

Brandy, in its broadest definition, is a spirit made from fruit juice or fruit pulp and skin. More specifically, it is broken down into three basic groupings.

Grape Brandy is Brandy distilled from fermented grape juice or crushed but not pressed grape pulp and skin. This spirit is aged in wooden casks (usually oak), which colors it, mellows the palate, and adds additional aromas and flavors.

Pomace Brandy (Italian Grappa and French Marc are the best-known examples) is Brandy made from the pressed grape pulp, skins, and stems that remain after the grapes are crushed and pressed to extract most of the juice for wine. Pomace Brandies, which are usually minimally aged and seldom see wood, are an acquired taste. They often tend to be rather raw, although they can offer a fresh, fruity aroma of the type of grape used, a characteristic that is lost in regular oak-aged Brandy.

Fruit Brandy is the default term for all Brandies that are made from fermenting fruit other than grapes. It should not be confused with Fruit-Flavored Brandy, which is grape Brandy that has been flavored with the extract of another fruit. Fruit Brandies, except those made from berries, are generally distilled from fruit wines. Berries tend to lack enough sugar to make a wine with sufficient alcohol for proper distillation, and thus are soaked (macerated) in high-proof spirit to extract their flavor and aroma. The extract is then distilled once at a low proof. **Calvados**, the Apple Brandy from the Normandy region of northwestern France, is probably the best known type of Fruit Brandy. **Eau-de-vie** ("water of life") is the default term in French for spirits in general, and specifically for colorless fruit brandy, particularly from the Alsace region of France and from California.

Brandy, like Rum and Tequila, is an agricultural spirit. Unlike grain spirits such as Whisky, Vodka, and Gin, which are made throughout the year from grain that can be harvested and stored, Brandy is dependent on the seasons, the ripening of the base fruit, and the production of the wine from which it is made. Types of Brandies, originally at least, tended to be location-specific. (Cognac, for example, is a town and region in France that gave its name to the local Brandy.)

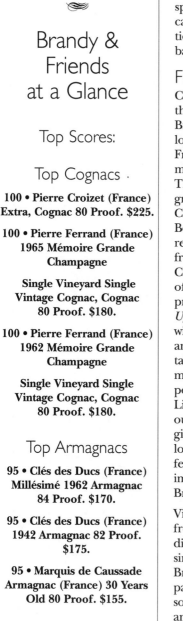

Brandy & Friends at a Glance

Top Scores:

Top Cognacs ·

100 • Pierre Croizet (France) Extra, Cognac 80 Proof. $225.

100 • Pierre Ferrand (France) 1965 Mémoire Grande Champagne

Single Vineyard Single Vintage Cognac, Cognac 80 Proof. $180.

100 • Pierre Ferrand (France) 1962 Mémoire Grande Champagne

Single Vineyard Single Vintage Cognac, Cognac 80 Proof. $180.

Top Armagnacs

95 • Clés des Ducs (France) Millésimé 1962 Armagnac 84 Proof. $170.

95 • Clés des Ducs (France) 1942 Armagnac 82 Proof. $175.

95 • Marquis de Caussade Armagnac (France) 30 Years Old 80 Proof. $155.

Important Brandy-making regions, particularly in Europe, further differentiate their local spirits by specifying the types of grapes that can be used and the specific areas (appellation) in which the grapes used for making the base wine can be grown.

French Brandies

Cognac is the best known type of Brandy in the world, a benchmark by which most other Brandies are judged. The Cognac region is located on the west-central Atlantic coast of France, just north of Bordeaux, in the departments of Charente and Charente-Maritime. The region is further subdivided into six growing zones: Grande Champagne, Petite Champagne, Bois Ordinaires, Borderies, Fins Bois, and Bons Bois. The first two of these regions produce the best Cognac and will frequently be so designated on bottle labels. Cognacs labeled *Fine Champagne* are a blend of Petite and Grande Champagne. The primary grapes used in making Cognac are *Ugni Blanc, Folle Blanche,* and *Colombard.* The wines made from these grapes are thin, tart, and low in alcohol; poor characteristics for table wines, but oddly enough, perfect for making Brandy. Cognac is double distilled in pot stills and then aged in casks made from Limousin or Troncais oak. All Cognacs start out in new oak to mellow the fiery spirit and give them color. Batches that are chosen for long-term aging are, after a few years, transferred to used, or "seasoned," casks that impart less of the oak flavor notes while the Brandy matures.

Virtually all Cognacs are a blend of Brandies from different vintages, and frequently, different growing zones. Even those from single vineyards or distilleries will be a mix of Brandies from different casks. As in Champagne, the production of local vineyards is sold to Cognac houses, each of which stores and ages Cognacs from different suppliers and then employs master blenders to draw from these disparate Brandies to create continuity in the house blends. Because there are no age statements on Cognacs, the industry has adopted some generally accepted terms to differentiate Cognacs. It is important to note that these terms have no legal status, and each Cognac shipper uses them according to his own criteria.

V.S./V.S.P./Three Star: (V.S., very superior; V.S.P.,very superior pale) A minimum of two years aging in a cask, although the industry average is four to five years.

V.S.O.P.: (very superior old pale) A minimum of four years cask aging for the youngest Cognac in the blend, with the industry average being between 10 and 15 years.

X.O./Luxury: (X.O., extra old) A minimum of six years aging for the youngest cognac in the blend, with the average age running 20 years or older. All Cognac houses maintain inventories of old vintage Cognacs to use in blending these top-of-the-line brands. The oldest Cognacs are removed from their casks in time and stored in glass demijohns (large jugs) to prevent further loss from evaporation and to limit excessively woody and astringent flavors. Luxury Cognacs are the very finest Cognacs of each individual Cognac house.

Armagnac is the oldest type of Brandy in France, with documented references to distillation dating back to the early 15th century. The Armagnac region is located in the heart of the ancient province of Gascony in the southwest corner of France. As in Cognac, there are regional growing zones: Bas-Armagnac, Haut-Armagnac, and Ténarèze. The primary grapes used in making Armagnac are likewise the *Ugni Blanc, Folle Blanche*, and *Colombard*. But distillation takes place in the unique *alambic Armagnacais*, a type of column still that is even more "inefficient" than a typical Cognac pot still.

The resulting brandy has a rustic, assertive character and aroma that requires additional cask aging to mellow it out. The best Armagnacs are aged in casks made from the local Monlezun oak. In recent years Limousin and Troncais oak casks have been added to the mix of casks as suitable Monlezun oak becomes harder to find.

Most Armagnacs are blends, but unlike Cognac, single vintages and single vineyard bottlings can be found. The categories of

Top Brandy

93 • RMS Distillery (CA) QE 14 Year Old Rare French Oak Aged Alambic Brandy 80 Proof. $116.

Top Calvados

95 • Coeur de Lion (France) 1977 Calvados Pays d'Auge 84 Proof. $223.95.

Top Spanish Brandy

93 • Antonio Barbadillo (Spain) Gran Reserva, Brandy de Jerez $27.

Top Grappa

98 • Jacopo Poli (Italy) 1997 Grappa Amorosa di Torcolato 86 Proof. $55/100ml.

Top Eau de Vie

96 • Moletto (Italy) Distillato D'Uva 80 Proof. $34.

Top Fruit Eau de Vie

100 • Jacopo Poli (Italy) 1997 Pear Brandy Stagione di Pere 86 Proof. $30/375 ml.

Armagnac are generally the same as those of Cognac (V.S., V.S.O.P., X.O., etc.). Blended Armagnacs frequently have a greater percentage of older vintages in their mix than comparable Cognacs, making them a better value for the discerning buyer.

Have Still, Will Travel

Up until the 1970s, portable *alambic Armagnacais* mounted on two-wheel carts were hauled among small vineyards in Armagnac by itinerant distillers called *bouillers de cru*. These traveling stills, alas, have mostly given way to larger fixed-in-place setups operated by farmer cooperatives and individual operators.

French Brandy is the catch-all designation for Brandy produced from grapes grown in other regions. These Brandies are usually distilled in column stills and aged in oak casks for varying periods of time. They are frequently blended with wine, grape juice, oak flavorings, and other Brandies, including Cognac, in order to smooth out the rough edges. Cognac-like quality designations such as V.S.O.P. and Napoleon are frequently used, but they have no legal standing.

Spanish Brandies

Brandy de Jerez is made by the Sherry houses centered around the city of Jerez de la Frontera in the southwest corner of Spain. Virtually all Brandy de Jerez, however, is made from wines produced elsewhere in Spain—primarily from the *Airen* grape in La Mancha and Extremadura—as the local Sherry grapes are too valuable to divert into Brandy production. Nowadays most of the distilling is likewise done elsewhere in Spain using column stills. It is then shipped to Jerez for aging in used Sherry casks in a solera system similar to that used for Sherry wine. A *solera* is a series of large casks (called butts), each holding a slightly older spirit than the previous one beside it. When brandy is drawn off (racked) from the last butt (no more than a third of the volume is removed) it is replenished with brandy drawn from the next butt in line all the way down the solera line to the first butt, where newly distilled brandy is added. This system of racking the brandy through a series of casks blends together a variety of vintages (some soleras have over 30 stages) and results in a speeding up of the maturation process.

Basic Brandy de Jerez Solera must age for a minimum of six months, *Reserva* for one year, and *Gran Reserva* for a minimum of three years. In practice, the best *Reservas* and *Gran Reservas* are frequently aged for 12 to 15 years. The lush, slightly sweet and fruity notes to be found in Brandy de Jerez come not only from aging in Sherry casks but also from the judicious use of fruit-based flavor concentrates and oak essence (*boise*).

Penedés Brandy comes from the Penedés region of Catalonia in the northeast corner of Spain near Barcelona. Modeled after the Cognacs of France and made from a mix of regional grapes and locally grown *Ugni Blanc* of Cognac, it is distilled in pot stills. One of the two local producers (Torres) ages in soleras consisting of butts made from French Limousin oak, whereas the other (Mascaro) ages in the standard non-solera manner, but also in Limousin oak. The resulting Brandy is heartier than Cognac, but leaner and drier than Brandy de Jerez.

Italian Brandies

Italy has a long history of Brandy production dating back to at least the 16th century, but unlike Spain or France there are no specific Brandy-producing regions. Italian Brandies are made from regional wine grapes, and most are produced in column stills, although there are now a number of small artisanal producers using pot stills. They are aged in oak for a minimum of one to two years, with six to eight years being the industry average. Italian Brandies tend to be on the light and delicate side with a touch of residual sweetness.

German Brandies

German monks were distilling Brandy by the 14th century and the German distillers had organized their own guild as early as 1588. Yet almost from the start, German Brandy (called *weinbrand*) has been made from imported wine rather than from the more valuable local varieties. Most German Brandies are produced in pot stills and must be aged for a minimum of six months in oak. Brandies that have been aged in oak for at least one year are called *uralt* or *alter* (meaning "older"). The best German Brandies are smooth, somewhat lighter than Cognac, and finish with a touch of sweetness.

U.S. Brandies

Brandy production in California dates back to the Spanish missions in the late 18th and early 19th centuries. In the years following the Civil War, Brandy became a major industry, with a substantial export trade to Europe by the end of the century. For a time Leland Stanford, founder of Stanford University, was the world's largest brandy producer. *Phylloxera* and National Prohibition almost shut down the industry in the 1920s.

Repeal started things up again, but as with the bourbon industry, the advent of World War II resulted in the brandy producers further marking time. Soon after the end of the war the industry commissioned the Department of Viticulture and Oenology at the University of California at Davis to develop a prototype "California-style" brandy. It had a clean palate, was lighter in style than most European Brandies, and had a flavor profile that made it a good mixer. Starting in the late 1940s, the California brandy producers began to change over to this new style.

Contemporary California Brandies are made primarily in column stills from table grape varieties such as the *Thompson Seedless* and *Flame Tokay*, although a handful of small new-generation Cognac-inspired pot distillers, such as Jepson and RMS, are using the classic *Ugni Blanc, Colombard,* and *Folle Blanche* grapes. California Brandies are aged for two to 12 years in used American oak (both Brandy and Bourbon casks) to limit woodiness in the palate, although the pot distillers also use French oak. Several California distillers, most notably Korbel, have utilized the Spanish solera method of maturing their Brandy. California Brandies do not use quality designations such as V.S.O.P. or stars. The more expensive brands will usually contain a percentage of older vintages and pot-distilled Brandies in the blend.

Latin American Brandies

In **Mexico** a surprising amount of wine is made, but it is little known outside of the country because most of it is used for Brandy production. Mexican Brandies are made from a mix of grapes, including *Thompson Seedless, Palomino,* and *Ugni Blanc.* Both column and pot stills are used in production whereas the solera system is generally used for aging. Brandy now outsells tequila and rum in Mexico.

South American Brandies are generally confined to their domestic markets. The best-known type is Pisco, a clear, raw Brandy from **Peru** and **Chile** that is made from *Muscat* grapes and double-distilled in pot stills. The resulting Brandy has a perfumed fragrance and serves as the base for a variety of mixed drinks, including the famous Pisco Sour.

Other Brandy Regions

Greece produces pot-distilled Brandies, many of which, such as the well-known Metaxa, are flavored with Muscat wine, anise, or other spices. Winemaking in **Israel** is a well-established tradition dating back thousands of years. But Brandy production dates back only to the 1880s when the French Jewish philanthropist Baron Edmond de Rothschild established what has become the modern Israeli wine industry along French lines. Israeli brandy is made in the manner of Cognac from *Colombard* grapes, with distillation in both pot and column stills and maturation in French Limousin oak casks. In the Caucasus region, along the eastern shore of the Black Sea, the ancient nations of **Georgia** and **Armenia** draw on monastic traditions to produce rich, intensely flavored pot still Brandies both from local grapes and from such imported varieties as *Muscadine* (from France), *Sercial,* and *Verdelho* (most famously from Madeira). **South Africa** has produced Brandies since the arrival of the first Dutch settlers in the 17th century, but these early spirits from the Cape Colony earned a reputation for being harsh firewater (*witblits,* white lightning, was a typical nickname). The introduction of modern production techniques and government regulations in the early 20th century gradually led to an improvement in the quality of local Brandies. Modern South African Brandies are made from *Ugni Blanc, Colombard, Chenin Blanc,* and *Palomino* grapes, produced in both pot and column stills, and aged for a minimum of three years in oak.

Pomace Brandies

Italy produces a substantial amount of Grappa, both of the raw, firewater variety and the more elegant, artisanal efforts that are made from one designated grape type and frequently packaged in hand-blown bottles. Both types of Grappa can be unaged or aged for a few years in old casks that will tame the hard edge of the spirit without imparting much flavor or color. Marc from **France** is produced in all of the nation's wine-producing regions, but is mostly consumed locally. Marc de gewürztraminer from Alsace is particularly noteworthy because it retains some of the distinctive perfumed nose and spicy character of the grape. California pomace Brandies from the **United States** are broadly in the Italian style and are usually called Grappas, even when they are made from non-Italian grape varieties. This is also true of the pomace Brandies from **Canada**.

Apple and Other Fruit Brandies

Normandy is one of the few regions in **France** that does not have a substantial grape wine industry. Instead it is apple country, with a substantial tradition of producing hard and sweet cider that in turn can be distilled into an Apple Brandy known as Calvados. The local cider apples, which tend to be small and tart, are closer in type to crab apples than to modern table apples. This spirit has its own *appellations*, with the best brands coming from *Appellation Contrôlée Pays d'Auge* near the Atlantic seaport of Deauville, and the rest in 10 adjacent regions that are designated *Appellation Réglementée*. Most *Pays d'Auge* and some of the better *Appellation Réglementée* are produced in pot stills. All varieties of Calvados are aged in oak casks for a minimum of two years. Cognac-style quality and age terms such as V.S.O.P. and Hors d'Age are frequently used on labels, but have no legal meaning. In the **United States**, Applejack, as Apple Brandy is called locally, is thought by many to be the first spirit produced in the British colonies. This colonial tradition has continued on the East Coast with the Laird's Distillery in New Jersey (established in 1780 and the oldest distillery in America). Apple Brandies that are more like eau-de-vie are produced in California and Oregon.

The fruit-growing regions of the upper Rhine River are the prime eau-de-vie production areas of Europe. The Black Forest region of Bavaria in **Germany**, and Alsace in **France**, are known for their Cherry Brandies (*Kir* in France, *Kirschwasser* in Germany), Raspberry Brandies (*Framboise* and *Himbeergeist*), and Pear Brandies (*Poire*). Similar eaux-de-vies are now being produced in the United States in California and Oregon. Some Plum Brandy is also made in these regions (*Mirabelle* from France is an example), but the best known type of Plum Brandy is *Slivovitz*, which is made from the small blue *Sljiva* plum found throughout **Eastern Europe** and the **Balkans**.

Brandy Reviews

Antinori (Italy)
Marchesi Antinori Tignanello Grappa 84 proof $30/375 ml.　　　**93**

Clear with a grayish cast. Medium-bodied. Sweet citrus, dried herbs, berries. Pungent aromas are complex and stylish. Smooth and well balanced in the mouth with a sense of delicacy. Finishes with a terrific persistence of flavor.

Asbach Uralt (Germany)
Asbach Uralt 80 proof $21.99.　　　**NR**

Askalon (Israel)
Askalon Grappa Di Segal 80 proof $12.99/375 ml.　　　**81**

Clear. Light- to medium-bodied. Oily texture. Slightly hot. Faint floral and pear flavors.

Antonio Barbadillo (Spain)
Antonio Barbadillo Gran Reserva, Brandy de Jerez. $27.　　　**93**

Dark mahogany. Full-bodied. Notes of dates, molasses, flan, leather. Rich, deep texture. Although heavily oriented toward brown spice elements, there is a rich core of fruit beautifully accented by soft wood notes. Very pungent finish. A powerhouse style that will enhance a good cigar.

Bisquit Dubouche (France)
Bisquit Dubouche Cognac Classique V.S. 80 proof $26.　　　**88**

Pale amber. Light-bodied. Golden raisins, herbs, honey. Soft and elegant. Delicate fruity notes in the finish.

Bisquit Dubouche VSOP Fine Champagne 80 proof $38.　　　**92**

Amber-orange. Medium-bodied. Soft texture. Perfume, dried peach, hazelnut. Flavors build with a warming, tangy and fruity finish.

Bisquit Dubouche Napoleon Fine Champagne 80 proof $69.　　　**93**

Dark amber, gold tint. Rich, creamy. Hot. Medium-bodied. Apricot, orange peel, bittersweet chocolate. Strong oak flavors. Superb range of flavors combined in a great structure. Lush fruity notes without being sweet.

Antonella Bocchino (Italy)
Antonella Bocchino Grappa di Moscato d'Asti 90 proof $37.99/375 ml.　　　**84**

Clear. Medium-bodied. Dried herbs, minerals. Relatively aromatic with a big herbal streak that plays out in the mouth. Oily on the palate with a mild burn to the finish.

Antonella Bocchino Grappa di Barbaresco 90 proof $43.99/375 ml.　　　**90**

Bright copper hue. Medium-bodied. Earth, roasted nuts, minerals. A wood-aged product that is complex both in aromatics and flavor. Quite smooth in the mouth with a slight perception of sweetness. Finishes with notable burn but retains fine length.

Brandy Peak Distillery (USA)
Brandy Peak Distillery Grappa 81.8 proof $21/375 ml.　　　**NR**

Brandy Peak Distillery Marc Brandy of Gewürztraminer 86.6 proof $24.95/375 ml.　　　**82**

Clear. Moderately light-bodied. Sweet herbs, minerals, slate. Very subtle aromatically with a lighter-styled palate that is well balanced with just a hint of heat on the finish.

Brillat Savarin (France)
Brillat Savarin VSOP, Armagnac 80 proof $29.99.   85
Gold with a light cast. Moderately light-bodied. Lightish sweet vanilla and earth aromas precede a rounded palate with hints of sweetness and an herbal backnote through the finish.

Busnel (France)
Busnel Calvados du Pays d'Auge, Vieille Réserve VSOP 80 proof $32.   89
Deep amber-orange hue. Attractive baked apple and caramel aromas. A smooth attack leads to a medium-bodied, slightly viscous mouthfeel. Drying, woody, smooth finish. Well rounded, with just a hint of fiery rusticity.

Ca' del Solo (USA)
Ca' del Solo Grappa di Moscato 84 proof $17.49/375 ml.   83
Clear. Medium-bodied. Peaches, sweet herbs, citrus. Quite fruity with a very aromatic quality. In the mouth this Grappa is rustic in style with a burn that builds at the finish, cutting short the delicate flavors.

Ca Rugate (Italy)
Ca Rugate Grappa di Recioto di Soave 86 proof $40/375 ml.   88
Clear. Medium-bodied with a creamy texture. Slight sweetness. Very warm. Some grassy flavors, with dried apricot and black pepper.

California Five Star (USA)
California Five Star Brandy 80 proof $6.99.   NR

Candolini (Italy)
Candolini Grappa Ruta 80 proof $35/L.   83
Sweet floral scents clash against oil and dirty solvent aromas. Lightly spiced, with a clean, tight palate. Bit of heat sneaks into the finish.

Caparzo (Italy)
Caparzo Grappa di Brunello 86 proof $55.   NR

Capezzana (Italy)
Capezzana Grappa di Carmignano Riserva 84 proof $65.   80
Pale copper hue with greenish highlights. Medium-bodied. Dried leaves, incense, wood, marjoram. Quite subtle aromatically with a straightforward brawny palate. A measure of heat cuts the finish short.

Carlos I (Spain)
Carlos I Solera Gran Reserva, Brandy de Jerez 80 proof $34.99.   82
Dark amber with a mahogany cast. Full-bodied. Notes of flan, walnuts, pipe tobacco. Heavy, rich texture. For all its weight, this is quite smooth on the palate. High dose of fragrance carries into the finish.

Carmel (Israel)
Carmel 3 Year Old Rishon Brandy 777 80 proof $13.99.   NR

Carmel 9 Year Old Rishon Brandy 100 80 proof $15.99.   NR

Castarède (France)

Castarède VSOP, Armagnac 80 proof $35.   **87**

Dark amber with a copper cast. Medium-bodied. Very pronounced complex aromas reminiscent of herbs and earth translate well onto a strongly flavored, rounded palate with a smooth, somewhat short finish. This has strong character and should appeal to connoisseurs.

Cerbois (France)

Cerbois VSOP, Bas-Armagnac 80 proof $28.   **80**

Amber with gold highlights. Moderately light-bodied. Quite a light perfumed style with mild citrus and vanilla flavors through to a brief finish. An easy drinking style.

Cerbois Réserve Personnelle, Bas-Armagnac 80 proof $50.   **83**

Amber with copper-tinted highlights. Medium-bodied. Sweet herbal and citrus-oil aromas reveal attractive caramel flavors on the sweetly nuanced palate. Rather pleasant though not hugely complex.

Ceretto (Italy)

Ceretto Grappa di Moscato 86 proof $62.99.   **97**

Clear. Moderately full-bodied. Citrus, tropical fruits, sweet herbs. Pungent in style, the aromatics are both forceful and appealing. The attack is extremely flavorful and well rounded, then clipped by a touch of heat at the finish. The flavors reemerge in a lengthy finale.

Ceretto Grappa di Nebbiolo da Barolo, "Brunate" 100 proof $71.50.   **88**

Clear. Moderately full-bodied. Pencil shavings, black fruits, minerals. Quite forceful in the nose with complex aromas and a hint of spirit. Quite fiery in the mouth but manages to finish flavorfully. Potent but well crafted.

Ceretto Wood Aged Grappa di Blange 86 proof $91.   **96**

Medium gold. Medium-bodied. Moderate sweetness. Very warm. Perfumed floral and herbal notes with honey and lemon. Well-integrated components.

William Chevaliers (Switzerland)

William Chevaliers Eau de Vie du Valais, Valais 84 proof $20/500 ml.   **88**

Rich scents of confection, pear, and minerals. Lightly textured with an elegant feel. Softer to the finish as sweet berry nuances are noted.

César Chiarella (Peru)

César Chiarella Pisco Puro 85.9 proof $24.95.   **86**

Clear. Interesting, perfumed flower and green herb aromas. A fiery entrance leads to a medium-bodied palate with a marked burn. Hot, clipped finish.

César Chiarella Pisco Italia 89.4 proof $32.50.   **89**

Clear. Unusual, sugar cane, citrus aromas. A rounded, textured entrance leads to a medium-bodied palate. Flashes a touch of heat in the drying finish. Exotically flavored and surprisingly smooth.

Michele Chiarlo (Italy)

Michele Chiarlo Grappa di Vinacce di Barbera d'Asti 84 proof $34.99/375 ml.   **85**

Clear. Medium-bodied. Dried herbs, minerals, anise. Rather subdued aromatically with a touch of heat. Full but drying in the mouth with a noticeable burn to the finish.

Michele Chiarlo Grappa di Vinacce di Barolo 84 proof $34.99/375 ml.   **93**

Clear. Moderately full-bodied. Dried herbs, hay, black grapes. Forward pungent aromas show great style and complexity. Full and rich in the mouth with a big viscous mouthfeel. Quite smooth, with very little burn and a lengthy finish.

Scale: Superlative (96-100), Exceptional (90-95), Highly Recommended (85-89), Recommended (80-84), Not Recommended (Under 80)

Michele Chiarlo Grappa di Vinacce di Gavi 84 proof $34.99/375 ml.　　**88**

Clear. Medium-bodied. Vanilla, sweet herbs. Quite aromatic with a sweet, perfumed quality. Full and rounded in the mouth but shows a bit of fire that bites into the finish. Stylish.

Michele Chiarlo Grappa di Vinacce di Moscato d'Asti
84 proof $34.99/375 ml.　　**87**

Clear. Medium-bodied. Citrus oil, pine, flowers. Forward and aggressive aromas walk the wild side of Moscato Grappas. Full and viscous in the mouth with a continuation of these unusual nuances. Interesting and powerfully flavored. Proceed with caution.

The Christian Brothers (USA)

The Christian Brothers Brandy 80 proof $8.99.　　**85**

Dark gold. Light- to medium-bodied. Mandarin orange, toasted almond. Easy, delicate, very fruity style.

Clear Creek Distillery (USA)

Clear Creek Distillery Bartlett Pear Brandy 80 proof $20/375 ml.　　**91**

Clear. Medium-bodied. Aromas are high-toned and spirity with floral backnotes and a huge blast of fleshy pears. Pear flavors are marked on the palate with a faint background sweetness, though the finish is rather hot.

Clés des Ducs (France)

Clés des Ducs Napoleon, Armagnac 80 proof $49.95.　　**84**

Amber with a gold hue. Medium-bodied. Rather intense earthy herbaceous aromas lead into a dry flinty palate with burnt butter nuances and subtle flavors overall.

Clés des Ducs XO, Armagnac 80 proof $74.95.　　**93**

Amber with orange highlights. Moderately full-bodied. Honeyed aromas with herbal nuances translate well to an oily, rich mouthfeel with warm spicy caramel flavors and a refined character. A rather classy after-dinner style that could complement most cigars.

Clés des Ducs Millésimé 1962 Armagnac 84 proof $170.　　**95**

Very deep mahogany hue with greenish highlights. Medium-bodied. Powerful rancio, caramel, and salted nut aromas. A smooth attack leads to a full-bodied palate. Quite warm and exploding with flavor, but remarkably smooth given its size. Persistent, nutty finish. Could stand up to the richest of cigars.

Clés des Ducs 1942, Armagnac 82 proof $175.　　**95**

Deep tawny appearance. Moderately full-bodied. Richly aromatic. Very dry on the palate with intense and complex flavors reminiscent of burnt sugar and dried herbs. Quite austere overall. Certainly not something to drink in large quantities, and its appeal will be to the connoisseur.

Coeur de Lion (France)

Coeur de Lion Calvados Pays d'Auge VSOP 80 proof $62.50.　　**84**

Pale yellow-amber hue. Subdued woody aromas. A firm entrance leads to a medium-bodied, drying palate. Flashes some heat on the finish. Aromatically interesting, but doesn't quite follow through.

Coeur de Lion 1969 Calvados Pays d'Auge 84 proof $223.95.　　**94**

Very deep amber-orange hue. Opulent sweet wood and caramel aromas belie a mellow, aged Brandy. A firm entry leads to a drying, medium-bodied palate. Years in cask shine through the woody finish. Exceptionally interesting in flavor with a fiery undercurrent of rusticity.

Coeur de Lion 1977 Calvados Pays d'Auge 84 proof $223.95.　　**95**

Very deep amber-orange hue. Exotic, pungent rancio and caramel aromas. A rounded attack leads to a supple, medium-bodied palate. Fairly smooth given the genre, with very little burn. Drying, flavorful finish. Great synergy among wood, apple, and alcohol.

Conde de Osborne (Spain)

Conde de Osborne Solera Gran Reserva, Brandy de Jerez 81 proof $50.   **88**

Deep amber. Medium-bodied. Notes of citrus, leather, flowers. Delicately textured. Bright and lively on the palate. Excellent blending of diverse components helps showcase elegance and refinement.

Courvoisier (France)

Courvoisier VS, Cognac 80 proof $18.99.   **NR**

Courvoisier VSOP, Fine Champagne Cognac 80 proof $29.99.   **80**

Medium amber with copper highlights. Medium-bodied. Slightly muted though delicate floral aromas lead to an assertively flavored palate with some fig notes and big, dry spicy oak flavors through the finish.

Courvoisier Napoleon, Fine Champagne Cognac 80 proof $69.99.   **86**

Medium amber with a red-copper cast. Moderately light-bodied. Mild brown spices with light floral notes in the aromatics. Displays a rather subtly flavored, high-toned palate with some spicy heat in the finish.

Courvoisier XO Imperial Cognac 80 proof $100.   **90**

Amber-chestnut with a tawny cast. Medium-bodied. Some rich vanilla and butterscotch aromas are well translated on the palate. Shows balance overall, with a lingering creamy viscous finish.

Courvoisier Initiale Extra, Cognac 80 proof $259.99.   **92**

Deep amber with a tawny cast. Moderately full-bodied. Rich maple and nut aromas reveal a rich but spicy palate balanced by sweet notes that linger through to the spiced finish. A succulent and spicy style.

Pierre Croizet (France)

Pierre Croizet XO, Cognac 80 proof $99.   **89**

Medium amber-copper color with an orange cast. Medium-bodied. Very pronounced and distinct aromas of mushrooms and herbs translate well onto the silky palate. Smooth and seamless through to the lengthy finish. The mouthfeel and finish are flawless. However, the flavors and associated aromas may be off-putting to the uninitiated. Cognac Gastronomique.

Pierre Croizet Extra Extra, Cognac 80 proof $225.   **100**

Deep orange with a tawny cast. Moderately full-bodied. Marked by delicate mushroom aromas. The style is characterized by a refined silky palate with complex integrated flavors that persist remarkably on the finish. A hugely elegant and textured Cognac. A gastronomique experience.

Francis Darroze (France)

Francis Darroze Francis Darroze Réserve Speciale Bas Armagnac 86 proof $74.   **84**

Very deep amber-orange hue. Forward sweet wood and salty aromas. A lean attack leads to a medium-bodied palate with marked heat. Fiery finish. Flavorful but a bit rough.

Francis Darroze Francis Darroze 1975 Domaine de St Aubin Bas Armagnac 90 proof $139.99.   **91**

Bright amber-copper hue. Attractive, forward sweet wood, salted nut, and caramel aromas. A supple entry leads to a medium-bodied palate. Shows a drying woody character. Lean, clean finish with a touch of heat. A rather refined style of Armagnac, with a touch of Cognac elegance.

Davidoff (France)

Davidoff Classic Cognac 80 proof $59.99.   **87**

Deep mahogany hue. Unusual burnt wood, marmalade, and earth aromas. A rich, rounded attack leads to a full-bodied palate with a drying spicy character. Marked heat bites into the finish. A brawny style.

Davidoff Extra Cognac 86 proof $150.   **90**

Dark amber with a deep tawny cast. Moderately full-bodied. Rich, deep woody aromas precede a wave of nutty brown spice on entry that gives way to a thick finish with sweet notes. The richness in texture and the sweet sensation should make this a good foil for all but the most ferocious cigars.

Delamain (France)

Delamain Pale & Dry, Grande Champagne, XO Cognac 80 proof $76.99.   **88**

Bright copper hue. Generous wood and mineral aromas. A soft and luxuriant mouthfeel leads to a rounded, wood-accented palate. Rich, flavorful finish. A supple, rounded style that shows restraint and elegance.

Delamain Vesper, Grande Champagne Cognac 80 proof $112.99.   **90**

Medium amber with a light tawny cast. Moderately full-bodied. Big floral and dried fruit nose reveals an exotic high-toned style that is dry with a lush, almost fruity component. Lengthy dry finish. A standout style with ephemeral complexity.

Delamain Très Vénérable, Grande Champagne Cognac 80 proof $241.99.   **90**

Dark orange with a brilliant red-copper cast. Medium-bodied. A delicate style with ample sweet stone fruit aromas, plenty of complex spicy flavors, and a dryish character on the palate that make this stand out from the more viscous styles at this price point.

Delamain Réserve de la Famille, Rare Unblended Grande Champagne Cognac 86 proof $300/500 ml.   **96**

Deep, rich amber, with a chestnut cast. Citrus, tobacco, walnut, and sweet flowers. Rich, plush texture. Bold palate replete with complexity and fire. Packed with strong aromatics and great depth. Light smoke and mineral notes layer the soft fruity flavors and brown spices. Lovely warming, and ever lasting finish.

Pedro Domecq (Mexico)

Pedro Domecq Brandy Presidente 80 proof $9.99.   **NR**

Pierre Ferrand (France)

Pierre Ferrand 1er Cru Ambre, Grande Champagne Cognac 80 proof $35.   **85**

Bright gold with amber highlights. Moderately light-bodied. Sweet herbal-tinged vanilla accents reveal a spicy palate that refreshes with some brown spice. Lively and dry enough to be enjoyed on the rocks as an aperitif.

Pierre Ferrand 1er Cru Sélection des Anges, Grande Champagne Cognac 80 proof $85.   **96**

Dark orange with a reddish-gold cast. Moderately full-bodied. Rather fruity, mineral aromatics follow a delicate, nuanced style with caramel cream notes. Impressive viscosity on the mouthfeel for such a delicate style. Too delicate for smoking.

Pierre Ferrand 1er Cru Abel, Grande Champagne Cognac 80 proof $175.   **97**

Medium amber with a deep tawny cast. Moderately full-bodied. Ample and rich sandalwood aromas translate well on the palate, which is lifted by fruity nuances. Extraordinarily smooth with viscous notes through to the long finish. A little fruitier than its "ancestrale" brother, but it still has great presence on the palate.

Pierre Ferrand 1962 Mémoire Grande Champagne Single Vineyard Single Vintage Cognac, Cognac 80 proof $180. 100

Deep amber-orange hue. Generous marmalade, crème brûlée, and date aromas. A smooth attack leads to a weightless palate with a slight drying character. Outrageously lush. Lengthy, sweetly flavored finish. Elegant and refined, with opulent sweet flavors and amazing smoothness. Incredibly complex.

Pierre Ferrand 1965 Mémoire Grande Champagne Single Vineyard Single Vintage Cognac, Cognac 80 proof $180. 100

Deep amber-orange hue. Generous marmalade, caramel, and mineral aromas. A supple attack leads to a medium-bodied palate. So smooth as to be almost weightless in the mouth. Refined, flavorful finish. Shows no heat whatsoever. A hint of viscosity and lingering flavors. Outrageously smooth.

Pierre Ferrand 1968 Mémoire Grande Champagne Single Vineyard Single Vintage Cognac, Cognac 80 proof $180. 95

Deep amber-orange hue. Elegant, high-toned floral, mineral, orange-rind aromas. A lean entry leads to an exceptionally smooth and stylish mouthfeel. Medium-bodied and refined with no burn whatsoever. Lengthy, perfectly balanced, flavorful finish. Shows great style and grace without being obvious.

Pierre Ferrand 1er Cru Ancestrale, Grande Champagne Cognac 80 proof $380. 99

Dark amber with a very deep tawny cast. Full-bodied. Brooding nutty and lacquer aromas show a slight hint of alcohol vapors. An imposing style derived from weighty integrated components that linger through an exceptional finish. An extraordinary marriage of viscous texture and elegant nut flavors. This should complement a similarly proportioned cigar.

Jean Fillioux (France)

Jean Fillioux Cigar Club 1er Cru du Grande Champagne Cognac 80 proof $136.50. 90

Bright orange-amber hue. Forward sweet wood, orange peel, and mineral aromas. A rounded, viscous attack leads to a moderately full-bodied palate. Smooth, warming finish. A rich but elegant style, with a warming finish.

Jean Fillioux Tres Vieille Grande Champagne 1er Cru du Cognac 80 proof $255. 93

Very deep amber-orange hue. Generous caramel, sweet wood, and mineral aromas. A supple, rounded entry leads to a moderately full-bodied palate. Fat, oily finish. Exceptionally smooth and stylish through the finish.

Jean Fillioux 1948 Grande Champagne 1er Cru du Cognac 86 proof $372.95. 94

Very deep amber-orange hue. Subdued honey, spice, rancio, and date aromas show a touch of heat. A smooth attack leads to a moderately full-bodied palate with a smooth drying character. Exceptionally flavorful, lengthy finish. Powerful and robust, yet shows very little burn. Exceptionally well balanced for such an aged spirit.

Pierre Frapin (France)

Pierre Frapin VS Cognac 80 proof $31.   **84**

Deep amber-orange hue. Lean mineral, almond, and forest aromas show a distinctive note of terroir. A supple, viscous entry leads to a medium-bodied palate. Drying, flavorful finish. An outstanding VS showing real complexity.

Pierre Frapin VSOP Réserve Grande Champagne Premier Cru du Cognac 80 proof $46.   **88**

Deep amber hue. Subdued, warming mineral aromas. A supple attack leads to a medium-bodied palate. Expands in flavor and shows marked complexity. Lengthy, smooth finish. Exceptionally refined and stylish for a VSOP.

Pierre Frapin Château Fontpinot Grande Champagne Premier Cru du Cognac 80 proof $83.   **89**

Deep amber-orange hue. Subdued wood and mineral aromas. A lush, supple attack leads to a moderately full-bodied palate. Smooth, refined finish. Texturally exciting, with subtle, elegant flavors.

Pierre Frapin Ch. Fontpinot Premier Cru, Très Vieille Réserve, Grande Champagne Cognac 82 proof $110.   **87**

Dark amber with a chestnut cast. Medium-bodied. Maple and brown spice aromas reveal a rich style with a generous entry that tapers to a spicy finish. A rather subtle finish, showing finesse in the flavors.

Pierre Frapin V.I.P. XO Grande Champagne Premier Cru du Cognac 80 proof $154.   **93**

Deep amber-orange hue. Subdued earth, walnut, and wood aromas. A rounded attack leads to a medium-bodied palate with a drying, wood-accented character. Lean, warming finish. A delicate style, showing refined complexity.

Pierre Frapin Réserve Patrimoniale Extra, Grande Champagne Cognac 80 proof $495.   **97**

Medium amber. Moderately full-bodied. Rich brown-butter aromas reveal a sumptuous and elegant palate with delicate fruity flavors lingering on the subtle dry finish. A luxury Cognac of great finesse that would be overwhelmed by powerful cigars.

A. de Fussigny (France)

A. de Fussigny Sélection, Cognac 80 proof $27.   **89**

Dark gold with a copper cast. Moderately light-bodied. Very distinctive and complex nose reminiscent of earth, herbs, and dried fruits translates well onto the oily textured palate, with an impressively lengthy and smooth finish. Rather distinctively aromatic and flavorsome, as with others tasted from Fussigny.

A. de Fussigny XO, Cognac 80 proof $85.   **90**

Dark gold with a light copper cast. Medium-bodied. Spicy fragrant aromatics reveal a high-toned character showing great finesse and subtlety of flavors. Smooth, lingering herbal and toasty finish. Quite complex and delicate. A match for milder cigars.

A. de Fussigny Alain Royer Cigare Blend Fine Champagne Cognac, Special Reserve, Cognac. $95.   **91**

Deep mahogany hue with greenish highlights. Powerful rancio, wood, and earth aromas. A firm attack leads to a moderately full-bodied palate with a drying woody quality. Flavorful, warming finish. Shows real complexity with an Amontillado-like intensity to the aged flavors.

A. de Fussigny Vieille Réserve Séries Rares, Fine Champagne Cognac 80 proof $110.   **90**

Medium amber with a dark orange cast. Medium-bodied. Delicate sweet smoky aromas reveal a lively fruity style well balanced by some brown spice and aged components. Displays great finesse and subtlety on the classy lingering finish.

A. de Fussigny Très Vieille Séries Rares,
Grande Champagne Cognac 80 proof $190.   **92**
Medium-deep amber with a copper cast. Moderately full-bodied. Deep, rich wood aromas with sweet nuances reveal a palate impression of dark honey and brown spicy notes that carry through to the lingering finish. Should be a good match with milder spiced cigars.

Gabriel & Andreu (France)

Gabriel & Andreu Lot 10, Fins Bois Cognac 80 proof $25.   **90**
Deep amber with a dark copper cast. Moderately full-bodied. Rather engaging full floral aromas reveal a nuanced and seductive style with complex fruity and earthy flavors evolving on the long finish. Leaning toward a digestive style.

Gabriel & Andreu Lot 8, Fins Bois Cognac 80 proof $25.   **87**
Brilliant deep gold with an amber cast. Moderately light-bodied. Very aromatic with whiffs of herbs and sweet vanilla translating well onto the palate. The mouthfeel is silky without being heavy and the finish is elegant. A dry versatile style, flavorsome without being hugely complex.

Gabriel & Andreu Lot 3, Borderies Cognac 80 proof $45.   **89**
Medium to deep amber with an orange cast. Medium-bodied. A soft buttery style with a rounded smoky character and an elegantly textured mouthfeel. Quite easy on the palate. Leans toward an after-dinner style or with lighter cigars.

Gabriel & Andreu Lot 23, Petite Champagne Cognac 84 proof $65.   **88**
Amber with reddish-gold highlights. Medium-bodied. Racy and pungent aromas reveal a flinty palate with some silky texture through to a medium length finish. The mouthfeel is weighty, but the overall style is delicate.

Gabriel & Andreu Lot 18, Grande Champagne Cognac 86 proof $90.   **92**
Dark amber with a light tawny cast. Moderately full-bodied. Rich aromas of sweet herbs precede a deep full palate with some sweet notes and subtle flavors. Finishes elegantly.

Gautier (France)

Gautier VS, Cognac 80 proof $18.99.   **NR**

Gautier VSOP, Cognac 80 proof $25.   **82**
Medium amber with a light tawny cast. Moderately light-bodied. Assertive leathery and smoky aromas translate to a robustly flavored style with a salty, mineral tang on the finish. Quite unusual, and it certainly has character.

Gautier XO, Cognac 80 proof $60.   **82**
Dark amber with a tawny chestnut cast. Moderately full-bodied. Herbal, woody aromas lead into an oily mouthfeel with some subtle flavors that linger on a mineral finish.

Gautier Maison Gautier 10th Generation Tradition Rare,
Cognac 86 proof $199.   **87**
Very dark amber with a deep tawny cast. Full-bodied. An assertive broad-shouldered style displaying big nutty wood aromas. A heavy duty, mouth-filling palate and prominent brown spice flavors put this in the powerhouse style that would stand up to a pugnacious cigar.

Germain-Robin (USA)

Germain-Robin Hand Distilled Alambic Brandy 80 proof $29.   **83**
Light amber. Light- to medium-bodied. Slightly grainy texture. Dried flowers and succulent fruity flavors reminiscent of pears and figs.

Godet (France)

Godet Sélection Spéciale Cognac VSOP 80 proof $24.99. **87**

Deep amber hue. Generous caramel and sweet wood aromas. A viscous attack leads to a moderately full-bodied palate with a touch of heat. Warming, rounded finish. A supple, sweet, easygoing style.

Golden State Vintners (USA)

Golden State Vintners Growers Old Reserve Aged 16 Years, 9 Months, and 3 Days 80 proof $33.50. **84**

Medium amber. Medium-bodied. Perfumy nose. Smooth caramel texture with lingering notes of praline, pear, almond. Lingering warm finish. Fine balance.

Grand Duque d' Alba (Spain)

Grand Duque d'Alba Gran Reserva Solera Brandy de Jerez 80 proof $39.99. **87**

Very deep mahogany hue. Forward caramel aromas carry a slightly earthy cast. A firm, drying entrance leads to a full-bodied palate. Woody through the finish. A drier style.

Grand Solage Boulard (France)

Grand Solage Boulard Calvados Pays d'Auge 80 proof $24. **87**

Pale amber-orange hue. Generous sweet wood and apple aromas come with a touch of heat. A fiery attack leads to a medium-bodied palate with marked burn. Hot, drying finish. Flavorful, but quite rustic.

Friedrich-Wilhelm Gymnasium (Germany)

Friedrich-Wilhelm Gymnasium Alter Riesling Weinbrand VSOP 80 proof $20/500 ml. **85**

Deep amber-orange hue. Pungent sweet caramel aromas. A fat, supple entry leads to a rich, viscous, moderately full-bodied palate. Finishes with very little burn. Exceptionally smooth.

Hardy (France)

Hardy Red Corner Fine Cognac 80 proof $7/L. **83**

Dark amber-orange hue. Unusual burnt wood and caramel aromas come with a touch of heat. A supple attack leads to a moderately full-bodied palate. A fading, viscous finish shows a hot edge.

Hardy VSOP, Cognac 80 proof $29.95. **85**

Light reddish-amber. Moderately light-bodied. Light floral aromas translate to a light and subtly flavored style with vanilla and stone fruit accents through a brief finish. A lighter style that will not overpower the tastebuds.

Hardy Napoleon, Cognac 80 proof $45.95. **86**

Medium dark amber. Medium-bodied. Deep aromas of herbs and earth lead into a palate with a rich, elegant mouthfeel. Distinguished by a lengthy finish with lingering mineral and caramel notes. Very distinct flavors and aromas.

Hardy XO, Fine Champagne Cognac 80 proof $99.95. **89**

Amber with a coppery orange cast. Medium-bodied. Aromatically very distinctive, with leather and herbal nuances. Rather complex mineral and spicy flavors distinguish the palate. Flavors show great persistence on the finish.

Hardy Noces d'Or, Grande Champagne Cognac 80 proof $250. **96**

Deep orange with a copper cast. Moderately full-bodied. Inviting rich, fat aromas reveal a silky honeyed character with lighter, elegant wood-spiced flavors lingering on the finish. A richly textured but gracefully proportioned style.

CRG Hellinger (South Africa)

CRG Hellinger Grappa Reserve, Franschhoek 86 proof $30/500 ml.　　**81**

Stone, dried herbs, and hot peppers. Offers a tequila-like profile with a brawny, pungent palate. Opens up a chalky, mineral dimension.

Hennessy (France)

Hennessy Privilège VSOP Cognac. $42.　　**87**

Deep amber-orange hue. Subdued earth and mineral aromas carry a touch of heat. A lean attack leads to a medium-bodied palate. Smooth and drying with a woody character. Lingering, complex finish. A low-key, refined style showing some complexity.

Hennessy Camp Romain Single Distillery Fine Cognac. $50.　　**84**

Bright copper hue. Perfumed, complex sweet wood and mineral aromas. A smooth attack leads to a medium-bodied palate with fiery warmth. Hot, drying finish. Flavorful but very warm.

Hennessy Izambard Single Distillery Cognac. $50.　　**90**

Deep amber hue. Forward, elegant mineral and wood aromas. A smooth attack leads to a lean and refined mouthfeel. Shows complex flavors throughout. Smooth, lengthy finish. Exceptionally well balanced and distinctive in a more delicate style.

Hennessy Le Peu Single Distillery Cognac. $50.　　**86**

Bright copper hue. Subdued mineral and earth aromas. A lean attack leads to a medium-bodied palate. Smooth, drying finish. A lighter style with distinctive flavors and a sense of elegance.

Hennessy XO Cognac. $110.　　**93**

Deep amber hue. Powerful, generous sweet wood and caramel aromas. An exceptionally smooth and viscous attack leads to a moderately full-bodied palate with explosive sweet flavors. Rich, warming finish. A big, sweet, smooth, eminently drinkable style.

Hennessy Paradis Rare Cognac. $249.　　**98**

Very deep mahogany hue. Explosive, enticing spice, caramel, and sweet wood aromas. A smooth, supple attack leads to a full-bodied palate with outrageous smoothness and viscosity. Lengthy, rounded, warming finish. A generous, sweet, exceptionally stylish Cognac.

Hine (France)

Hine Rare & Delicate, Fine Champagne Cognac 80 proof $35.　　**84**

Deep amber with an orange cast. Medium-bodied. Marked by highly spiced toasty aromas that lead into a cedary vanilla palate with a warm spicy finish.

Hine 1960 Glenhaven Bottling, Grande Champagne Cognac 96 proof $195.　　**91**

Dark amber. Medium- to full-bodied. Coconut note dominates with butterscotch, pear, and smoke. Intense and strong. A sensation of sweetness without being sweet.

Inga (Italy)

Inga, Grappa di Gavi di Gavi 84 proof $23.99/375 ml.　　**90**

Clear. Medium-bodied. Slight note of sweetness. Pleasant warmth. Sweet hay, bright floral flavors, and green vegetables. Well-balanced florals with a clean finish.

Inga Grappa di Moscato 84 proof $23.99/375 ml.　　**93**

Clear. Medium-bodied. Dried herbs, citrus, flowers. Clean and vibrant aromatics show complexity and style. Exceptionally smooth in the mouth with an oily, viscous palate feel and very little burn. Intense and flavorful.

Inga Grappa di Nebbiolo da Barolo 84 proof $23.99/375 ml.　　**88**

Clear. Medium-bodied. Pepper, black grapes. Forward pungent aromatics lead to a rounded mouthfeel. Finishes on a drying note with a touch of heat.

Jacopo Poli (Italy)

Jacopo Poli Sarpa di Poli Grappa 86 proof $19/750 ml.　　**88**

Clear. Pungent mineral and "wet paint" aromas. A soft entry leads to a rounded, medium-bodied palate feel. Intense through the finish with a touch of heat.

Jacopo Poli Uva Viva di Poli, Distillato d'Uva 78 proof $22/750 ml.　　**86**

Clear. Complex mineral aromas show marked heat. A rich, oily attack leads to a medium-bodied, rounded palate feel. Smooth through the finish with just a touch of heat. Not overly flavorful, but quite clean.

Jacopo Poli 1987 L'Arzente Brandy Italiano 86 proof $28/375 ml.　　**91**

Pale, brilliant copper hue. Perfumed toasted nut, rancio, and sea salt aromas come with a touch of heat. A rounded entry leads to a moderately full-bodied palate with exceptional smoothness and generosity. Generous, supple finish. A lighter style of Brandy, with piercing complexity to the aromatics. Unusual and intriguing.

Jacopo Poli 1996 Grappa Amorosa di Cabernet 86 proof $32/375 ml.　　**93**

Clear. Pungent, forceful hay and black fruit aromas show an intense perfumed quality. A smooth attack leads to a medium-bodied and viscous palate. Exceptionally smooth and quite flavorful. Robust finish with very little burn.

Jacopo Poli 1996 Grappa Amorosa di Merlot 86 proof $32/375 ml.　　**94**

Clear. Generous and complex violet, fresh fruit, and mineral aromas. A smooth attack leads to a moderately full-bodied palate with a touch of heat and exceptional flavor intensity. Lengthy, generous finish.

Jacopo Poli 1996 Grappa Amorosa di Pinot 86 proof $32/375 ml.　　**89**

Clear. Unusual sweet herb and spearmint aromas. A lush entry leads to a medium-bodied palate with some noticeable heat. Soft, tapered finish.

Jacopo Poli 1996 Grappa Amorosa di Vespaiolo 86 proof $32/375 ml.　　**90**

Clear. Unusual apricot and lavender aromas are pure and intense. A supple entry leads to a medium-bodied palate with a touch of heat. Generous, persistent finish.

Jacopo Poli 1997 Grappa Amorosa di Torcolato 86 proof $32/375 ml.　　**98**

Clear. Outrageous perfumed hay and flower aromas. A supple entry leads to a lush, medium-bodied mouthfeel. Exhibits great delicacy and complexity with very little burn. Haunting, persistent finish.

Jacopo Poli 1997 Pear Brandy Stagione di Pere 86 proof $33/375 ml.　　**100**

Clear. Intensely piercing and pure ripe pear aromas. A rich entry leads to a full-bodied palate with an explosion of pear-like flavors. Shows great intensity. Complex, rounded finish with just a touch of heat. An extraordinarily pure interpretation of a classic Poire William, showing great delicacy and refinement.

Jacopo Poli 1997 Raspberry Brandy Stagione di Lamponi 86 proof $33/375 ml.　　**94**

Clear. Pure and exotic ripe raspberry aromas literally jump from the glass with no heat whatsoever. A lush entry leads to a full-bodied, viscous mouthfeel with a wave of sweet raspberry flavors. Lengthy, rounded finish with just a touch of heat. Opulent and complex. A very flavorful eau de vie.

Jacopo Poli 1997 Immature Grape Brandy, Chiara di Moscato 86 proof $35/375 ml.　　**88**

Clear. Intense, clean, citrus and mineral aromas. A soft attack leads to a moderately full-bodied palate with marked heat. Fiery, zesty finish. On the rustic side, but powerful and cleansing.

Janneau (France)

Janneau Réserve de la Maison, Armagnac 80 proof $45.　　**90**

Amber with reddish highlights. Medium-bodied. Sweet, fresh vanilla aromas reveal a rich brown-spiced palate with rather refined and layered presence through to a lengthy finish.

Jepson (USA)

Jepson Rare Brandy 80 proof $34.   89

Bright bronzed-copper hue. Lean, mineral, loamy aromas. A soft attack leads to a moderately full-bodied palate with distinctive, earthy, complex flavors. Quite smooth with very little heat. Lean, woody finish. A drying, complex style.

Jepson Signature Reserve Mendocino Alambic Brandy 80 proof $100.   91

Deep amber hue. Pronounced, complex mushroom, forest, and sweet wood aromas. A supple attack leads to a medium-bodied palate with a touch of heat. Shows a drying woody character. Clean, persistent finish. Distinctive, with a sweeter beginning and a dry finish.

Pierre Joseph (France)

Pierre Joseph Sélection 1er Cru, Grande Champagne Cognac 80 proof $47.   92

Medium amber with a red-copper cast. Moderately full-bodied. Aromatically complex with floral, herbal, and mushroom nuances that translate well on the palate. Textured, with some good viscosity on the mouthfeel through the finish. The overall impression is luxurious and complex.

Pierre Joseph Réserve Famille 1er Cru,
Grande Champagne Cognac 80 proof $65.50.   89

Amber with a red-copper cast. Medium-bodied. Fragrant sweet woody aromas lead into a rich and smooth palate through to a mild caramel and spice finish. Not hugely complex but very stylish and elegant.

Pierre Joseph 1er Cru Age d'Or, Grande Champagne Cognac
80 proof $120.   89

Dark amber with a bright red-orange cast. Medium-bodied. Distinctive salt and herbal nuanced aromatics reveal an almost honeyed palate feel with complex flavors that linger with very mild spicy heat on the finish.

Kelt (France)

Kelt Tour du Monde VSOP Grande Champagne Cognac 80 proof $49.95.   88

Deep amber hue. Forward sweet wood, spice, and caramel aromas. A rounded attack leads to a moderately full-bodied palate with marked viscosity. Finishes with a touch of heat. More rewarding in texture than flavor.

Kelt Tour du Monde XO Grande Champagne Cognac 80 proof $130.   93

Dark gold with an amber cast. Medium-bodied. Delicate caramel, citrus, and herbal aromas lead into a smooth palate with a pleasing oily texture and an extraordinarily persistent finish. Elegance and finesse are the pointers here. The connoisseur's session Cognac: it should still be going down smoothly with the last glass.

Kelt Petra, Tour du Monde 80 proof $650.   97

Dark reddish chestnut. Medium-bodied. Deep, rich, broad, and oily palate. Intense floral nose that commands attention. Concentrated notes of dried herbs, toffee, mint, dried peaches. Strong spicy oak base that gives a firm structure. Decadent, full finish.

Korbel (USA)

Korbel Brandy 80 proof $8.99.   84

Deep amber-orange hue. Rather subdued aromatically, with some heat to the oaky nose. A rounded attack leads to a medium-bodied palate with subtle sweet wood flavors. Brief, drying finish.

Korbel Sonoma County Grappa 90 proof $29.95/375 ml.   NR

KWV (South Africa)

KWV Superior Three Star Brandy - 3 Years Old 86 proof $12.   NR

KWV V.S.O.P. Brandy - Average Age 7 Years 80 proof $16.   NR

Scale: Superlative (96-100), Exceptional (90-95), Highly Recommended (85-89), Recommended (80-84), Not Recommended (Under 80)

Laberdolive (France)

Laberdolive 1976 Domaine de Jaurrey, Bas-Armagnac 92 proof $91.99.   **92**

Amber with a reddish hue. Medium-bodied. Big full buttery aromas reveal a refined
oily textured palate with maple and butterscotch flavors through to a rich finish.
The overall impression is of a decadent and luxurious style that would sit well after
a multi-course dinner.

Larressingle (France)

Larressingle VSOP, Armagnac 80 proof $36.99.   **80**

Reddish-gold appearance. Medium-bodied. A mid-weight style with a rather assertive
earthy palate presence and a spiky herbaceous finish.

Larressingle XO, Armagnac 86 proof $76.99.   **89**

Dark amber with copper highlights. Rich, fat aromas lead into a luxuriously textured,
maple syrup-like, if not highly complex, palate. Lingering warm brown spice finish.

Lepanto (Spain)

Lepanto Solera Gran Reserva, Brandy de Jerez 80 proof $49.99.   **92**

Deep amber with a copper cast. Moderately full-bodied. Notes of citrus, flowers, walnuts.
Soft yet rich texture. Very wine-like feel on the palate offering ample fruit and pretty
fragrance with a touch of spice. Wonderful expression of elegant structure.

Luxardo (Italy)

Luxardo Grappa Euganea 80 proof $27.50.   **88**

Clear. Pungent, unusual citrus, lavender, and stone fruit aromas. Viscous attack leads to a
medium-bodied palate with great smoothness. Shows little burn. Neutral, rounded finish.

Magnotta (Canada)

Magnotta Fine Alambic Grappa, Ontario 80 proof $21.40.   **84**

Clear. Medium-bodied. Dried herbs, citrus. Forward, clean aromas lead to a lighter palate
feel with racy, almost minty flavors. Clean and smooth with a lengthy finish.

Magnotta 1996 Vidal Ice Grappa, Ontario 90 proof $25/500 ml.   **82**

Clear with a grayish tint. Medium-bodied. Plums, sweet herbs, citrus. Forward, pungent
aromatics lead to a hot and fiery mouthfeel. Shows a real burn to the finish. On the rustic side.

Magnotta 1997 Riesling Ice Grappa, Ontario 90 proof $25/500 ml.   **86**

Clear. Medium-bodied. Sweet herbs, earth, plums. Quite pungent in aroma with a
touch of heat. Shows an oily quality on the entry before fiery alcohol bites into the
drying finish.

Makedoniko (Greece)

Makedoniko Apostagma Apo Stafyli Eau de Vie 75 proof $22/500 ml.   **83**

Clear. Faintly sweet, grape aromas. Smooth, mildly glycerous mouthfeel with traces of
sweet vinous flavors lingering on the finish. Very clean.

Marcel Trepout Apotheose Armagnac (France)

Marcel Trepout Apotheose Armagnac 80 proof $95.   **91**

Dark amber. Full-bodied. Rich. Hot. Dates, sweet tobacco, custard. Strong oak flavors.
Thick, almost syrupy finish. A sensation of fruitiness, but not sweet.

Marchesi di Gresy (Italy)

Marchesi di Gresy Grappa Martinenga 84 proof $45.   **86**

Clear. Medium-bodied. Plums, sweet herbs, minerals. The nose richly belies black grape
origins. In the mouth this Grappa is forceful with some heat through the finish and a
brawny straightforward character.

Marnier-Lapostolle (France)

Marnier-Lapostolle XO, Armagnac 80 proof $47.   **90**

Medium amber with an orange hue. Moderately full-bodied. Lacquer notes on the nose reveal a sweetly fruity palate with a textured, complex mouthfeel through to a mildly spicy finish.

Marnier-Lapostolle XO, Grande Fine Champagne Cognac 80 proof $76.   **87**

Dark amber with a deep chestnut cast. Moderately full-bodied. Ample smoky wood aromas reveal a dark rich style with a textured mouthfeel. Some mild dry notes on the finish give this an imposing palate presence. Certainly more than a match for strong cigars.

Marquis de Caussade (France)

Marquis de Caussade Armagnac 10 Years Old 80 proof $40.   **90**

Dark amber. Medium-bodied. Smooth velvety texture. Lush notes of sweet herbs, figs, buttery popcorn, fruity pipe tobacco. Rich, lingering finish.

Marquis de Caussade Armagnac 17 Years Old 80 proof $48.   **88**

Dark amber, orange glow. Full-bodied. Hot. Dried peach, leather, cinnamon. Strong oak flavors. Although wood dominates, there is sufficient fruit to back up the flavors without being sweet.

Marquis de Caussade Armagnac 30 Years Old 80 proof $155.   **95**

Dark amber. Moderately full-bodied with a viscous mouthfeel. Smoke, toffee, peanuts, prune. Strong charred oak note. A panorama of flavors, especially nutty components. Broad texture. Powerful, rich finish. Dried fruit notes without being sweet.

Marquis de Montesquiou (France)

Marquis de Montesquiou Napoleon, Armagnac 80 proof $29.99.   **84**

Light amber with a reddish hue. Medium-bodied. High-toned and slightly pungent aromas translate well to herb-accented flavors through to a delicate finish with some delicately spicy heat.

Marquis de Montesquiou XO, Armagnac 80 proof $50.   **86**

Dark amber with a copper hue. Medium-bodied. Rather smooth aromas of smoke and delicate brown herbs reveal a flavorsome entrance that quietly tapers subtly to a lingering finish.

Martell (France)

Martell VS, Cognac 80 proof $20.   **NR**

Martell Cordon Bleu, Cognac 80 proof $100.   **90**

Dark chestnut with a deep cast. Moderately full-bodied. Ample rich caramel and wood aromas reveal a viscous and rich mouthfeel with a very smooth palate presence. Oak flavors carry through and onto the finish. A burly and impressive wood-dominated style that should complement strong cigars.

Martin Brothers (USA)

Martin Brothers Grappa di Moscato 80 proof $34/375 ml.   **87**

Clear. Moderately light-bodied. Citrus peel, sweet herbs, minerals. Pleasantly aromatic with a distinct citrus character. Delicate and smooth with a lingering finish and very little burn.

Martin Brothers Grappa di Nebbiolo 80 proof $34/375 ml.   **86**

Clear. Medium-bodied. Plums, brown spices, anise. Forceful in nature, with deep flavors and a touch of viscosity to the palate. Pleasant straightforward finish with a touch of spice and very little burn.

Mascaro Narciso Brandy (Spain)

Mascaro Narciso Brandy 80 proof $29. **80**

Amber-copper glow. Light- to medium-bodied. Allspice, honey, tart citrus. Strong oak flavors. Flavors and spices build to a plush finish.

G.E. Massenez (France)

G.E. Massenez Eau-de-Vie de Poire Williams, Williams Pear Brandy 80 proof $34/375 ml. **87**

Clear. Muted aromas are rather mineral with a faint suggestion of pear. On the palate, faint suggestions of sweet pear are evident with some heat on the long finish.

Paul Masson (USA)

Paul Masson Grande Amber Brandy 80 proof $13.99. **86**

Tawny amber. Medium- to full-bodied. Pralines, raisins, maple, bittersweet chocolate. Fruity elements without being sweet.

Mastroberardino (Italy)

Mastroberardino Grappa Novia di Greco di Tufo 80 proof $48. **87**

Clear. Light-bodied. Apples, flowers, citrus. Quite interesting aromatically, with an intensely fruity quality. Light and delicate quality with very little heat. Intense and lingering finish.

Mastroberardino Grappa Novia di Taurasi 90 proof $50. **89**

Clear. Medium-bodied. Plums, straw, citrus peel. Quite aromatic, with a lush, viscous mouthfeel. Very smooth on the palate with a pleasant lingering finish.

Mazzetti d'Altavilla (Italy)

Mazzetti d'Altavilla Grappa di Arneis, "Le Rose" 86 proof $85/375 ml. **82**

Clear. Medium-bodied. Dried herbs, tomatoes, cheese. Unusual aromatics are forceful and persistent. In the mouth this Grappa is well rounded with a touch of heat and lingering flavors.

Mazzetti d'Altavilla Grappa di Barbera, "I Frutti Di Vetro" 86 proof $85/375 ml. **91**

Clear. Medium-bodied. Plums, brown spices, earth. Deeply aromatic, this Grappa is rich yet well balanced on the palate with a sense of viscosity. Lingering and flavorful finish with a touch of heat.

Mazzetti d'Altavilla Grappa di Nebbiolo Da Barolo, "Le Gemme" 86 proof $85/100 ml. **95**

Very pale straw cast. Moderately light-bodied. Citrus, flowers, sweet herbs. Extremely aromatic with a superbly balanced palate that has a real sense of lightness. Lengthy and flavorful finish with very little heat.

Menuet (France)

Menuet VS Grande Champagne 1er Cru du Cognac 80 proof $20/. **80**

Deep amber-orange hue. Unusual and forceful fruity aromas. A supple attack leads to a hot, drying palate. Lean, fiery finish.

Menuet 1er Cru VSOP, Grande Champagne Cognac 80 proof $26.95. **85**

Light amber with a light tawny cast. High-toned floral, fruity aromas translate well onto a palate with vanilla and citrus oil accents, and a subtle spicy finish. A beautifully balanced style characterized by complexity and elegance.

Menuet XO Grande Champagne 1er Cru Cognac 80 proof $60. **89**

Deep amber with greenish highlights. Forward, unique mushroom, earth and herb aromas carry a touch of heat. A supple attack leads to a medium-bodied palate with a lean drying character. Lengthy, angular finish. An interesting and distinctive style showing a note of terroir.

Metaxa (Greece)

Metaxa Amphora 7 Star Brandy 80 proof $22. **NR**

F. Meyer (France)

F. Meyer Eau-de-vie de Mirabelle, Plum Brandy 90 proof $22.50/375 ml. **89**

Transparent. Delicate fruit-skin aromas. Very attractive. On the palate, silky smooth with a deep, persistent sensation of fruit-skin extract that is bone dry and fruity at the same time.

F. Meyer Eau-de-vie de Kirsch, Cherry Brandy 90 proof $22.95/375 ml. **95**

Clear. Displays distinctive fruit-skin essence. Silky smooth and bone dry with an underlying suggestion of cherry fruit pulp that lingers eternally on the finish. Fruit flavors are not very specific, but very pleasing nonetheless.

F. Meyer Eau-de-vie de Poire Williams, Williams Pear Brandy 90 proof $23.95/375 ml. **87**

Clear. Outstanding floral pear blossom with deeper pear flesh notes. Flavors follow the aromas with an outstanding, assertive oily texture complimenting the fleshy pear accents. Decidedly smooth and lingering finish.

F. Meyer Eau-de-vie de Framboise, Raspberry Brandy 90 proof $24.95/375 ml. **89**

Clear. Outstanding raspberry scents are quite subtle. Smooth on entry, rather hot on the finish with faint fruit flavors not quite latching onto anything specific.

Moletto (Italy)

Moletto Distillato D'Uva 80 proof $34. **96**

Clear. Medium-bodied. Packed, dense mouthfeel. Pleasant throughout. Soft warmth. Beautiful floral flavors with apple and nectarines. Wonderfully balanced with a slow warm finish and cool mintiness.

Château Montifaud (France)

Château Montifaud Fine Petite Champagne Cognac 80 proof $38. **82**

Deep amber-orange hue. Subdued mineral and earth aromas. A lean attack leads to a medium-bodied palate with marked heat. Fiery, drying finish.

Château Montifaud VSOP Fine Petite Champagne Cognac 80 proof $50.50. **85**

Deep amber hue. Muted woody aromas are restrained by some heat in the nose. A rounded attack leads to a moderately full-bodied, fiery palate. Hot, clipped finish. On the warm side.

Château Montifaud Napoleon, Fine Petite Champagne Cognac 80 proof $53.99. **86**

Deep amber with orange highlights. Medium-bodied. Some rich woody aromas precede a flavorful entry with generous nutty notes through the middle. Characterized by a generally lively palate and some lingering, warm brown spicy notes on the finish that leave a nice tingle.

Château Montifaud XO Fine Petite Champagne Cognac 80 proof $102.95. **94**

Deep amber-orange hue. Forward spice, toasted coconut, and mineral aromas. A supple, viscous attack leads to a moderately full-bodied palate with a rich and rounded character. Generous, drying finish. A texturally smooth style with typical sweet, warming flavors that linger on and on.

Château Montifaud Grand Siècle 2000 Fine
Petite Champagne Cognac 80 proof $118.50.   **95**

Deep amber-orange hue. Generous mineral, wood, and marmalade aromas. A supple entry leads to a moderately full-bodied palate with explosive flavors. Lengthy, exotic, spicy finish. Big and flavorful, but in a refined, elegant framework.

Mosby (USA)

Mosby, Grappa di Traminer 80 proof $27/375 ml.   **90**

Clear. Pleasant viscosity. Medium-bodied. Light hints of sweetness. Moderately warm. Complex layering of fragrant floral notes, dried peaches, and refreshing spearmint.

Nonino (Italy)

Nonino Grappa di Moscato 80 proof $104.49.   **95**

Clear. Medium-bodied. Lemon peel, lilacs, lavender. Very clean aromatics with tangy citrus flavors. Racy and vibrant on the palate with an expansion of flavor at the finish. Very little heat.

Nonino Grappa di Monovitigno Picolit 1993 100 proof $153.49.   **88**

Clear. Medium-bodied. Fresh hay, citrus, currant. Aromatics are delicate yet forceful. In the mouth the entry is graceful, well balanced, and flavorful. Finishes with a decided burn that belies its overproof character and cuts the finish a bit short.

Ornellaia (Italy)

Ornellaia Grappa di Merlot 84 proof $60.99/375 ml.   **94**

Deep pale-copper cast. Moderately full-bodied. Spice, hay, wood. Shows an attractive, nuanced, spicy quality to the nose. Smooth and full in the mouth with very little burn. Viscosity belies a sense of richness. Very lengthy finish.

Otard (France)

Otard VSOP Fine Champagne Cognac 80 proof $29.   **84**

Deep bronzed-copper hue. Forward earthy, loamy, forest floor aromas. A smooth attack leads to a medium-bodied palate. Finishes with a touch of heat. Elegant if somewhat subdued.

Planat (France)

Planat V.S. Cognac $14.99.   **90**

Medium amber. Medium- to full-bodied. Roast coffee, figs, vanilla. Excellent integration of components. Sweet feel at finish.

Andrea da Ponte (Italy)

Andrea da Ponte Vecchia Grappa di Prosecco 84 proof $7/Other.   **83**

Very pale yellow-straw hue. Generous honey, herb, and spice aromas. A rounded entry leads to a medium-bodied palate with a subtle fiery quality. Spirity through the finish with a marked burn.

Andrea da Ponte Uve Bianche Acquavite d'Uva 80 proof $7.50/Other.   **80**

Colorless. Muted, slightly hot, peppery aromas. A smooth attack leads to a moderately light-bodied palate with a marked burn. Spirity, neutral finish. Resembles a vodka, but quite clean.

Quady (USA)

Quady Spirit of Elysium Black Muscat Distillate 80 proof $33.   **92**

Clear. Citrus, flowers. Clean, forward, attractive fruity aromas lead to a smooth and oily mouthfeel. Finishes with very little burn and generous citrus flavors.

Marcel Ragnaud (France)

Marcel Ragnaud Premier Cru Réserve Spéciale,
Grande Champagne Cognac 86 proof $50.   85

Deep gold with a reddish-gold cast. Medium-bodied. Vibrant fruity spiced aromas reveal some flavor complexity and smooth viscous character on the palate. Distinguished by a pronounced spicy element, especially on the finish. A versatile palate awakener.

Raynal (France)

Raynal VSOP Napoleon Brandy 80 proof $11.99.   NR

Raynal 5 Year Old French Brandy 80 proof $15.99.   81

Deep amber-orange hue. Heavy caramel aromas with emphatic heat to the nose. A fat entry leads to a full-bodied palate. Finishes with some drying heat.

Remy Martin (France)

Remy Martin VSOP, Fine Champagne Cognac 80 proof $40.   84

Dark gold-amber with a copper cast. Medium-bodied. A delicate sweet vanilla nose reveals flavors of honey and dried apricots. Quite lush in flavors but not rich. Very delicate and pleasant.

Remy Martin XO Special Fine Champagne Cognac 80 proof $100.   90

Mahogany. Full-bodied. Rich mouthfeel. Creamy. Hot. Flowers, dried peaches, toasted almonds, smoke. Strong oak flavors. Palate has a degree of complexity and depth from aging that is felt under thick wood and spices. Very long, fragrant finish. Lingering fruit notes without being sweet.

Remy Martin Extra, Fine Champagne Cognac 80 proof $300.   93

Dark orange with a deep tawny cast. Full-bodied. Marked herbal nuances in the nutty aromas. Palate presence is rich and oily in texture with mild brown spicy notes lingering through to the elegant, lengthy finish. An impressively aged and elegantly proportioned spirit.

Renault (France)

Renault Carte Noir VSOP, Cognac 80 proof $29.99.   82

Deep reddish-amber with a chestnut cast. Medium-bodied. Some deep oaky notes reveal nutty butterscotch flavors and a hint of sweetness through to the finish. Quite satisfyingly rich.

RMS Distillery (USA)

RMS Distillery Special Reserve 7 Year Old Rare Alambic Brandy
80 proof $30.   88

Deep amber-orange hue. Generous caramel and sweet wood aromas. A soft, supple attack leads to a medium-bodied palate with a drying woody character. Finishes with a touch of heat. Quite stylish.

RMS Distillery Folle Blanche 10 Year Old
Rare Alambic Brandy 80 proof $60.   89

Deep copper-amber hue. Exotic, unusual orange peel and mineral aromas show a distinctive signature. A smooth entry leads to a lean, medium-bodied palate with a touch of heat. Lingering, mineral. A distinctive, elegant, drying, Cognac-like style.

**RMS Distillery QE 14 Year Old Rare French
Oak Aged Alambic Brandy 80 proof $116.**   93

Very deep tawny amber hue. Profoundly generous sweet wood,
caramel, and marmalade aromas. A smooth and supple entry
leads to a moderately full-bodied palate. Exceptionally smooth
with a pronounced sweetness to the flavors. Supple, velvety,
warming finish. Shows great balance and length.

Louis Royer (France)

Louis Royer XO Cognac 80 proof $99.   89

Dark amber. Full-bodied. Rich and smooth. Hot. Lilacs, figs,
almond, toffee. Strong oak flavors with a powerful impression
on the palate with a nice, warming finish.

Ruffino (Italy)

Ruffino Grappa di Cabreo Il Borgo 90 proof $25/375 ml.   86

Clear. Medium-bodied. Black fruits, sweet herbs, citrus. Pleasantly aromatic, this Grappa
has a rounded presence in the mouth and finishes with a sense of sweetness to the fruit
flavors. Features just a touch of heat on the palate.

Ruffino Grappa Riserva Ducale 90 proof $25/375 ml.   88

Clear. Medium-bodied. Plums, dried herbs, minerals. Pleasantly aromatic though spirited
in the nose. Smooth on the palate with a flavorful lingering finish.

St. George (USA)

St. George Grappa of Traminer, California 80 proof $21.95/375 ml.   93

Clear. Pungent, exotic citrus, perfume, and flower aromas. A smooth attack leads to a
medium-bodied palate. Lengthy, flavorful finish with minimal burn. Outrageously aromatic, with great complexity.

St. George Grappa of Zinfandel, California 80 proof $21.95/375 ml.   89

Clear. Forward, intense hay, black fruit, and mineral aromas. A smooth, somewhat fiery
attack leads to a medium-bodied, flavorful palate. Exceptionally flavorful through the
finish with a mild burn.

St. George Pale Brandy 80 proof $30/375 ml.   81

Pale yellow. Light-bodied. Ephemeral floral nose. Delicate dried fruit palate with notes of
pine, golden raisin, Fino Sherry. Hot, grainy finish.

St. Remy (France)

St. Remy Napoleon VSOP French Brandy 80 proof $11.99/.   83

Deep amber hue. Rich Oloroso Sherry and caramel aromas. A weighty attack leads to a
full-bodied palate. Shows a touch of heat and rather obvious sweet flavors. Thick, sweet
finish. Rather like a rustic Spanish Brandy.

Samalens (France)

Samalens VSOP, Bas-Armagnac 80 proof $40.   87

Dark amber with a reddish cast. Medium-bodied. Earthy, fruity
aromas lead into an herbal, woody palate through to a dry finish. A masculine style for those who like assertive flavors.

**Samalens Vieille Relique Bas-Armagnac
84 proof $110.**   89

Very deep amber-mahogany hue. A big, powerful, salty,
caramel-accented nose shows marked heat. A fiery attack leads to a moderately full-
bodied palate. Quite flavorful through the finish. Very smooth.

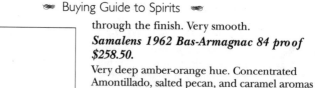

Brandy Cocktails

Sidecar

Fill a short glass with ice.
In a shaker combine:

1 oz. brandy
1 oz. triple sec
1 oz. lemon juice
Ice to fill

Shake and strain
into the glass.

Stinger

Fill a short glass with ice.
Add:

1 oz. brandy
1 oz. white crème de menthe

Stir and serve.

Brandy Alexander

In a shaker combine:

1 oz. brandy
1 oz. dark crème de cacao
1 oz. cream
Ice to fill

Shake and strain into a
large brandy snifter.
Dust with nutmeg.

---

through the finish. Very smooth.

*Samalens 1962 Bas-Armagnac 84 proof
$258.50.*   **94**

Very deep amber-orange hue. Concentrated
Amontillado, salted pecan, and caramel aromas
show a ton of barrel age and come with a measure
of heat. A lean attack leads to a full-bodied,
fiery palate. Shows a heavy, drying wood accent.
Flavorful, but hot through the finish. Complex,
but rather rustic in structure.

Sanchez Romate (Spain)

*Sanchez Romate Cardenal Mendoza Solera
Gran Reserva
Brandy de Jerez 80 proof $39.99.*   **90**

Very deep mahogany hue. Intense, pronounced
rancio and caramel aromas. A smooth, rounded
entrance leads to a supple, moderately full-bodied,
and gentle palate. Generous caramel finish with a
touch of heat.

Sassicaia (Marchesi Incisa della Rocchetta) (Italy)

*Marchesi Incisa della Rocchetta
Grappa da Vinacce di Sassicaia
84 proof $114.99/375 ml.*   **88**

Pale old-gold cast. Moderately light-bodied.
Wood, minerals. Aromatically reserved with
a subtle woody overtone indicating some light
barrel aging. Lighter in style with a smooth mouthfeel that turns drying on the mildly hot finish.

Emil Scheibel (Germany)

*Emil Scheibel Black Forest
Waldhimbeergeist,
Wild Raspberry Brandy
80 proof $29.95/375 ml.*   **84**

Clear. Dark berry skin aromas are pronounced,
though rather hot, fusel-like. Dry and rather
spirity on the palate with well-meshed fruit flavor
playing out through the finish. Berry flavors
are rather indistinct.

*Emil Scheibel Black Forest Kirschwasser,
Cherry Brandy 80 proof $33.50/375 ml.*   **92**

Clear. Very aromatic, with a big blast of cherry
fragrance. On the palate this is bone dry, oily, and
smooth with underlying cherry skin flavors that
linger impressively.

Scale: Superlative (96-100), Exceptional (90-95), Highly Recommended (85-89),
Recommended (80-84), Not Recommended (Under 80)

Emil Scheibel Black Forest Williams-Birnen-Brand,
Williams Pear Brandy 80 proof $33.50/375 ml.   **95**

Clear. Outstanding waxy pear aromas are very faithful. Smooth, oily, and textured on the palate, with wonderful pear flavors throughout. Finishes rather smoothly.

Sebastiani (USA)

Sebastiani Grappa di Sebastiani Arnold Holstein Pot Still,
Sonoma Valley 91.6 proof $19.99/375 ml.   **83**

Clear. Medium-bodied. Pleasant mouthfeel. Moderately sweet notes. Warm. Very floral with mint and orange flavors.

Stock (Italy)

Stock '84 Brandy 80 proof $8.99.   **82**

Light amber. Light-bodied. Soft texture. Dates, pecan, clove. Delicate and easy on the palate. Delicate dried fruit notes linger on the finish.

Stock Grappa Julia Riserva Stravecchia 80 proof $15.   **83**

Pale straw. Medium-bodied with a smooth mouthfeel. Moderate sweetness. Spicy and herbal notes combine with soft leather and caramel. Long finish.

Château du Tariquet (France)

Château du Tariquet VSOP, Bas-Armagnac 80 proof $35.   **88**

Pale amber with gold highlights. Medium-bodied. Mild earthy, leafy aromas reveal a lighter style with a rounded almost buttery feel. Soft fruity nuances on the finish.

Tbilisi (Georgia)

Tbilisi Rare Extra 17 Year Old Deluxe Georgian Brandy 80 proof $28.99.   **86**

Very deep amber hue. Pronounced candied orange and caramel aromas. A weighty attack leads to a full-bodied palate with a drying woody quality. Fiery, rustic finish. Rich but a tad coarse.

Terre Rouge (USA)

Terre Rouge Eau-de-Vie de Prune d'Agen, Plum Brandy
80 proof $25/375 ml.   **83**

Clear. Herbal, floral aromas are very distinctive and complex. Very flavorful. Quite dry with earthy flavors lingering through the finish.

Terry (Spain)

Terry Solera Gran Reserva, Terry Primero, Brandy de Jerez 80 proof $32.99. **88**

Dark amber. Moderately full-bodied. Notes of prunes, nutmeg, pralines. Deep, thick texture. Unctuous and fat on the palate, with a broad spectrum of pungent brown spices and heavy fragrance. Big, chewy finish. Quite succulent.

Torres (Spain)

Torres Miguel Torres Imperial Brandy, Penedes 80 proof $34.99.   **90**

Amber with an orange cast. Medium-bodied. Notes of orange peel, mocha, perfume. Round, soft texture. Smooth and delicate on the palate. Effusively fruity and fragrant with a slight impression of sweetness. A very elegant, refined style.

Villa de Varda (Italy)

Villa de Varda Grappa di Moscato 80 proof $60.   **83**

Clear. Citrus, white pepper, minerals. Very clean in aroma with a touch of viscosity to the palate. Finishes on a hot note.

Highly Rated Brandy, Eau de Vie, and Grappa

Cognac

VS Cognac

90 • Planat (France) V.S. $14.99.

88 • Bisquit Dubouche (France) Cognac Classique V.S. 80 Proof. $26.

VSOP Cognac

92 • Bisquit Dubouche (France) VSOP Fine Champagne 80 Proof. $38.

89 • A. de Fussigny (France) Sélection, Cognac 80 Proof. $27.

88 • Pierre Frapin (France) VSOP Réserve Grande Champagne Premier Cru du Cognac 80 Proof. $46.

88 • Kelt (France) Tour du Monde VSOP Grande Champagne Cognac 80 Proof. $49.95.

87 • Godet (France) Sélection Spéciale Cognac VSOP 80 Proof. $24.99.

87 • Hennessy (France) Privilège VSOP Cognac $42.

85 • Hardy (France) VSOP, Cognac 80 Proof. $29.95.

85 • Menuet (France) 1er Cru VSOP, Grande Champagne Cognac 80 Proof. $26.95.

85 • Château Montifaud (France) VSOP Fine Petite Champagne Cognac 80 Proof. $50.50.

XO Cognac

94 • Château Montifaud (France) XO Fine Petite Champagne Cognac 80 Proof. $102.95.

93 • Pierre Frapin (France) V.I.P. XO Grande Champagne Premier Cru du Cognac 80 Proof. $154.

93 • Hennessy (France) XO Cognac $110.

93 • Kelt (France) Tour du Monde XO, Grande Champagne Cognac 80 Proof. $130.

90 • Courvoisier (France) XO Imperial 80 Proof. $100.

90 • A. de Fussigny (France) XO, Cognac 80 Proof. $85.

90 • Remy Martin (France) XO Special Fine Champagne Cognac 80 Proof. $100.

89 • Pierre Croizet (France) XO, Cognac 80 Proof. $99.

89 • Hardy (France) XO, Fine Champagne Cognac 80 Proof. $99.95.

89 • Louis Royer (France) XO 80 Proof. $99.

89 • Menuet (France) Menuet XO Grande Champagne 1er Cru Cognac 80 Proof. $60.

88 • Delamain (France) Pale & Dry, Grande Champagne, XO Cognac 80 Proof. $76.99.

87 • Marnier-Lapostolle (France) XO, Grande Fine Champagne Cognac 80 Proof. $76.

Cigar Blend Cognac

91 • A. de Fussigny (France) Alain Royer Cigare Blend Fine Champagne Cognac, Special Reserve, Cognac $95.

90 • Jean Fillioux (France) Cigar Club 1er Cru du Grande Champagne Cognac 80 Proof. $136.50.

87 • Davidoff (France) Classic Cognac 80 Proof. $59.99.

Napoleon Cognac

93 • Bisquit Dubouche (France) Napoleon Fine Champagne 80 Proof. $69.

90 • Martell (France) Cordon Bleu, Cognac 80 Proof. $100.

86 • Courvoisier (France) Napoleon, Fine Champagne Cognac 80 Proof. $69.99.

86 • Hardy (France) Napoleon, Cognac 80 Proof. $45.95.

Single Distillery Cognac

90 • Hennessy (France) Izambard Single Distillery Cognac $50.

86 • Hennessy (France) Le Peu Single Distillery Cognac $50.

Single District Cognac

92 • Pierre Joseph (France) Sélection 1er Cru, Grande Champagne Cognac 80 Proof. $47.

90 • Gabriel & Andreu (France) Lot 10, Fins Bois Cognac 80 Proof. $25.

89 • Gabriel & Andreu (France) Lot 3, Borderies Cognac 80 Proof. $45.

89 • Pierre Joseph (France) Réserve Famille 1er Cru, Grande Champagne Cognac 80 Proof. $65.50.

88 • Gabriel & Andreu (France) Lot 23, Petite Champagne Cognac 84 Proof. $65.

87 • Gabriel & Andreu (France) Lot 8, Fins Bois Cognac 80 Proof. $25.

86 • Château Montifaud (France) Napoleon, Fine Petite Champagne Cognac 80 Proof. $53.99.

85 • Pierre Ferrand (France) 1er Cru Ambre, Grande Champagne Cognac 80 Proof. $35.

85 • Marcel Ragnaud (France) Premier Cru Réserve Spéciale, Grande Champagne Cognac 86 Proof. $50.

Luxury Cognac

100 • Pierre Croizet (France) Extra Extra, Cognac 80 Proof. $225.

100 • Pierre Ferrand (France) 1965 Mémoire Grande Champagne Single Vineyard Single Vintage Cognac, Cognac 80 Proof. $180.

100 • Pierre Ferrand (France) 1962 Mémoire Grande Champagne Single Vineyard Single Vintage Cognac, Cognac 80 Proof. $180.

99 • Pierre Ferrand (France) 1er Cru Ancestrale, Grande Champagne Cognac 80 Proof. $380.

98 • Hennessy (France) Paradis Rare Cognac, Cognac $249.

97 • Pierre Ferrand (France) 1er Cru Abel, Grande Champagne Cognac 80 Proof. $175.

97 • Pierre Frapin (France) Réserve Patrimoniale Extra, Grande Champagne Cognac 80 Proof. $495.

97 • Kelt (France) Petra, Tour du Monde 80 Proof. $650.

96 • Delamain (France) Réserve de la Famille, Rare Unblended Grande Champagne Cognac, Cognac 86 Proof. $300/500 ml.

96 • Pierre Ferrand (France) 1er Cru Sélection des Anges, Grande Champagne Cognac 80 Proof. $85.

96 • Hardy (France) Noces d'Or, Grande Champagne Cognac 80 Proof. $250.

95 • Pierre Ferrand (France) 1968 Mémoire Grande Champagne Single Vineyard Single Vintage Cognac, Cognac 80 Proof. $180.

95 • Château Montifaud (France) Grand Siècle 2000 Fine Petite Champagne Cognac 80 Proof. $118.50.

94 • Jean Fillioux (France) 1948 Grande Champagne 1er Cru du Cognac 86 Proof. $372.95.

93 • Jean Fillioux (France) Très Vieille Grande Champagne 1er Cru du Cognac 80 Proof. $255.

93 • Remy Martin (France) Extra , Fine Champagne Cognac 80 Proof. $300.

92 • Courvoisier (France) Initiale Extra, Cognac 80 Proof. $259.99.

92 • A. de Fussigny (France) Très Vieille Séries Rares, Grande Champagne Cognac 80 Proof. $190.

92 • Gabriel & Andreu (France) Lot 18, Grande Champagne Cognac 86 Proof. $90.

91 • Hine (France) 1960 Glenhaven Bottling—Grande Champagne Cognac 96 Proof. $195.

90 • Davidoff (France) Extra, Cognac 86 Proof. $150.

90 • Delamain (France) Vesper, Grande Champagne Cognac 80 Proof. $112.99.

90 • Delamain (France) Très Vénérable, Grande Champagne Cognac 80 Proof. $241.99.

90 • A. de Fussigny (France) Vieille Réserve Séries Rares, Fine Champagne Cognac 80 Proof. $110.

89 • Pierre Frapin (France) Château Fontpinot Grande Champagne Premier Cru du Cognac 80 Proof. $83.

89 • Pierre Joseph (France) 1er Cru Age d'Or, Grande Champagne Cognac 80 Proof. $120.

87 • Pierre Frapin (France) Ch. Fontpinot Premier Cru, Très Vieille Réserve, Grande Champagne Cognac 82 Proof. $110.

87 • Gautier (France) Maison Gautier 10th Generation Tradition Rare, Cognac 86 Proof. $199.

Armagnac

VSOP Armagnac

90 • Marquis de Caussade Armagnac (France) 10 Years Old 80 Proof. $40.

88 • Château du Tariquet (France) VSOP, Bas-Armagnac 80 Proof. $35.

87 • Castarède (France) VSOP, Armagnac 80 Proof. $35.

87 • Samalens (France) VSOP, Bas-Armagnac 80 Proof. $40.

85 • Brillat Savarin (France) VSOP, Armagnac 80 Proof. $29.99.

XO Armagnac

93 • Clés des Ducs (France) XO, Armagnac 80 Proof. $74.95.

90 • Marnier-Lapostolle (France) XO, Armagnac 80 Proof. $47.

89 • Larressingle (France) XO, Armagnac 86 Proof. $76.99.

86 • Marquis de Montesquiou (France) XO, Armagnac 80 Proof. $50.

Napoleon Armagnac

90 • Janneau (France) Réserve de la Maison, Armagnac 80 Proof. $45.

88 • Marquis de Caussade Armagnac (France) 17 Years Old 80 Proof. $48.

Luxury Armagnac

95 • Clés des Ducs (France) Millésimé 1962 Armagnac 84 Proof. $170.

95 • Clés des Ducs (France) 1942 Armagnac 82 Proof. $175.

95 • Marquis de Caussade Armagnac (France) 30 Years Old 80 Proof. $155.

94 • Samalens (France) 1962 Bas Armagnac 84 Proof. $258.50.

92 • Laberdolive (France) 1976 Domaine de Jaurrey, Bas-Armagnac 92 Proof. $91.99.

91 • Francis Darroze (France) Francis Darroze 1975 Domaine de St Aubin Bas-Armagnac 90 Proof. $139.99.

91 • Marcel Trepout Apotheose Armagnac (France) 80 Proof. $95.

89 • Samalens (France) Vieille Relique Bas-Armagnac 84 Proof. $110.

Calvados

95 • Coeur de Lion (France) 1977 Calvados Pays d'Auge 84 Proof. $223.95.

94 • Coeur de Lion (France) 1969 Calvados Pays d'Auge 84 Proof. $223.95.

89 • Busnel (France) Calvados du Pays d'Auge, Vieille Réserve VSOP 80 Proof. $32.

87 • Grand Solage Boulard (France) Calvados Pays d'Auge 80 Proof. $24.

Spanish Brandy

93 • Antonio Barbadillo (Spain) Gran Reserva, Brandy de Jerez $27.

92 • Lepanto (Spain) Solera Gran Reserva, Brandy de Jerez 80 Proof. $49.99.

90 • Sanchez Romate (Spain) Cardenal Mendoza Solera Gran Reserva Brandy de Jerez 80 Proof. $39.99.

90 • Torres (Spain) Miguel Torres Imperial Brandy, Penedes 80 Proof. $34.99.

88 • Conde de Osborne (Spain) Solera Gran Reserva, Brandy de Jerez 81 Proof. $50.

88 • Terry (Spain) Solera Gran Reserva, Terry Primero, Brandy de Jerez 80 Proof. $32.99.

87 • Grand Duque d' Alba (Spain) Gran Reserva Solera Brandy de Jerez 80 Proof. $39.99.

Other Brandies

93 • RMS Distillery (CA) QE 14 Year Old Rare French Oak Aged Alambic Brandy 80 Proof. $116.

91 • Jacopo Poli (Italy) 1987 L'Arzente Brandy Italiano 86 Proof. $35/375 ml.

91 • Jepson (CA) Signature Reserve Mendocino Alambic Brandy 80 Proof. $100.

89 • Jepson (CA) Rare Brandy 80 Proof. $34.

89 • RMS Distillery (CA) Folle Blanche 10 Year Old Rare Alambic Brandy 80 Proof. $60.

88 • RMS Distillery (CA) Special Reserve 7 Year Old Rare Alambic Brandy 80 Proof. $30.

86 • Paul Masson (CA) Grande Amber Brandy 80 Proof. $13.99.

86 • Tbilisi (Georgia) Rare Extra 17 Year Old Deluxe Georgian Brandy 80 Proof. $28.99.

85 • The Christian Brothers (CA) Brandy 80 Proof. $8.99.

85 • Friedrich-Wilhelm Gymnasium (Germany) Alter Riesling Weinbrand VSOP 80 Proof. $20/500 ml.

Grappa

98 • Jacopo Poli (Italy) 1997 Grappa Amorosa di Torcolato 86 Proof. $55/100ml.

97 • Ceretto (Italy) Grappa di Moscato 86 Proof. $62.99.

96 • Ceretto (Italy) Wood Aged Grappa di Blange 86 Proof. $91.

95 • Mazzetti d'Altavilla (Italy) Grappa di Nebbiolo Da Barolo, "Le Gemme" 86 Proof. $85/100 ml.

95 • Nonino (Italy) Grappa di Moscato 80 Proof. $104.49.

94 • Jacopo Poli (Italy) 1996 Grappa Amorosa di Merlot 86 Proof. $55/100ml.

94 • Ornellaia (Italy) Grappa di Merlot 84 Proof. $60.99/375 ml.

93 • Michele Chiarlo (Italy) Grappa di Vinacce di Barolo 84 Proof. $34.99/375 ml.

93 • Inga (Italy) Grappa di Moscato 84 Proof. $23.99/375 ml.

93 • Jacopo Poli (Italy) 1996 Grappa Amorosa di Cabernet 86 Proof. $55/100ml.

93 • Marchesi Antinori (Italy) Tignanello Grappa 84 Proof. $30/375 ml.

93 • St. George (CA) Grappa of Traminer, California 80 Proof. $21.95/375 ml.

91 • Mazzetti d'Altavilla (Italy) Grappa di Barbera, "I Frutti Di Vetro" 86 Proof. $85/375 ml.

90 • Antonella Bocchino (Italy) Grappa di Barbaresco 90 Proof. $43.99/375 ml.

90 • Inga (Italy) Grappa di Gavi di Gavi 84 Proof. $19.95/375 ml.

90 • Jacopo Poli (Italy) 1996 Grappa Amorosa di Vespaiolo 86 Proof. $55/100ml.

90 • Mosby (CA) Grappa di Traminer 80 Proof. $27/375 ml.

89 • Jacopo Poli (Italy) 1996 Grappa Amorosa di Pinot 86 Proof. $55/100ml.

89 • Mastroberardino (Italy) Grappa Novia di Taurasi 90 Proof. $50.

89 • St. George (CA) Grappa of Zinfandel, California 80 Proof. $21.95/375 ml.

88 • Ca Rugate (Italy) Grappa di Recioto di Soave 86 Proof. $40/375 ml.

88 • Ceretto (Italy) Grappa di Nebbiolo da Barolo, "Brunate" 100 Proof. $71.50.

88 • Michele Chiarlo (Italy) Grappa di Vinacce di Gavi 84 Proof. $34.99/375 ml.

88 • Inga (Italy) Grappa di Nebbiolo da Barolo 84 Proof. $23.99/375 ml.

88 • Jacopo Poli (Italy) Sarpa di Poli Grappa 86 Proof. $22/50ml.

88 • Luxardo (Italy) Grappa Euganea 80 Proof. $27.50.

88 • Marchesi Incisa della Rocchetta (Italy) Grappa da Vinacce di Sassicaia 84 Proof. $114.99/375 ml.

88 • Nonino (Italy) Grappa di Monovitigno Picolit 1993 100 Proof. $153.49.

88 • Ruffino (Italy) Grappa Riserva Ducale 90 Proof. $25/375 ml.

87 • Michele Chiarlo (Italy) Grappa di Vinacce di Moscato d'Asti 84 Proof. $34.99/375 ml.

87 • Martin Brothers (CA) Grappa di Moscato 80 Proof. $34/375 ml.

87 • Mastroberardino (Italy) Grappa Novia di Greco di Tufo 80 Proof. $48.

86 • Magnotta (Canada) 1997 Riesling Ice Grappa, Ontario 90 Proof. $25/500 ml.

86 • Marchesi di Gresy (Italy) Grappa Martinenga 84 Proof. $45.

86 • Martin Brothers (CA) Grappa di Nebbiolo 80 Proof. $34/375 ml.

86 • Ruffino (Italy) Grappa di Cabreo Il Borgo 90 Proof. $25/375 ml.

85 • Michele Chiarlo (Italy) Grappa di Vinacce di Barbera d' Asti 84 Proof. $34.99/375 ml.

Eau de Vie

96 • Moletto (Italy) Distillato D'Uva 80 Proof. $34.

92 • Quady (CA) Spirit of Elysium Black Muscat Distillate 80 Proof. $33.

89 • César Chiarella (Peru) Pisco Italia 89.4 Proof. $32.50.

88 • Jacopo Poli (Italy) 1997 Immature Grape Brandy, Chiara di Moscato 86 Proof. $55/375 ml.

88 • William Chevaliers (Switzerland) Eau de Vie du Valais, Valais 84 Proof. $20/500 ml.

86 • César Chiarella (Peru) Pisco Puro 85.9 Proof. $24.95.

86 • Jacopo Poli (Italy) Uva Viva di Poli, Distillato d'Uva 78 Proof. $35/50ml.

Fruit Eau de Vie

100 • Jacopo Poli (Italy) 1997 Pear Brandy Stagione di Pere 86 Proof. $30/375 ml.

95 • F. Meyer (France) Eau-de-vie de Kirsch, Cherry Brandy 90 Proof. $22.95/375 ml.

95 • Emil Scheibel (Germany) Black Forest Williams-Birnen-Brand, Williams Pear Brandy 80 Proof. $33.50/375 ml.

94 • Jacopo Poli (Italy) 1997 Raspberry Brandy Stagione di Lamponi 86 Proof. $30/375 ml.

92 • Emil Scheibel (Germany) Black Forest Kirschwasser, Cherry Brandy 80 Proof. $33.50/375 ml.

91 • Clear Creek Distillery (OR) Bartlett Pear Brandy 80 Proof. $20/375 ml.

89 • F. Meyer (France) Eau-de-vie de Mirabelle, Plum Brandy 90 Proof. $22.50/375 ml.

89 • F. Meyer (France) Eau-de-vie de Framboise, Raspberry Brandy 90 Proof. $24.95/375 ml.

87 • G.E. Massenez (France) Eau-de-Vie de Poire Williams, Williams Pear Brandy 80 Proof. $34/375 ml.

87 • F. Meyer (France) Eau-de-vie de Poire Williams, Williams Pear Brandy 90 Proof. $23.95/375 ml.

Scale: Superlative (96-100), Exceptional (90-95), Highly Recommended (85-89), Recommended (80-84), Not Recommended (Under 80)

two

Scotch, Irish, New Zealand, and Japanese Whiskies

The reason that there are eighteen holes in a round of golf is that there are eighteen shots in a bottle of Scotch.

– Ancient Celtic sports lore

An Overview – The Basis of Scotch Whisky, Irish Whiskey, Japanese Whisky, and New Zealand Whisky

Scotland
There are two basic categories of Scotch whisky: malt whisky, which is made primarily from malted barley that has been dried over smoking peat fires, and grain whisky, which is made from unmalted wheat or corn. These whiskies are aged in used wooden Bourbon, Sherry, or other wine barrels for a minimum of three years, although five to 10 years is the general practice.

Ireland
There are two basic categories of Irish whiskey: malt whiskey, which is made primarily from malted barley that has been kiln-dried, but not over peat fires, and grain whiskey, which is made from unmalted wheat or corn. These whiskeys are aged in used wooden Bourbon or Sherry barrels for a minimum of three years, although five to eight years is the norm.

Japan
Japanese whiskies, both malt and blended, are broadly based on Scotch whiskies, with some top brands even being made with imported Scottish water and peat-smoked barley malt. The peat-smoke character of Japanese whiskies is generally more subtle and delicate than their Scottish counterparts. Japanese whiskies are aged in both new and used (usually Bourbon) wooden barrels, which may be either charred or uncharred.

New Zealand
New Zealand whiskies draw on Scottish, Irish, and American traditions. The water used for mashing and dilution comes from streams that draw off of peat bogs, and the resulting whisky is aged in American oak barrels for a minimum of six years for malt whisky and three years for grain whisky.

The Distillation of Scotch Whisky, Irish Whiskey, Japanese Whisky, and New Zealand Whisky

Scotland
All Scotch malt whiskies are double or triple distilled in pot stills, whereas Scotch grain whiskies are made in column stills.

Scotch at a Glance

Top Scores:

Top Highland Single Malt Scotch

98 • Ben Nevis (Scotland)
The Scotch Malt Whisky
Society Bottling, 15 Year Old
Single West Highland Malt
Scotch Whisky, Cask No. 78.8,
Distilled October 1978,
Bottled October 1993
111.6 Proof. $75.

Top Speyside Single Malt Scotch

100 • The Macallan (Scotland)
25 Year Old, Anniversary,
Single Highland Malt Scotch
Whisky 86 Proof. $175.

Top Island Single Malt Scotch

96 • Highland Park (Scotland)
12 Year Old Orkney Island
Single Malt Scotch Whisky
86 Proof. $40.99.

Top Lowland Single Malt Scotch

97 • Inverleven Stills,
Dumbarton (Scotland)
Cadenhead Bottling, 27 Year
Old, Cask Strength Lowland
Malt Scotch Whisky, Distilled
March 1969, Bottled
June 1996 97.6 Proof. $95.

Ireland

Irish whiskeys, both blended and malt, are usually triple distilled through both column and pot stills, although there are a few exclusively pot-distilled brands.

Japan

Japanese whiskies follow the Scottish tradition, with malt whiskies being double distilled in pot stills and grain whiskies in column stills.

New Zealand

New Zealand malt and grain whiskies are double distilled in pot stills.

Classifications of Scotch Whisky, Irish Whiskey, Japanese Whisky, and New Zealand Whisky

Scotland

Single Malt Scotch Whisky is malt whisky that has been produced at one distillery. It may be a mix of malt whiskies from different years (in which case the age statement on the bottle label gives the age of the youngest spirit in the mix). The barley malt for Scotch whisky is first dried over fires that have been stoked with dried peat (a form of compacted grass and heather compost that is harvested from the moors). The peat smoke adds a distinctive smoky tang to the taste of the malt whisky. **Vatted Malt Scotch Whisky** is a blend of malt whiskies from different Scottish distilleries. **Scotch Grain Whisky** (which is rarely bottled as such) is made primarily from wheat or corn with a small percentage of barley and barley malt (the latter not being dried over peat fires).

Blended Scotch Whisky is a blend of grain whisky and malt whisky.

Ireland

Irish Pure Pot Still Whiskey is generally labeled as such. Otherwise, Irish whiskeys are a mix of pot and column-distilled whiskeys. **Irish Malt Whiskey** is likewise so designated.

Standard Irish Whiskey is a blend of malt and grain whiskies.

Japan

Japanese Malt Whisky is produced in pot stills from lightly peated barley malt. **Standard Japanese Whisky** is a blend of malt whiskey (Japanese or Scotch) and domestically produced grain whiskey.

New Zealand

New Zealand Single Malt Whisky is pot-distilled malt whisky. **New Zealand Blended Whisky** is a mix of domestic malt and grain whiskies.

The Whiskey Regions

Scotland

The Highlands consist of the portion of Scotland north of a line from Dundee on the North Sea coast in the east to Greenock on the Irish Sea in the west, including all of the islands off the mainland except for Islay. Highland malt whiskies cover a broad spectrum of styles. They are generally aromatic, smooth and medium bodied, with palates that range from lushly complex to floral delicacy. The subregions of the Highlands include **Speyside**; the **North, East,** and **West Highlands**; the **Orkney Isles**; and the **Western Islands (Arran, Jura, Mull,** and **Skye)**.

The Lowlands encompass the entire Scottish mainland south of the Highlands except the Kintyre Peninsula where Campbeltown is located. Lowland malt whiskies are light bodied, relatively sweet, and delicate.

Islay is an island off the west coast. Traditional Islay malt whiskies are intensely smoky and pungent in character with a distinctive iodine or medicinal tang that is said to come from sea salt permeating the local peat that is used to dry the barley malt.

Campbeltown is a port located on the tip of the Kintyre Peninsula on the southwest coast that has its own distinctive spicy and salt-tinged malt whiskies.

Top Islay Single Malt Scotches

99 • **Lagavulin (Scotland) 16 Year Old Islay Single Malt Scotch Whisky 86 Proof. $50.**

99 • **Bowmore (Scotland) 30 Year Old Islay Single Malt Scotch Whisky 86 Proof. $189.99.**

Top Campbeltown Single Malt Scotch

92 • **«Springbank (Scotland) Murray, McDavid Bottling, 30 Year Old Campbeltown Single Malt Scotch Whisky, Sherry Wood Aged, Distilled in 1965 92 Proof. $100.**

Top Vatted Malt Scotch

93 • **Moidart (Scotland) 21 Year Old Pure Malt Vatted Scotch Whisky 92 Proof. $103.**

Top Blended Scotch

93 • **Johnny Walker (Scotland) Blue Label Blend of Rarest Scotch Whiskies 80 Proof. $180.**

Top Irish Whiskey

95 • **Midleton (Ireland) 1995 Very Rare Irish Whiskey 80 Proof. $99.99.**

Japanese Whisky

86 • **Suntory (Japan) Yamazaki 12 Year Old Pure Malt Whisky 86 Proof. $38.**

≈

Ireland

A series of corporate consolidations and resulting plant closures have left the island with only three distilleries, one in County Antrim at the northern tip of Ulster and two in the Republic of Ireland to the south.

Japan

The whisky distilleries of Japan are scattered throughout Honshu and Hokkaido, the two main northern islands of Japan, with the malt whisky distilleries being located for the most part in mountainous regions where there are good water supplies.

New Zealand

New Zealand currently has only one operating whisky distillery in Dunedin on the South Island.

Origins and History

Whisky is, in its most basic sense, a spirit that is distilled from grain. Sometimes the grain has been malted, sometimes not. It is aged, often for long periods of time, in wooden barrels (usually oak). This barrel-aging smoothes the rough palate of the raw spirit and adds aromatic and flavoring nuances along with the base amber hue, all of which set whiskies apart from white grain spirits such as Vodka, Gin, and Aquavit, which are distilled closer to neutrality in taste, and then generally not aged in wood.

Scotch Whisky

The basis of Scotch whisky is the heather-flavored ales made from barley malt that the Picts and their prehistoric ancestors brewed. Archeologists have found evidence of such brewing dating back to at least 2000 B.C. This ale (which is still produced today by at least one Scottish microbrewer) was low in alcohol and not very stable.

Starting in the 9th century, Irish monks arrived in Scotland to Christianize their Celtic brethren. Along with the Word of the Lord they brought the first primitive stills, which they had picked up during their proselytizing visits to mainland Europe during the Dark Ages. The local Picts soon found that they could create a stable alcoholic beverage by distilling their heather ale. Simple stills came to be found in most rural homesteads, and homemade whisky became an integral part of Gaelic culture.

As long as Scottish kings ruled the country from Edinburgh the status quo of whisky as just another farm product was more or less maintained. But the Act of Union in 1707 that combined England, Wales, and Scotland into the United Kingdom altered the Scotch whisky scene forever. The London government soon levied excise taxes on Scottish-made whisky (while at the same time cutting the taxes on English gin). The result was a predictable boom in illicit distilling. In 1790s Edinburgh it was estimated that over 400 illegal stills competed with just eight licensed distilleries. A number of present-day Scottish distilleries, particularly in the Highlands, have their origins in such illicit operations.

The Excise Act of 1823 reduced taxes on Scotch whisky to a tolerable degree. This act coincided with the dawn of the Industrial Revolution, and entrepreneurs were soon building new, state-of-the-art distilleries. The local moonshiners (called smugglers) did not go quietly. Some of the first licensed distillers in rural locations were threatened by their illicit peers, but in the end production efficiencies and the rule of law won out. The whisky that came from these distilleries was made primarily from malted barley that had been kiln-dried over peat fires. The smoke from these peat fires gave the malt a distinctive tang that made the Scottish product instantly identifiable by whisky drinkers all over the world.

The 19th century brought a rush of changes to the Scotch whisky industry. The introduction of column stills early in the 1830s led to the creation of grain whisky, a bland spirit made primarily from unmalted grains such as corn. Grain whisky in turn led to the creation of blended Scotch whisky in the late 1860s. The smooth blandness of the grain whisky toned down the assertive smoky character of the malt whiskies.

The resulting blended whisky proved to be milder and more acceptable to foreign consumers, particularly the English, who turned to Scotch whisky in the 1870s when a *Phylloxera* infestation in the vineyards of Europe disrupted supplies of Cognac and Port—two of the mainstays of civilized living. Malt whisky distilleries were bought up by blending companies and their output was blended with grain whiskies to create the great blended brands that have come to dominate the market. The malt whisky distilleries took a back seat to these brands and sold most or, in some cases, all of their production to the blenders. But the recent popular revival of malt whiskies has led most of the distilleries to come out with bottlings of their own products.

By the 1970s international liquor companies owned most of the malt whisky distilleries, a situation that continues to this day.

A Note on Spelling

For reasons that have yet to be adequately explained, American and Irish distillers tend to spell the word whiskey with an "e" while their Scotch, Canadian, Japanese, and New Zealand peers spell whisky without it.

Why Blended Scotch Whisky Is a Good Thing, Even If You Prefer Single Malts

It is a truism of religion that converts frequently become the most zealous of believers. Among freshly minted modern-day enthusiasts of Scotch malt whiskies, it is a frequently heard refrain that malt whiskies are superior to the blended article, and that the latter are just not worth bothering with. Personal taste is ultimately subjective of course, but single-malt drinkers should raise their hats in salute whenever a Dewar's or Johnnie Walker delivery truck drives by, because without these blended brands most of the remaining malt distilleries would not exist. Blended Scotch whiskies require a mix of dozens of different malt whiskies to be combined with grain whisky in order to create the desired blend. The individual percentages of each malt whisky may be small, but each contributes its unique character to the blend. A blender will thus need to buy or produce a large amount of different malt whiskies in order to maintain the consistency of the blend. Thus, for a malt whisky distillery, the single malt may get all of the glory, but the blends ultimately pay the bills.

Ghost Whiskies

The modern history of Scotch whisky has been a series of boom-and-bust cycles. In the late 1800s a large number of new distilleries were established, but at the turn of the 20th century came a crash when financial hijinks among wholesale whisky merchants were brought to light. The industry revived, only to be disrupted by the advent of World War I and a prohibitionist mood in the government (it was at this same time that Britain's famously odd hours of operation for pubs were established). National Prohibition in the United States disrupted sales to a major export market, but, oddly enough, far more whisky was shipped to Canada, the Bahamas, and Mexico than had hitherto been the case (perhaps for transshipment to the United States?). World War II resulted in many distilleries turning to industrial alcohol production, but in the postwar years whisky production was boosted by substantial exports to the United States. All of these ups and downs have led to the phenomenon of distilleries being mothballed, reopened, and mothballed again depending on the demands of the marketplace. In such cases, and also when plants are permanently closed down, their brands of single malt whiskies continue to live on in the marketplace for decades as the previously distilled whisky slowly finishes its aging time and is bottled. These "ghost" or "fossil" whiskies keep alive the proud names of distilleries that were torn down long ago and replaced by parking lots and housing developments.

Independent Merchant Bottlings

Before the present-day revival in popularity of single malt Scotch whiskies, a number of the 100 or so malt whisky distilleries did not bother to bottle their own product. Almost all of their production would be sold to blenders, directly or through brokers. The one exception to this rule was the relative handful of casks from each season's production that would be sold to independent retail merchants or bottlers who would mature the whisky on their own, then at an age of their own choosing, bottle and sell them to the public. This commercial tradition was more prevalent before the rise of supermarket and discount liquor chains, but a handful of independent bottlers remain in Scotland. The best known of these are Cadenhead, Gordon & McPhail, and The Malt Whiskey Society. These merchant bottlings can offer interesting variations on official distillery bottlings, but that variance is not always a good thing. Caveat emptor.

Irish Whiskey

The Scots most likely learned about distilling from the Irish (though they are loath to admit it). The Irish in turn learned about it, according to the Irish at least, from missionary monks who arrived in Ireland in the 7th century. The actual details are a bit sketchy for the next 700 years or so, but it does seem reasonable to believe that monks in the various monasteries were distilling *aqua vitae* ("water of life"), primarily for making medical compounds. These first distillates were probably grape or fruit brandy rather than grain spirit. Barley-based whiskey (the word derives from *uisce beatha,* the Gaelic interpretation of aqua vitae) first appears in the historical record in the mid-1500s when the Tudor kings began to consolidate English control in Ireland. Queen Elizabeth I was said to be fond of it and had casks shipped to London on a regular basis.

The imposition of an excise tax in 1661 had the same effect as it did in Scotland, with the immediate commencement of the production of *poteen* (the Irish version of moonshine). This did not, however, slow down the growth of the distilling industry, and by the end of the 18th century there were over 2,000 stills in operation around the country.

Under British rule Ireland was export oriented and, along with grains and assorted foodstuffs, Irish distillers produced large quantities of pot-distilled whiskey for export into the expanding British Empire. Irish whiskey outsold Scotch whisky in most markets because it was lighter in body. It is said that in the late 19th century over 400 brands of Irish whiskey were being exported and sold in the United States.

This happy state of affairs for Irish distillers lasted into the early 20th century when the market began to change. The Irish distillers, pot still users to a man, were slow to respond to the rise of blended Scotch whisky with its column-distilled, smooth grain whisky component. When National Prohibition in the United States closed off Irish whisky's largest export market, many of the smaller distilleries closed. The remaining distilleries then failed to adequately anticipate the coming of Repeal (unlike the Scotch distillers) and were caught short without adequate stocks when it came. The Great Depression, trade embargoes between the newly independent Irish Republic and the United Kingdom, and World War II caused further havoc among the distillers.

In 1966 the three remaining distilling companies in the Republic of Ireland—Powers, Jameson, and Cork Distilleries—merged into a single company, Irish Distillers Company (IDC). In 1972, Bushmills, the last distillery in Northern Ireland, joined IDC. In 1975 IDC opened a new mammoth distillery at Midleton, near Cork, and all of the other distilleries in the Republic were closed down with the production of their brands being transferred to Midleton. For a 14-year period the Midleton plant and Bushmills in Northern Ireland were the only distilleries in the country.

This sad state of affairs ended in 1989 when a potato-peel ethanol plant in Dundalk was converted into a whiskey distillery. The new Cooley Distillery began to produce malt and grain whiskeys, with the first three-year-old bottlings being released in 1992.

Japanese Whisky

The modern Japanese whisky industry can trace its beginnings back to one man, Masataka Taketsura. The son of a sake brewer, Taketsura went to Scotland in 1918 and spent two years studying chemistry at Glasgow University and working at a Scotch whisky distillery in the Highland village of Rothes. He returned to Japan in 1920 with a Scottish bride and a determination to change the Japanese distilling industry.

The Japanese were then, as they are now, major consumers of Scotch whisky. Locally produced spirits, however, were limited to the fiery sorghum or sweet potato-based *shochu*, and a handful of dubious "whiskies" that were little more than neutral spirits colored with caramel. Taketsura convinced the owners of what became the Suntory Company to begin production of barley malt and grain whiskies based on the Scottish model. These whiskies, some of which are made from imported peat-smoked Scottish malt, became very successful in the Japanese market. Other distilleries soon followed Suntory's lead, and these grain-based whiskies, based on single malt and blended Scotch whisky models (and later Bourbon whiskey), soon came to dominate the Japanese market.

Modern Japanese distillers (including the Nikka Whisky Distillery, which was founded by Taketsura in 1934) have followed this trend and nowadays produce and market a full range of malt and blended whiskies.

New Zealand Whisky

Scottish emigrants brought their whisky-making skills to New Zealand in the 1840s. A thriving whisky industry soon developed and operated until 1875, when new, excessively high excise taxes and heavy competition from imported British whiskies forced the local commercial distilleries to shut down. A new, almost commercial-sized moonshine trade quickly replaced them, a situation that continued for almost a century.

In 1968 a new whisky distillery opened in Dunedin. It produces a range of malt and grain whiskies, broadly in the Scottish style, from locally grown grain. Even the barley malt is kilned and smoked using local peat.

Whisky Reviews

Aberlour (Scotland)

Aberlour 10 Year Old Single Highland Malt Scotch Whisky 86 proof $25.　　　　　　**90**

Orange-amber hue. Fine aromas of Sherry, honey, and orange peel with a fine malt accent. Moderately full-bodied and impressively viscous, showing a mouth-coating quality and well-balanced flavors that follow the aromas. This could be drunk anytime but it is weighty enough for a digestif.

Aberlour 15 Year Old, Sherry Wood Finish, Single Highland Malt Scotch Whisky 86 proof $45.　　　**95**

Full amber-gold hue. Lush peach and sweet smoky malt aromas. Full-bodied, with lovely vanilla and fruit flavors that persist through the elegant, lingering finish that shows fine malt persistence. Very complete, balanced, and harmonious.

Ardbeg (Scotland)

Ardbeg 17 Year Old Islay Single Malt Scotch Whisky 86 proof $70.　　　**94**

Pale, bright yellow-straw hue. Wonderfully perfumed heather and peat aromas with only a touch of coal tar. Pure and clean, with a medium body and a silky mouthfeel. The flavors speak of fresh peat and heather and persist wonderfully. This is a cerebral malt whose charms will continue to reveal themselves as the glass empties.

Ardbeg, Gordon & MacPhail Bottling, 20 Year Old Single Islay Malt Scotch Whisky, Distilled in 1974, Bottled in 1995 80 proof $75.　　　**90**

Golden with orange highlights. Full-bodied. Notes of smoke, tar, peat, salt. Rich entry with big tarry flavors on the midpalate through a lengthy smoke-dominated finish. An assertive bottling leaning toward a digestif style.

Scale: Superlative (96-100), Exceptional (90-95), Highly Recommended (85-89), Recommended (80-84), Not Recommended (Under 80)

Ardbeg 1978 Limited Edition Ultimate Islay Single Malt Scotch Whisky 86 proof $125.   **96**

Pale yellow-straw hue. Aromas of wet peat, heather, and minerals with a suggestion of smoke. Moderately full-bodied with a markedly thick mouthfeel and intense stony quality. The subtle peat hits late in the finish and lingers. This spirit demands attention.

Ardbeg 1974 Provenance Limited Edition Very Old Islay Single Malt Scotch Whisky 101.2 proof $500.   **97**

Burnished golden hue. Intense, perfumed aromas suggest smoky peat and wet stone. Quite pungent, yet not overpowering. Full-bodied and viscous on the palate with stony flavor intensity that develops throughout the extraordinary finish. Different flavors emerge with each sip.

Auchentoshan (Scotland)

Auchentoshan 10 Year Old Single Lowland Malt Scotch Whisky 80 proof $35.   **82**

Pale gold. Moderately light-bodied. Notes of dried flowers, grass, oil. Delicate nose with a distinct oily note that is translated onto the mouthfeel. Flavors are particularly grassy through the finish. Quite low key with a dryish character overall. Versatile. A richer aperitif style.

Auchentoshan 21 Year Old Single Lowland Malt Scotch Whisky 86 proof $90.   **86**

Medium amber-gold hue. Markedly peaty on the nose with a distinctive smoky, toffee element. Moderately full-bodied with peat-rich flavors and a mineral presence that fills the palate and lingers well onto the finish. Very mellow in character.

Auchroisk (Singleton) (Scotland)

Auchroisk, The Singleton of Auchroisk,10 Year Old Single Malt Scotch Whisky, Distilled in 1981, Bottled in 1992 86 proof $40.   **85**

Straw with orange highlights. Moderately full-bodied. Notes of honey, apricot, vanilla, licorice. Soft caramelized malt nose leads a mellow, very smooth palate with a hint of sweetness and good viscosity through the finish. A full-blown digestif style.

Balblair (Scotland)

Balblair, Gordon & MacPhail Bottling,10 Year Old Single Highland Malt Scotch Whisky 40 proof $45.   **88**

Amber with slight orange highlights. Medium-bodied. Notes of brown spice, peat, charcoal. Rich malty nose with peaty accents translates well onto the very dry lengthy palate. Quite flavorsome, though austere on the finish.

Ballantine's (Scotland)

Ballantine's, Finest Blended Scotch Whisky 80 proof $15.99.   **86**

Gold, amber tint. Salted cashews and a touch of caramel dominate the nose with more subtle date and fig flavors peeking through. Full-bodied, yet delicate in texture, these flavors provide a tangy, deep finish.

Ballantine's Blended Scotch Whisky, Gold Seal 12 Year Old 80 proof $21.99.   **90**

Deep gold. Medium-bodied. Soft honey and pineapple flavors balance with deeper aromas of molasses, leather, and smoke. Buttery texture with a salty, nutty finish.

The Balvenie (Scotland)

The Balvenie 10 Year Old Founder's Reserve Single Malt Scotch Whisky
86 proof $25.99.   **85**

Deep golden luster. Extraordinarily aromatic with a sweet malt nose showing Bourbon-like complexity. Rich on the entry with fine viscosity and sweet, almost fruity character. Impressively date-like flavors linger. Stylish and mellow.

The Balvenie 12 Year Old Double Wood Single Malt Scotch Whisky
86 proof $32.99.   **89**

Deep orange-amber hue. Markedly rich aromas show a licorice-like note. Heavily wood influenced, with a deep smoky accent. Mouthfeel is viscous and rich with a powerful oak accent and well-spiced finish. A rich after-dinner style.

The Balvenie 15 Year Old Single Barrel Single Malt Scotch Whisky
100.8 proof $49.99.   **94**

Full, brilliant orange-amber hue. Bright floral aromas are very pronounced. This is showing a heavy Sherry-like character, almost flor-like. Intensely flavorful, with fine texture and mouthfeel, and a touch fiery on the finish. Fantastically salty and tangy throughout. This wakes up the palate.

The Balvenie 21 Year Old Port Wood Single Malt Scotch Whisky
86 proof $64.99.   **93**

Bright golden-yellow hue with a reddish tint. Aromas of violets and rich fruit. Marked by Port-wine fruitiness, dried apricot, and elegant wood spice. Very flavorful, yet delicate and persistent.

Ben Nevis (Scotland)

Ben Nevis, The Scotch Malt Whisky Society Bottling,
15 Year Old Single West Highland Malt Scotch Whisky, Cask No. 78.8,
Distilled October 1978, Bottled October 1993 111.6 proof $75.   **98**

Dark reddish-amber. Full-bodied. Notes of molasses, Oloroso Sherry. Decadent, smoky Oloroso aromas reveal a silky, dry toffee palate with great depth through a lingering smoked caramelized finish. This speaks loudly of the barrel in which it has rested for 15 years. Full-fledged digestif that should stand up to strong cigars.

Benriach (Scotland)

Benriach 10 Year Old Pure Highland Malt Scotch Whisky 86 proof $35.   **95**

Light straw appearance. Medium-bodied. Notes of light peat, pear, tropical dried fruit, vanilla. Full, complex, perfumed nose leads a crisp, elegant mouthfeel with a full array of lighter flavors on the midpalate through to a subtle peaty finish with a hint of sweetness. For tippling anytime.

Bladnoch (Scotland)

Bladnoch, Cadenhead Bottling, 16 Year Old, Cask Strength Lowland
Malt Scotch Whisky, Distilled June 1980, Bottled September 1996
116.4 proof $72.   **92**

Bright yellow-gold color. Medium-bodied. Lush notes of caramel, dried apricots, grass. Sweet creamy caramel aromas lead a subtle and mildly sweet palate with a warm peppery mouthfeel and a grassy finish that lingers. This tastes very fresh, even delicate, given its age. Benefits from a spot of water.

Scale: Superlative (96-100), Exceptional (90-95), Highly Recommended (85-89),
Recommended (80-84), Not Recommended (Under 80)

Bowmore (Scotland)

Bowmore 10 Year Old Islay Single Malt Scotch Whisky
86 proof $34.95.   **88**

Medium amber. Medium-bodied with a smooth texture. Flavors of tropical fruits, nuts, smoke, grass, and hazelnuts play together along with a light kiss of mint at the close.

Bowmore 12 Year Old Islay Single Malt Scotch Whisky
86 proof $37.99.   **82**

Bright amber-gold. Medium-bodied. Notes of vanilla, seaweed, dried fruits, heather. Attractive floral, heather-accented aromas with a hint of sweetness on the palate. Smooth mouthfeel with a subtle, lingering finish.

Bowmore Cask Strength Islay Single Malt Scotch Whisky 112 proof $60.   **90**

Bright amber-gold hue. Heather, peat, coal tar, and iodine aromas jump out of the glass. Pungent. A medium-bodied palate with assertively peaty flavors that parade across the mouth and linger on the finish. A very pure Islay expression that will fill a room with its bouquet.

Bowmore 17 Year Old Islay Single Malt Scotch Whisky 86 proof $70.   **93**

Amber-gold appearance. Rich aromas of heather, peat, butterscotch. Viscous, textured and rich on the mouthfeel. A full-bodied style with full peat flavors tempered by butterscotch accents make this a mouth-filling malt. An after-dinner style.

Bowmore Sherry Casked Darkest Islay Single Malt Scotch Whisky
86 proof $80.   **89**

Dark amber hue. Generous aromas of mocha, dried fruits, and peat. A full-bodied, rich style with very woody flavors that take a vinous note. The finish is quite fruity and rich, though this lacks the intensity of perfumed smoky Islay peat character. A fine after-dinner style.

Bowmore 21 Year Old Islay Single Malt Scotch Whisky 86 proof $99.99.   **90**

Full gold with amber hints. Moderately full-bodied. Notes of caramel, burnt orange, peat. Full aromas with rich Sherry notes and peaty undertones. Oily and viscous texture with a hint of sea spray and peat. Complex array of flavors through the finish.

Bowmore 22 Year Old Islay Single Malt Scotch Whisky 86 proof $128.99.   **91**

Bright orange-amber appearance. Moderately full-bodied. Notes of honeysuckle, smoky peat, Sherry wood. Big sweet floral nose leads a sweet entry of Sherry wood with an oily feel on the palate. Luxurious and well balanced with lots of soft heather notes lingering through to the finish.

Bowmore 25 Year Old Islay Single Malt Scotch Whisky 86 proof $190.   **95**

Rich amber hue. Generously aromatic with mocha, peat, and salt. Full-bodied with a luxurious mouthfeel and a viscous texture showing the age and class of this malt. Sweeter toffee and chocolate flavors upfront give way to a lingering honeyed, peaty finish. An outstanding after-dinner drink.

Bowmore 30 Year Old Islay Single Malt Scotch Whisky 86 proof $289.99.   **99**

Rich golden-amber. Full-bodied. Dried stone fruit, Sherry wood, iodine. Full nose of fruity aromas with peaty backnotes. Wonderfully rich, smooth texture with a long dry finish of lingering salty peat flavors. This is clearly a rich digestif style with plenty of Sherry cask character.

Bruichladdich (Scotland)

Bruichladdich 15 Year Old Single Islay Malt Scotch Whisky 86 proof $45.   **88**

Straw appearance. Moderately full-bodied. Notes of marzipan, flower blossoms, honey. Sweet floral nose leads a sweet creamy-textured mouthfeel with generous malty flavors that taper to a subtle finish with a hint of peat. A very accessible Islay style.

Bushmills (Ireland)

Bushmills Irish Whiskey (White Label) 80 proof $16. 84

Bright yellow with amber highlights. Moderately light-bodied. Notes of dried tropical fruits, salt, minerals. Pleasant, with a subtle Sherry nose. Light and tangy on the palate with a compact warming finish.

Bushmills Special Old Irish Whiskey 80 proof $25.99. 89

Bright orange-amber hue. Delicate vinous aromas show a dark Sherry character with a very subtle note of walnuts. Smooth, fruity attack develops into a spicy, smooth, rounded, medium-bodied palate. Finishes with lingering sweet oak spice. Well balanced and drinkable.

Bushmills 10 Year Old Single Malt Irish Whiskey 80 proof $28.99. 91

Amber with yellow highlights. Fragrant nose with subtle aromas. Moderately full-bodied. Dried tropical fruit and sweet pecan flavors develop on a rich and oily textured palate. Much of the pleasure lies with the luxurious texture.

Bushmills 16 Year Old Rare Irish Single Malt Whiskey 80 proof $55. 93

Full orange-amber luster. Medium-bodied. Very spicy aromas with complex spice and vinous accents. Rich on the attack, with a fine texture and rounded malty flavors. Sweet, lingering finish. Very smooth and rich with an oily texture.

Caol Ila (Scotland)

Caol Ila, Signatory Bottling, 21 Year Old Single Islay Malt Scotch Whisky, Distilled 27 December 1974, Bottled 26 July 1996 115.6 proof $79.99. 82

Light straw. Moderately light-bodied. Notes of peat, anise, sea salt, pepper. Full seaweed nose reveals a light and peppery palate with plenty of flavor through to the warm finish. An aperitif style.

Cardhu (Scotland)

Cardhu 12 Year Old Highland Single Malt Scotch Whisky 80 proof $38. NR

Chivas Regal (Scotland)

Chivas Regal 12 Year Old, Premium Scotch Whisky 80 proof $25. 88

Medium gold. Moderately light-bodied. Notes of dried citrus, salt, minerals. Subtle smoky malt nose reveals a firm mouthfeel with a mineral note complementing a fruity entry through to a subtle finish.

Clan MacGregor (Scotland)

Clan MacGregor Blended Scotch Whisky 80 proof $10.99. NR

Clynelish (Scotland)

Clynelish, Glenhaven Bottling, 12 Year Old Single Malt Scotch Whisky 122 proof $65. 89

Very pale yellow. Medium-bodied. Notes of citrus, peat, flowers. Very aromatic floral, heather-scented aromas lead a dry spicy palate with a subtle but very persistent peaty note through the lingering finish. Quite forcefully spicy and very much in the aperitif spectrum.

Connemara (Ireland)

Connemara Peated Single Malt Irish Whiskey 80 proof $22. 86

Yellow-amber. Moderately full-bodied. Notes of peat, smoke, minerals. Fragrant smoky peat nose with a pleasant warm entry. Great oily viscosity coats the palate. Light smoke and peat flavors linger on the medium-length, warm finish. Fascinating hybrid style.

Cragganmore (Scotland)

Cragganmore 12 Year Old Single Highland Malt Scotch Whisky
80 proof $40. **90**

Striking, brilliant yellow-gold. Very perfumed and aromatic with a heather, peaty note. Medium-bodied and silky with fine flavors following the aromas. Shows a touch of vinous character through a dry finish. Outstanding balance. For those who must drink whisky with their haggis.

Cutty Sark (Scotland)

Cutty Sark Blended Scotch Whisky 80 proof $19.99. **NR**

The Dalmore (Scotland)

The Dalmore 12 Year Old Single Highland Malt Scotch Whisky
86 proof $30. **87**

Deep golden amber. Moderately full-bodied. Notes of orange peel, dried flowers, dried fruit. Powerful Sherry cask aromas translate well onto the palate with big flavors and a hint of sweetness that persist well into the finish. Veering toward an after-dinner style.

The Dalmore Cigar Malt Single Highland Malt Scotch Whisky
86 proof $32. **90**

Dark reddish-amber hue. Rich aromas of vanillin, smoke, and dark Sherry. Full-bodied and rich with cherry and dried fruit notes and nutty, heavily oak-influenced flavors through a dry finish. A chewy style.

The Dalmore 21 Year Old Single Highland Malt Scotch Whisky
86 proof $69. **93**

Medium amber with a deep cast. Rich, complex aromas of peat, heather, and dark Sherry. Full-bodied and powerfully flavored with rich, spicy accents that linger through the finish. A contemplative after-dinner malt.

The Dalmore The Stillman's Dram 30 Year Old Limited Edition Single Highland Malt Scotch Whisky 90 proof $129. **96**

Deep red-amber hue. Powerfully aromatic with heavy barrel influence giving walnut and sherried character. Rich, full-bodied and showing dried vine fruit and peat characteristics that develop into powerful flavors through a spicy, assertive finish. A substantial after-dinner style.

Dalwhinnie (Scotland)

Dalwhinnie 15 Year Old Single Highland Malt Scotch Whisky
86 proof $45. **89**

Bright golden-yellow hue. Medium-bodied. Floral, subtly peaty, and aromatic, with a delicate nose. Silky and smooth on the palate with delicate wood, spice, and Fino Sherry notes on the finish. Refreshing and very well balanced.

Deanston (Scotland)

The Deanston Single Malt Highland Scotch Whisky, 12 Year Old
86 proof $26.95. **88**

Medium gold. Smooth, silky, medium-bodied. Notes of buttered popcorn, pear, caramel, hazelnuts, and smoke. Tangy, tart finish.

The Deanston 17 Year Old Single Highland Malt Scotch Whisky 86 proof $48. **89**

Pale golden hue. Moderately light-bodied. Aromas of peat, charcoal, citrus, Fino Sherry. A clean oily feel on the palate with a subtle malt influence and some overt wood flavors through the slightly nutty finish.

Dewar's (Scotland)

Dewar's White Label, Blended Scotch Whisky 80 proof $17. **82**

Straw appearance. Medium-bodied. Notes of lemon, dried fruit, salted butter. Simple and drinkable with a balanced subtly peaty character through the finish.

Dufftown-Glenlivet (Scotland)

Dufftown-Glenlivet Distillery, Glenhaven Bottling, 11 Year Old Single Malt Scotch Whisky 120 proof $89. **NR**

Duggan's Dew (Scotland)

Duggan's Dew Blended Scotch Whisky 86.8 proof $12. **NR**

Duggans (Scotland)

Duggans 12 Year Old, Blended Scotch Whisky 80 proof $19.95. **85**

Bright orange-gold. Moderately full-bodied. Notes of rose water, dried fruit, brown spice. Subtle malt aromas translate well onto the palate showing a slight oily note with a mild wood-spice finish.

The Edradour (Scotland)

The Edradour 10 Year Old Single Highland Malt Scotch Whisky 80 proof $34.99. **86**

Deep straw with an orange cast. Moderately light-bodied. Notes of popcorn butter, honey, dried flowers. Impressively rich malty nose leads a smooth mouthfeel with smoky flavors persisting through the finish. Mellow, in a lighter after-dinner style.

The Famous Grouse (Scotland)

The Famous Grouse Finest Blended Scotch Whisky 80 proof $18.99. **86**

Bright amber-gold hue. Perfumed peaty aromas. Medium-bodied with a sweet, malty attack and lingering peat notes on the mineral finish. Generously malty style, highly drinkable.

The Famous Grouse 12 Year Old, Gold Reserve, Deluxe Scotch Whisky 80 proof $22.99. **89**

Deep amber cast. Medium-bodied. Notes of dried fruit, brown spice, wood notes. Subtle malty aromas with spicy overtones reveal a full-flavored palate with generous wood-derived flavors through the finish. An assertive masculine style.

Fettercairn (Scotland)

Fettercairn, Glenhaven Bottling, 10 Year Old, Single Malt Scotch Whisky 126.2 proof $81. **89**

Amber. Moderately full-bodied. Notes of cedar, dried flowers, semisweet chocolate. Big floral aromas reveal a very dry but silky textured palate with a delicate and complex character that reveals itself with a little water.

Findlater's Mar Lodge (Scotland)

Findlater's Mar Lodge Pure Malt Scotch Whisky, 12 Year Old 86 proof $19.99. **86**

Amber-copper. Sweet nose of dried apricot, maple, and caramel. Soft, mellow body accented by brown spices. Vanilla wafer flavors in the sweet finish.

Glen Esk (Scotland)

Glen Esk, Cadenhead Bottling, 13 Year Old, Single Highland Malt Scotch Whisky, Distilled April 1982, Bottled June 1995 123 proof $75.　　83

Almost clear with yellow hue. Moderately light-bodied. Notes of light apple, pepper, grass. Aromatically muted. Clear and neutral spirit with a burning finish, even when well diluted. Almost grappa-like.

Glen Garioch (Scotland)

Glen Garioch 15 Year Old Single Highland Malt Scotch Whisky 86 proof $35.　　91

Deep gold. Medium-bodied. Notes of peat, heather, charcoal. Pronounced smoky-floral aromatics lead a silky, smoothly textured palate with a sweetish smoky note through the warming finish. A richer-styled aperitif.

Glen Moray (Scotland)

Glen Moray Single Highland Malt Scotch Whisky, 12 Year Old 80 proof $23.99.　　86

Medium gold. Cedar, salt, bread crust and honey. Light-bodied, with a smooth texture. Nutty, sweet finish.

Glen Moray Single Highland Malt Scotch Whisky, 15 Year Old 80 proof $40.　　89

Dark gold-amber hue. Penetrating smoky nose. Moderately full-bodied, with hints of sea salt, roasted nuts, citrus, and peat. Well rounded, with a particularly smooth finish.

Glen Scotia (Scotland)

Glen Scotia 14 Year Old Campbeltown Single Malt Scotch Whisky 86 proof $55.　　86

Full orange-gold hue. Medium-bodied. Very perfumed aromas show a fruity, sweet spicy note. A lighter style with delicate fruity flavors and elegant peat and mineral flavors on the finish.

Glen Scotia 17 Year Old Campbeltown Single Malt Scotch Whisky 86 proof $80.　　85

Golden straw. Moderately full-bodied. Notes of chocolate, honey, dried fruit. Expansive chocolate aromas lead a thick, viscous palate with a rich center and a quick finish. Impressively proportioned although not hugely aromatically complex.

The Glendronach (Scotland)

The Glendronach Single Highland Malt Scotch Whisky, 12 Year Old 86 proof $33.99.　　89

Deep tawny amber. Rich, heavy nose of mocha and roasted nuts. On the palate, citrus, dates, and pipe tobacco. Round, full-bodied, warm texture. Finishes with a soft toffee sweetness.

The Glendronach 15 Year Old Single Highland Malt Scotch Whisky, Sherry Cask Aged 80 proof $43.　　87

Dark amber. Moderately full-bodied. Notes of caramel, smoke, subtle peat, nuts. Big woody, Oloroso Sherry-accented aromas. Silky dry caramel flavors on entry that develop into complex Sherry flavors through the finish. A rich digestif style.

Glenfarclas (Scotland)

Glenfarclas 10 Year Old Single Highland Malt Scotch Whisky 86 proof $27.99.　　88

Light amber. Moderately full-bodied. Notes of smoke, peat, honey, soft green herbs, salt. Smoky sweet aromas translate well onto the palate. Distinguished by expansive sweet Sherry flavors and a generous malty character that tapers through the finish. Rich after-dinner style.

Glenfarclas 12 Year Old Single Highland Malt Scotch Whisky 86 proof $45. **86**

Brilliant amber-gold hue. Lighter aromas show a mild floral, Fino Sherry note. A lighter style on the palate with a delicate, sweetish note and a touch of walnut through the finish. An easy drinking, unfussy malt.

Glenfarclas 17 Year Old Single Highland Malt Scotch Whisky 86 proof $80. **93**

Deep golden-amber hue. Impressive fruity orange, dried fruit, smoke-scented aromas. Rich, intense, and full-bodied with a viscous mouthfeel and flavors that follow the aromas through a deeply spiced finish that has fine persistence.

Glenfarclas 21 Year Old Single Highland Malt Scotch Whisky 86 proof $74.99. **93**

Full reddish-copper. Full-bodied. Notes of orange, chocolate, molasses, roasted nuts. Expansive marmalade aromas lead a full flavorsome palate with a rich center and a lasting smoky, Sherry-inspired finish. A big, masculine after-dinner style.

Glenfarclas 105 Cask Strength Single Highland Malt Scotch Whisky 120 proof $70. **95**

Orange-amber hue. Full-bodied. Expansive smoky, rich malt nose. Explosively flavorsome and full-bodied with sweet, spicy barrel influences and an oily texture that turns hot through the finish. Very warming and potent with sensational flavors.

Glenfarclas-Glenlivet (Scotland)

Glenfarclas-Glenlivet, Glenhaven Bottling, 17 Year Old Single Malt Scotch Whisky 106.4 proof $99. **95**

Deep gold. Full-bodied. Sweet aromas of date and papaya. Richly textured with hazelnut, butterscotch, and cedar. The elements are beautifully married.

Glenfiddich (Scotland)

Glenfiddich Special Reserve Single Malt Scotch Whisky 80 proof $22.99. **83**

Very pale straw. A light but elegant nose showing light Sherry accents and subtle heather. Delicate, suggestively sweet and moderately light-bodied with a clean, fruity finish. This does not offer a lot of complexity but is very clean and refreshing.

Glenfiddich 15 Year Old Cask Strength Speyside Single Malt Scotch Whisky 102 proof $34.99. **90**

Straw. Moderately full-bodied. Notes of vanilla, smoke, anise. Sweet peppery nose leads a warm malty entry that tapers to a lingering brown spice finish with subtle smoky flavors. A fairly assertive style.

Glenforres (Scotland)

Glenforres All Highland Malt Scotch Whisky, 8 Year Old 86 proof $19.99. **80**

Medium amber. Medium-bodied. Aromas of tar, sea air, peat, and delicate flavors of black cherries and licorice.

Glenkeith (Scotland)

Glenkeith Single Highland Malt Scotch Whisky, Distilled Before 1983, Aged More Than Ten Years 86 proof $35. **86**

Bright straw yellow. Medium-bodied. Notes of dried grass, peach, flowers. Grassy aromas with a sweet malt accent. A nice clean expression of malt flavors through to a subtle,

Scale: Superlative (96-100), Exceptional (90-95), Highly Recommended (85-89), Recommended (80-84), Not Recommended (Under 80)

smoky finish. Mellow and focused.

Glenkinchie (Scotland)

Glenkinchie 10 Year Old Single Lowland Malt Scotch Whisky
86 proof $40.   **84**

Yellow-gold hue. Mineral and peat aromas with ginger ale notes. Medium-bodied with
a straightforward sweet malt middle and faintly nutty finish.

The Glenlivet (Scotland)

The Glenlivet, Glenhaven Bottling,
17 Year Old Single Malt Scotch Whisky 113 proof $99.   **99**

Amber-orange. Pecan pie and glazed citrus flavors soar on the nose. Coupled with the
familiar peat and smoke components, these flavors combine power and finesse. Massive
in weight, but all elements are in beautiful, harmonious balance.

The Glenlivet 12 Year Old Single Malt Scotch Whisky 80 proof $35.   **86**

Bright yellow-gold. Moderately light-bodied. Notes of lemon peel, dried flowers, soft
charred wood. Delicate or even subtle nose. Rounded, smooth palate with a soft malty
profile and a subtle smoky finish. Smooth as silk. A tippler well suited as an aperitif.

The Glenlivet Pure Single Malt Scotch Whisky,
18 Year Old 86 proof $44.95.   **85**

Medium amber. Full-bodied. Mild peat, nuts, apples, and cloves. Delicate, creamy texture.
Pine and vanilla in the finish.

Glenmorangie (Scotland)

Glenmorangie 10 Year Old, Highland Single Malt Whisky 86 proof $30.   **87**

Bright amber. Medium- to light-bodied. Citrus notes blend with peach, honey, a dry
Sherry nuttiness, and a kiss of heather. Soft finish with light strokes of peat and smoke.

Glenmorangie 12 Year Old, Madeira Wood Finish, Highland Single Malt
Whisky 86 proof $40.   **90**

Full straw with orange highlights. Medium-bodied. Notes of molasses, smoke, dried
tropical fruit. Enticing smoky aromas lead a vaguely sweet entry to a smooth buttery
palate with subtle salty flavors lingering through the finish.

Glenmorangie 12 Year Old, Port Wood Finish,
Highland Single Malt Whisky 86 proof $40.   **93**

Light orange with a faint reddish glint. Moderately full-bodied. Notes of dried stone
fruit, smoke, sweet tea leaf. Full sweet vinous nose leads a minty-sweet entry with a subtle
candied fruit accent on the midpalate through a nutty spice finish. Very complex with
clear Port wood character throughout. A natural digestif style.

Glenmorangie 12 Year Old, Sherry Wood Finish, Highland Single Malt
Whisky 86 proof $40.   **94**

Orange-amber. Moderately full-bodied. Notes of Sherry, smoke, honey, dried flowers,
nuts. Big, rich Oloroso aromas lead a smooth, sweet Sherry entry that expands on the
palate through a nutty finish. Distinguished by a particularly velvety mouthfeel that puts
this in the luxurious digestif style.

Glenmorangie 18 Year Old, Highland Rare Single Malt Whisky
86 proof $50.   **95**

Gold with an orange hue. Medium-bodied. The sweet nose of marzipan and clove
is inviting. Fruit flavors of pear and citrus play with light cedar. Neither brawny nor
fiery, these seamlessly integrated elements are woven into a smooth, medium-bodied,
silky-textured delight.

Glenrothes (Scotland)

The Glenrothes 1982 Vintage Single Malt Scotch Whisky 86 proof $50.   **86**

Golden with amber highlights. Medium-bodied. Notes of butterscotch, vanilla, dried fruit. Hints of dried tropical fruit and vanilla in the nose lead a sweetish entry with rich malt flavors lingering through the persistent finish.

The Glenrothes 16 Year Old Single Speyside Malt Scotch Whisky, Distilled in 1979, Bottled in 1995 86 proof $55.   88

Golden with amber highlights. Medium-bodied. Notes of dried flowers, lemon peel, assorted spices. Delicate floral peat-scented nose. Soft, fragrant entry with a broad palate of spicy flavors on a creamy textured palate. Mellow and elegant.

Grand Macnish (Scotland)

Grand Macnish Blended Scotch Whisky 80 proof $9.99.   81

Bright yellow-gold hue. Muted aromas show hints of malt and very subtle peat character. Sweet caramel notes upfront play out on a medium-bodied palate with a lingering, subtle finish. A cleaner, lighter style.

William Grant's (Scotland)

William Grant's Family Reserve Blended Scotch Whisky 80 proof $12.99.   82

Bright orange-gold hue. Floral sweet-caramel aromas. Crisp, subtle malty note with mineral dryness taking over on the finish. A lighter, dryer style.

Highland Park (Scotland)

Highland Park 12 Year Old Orkney Island Single Malt Scotch Whisky 86 proof $40.99.   96

Full orange-amber hue. Deeply smoky, with walnut aromas. A rich, full-bodied malt with fine viscosity and an oily, rich mouthfeel that displays peaty richness and sea salt notes through the finish. A rich after-dinner malt.

Highland Park, Glenhaven Bottling, 20 Year Old, Orkney Islands Single Malt Scotch Whisky, Distilled September 1975, Bottled June 1996 115.4 proof $98.   92

Pale gold. Medium-bodied. Notes of sweet flowers, honey, peat, smoke. Delicate, perfumed nose of heather and peat. Strong smoky peat flavors emerge with the addition of water to give this a full-flavored, assertive character.

Inchmurrin (Scotland)

Inchmurrin 10 Year Old Single Highland Malt Scotch Whisky 86 proof $40.   90

Golden straw with amber highlights. Medium-bodied. Notes of anise, herbs, rose water, pepper. Very distinctive herbal aromas are well translated onto the malty palate that is distinguished by a smooth-textured mouthfeel. Some peppery notes contribute to the warm finish.

Inver House (Scotland)

Inver House Very Rare Scotch Whisky 80 proof $7.99.   NR

The Inverarity (Scotland)

The Inverarity Blended Scotch Whisky 80 proof $18.   86

Light amber. Medium-bodied. Notes of caramelized orange peel, dried flowers, brown spice. Soft floral, heather-accented nose. Smooth mouthfeel with a soft, subtly sweet character through the finish.

The Inverarity 10 Year Old Speyside Single Malt Scotch Whisky 80 proof $35.   NR

Inverleven Stills, Dumbarton (Scotland)

Inverleven Stills, Dumbarton, Cadenhead Bottling, 27 Year Old, Cask Strength Lowland Malt Scotch Whisky, Distilled March 1969, Bottled June 1996 97.6 proof $95.   **97**

Deep amber with copper highlights. Full-bodied. Notes of orange peel, chocolate, vanilla, molasses. Rich chocolate aromas lead a sweet vanilla entry developing to a complex array of dessert flavors that linger through the finish. Complex and quite decadent. A dessert malt or even an accompaniment to cigars.

Isle of Jura (Scotland)

Isle of Jura 10 Year Old Isle of Jura Single Malt Scotch Whisky 86 proof $20.

NR

Jameson (Ireland)

Jameson Irish Whiskey 80 proof $20.   **86**

Yellow-gold hue. Delicate floral aromas with grainy notes and heat. Light-bodied, very smooth and clean, with a touch of astringency on the finish betraying the grain character.

Jameson 1780 Reserve 12 Year Old Irish Whiskey 80 proof $30.   **92**

Deep golden-amber hue. Rich woody aromas. Full-bodied, with rich brown spice flavors and Bourbon-like sweetness through the finish. A rich, mature, and mellow style.

Jameson Gold Special Reserve Irish Whiskey 80 proof $60.   **93**

Bright orange-gold hue. Floral, oily aromas are very intense. Full-bodied and richly textured with an oily mouthfeel and vinous complexity through the finish. Distinguished by a lingering flavorful finish. Intensely flavored, smooth, and elegant.

John Power & Son (Ireland)

John Power & Son Gold Label Irish Whiskey 80 proof $17.99.   **83**

Pale gold. Moderately full-bodied. Notes of flowers, almonds, honey. Subtle aromas and a weighty mouthfeel with some oily texture on the faintly Bourbon-sweet midpalate. Finishes promptly and cleanly.

Johnny Walker (Scotland)

Johnny Walker Red Label Blended Scotch Whisky 80 proof $16.   **85**

Orange-amber hue. Muted aromas show a smoky character. Mineral-dominated and dry with a subtle malt flavor profile and a hot, dry finish.

Johnny Walker Black Label 12 Year Extra Special Old Scotch Whisky 80 proof $25.   **89**

Orange-amber hue. Oak aromas lead a medium-bodied palate showing textural richness and spicy flavors through the warm finish. Well aged and complex.

Johnny Walker Blue Label Blend of Rarest Scotch Whiskies 80 proof $180. **93**
Bright orange-amber hue. Medium-bodied with elegant floral and high-toned peaty flavors that persist through the salty-tinged finish. A complex and flavorful whisky.

Justerini & Brooks (Scotland)

Justerini & Brooks J & B Select, Blended Scotch Whisky 80 proof $17.99. **89**
Pale gold. Medium-bodied. Notes of honey, herbs, hay. Delicate aromas reveal a subtle, rather gentle style. Smooth entry with a soft, rounded palate showing faint sweet impressions through the finish. An excellent aperitif that leaves the palate refreshed.

Justerini & Brooks J.E.T., Old Scotch Whisky 86 proof $24.99. **90**
Medium gold. Perfumed with flowers and herbs. Medium-bodied, pear-flavored entry. A dash of white pepper mixes well with light caramel in a satiny texture.

Kilbeggan (Ireland)

Kilbeggan Irish Whiskey 80 proof $16. **NR**

Knockando (Scotland)

Knockando 12 Year Old Single Malt Scotch Whisky 86 proof $38. **85**
Bright yellow-gold hue. Plenty of earth, barrel spice, and floral aromas with high-toned malty accents. Lighter on a medium-bodied palate with very subtle peaty character. Finishes in a dry manner with a note of earth.

Knockando 14 Year Old Single Malt Scotch Whisky, Distilled in 1979, Bottled in 1994 86 proof $49.99. **87**
Bright straw appearance. Medium-bodied. Notes of honey, heather, menthol. Fragrant, perfumed nose with minty accents. Delicate and smooth on the palate with a tapering dry finish. A fairly dry aperitif style.

Knockando 18 Year Old Single Malt Scotch Whisky, Distilled in 1976 86 proof $59.99. **87**
Full orange-straw color. Moderately full-bodied. Notes of licorice, oak shavings, dried flowers. Pronounced Sherry cask accents with a licorice note that translates well onto the assertive palate. Generous spicy flavors throughout.

Knockando 21 Year Old Single Cask Single Malt Scotch Whisky, Distilled in 1973, Bottled in 1996 86 proof $149.99. **91**
Gold with amber highlights. Medium-bodied. Notes of cinnamon, toasted almond, mild peat. Fragrant Sherry cask nose leads a mellow palate with some depth and a hint of sweetness that tapers to a dry finish. This maintains a sense of delicacy in style.

Lagavulin (Scotland)

Lagavulin 16 Year Old Islay Single Malt Scotch Whisky 86 proof $50. **99**
Deep golden amber. Outstanding aromas fill the glass with smoky peat, Sherry wood and sea salt. Extraordinarily perfumed. Moderately full-bodied with a viscous mouthfeel. A sweet Sherry note on entry and complex dry peaty flavors lingering on the finish. A sumptuous combination of luxurious mouthfeel and assertive flavors and aromas.

Lammerlaw (New Zealand)

Lammerlaw 10 Year Old Single Malt Whisky 86 proof $35.95. **81**
Bright yellow-gold hue. Interesting aromas are rather fruity and mineral. The medium-bodied palate shows brisk malt flavors, with a crisp, dry character emerging on the warm finish. The mouthfeel does not quite live up to the flavors.

Laphroaig (Scotland)

Laphroaig 10 Year Old Islay Single Malt Scotch Whisky 86 proof $40. **89**
Full golden hue. Medium-bodied. Notes of salt, iodine, peat, smoke. A fragrant nose of medicinal peat and heather leads an oily palate with a big kick of iodine and seaweed flavors racing through the finish. Essence of Islay, and not for the faint hearted.

Laphroaig 15 Year Old Islay Single Malt Scotch Whisky 86 proof $65.   **87**

Deep amber-gold. Moderately full-bodied. Notes of peat, heather, chocolate. Hints of rich peaty character restrained by a sweet Sherry note on an oily palate with a brief finish. Fairly luxurious in an after-dinner fashion.

Lauder's (Scotland)

Lauder's Blended Scotch Whisky 80 proof $8.99.   **82**

Orange-amber hue. Malty, subtly peaty aromas. Medium- to full-bodied with a rounded mouthfeel and fine texture through the finish. Shows subtle peaty, malty character throughout. A flavorsome style.

Ledaig (Scotland)

Ledaig 15 Year Old Isle of Mull Single Malt Scotch Whisky 86 proof $46.95.   **86**

Full yellow-gold hue. Sea air aromas are enchanting, with peaty notes. Lighter-bodied, with delicate floral flavors and honeysuckle notes. Finishes with a salty note.

Ledaig 20 Year Old Isle of Mull Single Malt Scotch Whisky, Distilled in 1974 86 proof $60.   **87**

Bright yellow-gold. Medium-bodied. Notes of honeysuckle, smoke, peat. Fragrant peat and heather nose, silky on palate with a touch of sweetness to complement the full peaty flavors. Assertive but very accessible island style.

Littlemill (Scotland)

Littlemill 8 Year Old 100% Malt Scotch Whisky 86 proof $28.   **90**

Pale straw with greenish highlights. Moderately full-bodied. Notes of grass, pear, mint. Big grassy aromas reveal a crisp palate with a glycerous texture through the finish. Quite steely overall with great refinement. Remarkably fresh-tasting palate wakener.

Longmorn (Scotland)

Longmorn 15 Year Old Highland Single Malt Scotch Whisky 90 proof $45.   **83**

Bright medium-amber appearance. Medium-bodied. Notes of dried stone fruit, honeysuckle, nuts. Soft malty aromas lead a rounded palate with big malty and Sherry cask flavors. A very smooth though light feel through to the lingering finish. Very attractive and easy on the palate.

The Macallan (Scotland)

The Macallan 12 Year Old Highland Single Malt Scotch Whisky 86 proof $35.   **89**

Deep golden-amber with reddish highlights. Outstanding smoky, sherried aromas. Silky, full-bodied, and round on the palate with some vinous qualities and a strong malt component. Plenty of wood spice through the finish.

The Macallan 18 Year Old Gran Reserva Single Malt Highland Scotch Whisky 80 proof $140.   **93**

Dark reddish-gold hue. Powerful Oloroso Sherry and walnut aromas with marked oak spice influence. Very rich, smooth, and deep on the palate with a silky texture and no heat on the finish. Exceptionally tactile. An outstanding after-dinner drink.

The Macallan 25 Year Old, Anniversary, Single Highland Malt Scotch Whisky 86 proof $175.   **100**

Full reddish-amber appearance. Full-bodied. Honey, heather, molasses, roasted nuts, sweet pipe tobacco. Beautifully fragrant Oloroso nose. Rich mouth-filling entry and smooth viscosity give this a luxurious feel. Particularly distinguished by a heavy smoky character and an exceptionally long nutty finish.

Magdalen (Scotland)

Magdalen Ultimate Blended Scotch Whisky 80 proof $18. **82**

Orange-amber hue. Subtle aromas have a malt accent. Medium-bodied, with a good nutty malt profile upfront, though the finish is rather short. Not much flavor or complexity.

Martin's (Scotland)

Martin's Blended Scotch Whisky, VVO 80 proof $11.99. **83**

Medium gold. A restrained nose offers a hint of herbs and sea air. Moderately light-bodied. Creamy, lighter entry with notes of hay, Sherry, and walnuts. A touch of smoke adds a layer of complexity.

McClellands (Scotland)

McClellands, Lowland Single Malt Scotch Whisky 80 proof $19.95. **NR**

Midleton (Ireland)

Midleton 1994 Very Rare Irish Whiskey 80 proof $99.99. **94**

Striking deep amber with reddish-orange highlights. Full-bodied. Notes of orange peel, citrus, minerals. Seductively aromatic with a classy cognac-like essence. Complex, with many layers of harmonious flavors and silky viscosity through the extraordinarily lengthy finish.

Midleton 1995 Very Rare Irish Whiskey 80 proof $99.99. **95**

Brilliant orange-gold hue. Wonderfully pure aromas of peach, apricot, and vanilla. Almost dessert-like. Outstandingly smooth, with a sweet Bourbon-like character, honey and toffee notes, and an outstandingly mellow, smooth character through the finish.

Millburn (Scotland)

Millburn, Signatory Bottling, 16 Year Old Single Highland Malt Scotch Whisky, Distilled in 1979 86 proof $50. **83**

Bright yellow-gold. Medium-bodied. Notes of grass, peat, lemon. Fragrant aromas reveal a dry palate with subtle peat notes with just a hint of Sherry on the entry. Smooth and well balanced, overall quite subtle in style.

Moidart (Scotland)

Moidart 21 Year Old Pure Malt Vatted Scotch Whisky 92 proof $103. **93**

Medium-amber hue. Coal tar, briny, and lightly peaty aromas. Shows a distinctive candied, taffy note. Flavors follow the aromas on the moderately light-bodied palate with honey and almond notes persisting through the finish. Very distinctive.

Muirheads (Scotland)

Muirheads, Blended Scotch Whisky 80 proof $8.99. **83**

Medium gold. Smoky campfire aromas signal what is to come. Moderately light-bodied. Lemon and honey dominate the easy, lighter-textured entry. Firewood and charcoal prevail in the warm finish.

Oban (Scotland)

Oban 14 Year Old Single West Highland Malt Scotch Whisky 86 proof $40. **89**

Bright orange-gold hue. Aromatically appealing with sweet caramel, peat, and sea salt aromas. Very smooth and silky on the moderately full-bodied palate. Texturally outstanding, showing a lovely, long, and complex finish with lingering peaty notes.

Old Pulteney (Scotland)

Old Pulteney 12 Year Old Single Malt Scotch Whisky 86 proof $32.99. **89**

Bright yellow-gold hue. Medium-bodied. Notably floral, attractive aromas with nutty accents. Smooth and silky on the palate with remarkably little heat. Shows a vanilla, apricot, and sweet spice character that lingers.

Old Pulteney, Gordon & MacPhail Bottling, 8 Year Old Single Highland Malt Scotch Whisky 40 proof $40. **86**

Bright yellow-orange. Medium-bodied. Notes of peat, malt, orange peel. Full malty, peat-infused aromas translate well onto the palate, which displays a rich malty profile with a subtle spicy finish.

Old Smuggler (Scotland)

Old Smuggler Blended Scotch Whisky 80 proof $11.99. **NR**

Royal Lochnagar (Scotland)

Royal Lochnagar 12 Year Old Single Highland Malt Scotch Whisky 80 proof $38. **83**

Pale yellow-straw. Medium-bodied. Earthy, mineral aromas with subtle sweet heather. Rather harsh and mineral on the palate with subtle malt flavors. Finishes quickly.

Scapa (Scotland)

Scapa 12 Year Old Orkney Islands Single Malt Scotch Whisky 80 proof $37. **80**

Bright orange-yellow. Medium-bodied. Notes of orange peel, flowers, tropical dried fruit. Bright almost fruity aromas lead a delicate entry with light flavors and an aromatic, lingering finish. A lighter aperitif style with an easy-drinking character.

Scoresby (Scotland)

Scoresby, Very Rare Blended Scotch Whisky 80 proof $11.99. **NR**

Spey Cast (Scotland)

Spey Cast Scotch Whisky, 12 Year Old 80 proof $29.99. **85**

Medium amber. Soft-textured, medium-bodied. Hazelnuts and sherried wood in the nose. Butterscotch flavors are accented by a dash of smoke. Sweet pipe tobacco and a smack of tar add a layering effect.

Speyburn (Scotland)

Speyburn 10 Year Old Single Highland Malt Scotch Whisky 86 proof $19.99. **86**

Full golden-yellow hue. Smooth sandalwood and malty aromas. Elegant mineral, sweet-malt flavors with a touch of caramel sweetness on the medium-bodied palate. Finishes crisply.

Springbank (Scotland)

Springbank 15 Year Old Campbeltown Single Malt Scotch Whisky 92 proof $49.95. **86**

Very pale straw appearance. Medium-bodied. Notes of green herbs, grass, Fino Sherry. Light fragrant nose with grassy aromas. Fragrant and delicate in the mouth with a distinct grassy note that lingers through the finish. A light though rather complex style that enlivens the tastebuds.

Springbank 12 Year Old Campbeltown Single Malt Scotch Whisky 92 proof $81.95. **NR**

Springbank Murray, McDavid Bottling, 30 Year Old Campbeltown Single Malt Scotch Whisky, Sherry Wood Aged, Distilled in 1965 92 proof $100. **92**

Deep orange-amber appearance. Full-bodied. Notes of peat, charcoal, vanilla, chocolate. Powerfully fragrant nose with fruity, peaty accents. Rich, oily textured palate with big flavors and nutty complexity through the lingering finish. An after-dinner style that has gained much character from 30 years in old Sherry casks.

Springbank 21 Year Old Campbeltown Single Malt Scotch Whisky 92 proof $149.95. **89**

Orange-amber hue. Outstanding aromas of walnuts, spice, and peat. Moderately full-bodied with coal tar and walnuts dominating the palate with marked heat on the finish. Very assertive and complex.

Strathisla (Scotland)

Strathisla 12 Year Old Pure Highland Malt Scotch Whisky 86 proof $40. **89**

Gold with orange highlights. Medium-bodied. Notes of vanilla, dried tropical fruit, smoke. Pretty vanilla-scented nose leads a sweet malty, dry, fruity entry that tapers to a long finish with subtle smoky nuances. Dry and elegant style.

Suntory (Japan)

Suntory Yamazaki 12 Year Old Pure Malt Whisky 86 proof $38. **86**

Brilliant orange-gold hue. Very aromatic, with a honeyed, Fino Sherry-like character. Moderately full-bodied with a rich texture and succulent malty flavors that finish with great persistence. Very impressive.

Talisker (Scotland)

Talisker 10 Year Old Isle of Skye Single Malt Scotch Whisky 91.6 proof $48. **89**

Brilliant orange-gold. Rich seaweed and peat aromas. Moderately full-bodied, with silky texture and sweet malty notes upfront that develop into a full-fledged salty, peaty character through the finish. Outstanding balance.

Tamdhu (Scotland)

Tamdhu Speyside Single Malt Scotch Whisky 80 proof $31.99. **88**

Pale yellow-gold hue. Floral, lighter aromas show a smoky note. Lighter-framed. Crisp on the entry with a dry palate and smooth, clean finish.

Teacher's (Scotland)

Teacher's Blended Scotch Whisky 86 proof $17.99. **85**

Light amber. Medium-bodied. Notes of flowers, charcoal, smoke. Full floral, perfumed nose reveals a lighter style with a subtly flavored palate and a dry feel through the finish. An easygoing, drink-anytime style.

Tomintoul (Scotland)

Tomintoul 14 Year Old Single Highland Malt Scotch Whisky 86 proof $40. **88**

Bright yellow-amber hue. Very attractive vinous aromas with wildflowers and tea leaves. Takes a sweetish note on the medium-bodied palate, with silky mouthfeel and a long and lingering floral finish.

Tullamore Dew (Ireland)

Tullamore Dew Irish Whiskey 80 proof $17.99. **83**

Yellow-gold hue. Clean floral, grainy aromas. Medium-bodied, with citrus fruit notes and spicy vanilla that fades quickly. Light on flavors, an easy drinking style.

Tullibardine (Scotland)

Tullibardine 10 Year Old Single Highland Malt Scotch Whisky
86 proof $35.   **86**

Golden straw. Medium-bodied. Notes of flowers, honeysuckle, grass, herbs. Sweet fragrant malt aromas lead a supple sweet-malt palate with clean grassy notes through the finish. Easygoing and unchallenging to the palate, in the best sense.

The Tyrconnell (Ireland)

The Tyrconnell Single Malt Irish Whiskey 80 proof $22.   **81**

Bright yellowish-gold with a light cast. Medium-bodied. Notes of sweet grains, hay, minerals. Pronounced hay-like aromas lead a crisp entry with very subtle sweet notes through the finish. Quite restrained in style.

Usher's (Scotland)

Usher's Green Stripe, Blended Scotch Whisky 80 proof $9.99.   **NR**

Usquaebach (Scotland)

Usquaebach Blended Scotch Whisky 86 proof $25.   **90**

Amber with pale golden highlights. Medium-bodied. Notes of peat, dried leather, caramel, vanilla. Richly aromatic nose with big malty notes and floral overtones. Delivers on the palate with generous wood-influenced flavors through the expanding finish. Distinguished by a rich mouthfeel and silky smoothness.

White Horse (Scotland)

White Horse Blended Scotch Whisky 80 proof $13.99.   **80**

Deep golden amber. Medium-bodied. Notes of light peat, sawdust, dried fruit. Subtle aromas lead a palate with some weight and an oily consistency through the finish, though without great flavor complexity.

White Horse 12 Year Old Extra Fine Blended Scotch Whisky
80 proof $25.99.   **84**

Full orange-amber luster. Mouthfeel and texture are the keynotes here. Sweetish caramel, nutty flavors finish with a note of mineral dryness.

Highly Rated Whisky

Highland Single Malt Scotch

98 • Ben Nevis (Scotland) The Scotch Malt Whisky Society Bottling, 15 Year Old Single West Highland Malt Scotch Whisky, Cask No. 78.8, Distilled October 1978, Bottled October 1993 111.6 Proof. $75.

96 • The Dalmore (Scotland) The Stillman's Dream 30 Year Old Limited Edition Single Highland Malt Scotch Whisky 90 Proof. $129.

95 • Glenmorangie (Scotland) 18 Year Old, Highland Rare Single Malt Whisky 86 Proof. $50.

95 • Aberlour (Scotland) 15 Year Old, Sherry Wood Finish, Single Highland Malt Scotch Whisky 86 Proof. $45.

94 • Glenmorangie (Scotland) 12 Year Old, Sherry Wood Finish, Highland Single Malt Whisky 86 Proof. $40.

93 • The Dalmore (Scotland) 21 Year Old Single Highland Malt Scotch Whisky 86 Proof. $69.

93 • Glenmorangie (Scotland) 12 Year Old, Port Wood Finish, Highland Single Malt Whisky 86 Proof. $40.

91 • Glen Garioch (Scotland) 15 Year Old Single Highland Malt Scotch Whisky 86 Proof. $35.

90 • The Dalmore (Scotland) Cigar Malt Single Highland Malt Scotch Whisky 86 Proof. $32.

90 • Inchmurrin (Scotland) 10 Year Old Single Highland Malt Scotch Whisky 86 Proof. $40.

90 • Glenmorangie (Scotland) 12 Year Old, Madeira Wood Finish, Highland Single Malt Whisky 86 Proof. $40.

90 • Aberlour (Scotland) 10 Year Old Single Highland Malt Scotch Whisky 86 Proof. $25.

89 • The Deanston (Scotland) 17 Year Old Single Highland Malt Scotch Whisky 86 Proof. $48.

89 • Old Pulteney (Scotland) 12 Year Old Single Malt Scotch Whisky 86 Proof. $32.99.

89 • Oban (Scotland) 14 Year Old Single West Highland Malt Scotch Whisky 86 Proof. $40.

89 • Fettercairn (Scotland) Glenhaven Bottling, 10 Year Old, Single Malt Scotch Whisky 126.2 Proof. $81.

89 • Dalwhinnie (Scotland) 15 Year Old Single Highland Malt Scotch Whisky 86 Proof. $45.

89 • Clynelish (Scotland) Glenhaven Bottling, 12 Year Old Single Malt Scotch Whisky 122 Proof. $65.

88 • Tomintoul (Scotland) 14 Year Old Single Highland Malt Scotch Whisky 86 Proof. $40.

88 • Deanston (Scotland) Single Malt Highland Scotch Whisky, 12 Year Old 86 Proof. $26.95.

88 • Balblair (Scotland) Gordon & MacPhail Bottling, 10 Year Old Single Highland Malt Scotch Whisky 40 Proof. $45.

87 •The Dalmore (Scotland) 12 Year Old Single Highland Malt Scotch Whisky 86 Proof. $30.

87 • Glenmorangie (Scotland) 10 Year Old, Highland Single Malt Whisky 86 Proof. $30.

86 • Tullibardine (Scotland) 10 Year Old Single Highland Malt Scotch Whisky 86 Proof. $35.

86 • The Edradour (Scotland) 10 Year Old Single Highland Malt Scotch Whisky 80 Proof. $34.99.

86 • Speyburn (Scotland) 10 Year Old Single Highland Malt Scotch Whisky 86 Proof. $19.99.

Scale: Superlative (96-100), Exceptional (90-95), Highly Recommended (85-89), Recommended (80-84), Not Recommended (Under 80)

86 • Old Pulteney (Scotland) Gordon & MacPhail Bottling, 8 Year Old Single Highland Malt Scotch Whisky 40 Proof. $40.

Speyside Single Malt Scotch

100 • The Macallan (Scotland) 25 Year Old, Anniversary, Single Highland Malt Scotch Whisky 86 Proof. $175.

99 • Glenhaven (Scotland) Single Malt Scotch Whisky Glenlivet Distillery, 17 Year Old 113 Proof. $99.

95 • Glenhaven (Scotland) Single Malt Scotch Whisky Glenfarclas-Glenlivet Distillery, 17 Year Old 106.4 Proof. $99.

95 • Glenfarclas (Scotland) 105 Cask Strength Single Highland Malt Scotch Whisky 120 Proof. $70.

95 • Benriach (Scotland) 10 Year Old Pure Highland Malt Scotch Whisky 86 Proof. $35.

94 • The Balvenie (Scotland) 15 Year Old Single Barrel Single Malt Scotch Whisky 100.8 Proof. $49.99.

93 • The Macallan (Scotland) 18 Year Old Gran Reserva Single Malt Highland Scotch Whisky 80 Proof. $140.

93 • The Balvenie (Scotland) 21 Year Old Port Wood Single Malt Scotch Whisky 86 Proof. $64.99.

93 • Glenfarclas (Scotland) 21 Year Old Single Highland Malt Scotch Whisky 86 Proof. $74.99.

93 • Glenfarclas (Scotland) 17 Year Old Single Highland Malt Scotch Whisky 86 Proof. $80.

91 • Knockando (Scotland) 21 Year Old Single Cask Single Malt Scotch Whisky, Distilled in 1973, Bottled in 1996 86 Proof. $149.99.

90 • Glenfiddich (Scotland) 15 Year Old Cask Strength Speyside Single Malt Scotch Whisky 102 Proof. $34.99.

90 • Cragganmore (Scotland) 12 Year Old Single Highland Malt Scotch Whisky 80 Proof. $40.

89 • The Macallan (Scotland) 12 Year Old Highland Single Malt Scotch Whisky 86 Proof. $35.

89 • The Glendronach (Scotland) Single Highland Malt Scotch Whisky, 12 Years Old 86 Proof. $33.99.

89 • The Balvenie (Scotland) 12 Year Old Double Wood Single Malt Scotch Whisky 86 Proof. $32.99.

89 • Strathisla (Scotland) 12 Year Old Pure Highland Malt Scotch Whisky 86 Proof. $40.

89 • Glen Moray (Scotland) Single Malt Scotch Whisky, 15 Year Old 80 Proof. $40.

88 • The Glenrothes (Scotland) 16 Year Old Single Speyside Malt Scotch Whisky, Distilled in 1979, Bottled in 1995 86 Proof. $55.

88 • Tamdhu (Scotland) Speyside Single Malt Scotch Whisky 80 Proof. $31.99.

88 • Glenfarclas (Scotland) 10 Year Old Single Highland Malt Scotch Whisky 86 Proof. $27.99.

87 • The Glendronach (Scotland) 15 Year Old Single Highland Malt Scotch Whisky, Sherry Cask Aged 80 Proof. $43.

87 • Knockando (Scotland) 18 Year Old Single Malt Scotch Whisky, Distilled in 1976 86 Proof. $59.99.

87 • Knockando (Scotland) 14 Year Old Single Malt Scotch Whisky, Distilled in 1979, Bottled in 1994 86 Proof. $49.99.

86 • The Glenlivet (Scotland) 12 Year Old Single Malt Scotch Whisky 80 Proof. $35.

86 • Glenrothes (Scotland) 1982 Vintage Single Malt Scotch Whisky 86 Proof. $50.

86 • Glenkeith (Scotland) Single Highland Malt Scotch Whisky, Distilled Before 1983, Aged More Than Ten Years 86 Proof. $35.

86 • Glenfarclas (Scotland) 12 Year Old Single Highland Malt Scotch Whisky 86 Proof. $45.

86 • Glen Moray (Scotland) Single Highland Malt Scotch Whisky, 12 Year Old
80 Proof. $23.99.

85 • The Glenlivet (Scotland) Pure Single Malt Scotch Whisky, 18 Year Old
86 Proof. $44.95.

85 • The Balvenie (Scotland) 10 Year Old Founder's Reserve Single Malt Scotch Whisky
86 Proof. $25.99.

85 • Knockando (Scotland) 12 Year Old Single Malt Scotch Whisky 86 Proof. $38.

85 • Auchroisk (Scotland) The Singleton of Auchroisk,10 Year Old Single Malt Scotch
Whisky, Distilled in 1981, Bottled in 1992 86 Proof. $40.

Island Single Malt Scotch

96 • Highland Park (Scotland) 12 Year Old Orkney Island Single Malt Scotch Whisky
86 Proof. $40.99.

92 • Highland Park (Scotland) Glenhaven Bottling, 20 Year Old, Orkney Islands Single
Malt Scotch Whisky, Distilled September 1975, Bottled June 1996 115.4 Proof. $98.

89 • Talisker (Scotland) 10 Year Old Isle of Skye Single Malt Scotch Whisky
91.6 Proof. $48.

87 • Ledaig (Scotland) 20 Year Old Isle of Mull Single Malt Scotch Whisky,
Distilled in 1974 86 Proof. $60.

86 • Ledaig (Scotland) 15 Year Old Isle of Mull Single Malt Scotch Whisky
86 Proof. $46.95.

Lowland Single Malt Scotch

97 • Inverleven Stills, Dumbarton (Scotland) Cadenhead Bottling, 27 Year Old, Cask
Strength Lowland Malt Scotch Whisky, Distilled March 1969, Bottled June 1996
97.6 Proof. $95.

92 • Bladnoch (Scotland) Cadenhead Bottling, 16 Year Old, Cask Strength Lowland
Malt Scotch Whisky, Distilled June 1980, Bottled September 1996 116.4 Proof. $72.

90 • Littlemill (Scotland) 8 Year Old 100% Malt Scotch Whisky 86 Proof. $28.

86 • Auchentoshan (Scotland) 21 Year Old Single Lowland Malt Scotch Whisky
86 Proof. $90.

Islay Single Malt Scotch

99 • Lagavulin (Scotland) 16 Year Old Islay Single Malt Scotch Whisky 86 Proof. $50.

99 • Bowmore (Scotland) 30 Year Old Islay Single Malt Scotch Whisky 86 Proof. $189.99.

97 • Ardbeg (Scotland) 1974 Provenance Limited Edition Very Old Islay Single Malt
Scotch Whisky 101.2 Proof. $500.

96 • Ardbeg (Scotland) 1978 Limited Edition Ultimate Islay Single Malt Scotch Whisky
86 Proof. $125.

95 • Bowmore (Scotland) 25 Year Old Islay Single Malt Scotch Whisky 86 Proof. $190.

94 • Ardbeg (Scotland) 17 Year Old Islay Single Malt Scotch Whisky 86 Proof. $70.

93 • Bowmore (Scotland) 17 Year Old Islay Single Malt Scotch Whisky 86 Proof. $70.

91 • Bowmore (Scotland) 22 Year Old Islay Single Malt Scotch Whisky 86 Proof. $128.99.

90 • Bowmore (Scotland) Cask Strength Islay Single Malt Scotch Whisky 112 Proof. $60.

90 • Bowmore (Scotland) 21 Year Old Islay Single Malt Scotch Whisky 86 Proof. $99.99.

90 • Ardbeg (Scotland) Gordon & MacPhail Bottling, 20 Year Old Single Islay Malt
Scotch Whisky, Distilled in 1974, Bottled in 1995 80 Proof. $75.

89 • Laphroaig (Scotland) 10 Year Old Islay Single Malt Scotch Whisky 86 Proof. $40.

89 • Bowmore (Scotland) Sherry Casked Darkest Islay Single Malt Scotch Whisky
86 Proof. $80.

88 • Bruichladdich (Scotland) 15 Year Old Single Islay Malt Scotch Whisky 86 Proof. $45.

88 • Bowmore (Scotland) Islay Single Malt Scotch Whisky, 10 Year Old 86 Proof. $34.95.

87 • Laphroaig (Scotland) 15 Year Old Islay Single Malt Scotch Whisky 86 Proof. $65.

Scale: Superlative (96-100), Exceptional (90-95), Highly Recommended (85-89),
Recommended (80-84), Not Recommended (Under 80)

Campbeltown Single Malt Scotch

92 • Springbank (Scotland) Murray, McDavid Bottling, 30 Year Old Campbeltown Single Malt Scotch Whisky, Sherry Wood Aged, Distilled in 1965 92 Proof. $100.

89 • Springbank (Scotland) 21 Year Old Campbeltown Single Malt Scotch Whisky 92 Proof. $149.95.

86 • Springbank (Scotland) 15 Year Old Campbeltown Single Malt Scotch Whisky 92 Proof. $49.95.

86 • Glen Scotia (Scotland) 14 Year Old Campbeltown Single Malt Scotch Whisky 86 Proof. $55.95.

85 • Glen Scotia (Scotland) 17 Year Old Campbeltown Single Malt Scotch Whisky 86 Proof. $65.

Vatted Malt Scotch

93 • Moidart (Scotland) 21 Year Old Pure Malt Vatted Scotch Whisky 92 Proof. $103.

86 • Findlater's Mar Lodge (Scotland) Pure Malt Scotch Whisky, 12 Year Old 86 Proof. $19.99.

Blended Scotch

93 • Johnny Walker (Scotland) Blue Label Blend of Rarest Scotch Whiskies 80 Proof. $180.

90 • Usquaebach (Scotland) Blended Scotch Whisky 86 Proof. $25.

90 • Justerini & Brooks (Scotland) J.E.T., Old Scotch Whisky 86 Proof. $24.99.

90 • Ballantine's (Scotland) Blended Scotch Whisky, Gold Seal 12 Year Old 80 Proof. $21.99.

89 • The Famous Grouse (Scotland) 12 Year Old, Gold Reserve, Deluxe Scotch Whisky 80 Proof. $22.99.

89 • Justerini & Brooks (Scotland) J & B Select, Blended Scotch Whisky 80 Proof. $17.99.

89 • Johnny Walker (Scotland) Black Label 12 Year Extra Special Old Scotch Whisky 80 Proof. $25.

88 • Chivas Regal (Scotland) 12 Year Old, Premium Scotch Whisky 80 Proof. $25.

86 • The Inverarity (Scotland) Blended Scotch Whisky 80 Proof. $18.

86 • The Famous Grouse (Scotland) Finest Blended Scotch Whisky 80 Proof. $18.99.

86 • Ballantine's (Scotland) Finest Blended Scotch Whisky 80 Proof. $15.99.

85 • Teacher's (Scotland) Blended Scotch Whisky 86 Proof. $17.99.

85 • Spey Cast (Scotland) Scotch Whisky, 12 Year Old 80 Proof. $29.99.

85 • Johnny Walker (Scotland) Red Label Blended Scotch Whisky 80 Proof. $16.

85 • Duggans (Scotland) 12 Year Old, Blended Scotch Whisky 80 Proof. $19.95.

Irish Whiskey

95 • Midleton (Ireland) 1995 Very Rare Irish Whiskey 80 Proof. $99.99.

94 • Midleton (Ireland) 1994 Very Rare Irish Whiskey 80 Proof. $99.99.

93 • Jameson (Ireland) Gold Special Reserve Irish Whiskey 80 Proof. $60.

92 • Jameson (Ireland) 1780 Reserve 12 Year Old Irish Whiskey 80 Proof. $30.

89 • Bushmills (Ireland) Special Old Irish Whiskey 80 Proof. $25.99.

86 • Jameson (Ireland) Irish Whiskey 80 Proof. $20.

Irish Malt Whiskey

93 • Bushmills (Ireland) 16 Year Old Rare Single Irish Malt Whiskey 80 Proof. $55.

91 • Bushmills (Ireland) 10 Year Old Single Malt Irish Whiskey 80 Proof. $28.99.

86 • Connemara (Ireland) Peated Single Malt Irish Whiskey 80 Proof. $22.

Japanese Whisky

86 • Suntory (Japan) Yamazaki 12 Year Old Pure Malt Whisky 86 Proof. $38.

three

North American
Whiskies

*"Taken sanely and in moderation whisky is
beneficial, aids digestion, helps throw off colds,
megrims and influenzas. Used improperly the effect is
just as bad as stuffing on too many starchy foods,
taking no exercise, or disliking our neighbor."*

– Charles H. Baker, Jr., The Gentleman's Companion, 1939

An Overview

North American whiskies are all-grain spirits that have been produced from a
mash bill that usually mixes together corn, rye, wheat, barley, and other grains
in different proportions, and then generally aged for an extended period of
time in wooden barrels. These barrels may be new or used, and charred or
uncharred on the inside, depending on the type of whiskey being made.

The Distillation of North American Whiskies

Most North American whiskies are made in column stills. The United States
government requires that all whiskies:

- Be made from a grain mash.
- Be distilled at 90% ABV or less.
- Be reduced to no more than 62.5% ABV (125° proof) before being aged in oak
  barrels (except for Corn whiskey, which does not have to be aged in wood).
- Have the aroma, taste, and characteristics that are generally attributed to
  whiskey.
- Be bottled at no less that 40% ABV (80° proof).

Classifications of North American Whiskies

North American whiskies are essentially classified by the type or variety of grains
in the mash bill, the percentage or proof of alcohol at which they are distilled,
and the length and manner of their aging.

Bourbon Whiskey must contain a minimum of 51% corn, be produced in the
United States, be distilled at less than 80% ABV (160° proof), and be aged for
a minimum of two years in new charred barrels, although in practice virtually
all straight whiskies are aged at least four years. Any Bourbon, or any other
domestic or imported whiskey, for that matter, that has been aged less than four
years must contain an age statement on the label. **Small Batch Bourbons**
are bourbons that are bottled from a small group of specially selected barrels
that are blended together. It should be noted though that each distiller has their
own interpretation of what constitutes a "small batch." **Single Barrel Bourbon** is
Bourbon from one specifically chosen cask.

Tennessee Whiskey must contain a minimum of 51% corn, be produced in
Tennessee, be distilled at less than 80% ABV (160° proof), be filtered through
a bed of sugar maple charcoal, and be aged for a minimum of two years in new
charred barrels.

North American Whiskies at a Glance

Top Score:

99 • Old Rip Van Winkle (KY) 20 Year Old, Pappy Van Winkle's Family Reserve Kentucky Straight Bourbon Whiskey 90.4 Proof. $70.

Rye Whiskey must contain a minimum of 51% rye grain, be distilled at less than 80% ABV (160° proof), and be aged for a minimum of two years in new charred barrels. Some straight Rye whiskey is bottled and marketed, but most of the industry production is blended into other whiskies to give them additional character and structure. Canadians frequently refer to their whisky as "Rye," though it is in fact made primarily from corn or wheat.

Blended American Whiskey is required to contain at least 20% straight whiskey, with the balance being unaged neutral spirit or, in a few cases, high-proof light whiskey. It has a general whiskey flavor profile (most closely resembling Bourbon), but lacks any defining taste characteristic.

Corn Whiskey is a commercial product that must contain at least 80% corn, be distilled at less than 80% ABV (160° proof), and be aged for a minimum of two years in new or used uncharred barrels.

Moonshine Whiskey (a.k.a. white lightning, Corn likker, or white dog) is distilled from a varied mix of corn and sugar and is aged in Mason jars and jugs for the length of time that it takes the customers to get home, or the Dukes of Hazzard to make a delivery in the General Lee.

Canadian Whisky is made primarily from corn or wheat, with a supplement of rye, barley, or barley malt. There are no Canadian government requirements when it comes to the percentages of grains used in the mash bill. Unlike Bourbons, they are aged, primarily in used oak barrels. The minimum age for Canadian Whisky is three years, with most brands being aged four to six years. Virtually all Canadian whiskys (except the pot-distilled malt whiskies of Glenora in Nova Scotia) are blended from different grain whiskies of different ages. **Bulk Canadian Whisky**s are usually shipped in barrels to their destination country where they are bottled. These bulk whiskies are usually bottled at 40% ABV (80° proof) and are usually no more than four years old. **Bottled in Canada Whiskys** generally have older components in their blends and are bottled at 43.4% ABV (86.8° proof).

North American Whiskey Regions

United States

Kentucky produces all types of North American whiskies except for Tennessee and Canadian. It has the largest concentration of distilleries on the continent.

Tennessee started out as Bourbon country, but today its two remaining distilleries specialize in the distinctive Tennessee style of whiskey.

Other states—primarily **Indiana**, **Illinois**, **Virginia**, and **Missouri**—have distilleries that produce straight whiskeys, although some of these plants are currently mothballed. **California** has one tiny micro-distillery that produces Rye. Additionally there are a number of distilling plants scattered around the country that rectify (dilute and blend), process, and bottle spirits that were originally distilled elsewhere. These distilleries, in addition to sometimes bottling Bourbon that has been shipped to them in bulk, may also create their own blended whiskies. These whiskies tend to be relatively inexpensive "well" brands that are sold mainly to taverns and bars for making mixed drinks.

Canada

Ontario has the largest concentration of whisky distilleries in Canada—three. **Alberta** has two and **Manitob**a, **Quebec**, and **Nova Scotia** each have one. With the exception of Glenora in Nova Scotia, which is a malt whisky distillery, all of the Canadian distilleries produce only blended Canadian whisky.

Top Whiskies by Style

Bourbon Whiskey

99 • **Old Rip Van Winkle (KY) 20 Year Old, Pappy Van Winkle's Family Reserve Kentucky Straight Bourbon Whiskey 90.4 Proof. $70.**

Rye Whiskey

95 • **Old Rip Van Winkle (KY) 13 Year Old, Van Winkle Family Reserve Kentucky Straight Rye Whiskey 95.6 Proof. $25.**

Tennessee Whiskey

89 • **George Dickel (TN) 10 Year Old Special Barrel Reserve Tennessee Whisky 86 Proof. $30.**

American Blended Whiskey

90 • **Seagram's Seven Crown (USA) Blended Whiskey 80 Proof. $9.99.**

Canadian Whisky

89 • **Alberta Springs (Canada) Blended Canadian Whisky 90 Proof. $9.49.**

89 • **Alberta Springs (Canada) 10 Year Old Canadian Rye Whisky 80 Proof. $20.50**

Bourbon, Tennessee, Rye, Blended American, Corn, and Canadian Whiskies – Origins and History

Bourbon Whiskey

The first waves of British settlers in North America were a thirsty lot. It is recorded that the Pilgrims chose to make final landfall at Plymouth, Massachusetts, even though their original destination was elsewhere, primarily because they were almost out of beer.

The first locally made alcoholic beverage was beer, although the limited supply of barley malt was frequently supplemented by such local substitutes as pumpkin pulp. Distilled spirits soon followed, with rum made from imported Caribbean molasses dominating in the northern colonies, and an assortment of fruit brandies in the south.

In the early 1700s a combination of bad economic times and religious unrest against the Established Church in Great Britain set off a great wave of emigration from Scotland and Ireland. These Scots, and the Protestant Scottish settlers from the northern Irish province of Ulster who came to be known as the "Scotch-Irish" in the new World, brought to North America their religion, their distrust of government control, and their skill at distilling whiskey.

This rush of humanity, augmented by German immigrants of a similar religious and cultural persuasion, passed through the seaboard colonies and settled initially in Pennsylvania, Maryland, and western Virginia. Mostly small farmers, they quickly adapted to growing rye because of its hardiness, and, in the western counties, Native American corn because of its high yields. Grain was awkward to ship to East Coast markets because of the poor roads; so many farmers turned to distilling their crops into whiskey. In Pennsylvania these were primarily Rye whiskies; farther to the west and south Corn whiskies predominated. By the end of the American War of Independence in 1784, the first commercial distilleries had been established in what was then the western Virginia county of Kentucky. From the start they produced corn-based whiskies.

In 1794 the new, cash-strapped Federal government imposed the first federal excise tax on distillers. The farmer-distillers of western Pennsylvania responded violently in what became known as the Whiskey Rebellion. Federal tax agents were assaulted and killed by angry mobs. Order was finally restored when the federal government sent in an army of 15,000 militiamen, under President George Washington, to put down the revolt. The ringleaders were convicted and sentenced to be hanged, but cooler heads prevailed, and after jail time they were pardoned and released.

This situation did provoke a new migration of settlers into the then-western frontier lands of Kentucky and Tennessee. In these new states farmers found ideal corn-growing country and smooth, limestone-filtered water—two of the basic ingredients of Bourbon whiskey.

The name "Bourbon" comes from a county in eastern Kentucky, which in turn was named for the Bourbon kings of France who had aided the American rebels in the Revolutionary War. Bourbon County was in the early 19th century a center of whiskey production and transshipping (ironically, at the present time, it is a "dry" county). The local whiskey, made primarily from corn, soon gained a reputation for being particularly smooth because the local distillers aged their products in charred oak casks. The adoption of the "sour mash" grain conversion technique served to further distinguish Bourbon from other whiskey styles.

By the 1840s Bourbon was recognized and marketed as a distinctive American style of whiskey, although not as a regionally specific spirit. Bourbon came to be produced in Kentucky, Tennessee, Indiana, Illinois, Ohio, Missouri, Pennsylvania, North Carolina, and Georgia, among other states. Nowadays Bourbon production is confined to Kentucky and Indiana, although the only legal location requirement for calling a whiskey "Bourbon" is that it be produced in the United States. Initially Bourbon was made in pot stills, but as the century progressed the new column still technology was increasingly adopted. The last old-line pot still plant closed in Pennsylvania in 1992, but the technique was revived in Kentucky in 1995 when the historic Labrot & Graham Distillery was renovated and reopened with a set of new, Scottish-built copper pot stills.

The late 19th century saw the rise of the Temperance Movement, a social phenomenon driven by a potent combination of religious and women's groups. Temperance societies, such as the Women's Christian Temperance Union and the Anti-Saloon League, operated nationally, but were particularly active in the southern states. The notion of temperance soon gave way to a stated desire for outright prohibition, and throughout the rest of the century an assortment of states and counties adopted prohibition for varying lengths of time and degrees of severity. This muddle of legal restrictions played havoc in

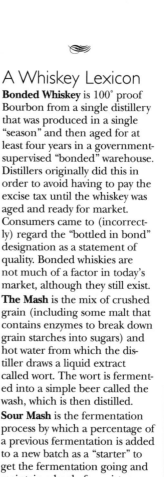

A Whiskey Lexicon

Bonded Whiskey is 100° proof Bourbon from a single distillery that was produced in a single "season" and then aged for at least four years in a government-supervised "bonded" warehouse. Distillers originally did this in order to avoid having to pay the excise tax until the whiskey was aged and ready for market. Consumers came to (incorrectly) regard the "bottled in bond" designation as a statement of quality. Bonded whiskies are not much of a factor in today's market, although they still exist.

The Mash is the mix of crushed grain (including some malt that contains enzymes to break down grain starches into sugars) and hot water from which the distiller draws a liquid extract called wort. The wort is fermented into a simple beer called the wash, which is then distilled.

Sour Mash is the fermentation process by which a percentage of a previous fermentation is added to a new batch as a "starter" to get the fermentation going and maintain a level of consistency from batch to batch. A sweet mash means that only fresh yeast is added to a new batch to start fermentation.

Straight Whiskey is unblended whiskey that contains no neutral spirit. Bourbon, Tennessee, Rye, and Corn whiskey are straight whiskies. There is also a spirit, simply called "straight whiskey," that is made from a mixture of grains, none of which accounts for 51% of the mash bill.

the Bourbon industry, as it interfered with the production and aging of stocks of whiskey.

National Prohibition in 1919 had effects on the Bourbon industry beyond shutting down most of the distilleries. Drinking did not stop, of course, and the United States was soon awash in illegal alcohol, much of it of dubious quality. What did change was the American taste in whiskey. Illicit moonshine and imported Canadian whiskeys were lighter in taste and body than Bourbon and Rye. The corresponding increase in popularity of white spirits such as Gin and Vodka further altered the marketplace. When Repeal came in 1933, a number of the old distilleries didn't reopen, and the industry began a slow consolidation that lasted into the early 1990s, at which time there were only 10 distilleries in Kentucky and two in Tennessee.

It may seem odd, but Scotch whisky may be Bourbon's inspiration for long-term revival. The steady growth in sales of single malt and high-quality Scotch whiskies has not gone unnoticed in Bourbon country. All of the Kentucky and Tennessee whiskey distilleries are now marketing high-end "single cask" and "small batch" whiskies that have found great success among upscale consumers. Two small specialty distilleries have opened in the last few years in Kentucky and California to cater to this increasing demand for quality over quantity. The United States may yet, in the words of one commentator, "turn away from foreign potions and return to its native spirit."

Tennessee Whiskey

Tennessee whiskey is a first cousin of Bourbon, with virtually an identical history. The same sort of people used the same sort of grains and the same sort of production techniques to produce a style of whiskey that, remarkably, is noticeably different. The early whiskey distillers in Tennessee, for reasons that are lost in the mists of history, added a final step to their production process when they began filtering their whiskey through thick beds of sugar maple charcoal. This filtration removes some of the congeners (flavor elements) in the spirit and creates a smooth, mellow palate. The two remaining distillers in the state continue this tradition, which a distiller at the Jack Daniel's Distillery once described as being "same church, different pew."

Rye Whiskey

The Scotch-Irish immigrant distillers had some exposure to using rye in whiskey production, but for their German immigrant neighbors rye had been the primary grain used in the production of Schnapps and Vodka back in northern Europe. They continued this distilling practice, particularly in Pennsylvania and Maryland, where Rye whiskey, with its distinctive hard-edged, grainy palate, remained the dominant whiskey type well into the 20th century.

Rye whiskey was even more adversely effected by National Prohibition than Bourbon. A generation of consumers weaned on light-bodied and relatively delicate white spirits turned away from the uncompromising, pungent, full-bodied straight Rye whiskies. Production of Rye whiskies had vanished altogether from its mid-Atlantic homeland by the 1980s. A handful of modern Rye whiskies are currently being made by Bourbon distilleries in Kentucky and Indiana. America's first indigenous whiskey style is today only barely surviving in the marketplace. Its primary use is for blending to give other whiskies more character and backbone, although a small but vocal group of Rye whisky enthusiasts continue to champion it.

Blended American Whiskey

Blended whiskies date from the early 19th century when the invention of the column still made possible the production of neutral spirits. Distillers would blend one or more straight whiskies (Bourbon and Rye) with these neutral spirits in varying proportions to create their own branded blend. The taste and quality of these whiskies, then as now, varies according to the ratio of straight whiskey to neutral grain spirit. Early blends were frequently flavored with everything from sherry to plug tobacco. Compared to straight whiskies they were relatively inexpensive and bland in character. Modern blends utilize dozens of different straight whiskies to insure a consistent flavor profile. Blended American whiskies had a great sales boost during and just after World War II when distillers promoted them as a way of stretching their limited supply of straight whiskey. This sales spike did not last, however. Blended whiskies were considered to be too bland by Bourbon and Rye drinkers, and consumers with a taste for lighter spirits soon migrated to Vodka and Gin. Blended whiskies have been leading the pack in declining sales over the past few decades.

Corn Whiskey

Corn whiskey was the first truly American whiskey, and the precursor to Bourbon. An unaged, clear spirit, it was the type of whiskey that Scotch-Irish farmers produced in their stills for family consumption or to trade for store goods. When state and federal excise taxes were permanently introduced during the Civil War, most of the production of Corn whiskey went underground to become moonshine, where it has remained ever since. A modest amount of commercial Corn whiskey is still produced and consumed in the South.

Canadian Whisky

Canadian whiskies, as with their American cousins, originated on the farm. These early whiskies were made primarily from rye. In time most Canadian distillers turned to corn, wheat, and other grains, but Canadians continue to refer to their whisky as "Rye" even though the mash bill for most Canadian Whisky is now predominantly a mix of corn, wheat, and barley, with only a modest preportion of rye for flavor, which results in a lighter-bodied spirit.

Reviews

Alberta Springs (Canada)
Alberta Springs Blended Canadian Whisky 90 proof $9.49.   **89**

Dark gold with an amber glow. Full-bodied. Notes of peach, apricot, vanilla, walnut. Rich, deep texture. Bold flavors are beautifully merged with fragrant wood. Lush, full finish. Complex.

Alberta Springs 10 Year Old Canadian Rye Whisky 80 proof $20.50.   **89**

Full orange-amber hue. Smoky, vanilla-rich aromas. Full-bodied palate with heavy wood-spiced flavors that develop nutty complexity through the finish. Rich, generously oaky style.

Ancient Age (KY)
Ancient Age Kentucky Straight Bourbon Whiskey 80 proof $7.99.   **81**

Gold with a light copper cast. Medium-bodied. Notes of chalk, nutmeg, lemon. Tight, grainy texture. Compact feel on the palate with a refreshing sensation. Has a nice blend of tartness with brisk spice.

Ancient Age Kentucky Straight Bourbon Whiskey 90 proof $9.49.   **85**

Deep gold with an amber cast. Medium-bodied. Notes of flan, fig, bread dough, flowers. Broad and smooth on the palate. Pretty, slightly rich dried fruit is enhanced by soft fragrance and weighty brown spice. Silky finish.

Baker's (KY)
Baker's 7 Year Old Kentucky Straight Bourbon Whiskey, 107 proof $38.   **92**

Deep amber with a copper cast. Full-bodied. Notes of citrus, roasted nuts, sea air, cedar. Rich, full texture. A rush of deep flavors attack the palate accompanied by a good dose of heat. Quite complex with a peculiar, refreshing note in the middle. Sensational aromatics never cease. Greater depth is realized in the broad, lush finish. A tour de force.

Banker's Club (KY)
Banker's Club 4 Year Old Kentucky Sour Mash Bourbon 80 proof $6.99.   **82**

Amber with a dark copper cast. Medium-bodied. Notes of minerals, dried herbs, dried citrus. Bright and assertive on the palate. A hint of complexity as various spicy, piquant nuances and strong aromatics are showcased. Racy, fruity finish.

Basil Hayden's (KY)
Basil Hayden's 8 Year Old Kentucky Straight Bourbon Whiskey 80 proof $30.   **90**

Amber with an orange cast. Medium-bodied. Notes of pear, peach, flowers, fresh herbs. Medium texture. Soft and light on the palate with a potpourri of attractive fragrances. Displays a sense of elegance and grace. Fruity and lively at the finish.

Black Velvet (Canada)
Black Velvet Blended Canadian Whisky 80 proof $7.99.   **NR**

Blanton's (KY)
Blanton's Single Barrel Kentucky Straight Bourbon Whiskey 93 proof $45.99.   **91**

Amber-copper with an orange cast. Moderately full-bodied. Notes of flowers, sweet herbs, peach, smoke. Soft, smooth texture. Lovely fragrances are married with fruit and light spice. Complex, lingering finish. A very elegant, refined style.

Booker's (KY)

Booker's Kentucky Straight Bourbon Whiskey, Batch C89-6-13:
Aged 6 Years 5 Months 126.6 proof $50. **95**
Dark amber with a chestnut cast. Full-bodied. Elements of molasses, butterscotch, pecan, dried tropical fruits. Deep, thick texture. Loaded with richness in flavors, woody notes, and rich spices. A pleasant, syrupy sensation keeps evolving. For all its power and heat, there is a remarkable velvety, elegant finish. A potent, soaring spirit.

Canadian Club (Canada)

Canadian Club Six Year Old Blended Canadian Whisky 80 proof $8.99. **84**
Dark yellow-gold tint. Medium- to light-bodied. Notes of apple, peach, smoky butter. Creamy, light texture. Smooth and easy with a fruity, clean finish.

Canadian Club Classic Twelve Year Old Blended Canadian Whisky
80 proof $15.99. **86**
Deep gold. Medium-bodied. Notes of peach, walnut, tea. Medium, delicate texture. Pretty fruit and a touch of nut spice add to the refined style.

Canadian LTD (Canada)

Canadian LTD Blended Canadian Whisky 80 proof $6.99. **NR**

Canadian Mist (Canada)

Canadian Mist Blended Canadian Whisky 80 proof $8.99. **NR**

Corby's (USA)

Corby's 4 Year Old Reserve Blended American Whiskey 80 proof $5.99. **84**
Dark amber with a chestnut-orange cast. Medium-bodied. Notes of dried peach, cedar, herbs. Moderately rich texture. Quite aromatic, offering an interesting mix of spice and fruit. Lively finish.

Corner Creek (KY)

Corner Creek 8 Year Old Reserve Kentucky
Bourbon Whiskey 88 proof $26. **90**
Deep amber hue. Hedonistic sweet wood, smoke, and charred barrel aromas. A very smooth attack leads to a medium-bodied palate. Refined, supple, flavorful finish. Rounded and elegant, this is a very refined style.

Crown Royal (Canada)

Crown Royal Blended Canadian Whisky 80 proof $15.99. **87**
Amber with a copper glow. Medium- to full-bodied. Notes of citrus, date, pecan. Rich flavors are supported by ample weight. Full, deep, and lingering finish.

Eagle Rare (KY)

Eagle Rare 10 Year Old Kentucky Straight Bourbon Whiskey
101 proof $18/L. **89**
Deep tawny amber hue. Pleasant sweet wood and toasted coconut aromas. A weighty, viscous attack leads to a full-bodied palate. Smooth, flavorful, warming finish. Well balanced and supple, with a rustic sense of refinement.

Early Times (KY)

Early Times Old Style Kentucky Whisky 80 proof $8.99. **NR**

Elijah Craig (KY)

Elijah Craig 12 Year Old Double Distillation Straight Bourbon Whiskey 94 proof $12.95.　　　　**86**

Deep amber. Perfume and clover honey fill the nose. Deep and rich in structure. Well-integrated elements combine with a high alcohol feel. Still perfumed at the end. Best served neat.

Elijah Craig Single Barrel 18 Year Old Kentucky Bourbon Whiskey, Barrel #148, Barreled on 3/28/78 90 proof $39.95.　　　　**88**

Deep amber with a chestnut cast. Medium-bodied. Notes of mincemeat pie, maple, minerals. Lush texture. Grainy, tight sensation on the palate. Opens up to display a complex range of flavors with lively aromatics with an assertive finish.

Elmer T. Lee (KY)

Elmer T. Lee Kentucky Sour Mash Bourbon Whiskey 90 proof $12/.　　　　**83**

Deep tawny amber hue. Powerful charred barrel, spice, and mineral aromas. A smooth attack leads to a medium-bodied palate. Lean, fiery finish. Nicely flavored with a slight burn.

Evan Williams (KY)

Evan Williams 7 Year Old Sour Mash Straight Bourbon 90 proof $8.95.　　　　**NR**

Evan Williams Single Barrel Vintage 1988 Kentucky Bourbon Whiskey, Barrel #132, Barreled on 8/30/88 86.6 proof $21.99.　　　　**90**

Amber-copper with a golden cast. Moderately light-bodied. Notes of walnut, dried citrus, dried herbs, tea. Racy feel on the palate with an elegant balance of dried fruit, spice, and dusty aromatics. Pretty, delicate finish.

Ezra Brooks (KY)

Ezra Brooks Kentucky Straight Bourbon Whiskey 90 proof $9.99.　　　　**89**

Dark gold with a dark orange cast. Moderately full-bodied. Notes of dried citrus, smoke, sea air. Very broad on the palate, full of lively fruit accented by refreshing, zesty aromatics. Contains a curious, almost briny note. A sense of depth is evident in the rich, lush finish.

Fleischmann's (USA)

Fleischmann's 4 Year Old Preferred Blended American Whiskey 80 proof $5.99.　　　　**NR**

G & W (KY)

G & W 4 Year Old Five Star Blended Whiskey 80 proof $6.49.　　　　**81**

Dark amber. Medium-bodied. Notes of molasses, fig, smoke. Pungent feel with an earthy, smoked note permeating lighter fruit and brown spice. Grainy on the palate with a compact finish.

G & W 4 Year Old Private Stock Kentucky Bourbon 80 proof $6.99.　　　　**81**

Dark gold with an amber cast. Moderately light-bodied. Notes of lemon, honey, straw. Grainy texture. Although relatively light in profile, there is a strong dose of sour lemon-drop candy upfront. Nice, lingering finish.

　Scale: Superlative (96-100), Exceptional (90-95), Highly Recommended (85-89), Recommended (80-84), Not Recommended (Under 80)

Gentleman Jack (TN)

Gentleman Jack Rare Tennessee Whiskey 80 proof $20.   **87**

Deep gold with an amber cast. Medium-bodied. Notes of citrus, honey, dried herbs, almonds. Moderately rich texture. Slightly tangy on the palate. While not overly herbaceous, there are ample fragrances straight out of a country meadow. A dollop of lightly sweet brown spice complements easy, soft fruit.

George Dickel (TN)

George Dickel Original No. 12 Tennessee Sippin' Whisky 90 proof $14.99.   **82**

Amber with a copper-orange cast. Medium-bodied. Notes of citrus, dried herbs, honey. Round, bold texture. Fairly assertive in style, displaying a high degree of aromatics and lighter fruit notes. Good intensity in the finish.

George Dickel 10 Year Old Special Barrel Reserve Tennessee Whisky 86 proof $30.   **89**

Amber with a light copper cast. Moderately full-bodied. Notes of vanilla, dried peach, almonds, ashwood. Full, rich texture. Thick and forceful on the palate, showing a heavy woody note. Quite warming in style, with graceful harmony of nutty and spicy elements. Soft fruit nuances are evident in the finish.

Hancock's (KY)

Hancock's President's Reserve Single Barrel Sour Mash Kentucky Bourbon Whiskey 88.9 proof $48.   **91**

Amber with an orange cast. Moderately full-bodied. Notes of citrus, flowers, nuts. Rich texture. Moderately soft with a compact feel on the palate. Fruity and amply spiced with rich nutty and herbal nuances. Very elegant, refined finish.

I.W. Harper (KY)

I. W. Harper Straight Bourbon Aged 12 Years 86 proof $20.   **82**

Deep amber. Medium-bodied. Vanilla, clove, and nutmeg emerge from the first few sniffs. Figs and roasted almonds follow.

I. W. Harper 15 Year Old Kentucky Straight Bourbon Whiskey 80 proof $30.   **86**

Deep amber with a copper cast. Medium-bodied. Notes of maple, ashwood, smoke, peach. Soft, smooth texture. A light entry on the palate. Displays deft fruit nuances in an elegant frame with an earthy, smoky finish.

A.H. Hirsch (KY)

A. H. Hirsch 13 Year Old Kentucky Straight Rye Whiskey 95.6 proof $42.50.   **89**

Deep brilliant amber cast. Opulent caramel, kipper, and spice box aromas. A supple attack leads to a full-bodied and exceptionally smooth palate with very little burn. Fades toward the spicy finish with a gentle, lingering warmth.

A. H. Hirsch 16 Year Old Reserve Pot Stilled Sour Mash Straight Bourbon Whiskey 91.6 proof $74.50.   **94**

Deep amber hue. Generous sweet caramel, fig, and mineral aromas. A smooth attack leads to a moderately full-bodied, viscous palate. Smooth and supple with a drying woody finish. Rich, rounded, and refined.

A. H. Hirsch Finest Reserve 20 Year Old Pot Stilled Sour Mash Straight Bourbon Whiskey 91.6 proof $99.95.   **98**

Very deep tawny amber hue. Hedonistic caramel, maple, and vanilla aromas. A wonderfully smooth entry leads to a full-bodied palate with gentle, drying wood astringency. Exceptionally flavorful and rich through the warming finish. Weighty and powerful.

Imperial (USA)

Imperial Blended American Whiskey 80 proof $5.99.   **80**

Dark gold with an amber cast. Medium-bodied. Notes of peach, orange peel, honey. Slightly lush texture. Assertive on the palate with a rough edge of tart fruit. Smoother toward the tangy finish.

Jack Daniel's (TN)

Jack Daniel's Old No. 7 Tennessee Sour Mash Whiskey 86 proof $13.99.   **84**

Deep gold with an amber cast. Medium-bodied. Notes of peach, apricot, almonds. Soft, smooth texture. Slightly round and lush on the palate. Pleasantly fruity, with engaging notes of nutty spice. Lively, persistent finish.

Jacob's Well (KY)

Jacob's Well Kentucky Straight Bourbon Whiskey 84 proof $18.99.   **87**

Amber with a copper-orange cast. Medium-bodied. Notes of minerals, dried herbs, dried peach, cocoa. Pleasantly pungent on the palate. Brisk feel of dried elements are nicely woven in a compact format. Softer in the finish with attractive fruit note.

Jim Beam (KY)

Jim Beam Jim Beam Rye 80 proof $8.50.   **83**

Gold with a light amber cast. Moderately light-bodied. Notes of toasted oats, hazelnuts, lemon. Delicate, soft texture. Brisk and slightly tart on the palate. Easy on the lighter citrus notes as more seasoned grainy and nutty elements dominate. Quite pungent in the finish, showing a little heat.

Jim Beam Kentucky Straight Bourbon Whiskey 80 proof $8.50.   **87**

Amber with a copper cast. Medium-bodied. Notes of minerals, dried herbs, nutmeg, dried citrus. Rather tight on the palate, displaying ample spice and an angular, yet bracing sensation. Very brisk, refreshing style.

Kentucky Bourbon Distillers Ltd. (KY)

Kentucky Bourbon Distillers Ltd. 8 Year Old Kentucky Vintage Bourbon Whiskey. $19.   **88**

Amber with a golden cast. Medium-bodied. Notes of clove, citrus, smoke, dried herbs. Buttery, smooth texture. Attractive in its viscosity and warmth on the palate. Nicely balanced by whiffs of campfire scents, soft fruit notes, and a light streak of fragrance.

Kentucky Bourbon Distillers Ltd. 12 Year Old Pure Kentucky XO Bourbon Whiskey. $26.   **89**

Amber with a golden-orange cast. Moderately full-bodied. Notes of dried peach, dried herbs, smoke, walnuts. Bold texture. Very rich and pungent, showing its force and power right on the nose through the palate. Notes of smoke and nuts are woven with light herbal nuances. Fruity yet hot finish. Not for the timid.

Kentucky Gentleman (KY)

Kentucky Gentleman Kentucky Straight Bourbon Whiskey 80 proof $5.99. **83**

Deep amber hue. Generous sweet wood and caramel aromas. A relatively viscous attack leads to a moderately full-bodied palate. Lingering, flavorful finish. Well balanced and straightforward with a slight burn.

Kentucky Tavern (KY)

Kentucky Tavern Straight Bourbon Whiskey 80 proof $6.99.   **80**

Bright amber hue. Fiery wood-accented aromas. A soft attack leads to a medium-bodied palate. Slightly hot, woody finish. Straightforward and a bit coarse.

Kessler (USA)

Kessler American Blended Whiskey 80 proof $8. 83

Dark amber. Medium-bodied. Notes of licorice, dried citrus, leather. Soft texture. Assertive and brisk on the palate. Ample spice and horse saddle notes are nicely complemented by fruity nuances. Lively, engaging finish.

Knob Creek (KY)

Knob Creek Kentucky Straight Bourbon Whiskey 100 proof $24. 93

Amber with a copper cast. Moderately full-bodied. Notes of marmalade, honey, maple. Rounded and quite fragrant on the palate. Ample fruit is brought forth with rich woody components and deep spice. Long, smooth, sweet, and delicious finish.

Labrot & Graham (KY)

Labrot & Graham Woodford Reserve Distiller's Select Kentucky Straight Bourbon Whiskey 90.4 proof $26.99. 89

Very deep amber hue. Powerful and hedonistic caramel, date, and vanilla aromas. An exceptionally smooth, viscous attack leads to a full-bodied palate. Supple, flavorful finish. Intensely flavored but refined, with a gentle warming quality.

Lord Calvert (Canada)

Lord Calvert Blended Canadian Whisky 80 proof $7.99. 80

Medium gold. Light-bodied. Notes of apple, herbs, honey. Soft, light texture. A good blend of fruit and spices in a delicate style.

Maker's Mark (KY)

Maker's Mark Old Style Sour Mash Straight Bourbon Whisky 90 proof $15. 92

Bright, deep amber. Medium- to full-bodied. Caramel, banana, and charcoal prevail in the nose. Traces of leather and tart fruits emerge. In the middle more honey, wood, and vanilla blend together. A big, brawny style.

Maker's Mark Select Straight Bourbon Whisky, Black Label 95 proof $68. 96

Deep amber. Full-bodied. A rich orange liqueur-like nose marries with lush butterscotch and vanilla flavors. Accents of nutmeg and clove add complexity. Deep and powerful, with tremendous length.

Noah's Mill (KY)

Noah's Mill 15 Year Old Straight Kentucky Bourbon Whiskey. $46. 96

Deep amber with a copper-orange cast. Moderately full-bodied. Notes of pralines, mocha, dried apricot, and minerals. Bold, rich texture. Very dry and assertive on the palate. Nutty, spicy components dominate soft fruit notes. Amid all the power lies a fascinating element of zesty, bright succulence. Beautifully structured, this is a sensual delight.

Northern Light (Canada)

Northern Light Blended Canadian Whisky 80 proof $5.99. 80

Orange-amber hue. Sweet, syrupy aromas. Medium-bodied. Caramel flavors with a touch of spice finish quickly. Flavors seem rather confected.

Old Charter (KY)

Old Charter Straight Bourbon Whiskey 10 Years Old 86 proof $10.99. 82

Medium amber. Medium-bodied. Burnt butter, pecan, and orange in the nose. Adding water brings out caramel and honey.

***Old Charter 13 Year Old Proprietor's Reserve Kentucky
Straight Bourbon Whiskey 90 proof $30.***   **89**

Amber with an orange cast. Full-bodied. Notes of walnut, peach-citrus, herbs. Buttery, lush texture. Quite rich and full on the palate. A strong measure of fruit interplays with brown spice and nuts. Notable for its glorious, deep finish, with a touch of heat.

Old Crow (KY)

Old Crow Straight Bourbon Whiskey 80 proof $7.99.   **91**

Bright amber. Medium-bodied. A great old-time favorite. Lilac, wet stone, and licorice are dominant in the leadoff and indicate unusual elements. Richness in the middle serves up walnut with custard and more licorice. A landmark of old Bourbons.

Old Ezra (KY)

Old Ezra 7 Years Old Straight Bourbon Whiskey 101 proof $13.99.   **84**

Medium amber. Medium-bodied. Corn and roasted almonds lead off. Tough, hot feel on entry. A few drops of water opens it up, revealing marzipan. Custard and almonds cap off the finish.

Old Fitzgerald (KY)

***Old Fitzgerald 1849 Straight Bourbon Whiskey 8 Years Old
90 proof $14.99.***   **85**

Deep amber. Medium-bodied. A spicy style, combining notes of pumpkin, allspice and licorice. There is a core of glazed apple and apricot in the midpalate.

***Old Fitzgerald 12 Year Old Very Special Kentucky Straight Sour Mash
Bourbon Whiskey 90 proof $30.***   **90**

Deep amber with a copper cast. Medium-bodied. Notes of flowers, sweet herbs, nuts, pear, custard. Soft, smooth texture. Glides across the palate, in a velvety frame. Lovely fragrances are accented by nutty spices. Fruity, full finish.

Old Forester (KY)

Old Forester 4 Year Old Kentucky Straight Bourbon Whisky 86 proof $8.   **86**

Dark gold with an amber cast. Moderately full-bodied. Notes of nutmeg, dried peach, walnut. Broad, richly spiced, and quite nutty on the palate. A softer note of fruit helps accent the impression. Subtle, elegant finish.

Old Forester Kentucky Straight Bourbon Whisky 100 proof $12.99.   **88**

Deep tawny amber hue. Lean sweet wood and mineral aromas with a touch of heat to the nose. A supple attack leads to a full-bodied palate. Fiery, drying finish. Rounded and viscous with a decided burn and a rustic woody edge.

Old Grand Dad (KY)

Old Grand Dad Kentucky Straight Bourbon Whiskey 86 proof $11.50.   **89**

Dark amber with a chestnut cast. Moderately full-bodied. Notes of walnuts, dried citrus, flowers, allspice. Rich, silky texture. Deep sensations of nuts and fragrance are followed by a spicy core of fruit. Quite rounded in the finish. An elegant sipper.

Old Grand Dad Kentucky Straight Bourbon Whiskey 100 proof $13.50.   **92**

Dark amber with an orange-copper cast. Full-bodied. Notes of pecan pie, marmalade, sweet pipe tobacco, toffee. Viscous texture. Lovely buttery feel on the palate showcasing rich, tangy fruit and deep baked-pie flavors. Quite lush and broad in the finish. A terrific old-style spirit that has paved the way for the new "hand-crafted" brands.

Old Overholt (KY)

Old Overholt 4 Year Old Straight Rye Whiskey 80 proof $9.99.   **87**

Deep amber with a copper cast. Moderately full-bodied. Notes of toffee, dried pear, smoke. Round, smooth texture. Fairly soft and lush on the palate. Quite powerful with a nice balance of brown spice notes, delicate fruit, and a whiff of campfire embers. Elegant, engaging finish.

Old Rip Van Winkle (KY)

Old Rip Van Winkle 13 Year Old, Van Winkle Family Reserve Kentucky Straight Rye Whiskey 95.6 proof $25.   **95**

Deep mahogany hue. Forward tobacco, marmalade, and mineral aromas. A soft attack leads to a full-bodied palate with a rounded viscous texture. Finishes with a drying woody quality, a touch of heat, and persistent sweet flavors.

Old Rip Van Winkle 15 Year Old, Old Rip Van Winkle Handmade Kentucky Straight Bourbon Whiskey 107 proof $55.   **97**

Dark amber with a mahogany cast. Full-bodied. Notes of dried tropical and stone fruits, figs, sweet pipe tobacco, mocha, toasted pecans. Nectar-like, thick texture. This burst of rich flavors is beautifully enhanced by dramatic fragrance and luscious, layered spices. This spirit crescendos with a symphonic range of elements echoing through a seemingly never-ending finish.

Old Rip Van Winkle 20 Year Old, Pappy Van Winkle's Family Reserve Kentucky Straight Bourbon Whiskey 90.4 proof $70.   **99**

Dark amber–dark orange cast. Full-bodied. Notes of oiled leather, smoke, minerals, coffee, cigar box. Viscous, with a thick layered texture without being overly hot. Pungent and angular on the palate. Demonstrates a broad (endless) range of aromatics and wealth of flavors that just keep building and expanding into an infinite finish. Cigar and pipe lovers take note: you have found a challenge.

Old Rip Van Winkle 23 Years Old, Pappy Van Winkle's Family Reserve Kentucky Straight Bourbon Whiskey 95.6 proof $150.   **96**

Deep, rich mahogany hue. Profound, generous pipe tobacco, date, and treacle aromas. A soft attack leads to a moderately full-bodied palate with gentle woody astringency. Lengthy, sweet finish. Very smooth and refined with exceptional balance and complex mineral undercurrents.

Old Thompson (USA)

Old Thompson 4 Year Old Blended American Whiskey 80 proof $5.99.   **81**

Dark gold with an amber cast. Moderately light-bodied. Notes of citrus, dried herbs, minerals. Flinty, lightly spiced impression with a slightly tangy fruity note. Vibrant finish.

Olde St. Nick (KY)

Olde St. Nick Kentucky Winter Rye Whiskey 101 proof $36.   **94**

Deep mahogany hue. Lean mineral, dried apricot, and charred barrel aromas. An exceptionally smooth and viscous attack leads to a full-bodied, rich mouthfeel. Weighty and intense, yet rounded. Lengthy, flavorful, warming finish. A gentle giant...big and rich but oh so smooth.

Olde St. Nick Very Old St. Nick Rare Bourbon Whiskey Aged 20 Years 94 proof $85.   **95**

Deep mahogany hue with greenish highlights. Complex and unusual burnt caramel, ginger, and sweet corn aromas. A lean attack leads to a medium-bodied palate with a drying woody character. Profound, flavorful finish. Has traded the sweet viscosity of youth for drying, complex, woody flavors. Intense, with a decided burn.

Rebel Yell (KY)

Rebel Yell Straight Bourbon 80 proof $8.99. **83**

Medium amber. Medium-bodied. Banana and Turkish taffy are evident in the nose. Soon more tropical (pineapple, date) flavors develop. A controversial style, but unique. Great value.

Rock Hill Farms (KY)

Rock Hill Farms Single Barrel Kentucky Straight Bourbon Whiskey 100 proof $33. **92**

Rich dark amber hue. Forward sweet wood, caramel and salted-nut aromas with a touch of heat to the nose. A supple, smooth attack leads to a moderately full-bodied, drying palate. Rich, woody finish. Big and weighty with a fiery note.

Rowan's Creek (KY)

Rowan's Creek 12 Year Old Straight Kentucky Bourbon Whiskey 105 proof $38. **91**

Amber with a dark golden cast. Medium-bodied. Notes of pear, lemon, honey, and flowers. Smooth texture. Elegant and attractive on the palate. Stunning, velvety mouthfeel of delicate fruit and spice elements that carry forth in a highly fragrant, lingering finish.

Royal Canadian (Canada)

Royal Canadian Blended Canadian Whisky 80 proof $8.99. **83**

Amber-orange hue. Sweet caramel aromas. Sweet attack with nutty, spicy rye flavors that finish with a lingering dryness. Well balanced, smooth.

Schenley (USA)

Schenley 4 Year Old Reserve American Whiskey 80 proof $5.99. **82**

Dark gold with a copper cast. Medium-bodied. Notes of caramel, citrus, cedar. Soft texture. Quite aromatic, showing pretty wood and spice elements over a moderate dose of fruit. An easy sipper or mixer.

Seagram's Seven Crown (USA)

Seagram's Seven Crown Blended Whiskey 80 proof $9.99. **90**

Deep amber. Medium-bodied. A lovely bouquet of smoky, herbal, Grade B maple syrup elements. A smooth-bodied, apricot-flavored, buttery delight. A sleeper, and a fine value.

Seagram's V.O. (Canada)

Seagram's V.O. Six Year Old Blended Canadian Whisky 80 proof $9.99. **83**

Gold with a light amber glow. Medium- to light-bodied. Notes of pear, caramel, butter, brown spices. Light, slightly coarse texture. Fruit is complemented by soft brown spices.

Senator's Club (USA)

Senator's Club 4 Year Old Blended Whiskey 86 proof $6.49. **NR**

Tangle Ridge (Canada)

Tangle Ridge 10 Year Old Double Casked Canadian Whisky 80 proof $21.95. **87**

Dark amber orange. Honeyed, vanilla-rich aromas. Textured and rich with a velvety mouthfeel and honeyed, nutty flavors persisting through the finish. Elegant and sophisticated, not unlike a fine brandy.

Scale: Superlative (96-100), Exceptional (90-95), Highly Recommended (85-89), Recommended (80-84), Not Recommended (Under 80)

Ten High (KY)

Ten High Kentucky Straight Sour Mash Bourbon Whiskey 80 proof $6.99. **80**

Bright amber hue. Restrained grainy, woody aromas. A lean entry leads to a medium-bodied palate. Fiery, drying finish. Rather coarse, with a decided burn.

Tom Moore (KY)

Tom Moore 4 Year Old Straight Kentucky Bourbon Whiskey 80 proof $5.99. **81**

Amber with a copper cast. Medium-bodied. Notes of minerals, dried peach, dried herbs. Bright on the palate, though slightly pungent and astringent. Very refreshing, with a harmonious blend of aromatics. Lively, tart fruit finish.

Very Old Barton (KY)

Very Old Barton 6 Year Old Kentucky Straight Bourbon Whiskey 80 proof $6.99. **84**

Rich tawny amber hue. Lean woody aromas. A firm attack leads to a medium-bodied palate with a drying woody character. Dry, warming finish.

Virginia Gentleman (VA)

Virginia Gentleman 4 Year Old Straight Bourbon 80 proof $8.65. **NR**

Wathen's (KY)

Wathen's Single Barrel Kentucky Straight Bourbon Whiskey 94 proof $24.99. **86**

Deep tawny amber hue. Rich sweet wood, roasted pecan, and kipper aromas. A smooth attack leads to a medium-bodied palate. Persistent, woody finish. Lighter in style, but refined and supple.

W. L. Weller (KY)

W. L. Weller 10 Year Old Kentucky Straight Bourbon Whiskey 100 proof $30. **88**

Copper with a tawny cast. Moderately full-bodied. Notes of citrus, almonds, vanilla. Silky full texture. Pungent on the palate, offering a whiff of smoke and assertive brown spices. Slightly lush, soft finish. A complex, engaging style.

Old Weller Antique Straight Bourbon Whiskey, 7 Summers Old 107 proof $13.99. **83**

Medium amber. Medium-bodied. Notice is served by a strong assault on the nose. Notes of pear and peach over maple and toffee. Very smooth with good length of fruit and butterscotch in the finish.

Wild Turkey (KY)

Wild Turkey Straight Rye Whiskey 101 proof $14.99. **90**

Light amber with a copper cast. Moderately full-bodied. Notes of maple, dried peach, honey, walnuts. Full, rich texture. Pungent and fiery on the palate. Despite all the intensity there is an interesting undercoat of tart, ripe fruit. Beautiful balance keys in all wood and seasoning components. Deep nutty finish.

Whiskey Cocktails

Depth Charge

Fill a tall glass 3/4 full of beer. Pour 1-1/2 oz. Canadian whiskey into a shot glass. Drop the shot glass into the glass of beer and drink then together.

Whiskey Sour

Fill a short glass with ice. In a shaker combine:

**1-1/2 oz. blended whiskey
1 oz. lemon juice
1 tablespoon sugar
Crushed ice (half full)
Shake and strain into the glass.**

Manhattan

In a shaker combine:

**1-1/2 oz. Bourbon
3/4 oz. sweet vermouth
Ice**

Stir and strain into a Martini (cocktail) glass, or a short glass. Garnish with a maraschino cherry.

Sazerac

In a short glass combine:

**2 oz. rye whiskey
1 teaspoon white sugar
Stir to blend, then add:**

**Dash Peychaud bitters
Dash Angostura bitters
1/2 oz. Pernod
2 ice cubes**

Stir to blend. Garnish with lemon twist.Stir and serve.

101 proof $16.99. **86**
Rich amber hue. Subdued wood and mineral aromas. A lean attack leads to a medium-bodied palate. Firm, drying finish. Not exactly refined, but fiery and flavorful with a decided burn.

Wild Turkey Rare Breed Kentucky Straight Bourbon Whiskey 108.6 proof $29.99. **92**
Brilliant deep amber hue. Subdued caramel, pipe tobacco, and sweet wood aromas show a touch of heat to the nose. A rich and viscous attack leads to a full-bodied palate. Intense, flavorful, edgy finish. A weighty and warming style. Two parts refined, one part rustic.

Wild Turkey Kentucky Spirit Single Barrel Kentucky Straight Bourbon Whiskey 101 proof $35. **93**
Deep tawny amber hue. Perfumed bitter orange, praline, and vanilla aromas. A smooth attack leads to a full-bodied, drying palate. Intensely flavored, weighty finish with a marked burn. Big and rich in style. A warming blockbuster.

Wild Turkey 12 Year Old Kentucky Straight Bourbon Whiskey 101 proof (Gold Label) $50. **94**
Deep amber hue. Lean wood, spice, and date aromas. A smooth entry leads to a medium-bodied palate. Persistent, flavorful finish. Exceptionally smooth and refined with an underlying dry, woody quality.

Windsor Canadian (Canada)

Windsor Canadian Blended Canadian Whisky 80 proof $8.49. **81**
Dark gold. Medium-bodied. Notes of peach, honey, clove, pine. Rich, assertive texture. Packs in plenty of grainy wood notes with fruit and fragrance.

Highly Rated North American Whiskey

Bourbon Whiskey

99 • Old Rip Van Winkle (KY) 20 Year Old, Pappy Van Winkle's Family Reserve Kentucky Straight Bourbon Whiskey 90.4 Proof. $70.

98 • A. H. Hirsch (KY) Finest Reserve 20 Year Old Pot Stilled Sour Mash Straight Bourbon Whiskey 91.6 Proof. $99.95.

97 • Old Rip Van Winkle (KY) 15 Year Old, Old Rip Van Winkle Handmade Kentucky Straight Bourbon Whiskey 107 Proof. $55.

96 • Old Rip Van Winkle (KY) 23 Years Old, Pappy Van Winkle's Family Reserve Kentucky Straight Bourbon Whiskey 95.6 Proof. $150.

96 • Noah's Mill (KY) 15 Year Old Straight Kentucky Bourbon Whiskey $46.

96 • Maker's Mark (KY) Select Straight Bourbon, Black Label 95 Proof. $68.

95 • Olde St. Nick (KY) Very Old St. Nick Rare Bourbon Whiskey Aged 20 Years 94 Proof. $85.

95 • Booker's (KY) Kentucky Straight Bourbon Whiskey, Batch C89-6-13: Aged 6 Years 5 Months 126.6 Proof. $50.

94 • Wild Turkey (KY) 12 Year Old Kentucky Straight Bourbon Whiskey 101 Proof. $50.

94 • A. H. Hirsch (KY) 16 Year Old Reserve Pot Stilled Sour Mash Straight Bourbon Whiskey 91.6 Proof. $74.50.

93 • Wild Turkey (KY) Kentucky Spirit Single Barrel Kentucky Straight Bourbon Whiskey 101 Proof. $35.

93 • Knob Creek (KY) Kentucky Straight Bourbon Whiskey 100 Proof. $24.

92 • Wild Turkey (KY) Rare Breed Kentucky Straight Bourbon Whiskey 108.6 Proof. $29.99.

92 • Rock Hill Farms (KY) Single Barrel Kentucky Straight Bourbon Whiskey 100 Proof. $33.

92 • Old Grand Dad (KY) Kentucky Straight Bourbon Whiskey 100 Proof. $13.50.

92 • Maker's Mark (KY) Old Style Sour Mash Straight 90 Proof. $15.

92 • Baker's (KY) 7 Year Old Kentucky Straight Bourbon Whiskey 107 Proof. $38.

91 • Rowan's Creek (KY) 12 Year Old Straight Kentucky Bourbon Whiskey 105 Proof. $38.

91 • Old Crow (KY) Straight Bourbon 80 Proof. $7.99.

91 • Hancock's (KY) President's Reserve Single Barrel Sour Mash Kentucky Bourbon Whiskey 88.9 Proof. $48.

91 • Blanton's (KY) Single Barrel Kentucky Straight Bourbon Whiskey 93 Proof. $45.99.

90 • Old Fitzgerald (KY) 12 Year Old Very Special Kentucky Straight Sour Mash Bourbon Whiskey 90 Proof. $30.

90 • Evan Williams (KY) Single Barrel Vintage 1988 Kentucky Bourbon Whiskey, Barrel #132, Barreled on 8/30/88 86.6 Proof. $21.99.

90 • Corner Creek (KY) 8 Year Old Reserve Kentucky Bourbon Whiskey 88 Proof. $26.

90 • Basil Hayden's (KY) 8 Year Old Kentucky Straight Bourbon Whiskey 80 Proof. $30.

89 • Old Grand Dad (KY) Kentucky Straight Bourbon Whiskey 86 Proof. $11.50.

89 • Old Charter (KY) 13 Year Old Proprietor's Reserve Kentucky Straight Bourbon Whiskey 90 Proof. $30.

89 • Labrot & Graham (KY) Woodford Reserve Distiller's Select Kentucky Straight Bourbon Whiskey 90.4 Proof. $26.99.

89 • Kentucky Bourbon Distillers Ltd. (KY) 12 Year Old Pure Kentucky XO Bourbon Whiskey $26.

89 • Ezra Brooks (KY) Kentucky Straight Bourbon Whiskey 90 Proof. $9.99.

89 • Eagle Rare (KY) 10 Year Old Kentucky Straight Bourbon Whiskey 101 Proof. $18/L.

88 • W. L. Weller (KY) 10 Year Old Kentucky Straight Bourbon Whiskey 100 Proof. $30.

88 • Old Forester (KY) Kentucky Straight Bourbon Whiskey 100 Proof. $12.99.

88 • Kentucky Bourbon Distillers Ltd. (KY) 8 Year Old Kentucky Vintage Bourbon Whiskey $19.

88 • Elijah Craig (KY) Single Barrel 18 Year Old Kentucky Bourbon Whiskey, Barrel #148, Barreled on 3/28/78 90 Proof. $39.95.

87 • Jim Beam (KY) Kentucky Straight Bourbon Whiskey 80 Proof. $8.50.

87 • Jacob's Well (KY) Kentucky Straight Bourbon Whiskey 84 Proof. $18.99.

86 • Wild Turkey (KY) Brand Kentucky Straight Bourbon Whiskey 101 Proof. $16.99.

86 • Wathen's (KY) Single Barrel Kentucky Straight Bourbon Whiskey 94 Proof. $24.99.

86 • Old Forester (KY) 4 Year Old Kentucky Straight Bourbon Whisky 86 Proof. $8.

86 • I. W. Harper (KY) 15 Year Old Kentucky Straight Bourbon Whiskey 80 Proof. $30.

86 • Elijah Craig (KY) 12 Year Old Double Distillation Straight Bourbon 94 Proof. $12.95.

85 • Old Fitzgerald (KY) Straight Bourbon 1849 8 Years Old 90 Proof. $14.99.

85 • Ancient Age (KY) Kentucky Straight Bourbon Whiskey 90 Proof. $9.49.

Rye Whiskey

95 • Old Rip Van Winkle (KY) 13 Year Old, Van Winkle Family Reserve Kentucky Straight Rye Whiskey 95.6 Proof. $25.

94 • Olde St. Nick (KY) Kentucky Winter Rye Whiskey 101 Proof. $36.

90 • Wild Turkey (KY) Straight Rye Whiskey 101 Proof. $14.99.

89 • A. H. Hirsch (KY) 13 Year Old Kentucky Straight Rye Whiskey 95.6 Proof. $42.50.

87 • Old Overholt (KY) 4 Year Old Straight Rye Whiskey 80 Proof. $9.99.

Tennessee Whiskey

89 • George Dickel (TN) 10 Year Old Special Barrel Reserve Tennessee Whisky 86 Proof. $30.

87 • Gentleman Jack (TN) Rare Tennessee Whiskey 80 Proof. $20.

American Blended Whiskey

90 • Seagram's Seven Crown (USA) Blended Whiskey 80 Proof. $9.99.

Canadian Whisky

89 • Alberta Springs (Canada) Blended Canadian Whisky 90 Proof. $9.49.

89 • Alberta Springs (Canada) 10 Year Old Canadian Rye Whisky 80 Proof. $20.50.

87 • Tangle Ridge (Canada) 10 Year Old Double Casked Canadian Whisky 80 Proof. $21.95.

87 • Crown Royal (Canada) Blended Canadian Whisky 80 Proof. $15.99.

86 • Canadian Club (Canada) Classic Twelve Year Old Blended Canadian Whisky 80 Proof. $15.99.

Scale: Superlative (96-100), Exceptional (90-95), Highly Recommended (85-89), Recommended (80-84), Not Recommended (Under 80)

four

Rum

"There's nought no doubt so much the
spirit calms as rum and true religion."
– Lord Byron

An Overview

The Basis of Rum

Rum, and its fraternal twin, cane spirit, are made by distilling fermented sugar and water. This sugar comes from the sugarcane and is fermented from cane juice, concentrated cane juice, or molasses. Molasses is the sweet, sticky residue that remains after sugarcane juice is boiled and the crystallized sugar is extracted.

Most Rum is made from molasses. Molasses is over 50% sugar, but it also contains significant amounts of minerals and other trace elements, which can contribute to the final flavor. Rums made from cane juice, primarily on Haiti and Martinique, have a naturally smooth palate.

Depending on the recipe, the "wash" (the cane juice, or molasses and water) is fermented, using either cultured yeast or airborne wild yeasts, for a period ranging from 24 hours for light Rums up to several weeks for heavy, full varieties.

Distillation of Rum

Rum is distilled in the manner described in the introductory chapter of this book. The choice of stills does, however, have a profound effect on the final character of Rum. All Rums come out of the still as clear, colorless spirits. Barrel aging and the use of added caramel determine their final color. Since caramel is burnt sugar, it can be truthfully said that only natural coloring agents are used.

Lighter Rums are highly rectified (purified and blended) and are produced in column or continuous stills, after which they are usually charcoal-filtered and sometimes aged in old oak casks for a few months to add a degree of smoothness. Most light Rums have minimal flavors and aroma, and are very similar to Vodka, particularly those brands that have been charcoal-filtered. Heavier Rums are usually distilled in pot stills; similar to those used to produce Cognacs and Scotch whiskies. Pot stills are less "efficient" than column stills and some congeners (fusel oils and other flavor elements) are carried over with the alcohol. Some brands of Rum are made by blending pot- and column-distilled Rums in a manner similar to Armagnac production.

Classifications of Rum

White Rums are generally light-bodied (although there are a few heavy-bodied White Rums in the French islands). They are usually clear and have a very subtle flavor profile. If they are aged in oak casks to create a smooth palate they are then usually filtered to remove any color. White Rums are primarily used as mixers and blend particularly well with fruit flavors.

Golden Rums, also known as **Amber Rums**, are generally medium-bodied. Most have spent several years aging in oak casks, which give them smooth, mellow palates.

Dark Rums are traditionally full-bodied, rich, caramel-dominated Rums. The best are produced mostly from pot stills and frequently aged in oak casks for extended periods. The richest of these Rums are consumed straight up.

Rum at a Glance

Top Scores:

Top Amber/ Dark Rum

96 • Pampero (Venezuela)
Ron Añejo Aniversario
80 Proof. $29.99.

Top Flavored Rum

88 • Cruzan (Virgin Islands)
Coconut Rum 55 Proof. $10.

Top Vintage-Dated Rum

94 • Saint James (Martinique)
1979 Millesime Rhum
86 Proof. $59.99.

Top White/Silver Rum

88 • Ypióca (Brazil)
Cachaca Rum, Ceará
80 Proof. $19.95/L.

Spiced Rums can be white, golden, or dark Rums. They are infused with spices or fruit flavors. Rum punches (such as planter's punch) are blends of Rum and fruit juices that are very popular in the Caribbean.

Añejo and Age-Dated Rums are aged Rums from different vintages or batches that are mixed together to insure a continuity of flavor in brands of Rum from year to year. Some aged Rums will give age statements stating the youngest Rum in the blend (e.g., 10-year-old Rum contains a blend of Rums that are at least 10 years old). A small number of French island Rums are **Vintage Dated**.

Rum Regions

The Caribbean is the epicenter of world Rum production. Virtually every major island group produces its own distinct Rum style.

Barbados produces light, sweetish Rums from both pot and column stills. Rum distillation began here and the Mount Gay Distillery, dating from 1663, is probably the oldest operating Rum producer in the world.

Cuba produces light-bodied, crisp, clean Rums from column stills. It is currently illegal to ship Cuban Rums into the United States.

The Dominican Republic is notable for its full-bodied, aged Rums from column stills.

Guyana is justly famous for its rich, heavy Demerara Rums, named for a local river, which are produced from both pot and column stills. Demerara Rums can be aged for extended periods (25-year-old varieties are on the market) and are frequently used for blending with lighter Rums from other regions. Neighboring **Surinam** and **French Guyana** produce similar full-bodied Rums.

Haiti follows the French tradition of heavier Rums that are double-distilled in pot stills and aged in oak casks for three or more years to produce full-flavored, exceptionally smooth-tasting Rums. Haiti also still has an extensive underground moonshine industry that supplies the voodoo religious ritual trade.

Jamaica is well known for its rich, aromatic Rums, most of which are produced in pot stills. Jamaica has official classifications of Rum, ranging from light- to very full-flavored. Jamaican Rums are extensively used for blending.

Martinique is a French island with the largest number of distilleries in the eastern Caribbean. Both pot and column stills are used. As on other French islands such as **Guadeloupe**, both *rhum agricole* (made from sugarcane juice) and *rhum industriel* (made from molasses) are produced. These Rums are frequently aged in used French brandy casks for a minimum of three years. *Rhum vieux* (aged Rum) is frequently compared to high-quality French brandies.

Puerto Rico is known primarily for light, very dry Rums from column stills. All white Puerto Rican Rums must, by law, be aged a minimum of one year while dark Rums must be aged three years.

Trinidad produces mainly light Rums from column stills and has an extensive export trade.

Virgin Islands, which are divided between the United States Virgin Islands and the British Virgin Islands, both produce light, mixing Rums from column stills. These Rums, and those of nearby **Grenada**, also serve as the base for bay Rum, a classic aftershave lotion.

Central America has a variety of primarily medium-bodied Rums from column stills that lend themselves well to aging, particularly those from **Guatemala** and **Nicaragua**. They have recently begun to gain international recognition

South America produces vast quantities of mostly light Rums from column stills with unaged cane spirit from **Brazil**, called *Cachaça* (ca·sha·sa), being the best-known example. **Venezuela** bucks this general trend with a number of well-respected barrel-aged golden and dark Rums.

North America has a handful of Rum distilleries in the southern **United States**, producing a range of light and medium-bodied Rums that are generally marketed with Caribbean-themed names. In **Canada** the 300-year-old tradition of trading Rum for dried cod fish continues in the Atlantic Maritime provinces of Newfoundland and Nova Scotia where golden Rums from **Antigua**, **Barbados**, and **Jamaica** are imported and aged for five years. The resulting hearty Rum is known locally as *Screech.*

Europe is primarily a blender of imported Rums. Both the **United Kingdom** and **France** import Rums from their former colonies in the Caribbean for aging and bottling. Heavy, dark Jamaican Rums are imported into **Germany** and mixed with neutral spirit at a 1:19 ratio to produce *Rum verschnitt.* A similar product in **Austria** is called *inlander Rum.*

Australia produces a substantial amount of white and golden Rums in a double-distillation method utilizing both column and pot stills. Rum is the second most popular alcoholic beverage in the country after beer. Light Rums are also produced on some of the islands in the South Pacific such as **Tahiti**.

Asia Rums tend to follow regional sugarcane production, with white and golden Rums from column stills being produced primarily in the **Philippines** and **Thailand**.

Fifteen men on a dead man's chest,
Yo, ho, ho and a bottle of Rum.

– 17th century 401(k) savings plan for buccaneers

Rum: Its History and Significance

The history of Rum is the history of sugar. Sugar is a sweet crystalline carbohydrate that occurs naturally in a variety of plants. One of those is the sugarcane (*Saccharum officinarum*), a tall, thick grass that has its origins in the islands of present-day Indonesia in the East Indies. Chinese traders spread its cultivation to Asia and on to India. Arabs in turn brought it to the Middle East and North Africa where it came to the attention of Europeans during the Crusades in the 11th century.

As the Spanish and Portuguese began to venture out into the Atlantic Ocean, they planted sugarcane in the Canary and Azore Islands. In 1493 Christopher Columbus picked up cane cuttings from the Canaries while on his second voyage to the Americas and transplanted them to Hispaniola, the island in the Caribbean that is now shared by Haiti and the Dominican Republic. Portuguese explorers soon did likewise in Brazil.

The Caribbean basin proved to have an ideal climate for growing sugarcane, and sugar production quickly spread around the islands. The insatiable demand in Europe for sugar soon led to the establishment of hundreds of sugarcane plantations and mills in the various English, Spanish, French, Portuguese, and Dutch colonies. These mills crushed the harvested cane and extracted the juice. Boiling this juice caused chunks of crystallized sugar to form. The remaining unsolidified juice was called *melazas* (from "*miel,*" the French word for honey); in English this became *molasses.*

Molasses is a sticky syrup that still contains a significant amount of sugar. Sugar mill operators soon noticed that when it was mixed with water and left out in the sun it would ferment. By the 1650s this former waste product was being distilled into a spirit. In the English colonies it was called *Kill Devil* (from its tendency to cause a nasty hangover or its perceived medicinal power, take your choice) or *rumbullion* (origins uncertain), which was shortened over the years to our modern word Rum. The French render this word as *rhum,* while the Spanish call it *ron.*

Locally, Rum was used as cure-all for many of the aches and pains that afflicted those living in the tropics. Sugar plantation owners also sold it, at discounted prices, to naval ships that were on station in the Caribbean in order to encourage their presence in local waters and thus discourage the attentions of marauding pirates. The British navy adopted a daily ration of a half-pint of 160 proof Rum by the 1730s. This ration was subsequently modified by mixing it with an equal amount of water to produce a drink called *grog.* The grog ration remained a staple of British naval life until 1969.

This naval-Rum connection introduced Rum to the outside world and by the late 17th century a thriving export trade developed. The British islands shipped Rum to Great Britain (where it was mixed into Rum punches and replaced gin as the dominant spirit in the 18th century) and to the British colonies in North

America where it became very popular. This export of Rum to North America, in exchange for New England lumber and dried cod (the latter is still a culinary staple in the Caribbean) soon changed over to the export of molasses to distilleries in New England. This was done in order to avoid laws from the British parliament, which protected British distillers by forbidding the trade in spirits directly between colonies. This law was, at best, honored in the breech, and smuggling soon became rampant.

The shipping of molasses to make Rum in New England distilleries became part of the infamous "slavery triangle." The first leg was the shipment of molasses to New England to make Rum. The second leg was the shipment of Rum to the ports of West Africa to trade for slaves. The final leg was the passage of slave ships to the sugar plantations of the Caribbean and South America where many of the slaves were put to work in the sugarcane fields.

The disruption of trade caused by the American Revolution and the rise of whisky production in North America resulted in the slow decline of Rum's dominance as the American national tipple. Rum production in the United States slowly decreased through the 19th century, with the last New England Rum distilleries closing at the advent of National Prohibition in 1920. The famed rumrunners of the Prohibition era were primarily smuggling whiskey into the United States.

In Europe the invention of sugar extraction from the sugar beet lessened the demand for Caribbean sugar, reducing the amount of molasses being produced and the resulting amount of Rum being distilled. Many small plantations and their stills were closed. Rum production receded, for the most part, to countries where sugarcane was grown.

The modern history of Rum owes a lot to the spread of air conditioning and the growth of tourism. In the second half of the 20th century, modern air conditioning made it possible for large numbers of people to migrate to warm-weather regions where Rum remained the dominant spirit. Additionally, the explosive increase in the number of North American and European tourists into Rum-drinking regions lead to a steady rise in the popularity of Rum-based mixed drinks. Nowadays White Rum gives Vodka serious competition as the mixer of choice in a number of distinctively nontropical markets.

Aged Rums are gaining new standing among consumers of single malt Scotch whiskies, Armagnacs, and small-batch Bourbons who are learning to appreciate the subtle complexities of these Rums. The pot still Rums of Guyana and Jamaica have a particular appeal for Scotch whisky drinkers (it is no accident that the Scottish whisky merchant and bottler Cadenhead also ages and bottles Demerara Rum), while the subtle and complex rhums of Martinique and Guadeloupe mirror the flavor profiles of the top French brandies in Cognac and Armagnac.

Reviews

Admiral Nelson's (USA)

Admiral Nelson's Premium Spiced Rum 70 proof $8.99.   84

Pale, bronzed-copper hue. Fiery but subdued spice aromas. A viscous attack leads to a lighter-styled palate. Clean, mildly flavorful finish. Tasty, but a bit shy.

Appleton Estate (Jamaica)

Appleton Estate V/X Jamaican Rum 80 proof $14.99.   88

Amber with a deep copper cast. Moderately full-bodied. Notes of stone fruits, flan, herbs. Thick texture. Very viscous, with a rich silky feel that is delightful. Quite pronounced in its fruity components. Unctuous big finish.

Appleton Estate 12 Year Old Jamaican Rum 86 proof $24.99.   92

Dark amber with a dark copper cast. Moderately full-bodied. Notes of citrus, walnut, date, molasses. Rich texture. Smooth yet lively on the palate. Gives off a rush of thick nutty spices. Very lush and intense in the finish. A textbook style of well-aged, well-oaked Rum.

Bacardi (Puerto Rico)

Bacardi Dark Rum 80 proof $7.99.   81

Medium gold with an orange glow. Moderately light-bodied. Hint of sweetness. Notes of flowers, apple, lemon, pecan. Fruity style with an elegant, refined texture. Light finish.

Bacardi Spiced Rum 70 proof $10.99.   87

Amber. Moderately full-bodied. Notes of sweet potato pie, cinnamon, dried apricot. Rich texture. An unusual mixing of tart fruit and soft baked flavors provides depth. A creamy sensation, with toasty nuances and engaging spice that add complexity.

Bacardi Limon Rum 70 proof $11.99.   NR

Bacardi Select Rum 80 proof $11.99.   90

Dark amber with a chestnut-copper cast. Moderately full-bodied. Notes of toffee, leather, honey, lemon cream. Rich texture. Brawny, bold entry. Loaded with light sweet and tart flavors. Excellent integration of diverse components. Picks up plenty of wood tones near the buttery finish.

Bacardi Reserve Rum 80 proof $14.99.   85

Amber with an orange glow. Medium-bodied. Medium sweetness. Notes of tea, citrus, custard, oiled leather. Moderately rich mouthfeel. Leather adds complexity and contributes to a deep finish.

Bacardi 1873 Solera Rum 80 proof $15.99.   88

Dark amber with a dark copper cast. Medium-bodied. Notes of flowers, glazed orange, menthol, cedar. Soft, dry texture. A very pretty, Oloroso Sherry-like character is evident. Elegant, fragrant, lightly sweet fruit notes glide across the palate. In the finish, a kiss of wood comes through. Nice delicate touches throughout.

Bacardi, Casa Bacardi, 8 Year Old Limited Edition Rum 80 proof $39.99.   94

Dark amber with a dark copper cast. Moderately full-bodied. Notes of walnuts, cinnamon, pecan pie, maple. Soft, rich texture. A fascinating style: like drinking pie topped with cream. A hedonic delight packed with chewy brown spices. The sweet baked sensation keeps intensifying. An everlasting finish.

Rhum Baita (France)

Rhum Baita 80 proof $20/L.   **87**

Dark amber with a dark copper cast. Moderately full-bodied. Notes of lemon grass, pipe tobacco, peat. Rich texture. High on aromatics, as deep, pungent smoky notes hold forth. Quite like an Islay malt. Not for the timid. A winter warmer.

J. Bally (Martinique)

J. Bally 1989 Rhum Vieux Agricole Martinique Single Vintage, Plantation Lajus Carbet 90 proof $29.   **86**

Deep tawny amber hue. Generous caramel, sweet wood, and brown sugar aromas. A viscous attack leads to a moderately full-bodied, fiery, drying palate. Heat bites into the finish. Rather austere, but has some attractive qualities and interesting flavors.

J. Bally 1986 Rhum Vieux Agricole Martinique Single Vintage, Plantation Lajus Carbet 90 proof $45.   **90**

Deep amber with an orange-copper cast. Moderately full-bodied. Notes of minerals, dried herbs, figs, cocoa. Rounded, full texture. A truly grand spirit with great presence on the palate revealing a complex range of delicate yet pronounced flavors. Not overly aromatic, but with more delicate, restrained elements. Keeps on building to a seamless never-ending finish.

Barbancourt (Haiti)

Barbancourt 4 Year Old Rhum 86 proof $16.   **89**

Dark gold with an amber cast. Medium-bodied. Notes of apricot, butterscotch, white pepper, bananas Foster. Rich texture. Zippy, almost racy on the palate as sharp spices cut through a softer, layering structure. Enough components to keep one guessing what's next.

Barbancourt 8 Year Old Reserve Speciale Rhum 86 proof $20.   **92**

Dark amber with a deep copper cast. Moderately full-bodied. Notes of pecan pie, herbs, roasted coffee, dates. Deep, rich texture. Starts off with a soft note and a very forceful presence on the palate. Carries its weight with a measure of refinement. Lovely succulent, aromatic style.

Barbancourt 15 Year Old Estate Reserve Rhum 86 proof $32.   **93**

Dark amber with a dark copper cast. Full-bodied. Notes of marmalade, walnut, pipe tobacco, mincemeat pie. Rich, robust texture. Intense yet mellow, as deep fruit and wood components surge. Full earthy notes fill up the finish. A very complex, refined style. Savor this robust Rum slowly with a robusto cigar.

Barrows (Trinidad)

Barrows Grand Reserve Cigar Blend Rum 86 proof $49.99.   **80**

Bright amber hue. Very subtle, vaguely woody aromas. A smooth attack leads to a neutral, medium-bodied palate. Hot finish. Not much Rum flavor.

Barrows Hors d' Age Cigar Blend Rum 90.2 proof $59.95.   **83**

Bright golden-amber hue. Rather reserved aromas carry a slight wood accent. A smooth attack leads to a medium-bodied palate with a subtle drying, woody character. Smooth finish. Sound, but certainly not assertive.

Barton (U.S. Virgin Islands)

Barton Light Rum 80 proof $5.99.   **80**

Clear with a brilliant metallic cast. Lean, muted aromas come with a measure of heat. A smooth attack leads to a medium-bodied palate. Gentle finish. Provides a decent texture but very little flavor.

Ron Botran (Guatemala)

Ron Botran Anejo 80 proof $12.99.   **92**

Amber-copper glow. Full-bodied. Chewy sweet caramel palate with subtle notes of date, orange, pecan. Rich, smooth mouthfeel. Assertive character with strong oak notes. Sherry-like, succulent finish.

Brugal (Dominican Republic)

Brugal Anejo 80 proof $12.99.   **88**

Deep amber. Medium-bodied. Hint of sweetness. Notes of dates and buttery, smoky flan. Fat, rich texture. Broad flavors soar on the mouth. Heavy wood with great balance.

Ron Anejo Cacique (Venezuela)

Ron Anejo Cacique 80 proof $12.99.   **80**

Dark gold. Medium-bodied. Hint of sweetness. Notes of toffee, mocha, citrus, brown spices. Smooth. Wood-induced brown spices are strong. Rich, deep finish.

Cadenhead (Guyana)

Cadenhead 9 Year Old Green Label Guyanan Rum 92 proof $46.   **86**

Straw with a pale yellow cast. Medium-bodied. Notes of herbs, dried peach, minerals, flowers. Bold texture. Rather forward, with a brisk feel of light fruit accented by sharper mineral tones. Long, smooth finish. A more elegant, restrained style.

Cadenhead 25 Year Old Green Label Demerara Rum 92 proof $132.   **91**

Dark amber with a red-copper cast. Full-bodied. Notes of blood orange, walnut, pipe tobacco, molasses. Bold, rich texture. Fiery entry attacking the palate with an explosion of flavors and wicked fragrance. Although quite hot, there is incredible balance here, particularly for such a large-scale spirit. A chaser of espresso may be required.

Cadenhead (Jamaica)

Cadenhead 10 Year Old Green Label Jamaican Rum 92 proof $52.   **89**

Straw. Moderately full-bodied. Notes of clover honey, herbs, grass, citrus. Moderately rounded texture. Highly aromatic with an intriguing nose of tart fruit and Fino Sherry. Gains depth with a richer expansion. More finesse than power in the finish.

Captain Morgan (Puerto Rico)

Captain Morgan Original Spiced Rum 70 proof $8.99.   **83**

Medium amber, dark gold cast. Medium-bodied. Notes of toasted almonds, cream pie, mocha, allspice. Mild texture. A gentle yet brisk feel on the palate. Quite flavorful, although sweeter nuances dominate spices. Light, easy finish.

Chauffe Coeur (Martinique)

Chauffe Coeur Dark Rhum Martinique 94 proof $21.99.   **85**

Gold-orange hue. Full-bodied. Medium sweetness. Notes of flowers, lemon, honey. Deep, heavy on the palate. Smooth. Powerful tropical flavor.

Chauffe Coeur Light Rhum Martinique 108 proof $21.99.   **NR**

Rhum Chauvet (France)

Rhum Chauvet Red Label Rum 88 proof $23.   **86**

Dark amber with a light chestnut cast. Moderately full-bodied. Notes of dried citrus, flowers, mineral, sesame. Pungent texture. Aggressive, bold, mouth-filling style with lovely tart fruit and spice notes bouncing off rich fragrance. A sensuous range of components. Very exotic.

Rhum Chauvet Special Cocktail Rhum Traditionnel 88 proof $25/L.   **82**

Clear. Moderately full-bodied. Notes of herbs, smoke, nuts. Robust texture. Tequila-like in its pungency and stony profile. Has a telltale bite at the finish.

Scale: Superlative (96-100), Exceptional (90-95), Highly Recommended (85-89), Recommended (80-84), Not Recommended (Under 80)

Chauvet 10 Year Old Rhum Martinique 90 proof $45/L. **90**

Dark amber with a light chestnut cast. Moderately full-bodied. Notes of molasses, oil, tobacco, leather. Rich, deep texture. Fairly broad, with a burnt buttery note. Quite pungent with dramatic high-toned aromatics. Lushness pervades with a touch of rancio-style richness filling out the profile.

Cockspur (Barbados)

Cockspur 8 Year Old VSOR Rum 80 proof $23.99. **92**

Amber with a deep gold cast. Moderately full-bodied. Notes of dried tropical fruits, vanilla, walnuts, flan. Rich, smooth texture. Very lush with a plush, soft feel on the palate. A more fruity style, showcasing refinement with a sense of depth. Lovely, viscous finish.

Coruba (Jamaica)

Coruba Jamaican Rum 80 proof $9.99. **83**

Dark amber. Moderately full-bodied. Notes of nutmeg, molasses, pipe tobacco, orange peel. Thick, rich texture. Plush and soft on the palate with a nice flow of succulent flavors. Very invigorating finish. A fine libation with a pipe or cigar.

Cruzan (Virgin Islands)

Cruzan Pineapple Rum 110 proof $7.99. **NR**

Cruzan Premium Dark Rum 80 proof $9. **85**

Deep gold with a pale platinum cast. Medium-bodied. Notes of pear, baked dough, nuts, herbs. Compact texture. Has an initial sharp edge. Demonstrates vibrancy with a flinty, grainy sensation. A nice blend of light brown spice and delicate fruit flavor.

Cruzan Banana Rum 55 proof $10. **87**

Clear. Medium-bodied. Notes of talc, tropical fruits, flowers. Smooth texture. Rounded and slightly lush on the palate. Shows an expected strong banana note, with sweet oily fragrance. An ideal flavoring mixer.

Cruzan Coconut Rum 55 proof $10. **88**

Clear. Medium-bodied. Notes of coconut, banana, minerals. Compact texture. Vibrant, showing some assertion with a backdrop of stony, mineral notes. Has nice persistence with a toasty feel toward the finish.

Cruzan Premium Light Rum 80 proof $10. **85**

Clear. Medium-bodied. Medium sweetness. Notes of papaya and pineapple flavors. Strong perfumey character. Silky, elegant texture. Delicate, tropical flavors linger in a mild finish.

Cruzan Estate Diamond Rum, 4 Year Old 80 proof $15.99. **90**

Deep amber with a copper cast. Medium-bodied. Notes of coconut, citrus, flowers, vanilla. Smooth texture. Has an oily feel, with succulent touches of fruit and light, sweet aromas. Deliciously fragrant in the finish. Very elegant and polished throughout.

Cruzan Junkanu Citrus Stash 70 proof $17. **85**

Slightly pale platinum. Medium-bodied. Notes of orange, fresh herbs, ginger candy, quinine. Quite soft and silky, giving a touch of sweetness with interesting flavors and exotic fragrances. Has a whispering light, lingering finish.

Flor de Caña (Nicaragua)

Flor de Caña Five Year Old Black Label Anejo Rum 80 proof $11.69. **81**

Tawny amber. Medium-bodied. Hint of sweetness. Notes of cedar, banana, dates. Strong wood combined with the tropical flavors gives a touch of complexity.

Flor de Caña 12 Year Old Centenario Rum 80 proof $24.99. **89**

Deep tawny amber hue. Generous toffee, pecan, and caramel aromas show a refined wood accent. A supple entry leads to a medium-bodied palate. Exceptionally smooth. Finishes with some lingering sweet oak notes. A very refined and delicate style.

Gosling's (Bermuda)
Gosling's Black Seal Rum 80 proof $15. **90**

Mahogany. Moderately full-bodied. Notes of herbs, pecan, ginger, sandalwood. Smooth, bold texture. A potpourri of exotic, wild fragrances soars from the glass. Mouth-coating, layering feel on the palate. Elegant wood and nut components add refinement. Quite succulent in the lingering finish. Invigorating, heady style.

Havana Club (Bahamas)
Havana Club Gold Rum 80 proof $8.99. **NR**

Havana Club (Cuba)
Havana Club Añejo Rum 80 proof $16. **87**

Amber with an orange cast. Medium-bodied. Notes of citrus, straw, soy. Soft, delicate texture. A slightly tangy citrus note covers a lively pomace-like feel on the palate. Smooth, easy finish. A restrained, elegant style.

Havana Club 7 Year Old Aged Rum 80 proof $22. **92**

Amber-orange. Medium-bodied. Notes of minerals, citrus, wildflower honey, almond. Smooth, silky texture. A mouthful of rich fruit with light creamy tones and a stony backdrop. Harmonious and complex, with light spice notes blending into a velvety, full finish. If you have this Havana, you'll need a Cuban smoke. An utterly joyous drink.

Kaniche (Guadeloupe)
Kaniche 10 Year Old Rhum Guadeloupe 80 proof $25. **89**

Amber with an orange cast. Full-bodied. Notes of marmalade, vanilla, roasted nuts. Lively, broad texture. Tangy fruit notes help open this up. A sense of lushness comes forth, as soft brown spices fold in. Quite pungent at the finish, with a creamy, warming feel.

Kaniche (Martinique)
Kaniche Rum Martinique 80 proof $30. **89**

Deep mahogany hue. Unusual, distinctive egg, marmalade, and mineral aromas say unadulterated Martinique. A rich, rounded entry leads to a full-bodied palate. Exceptionally flavorful with sweet wood flavors and a drying quality. Clean, fiery finish.

Lemon Bay (Virgin Islands)
Lemon Bay Citrus Rum 70 proof $9.99. **80**

Clear. Piercing candied lemon and citrus aromas. A smooth attack leads to a full-bodied, viscous palate with marked sweetness. Lingering, thick finish with a slightly bitter citrus skin character. Rather candied, with the sweetness taking on a saccharine-like aftertaste.

Lemon Hart (Guyana)
Lemon Hart Demerara Rum 80 proof $15.99. **88**

Chestnut with a dark copper cast. Moderately full-bodied. Notes of flowers, pipe tobacco, citrus, toffee. Rich texture. Deep, revealing layers of plush, slightly sweet flavors, buttressed by heady, intense aromatics. Very broad, tangy finish. A very complex style.

Malibu (Barbados)
Malibu Coconut Flavored Rum 48 proof $13.99. **83**

Clear. Moderately light-bodied. Notes of coconut, almonds, mocha. Delicate, soft texture. Moderately light on the palate, with a syrupy feel. Smooth and easy finish.

Scale: Superlative (96-100), Exceptional (90-95), Highly Recommended (85-89), Recommended (80-84), Not Recommended (Under 80)

Mangoustan's (France)

Mangoustan's Rhum Carte Gris 84 proof $24/L.   **87**

Dark amber with a light chestnut cast. Moderately full-bodied. Notes of dried apricot, tobacco, allspice. Rich texture. Soft, yet mouthfilling. Quite creamy and seductive with an ample dose of deep wood and spice notes. Nice, lightly fruity finish.

Marie Galante (France)

Marie Galante Rhum Agricole Blanc 100 proof $29/L.   **84**

Clear. Medium-bodied. Moderately extracted. Notes of cheese, molasses, tomato vines. Bold texture. Quite pungent and austere on the nose. Carries a very soft, intriguing texture. A bizarre range of aromatics includes smoke and tomatoes. Quite different, and quite potent.

Marie Galante Rhum Agricole Gold 100 proof $29/L.   **83**

Deep amber with a dark copper cast. Medium-bodied. Notes of oilcloth, buttermilk biscuits, green vegetables. Soft texture. Pungent aromatics soar forth. Weedy, green notes dominate.

Ron Matusalem (West Indies)

Ron Matusalem Light Dry Rum, West Indies 80 proof $8.99.   **82**

Vegetal, herbal, and granite components. Light, tight texture. Some heat is felt on the palate as light oily nuances come forward. Will make an exotic mixer.

Ron Matusalem Golden Dry Rum, West Indies 80 proof $9.99.   **83**

Deep gold, with an amber cast. Peach, caramel, dates. Light, smooth texture. Moderately sweet palate, with a touch of fruit. Slight oily feel to the finish.

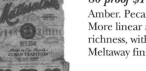

Ron Matusalem Classic Black Rum, West Indies 80 proof $10.99.   **90**

Deep copper, with a rich amber cast. Flan, coconut, and vanilla. Rich aromatics with a whiff of sweet tobacco adding accent. Very soft, lush texture. Sweetness is key, as Bourbon-like wood notes push the flavors. A very seductive libation.

Ron Matusalem Gran Reserva Rum, West Indies 80 proof $19.99.   **90**

Amber. Pecans, baked pie crust, and apricot. Compact texture. More linear and direct on the palate. Shows a slight sense of richness, with pronounced flavors and caramel sweetness. Meltaway finish.

Mekhong (Thailand)

Mekhong Rum 80 proof $14.99.   **85**

Light amber. Moderately light-bodied. Hint of sweetness. Notes of lemon grass, grain, and honey. Soft, easy texture. Assertive herbal components.

Monarch (USA)

Monarch Original Dark Rum 80 proof $8.95.   **81**

Deep tawny amber hue. Aggressive, unusual banana aromas. A supple attack leads to a relatively neutral, moderately full-bodied palate. Smooth finish. The palate does not deliver what the nose promises.

Mount Gay (Barbados)

Mount Gay Refined Eclipse Barbados Rum 86 proof $14.99.   **86**

Amber with a copper cast. Medium-bodied. Notes of clover honey, dried herbs, pineapple, orange blossom. Compact texture, a bit sharp on the palate. Flinty, dried-fruit components are key. Well balanced, with a nice fragrant finish.

Mount Gay Extra Old Barbados Rum 80 proof $19.99.   **92**

Dark amber with a dark copper cast. Medium-bodied. Notes of pine, minerals, roasted nuts, peach, caramel. Soft yet compact texture. Aromatic woody notes lie over light fruit. Lovely brown accents of nuts and spice add dimension. A beautifully balanced style.

Myers's (Jamaica)

Myers's Original Dark Jamaican Rum 80 proof $11.49.   **82**

Dark chestnut. Medium-bodied. Notes of figs, aromatic pipe tobacco, roasted grain. Moderately light texture. A bit soft, even diffuse on the palate. Sweet fragrances are the hallmark here.

N.O. Rum (USA)

N.O. Rum 86 proof $16.99.   **83**

Deep golden-amber. Moderately full-bodied. Maple sugar, walnut, and citrus. Compact texture. Pronounced aromas showcase rich brown spice components. Somewhat rich and intense, yet tightly wound, with a nice touch of fruit coming through on the palate. Picks up a bit of heat toward a leaner finish.

Pampero (Venezuela)

Pampero Ron Añejo Aniversario 80 proof $29.99.   **96**

Dark chestnut. Full-bodied. Notes of butterscotch, pipe tobacco, coffee, black walnut. Rich, creamy texture. So smooth and deep that one may be tempted to use a spoon. Has a buttery, thick feel with lovely baked, layered flavors. A world-class, slow-sipping spirit. Just match it with a rich Churchill.

Port Morant Still (Guyana)

Port Morant Still 11 Year Old Guyana Demerara Rum 92 proof $45.   **84**

Gold. Medium-bodied. Notes of dried banana, herbs, peanut brittle. Tight texture. Quite lively on the palate. Shows off a most interesting mix of lightly sweet, nutty elements with an old fruit note. Fairly spicy in the finish.

Pusser's (British Virgin Islands)

Pusser's British Navy Gold 80 proof $12.99.   **81**

Medium gold. Moderately light-bodied. Touch of sweetness. Notes of honey, lemon, molasses, herbs. On the lighter side with a grainy texture. Herbs are strong in the dry finish.

Pusser's (USA)

Pusser's Blended Rum 95.5 proof $15.99.   **NR**

Redrum (Virgin Islands)

Redrum Flavored Rum 70 proof $13.99.   **NR**

Ronrico (Puerto Rico)

Ronrico Silver Label Puerto Rican Rum 80 proof $8.49.   **NR**

Scale: Superlative (96-100), Exceptional (90-95), Highly Recommended (85-89), Recommended (80-84), Not Recommended (Under 80)

Saint James (Martinique)

Saint James Royal Ambre Rhum 90 proof $17.99.   **84**

Dark amber with a mahogany cast. Medium-bodied. Notes of lemon grass, pine, sweet herbs, flowers. Tight texture. Vibrant style as racy tart flavors dominate light sensations of sweet fragrance. Delicate finish.

Saint James Extra Old Rhum 84 proof $24.99.   **89**

Chestnut with a dark copper cast. Moderately full-bodied. Notes of orange blossom, pecan, nutmeg, licorice. Bold texture. Quite nutty with a profuse note of brown spice. Richer in the middle, as woody tones are noted. Fresh, vibrant, fruity finish.

Saint James Hors d'Age Rhum 86 proof $39.99.   **91**

Chestnut with a mahogany cast. Moderately full-bodied. Notes of pecan pie, glazed apricot, dried flowers, clove. Rich texture. Bold and dramatic feel on the palate. Lush, fruity nuances play off deep nutty, baked components. Very engaging, aromatic finish. A classy style.

Saint James 1979 Millesime Rhum 86 proof $59.99.   **94**

Chestnut with a mahogany cast. Moderately full-bodied. Notes of citrus, herbs, dried flowers, allspice. Soft, rich texture. Lovely, with a deep layering effect. Plush yet seamless feel throughout, with fresh fragrances. Wonderful spicy fruit flavors keep on building. A truly refined, elegant spirit.

San Juan (Virgin Islands)

San Juan Spiced Rum 70 proof $5.99/1.5 L.   **81**

Bright bronzed-copper hue. Powerful coconut, cola nut, and marshmallow aromas jump from the glass. A smooth attack leads to a moderately full-bodied palate with no sign of heat. Smooth, lingering finish, but loses some flavor impact. Well balanced but rather artificial.

San Miguel (Ecuador)

San Miguel Rum 7 80 proof $24.   **NR**

Rhum des Sargasses (Martinique)

Rhum des Sargasses Dark Rum 80 proof $16.99/L.   **89**

Dark amber with a chestnut cast. Moderately full-bodied. Notes of dried citrus, smoke, tobacco, almonds. Deep, bold texture. Lovely sense of richness is manifested by a broad range of mouth-coating flavors. Nice accents of earthy, nut, and spice elements help round it out. Engaging aromatics.

Rhum des Sargasses Agricole Blanc de la Martinique 108 proof $19.95/L.   **80**

Clear. Moderately full-bodied. Notes of cheese, oilcloth, herbs, poppy seeds. Quite rich and soft, with an interesting array of flavors. Deep, complex flinty-stony components and spice, especially at the finish.

Stubbs (Australia)

Stubbs Queensland Dry White Rum 85 proof $13.99.   **NR**

Toucano (Brazil)

Toucano Cachaca Rum 80 proof $20.95/L.   **84**

Pale yellow-copper hue. Intriguing, fiery egg, herb, and mineral aromas not unlike a Martinique white Rum. A viscous attack leads to a medium-bodied palate with remarkable smoothness. Rather neutral finish. An interesting, unusual spirit.

Ron Varadero (Cuba)

Ron Varadero Anejo Seven Years Old 76 proof $12.   **84**

Medium amber. Moderately full-bodied. Touch of sweetness. Notes of chili pepper, caramel, hazelnut. Dramatic fragrance. Highly spiced. Rich texture.

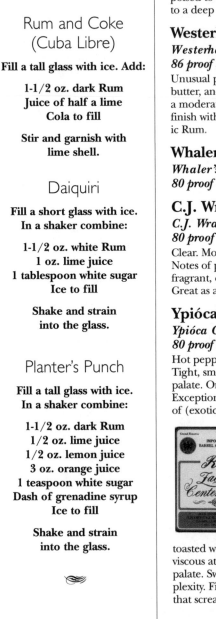

❧

Rum Cocktails

Rum and Coke (Cuba Libre)

Fill a tall glass with ice. Add:

**1-1/2 oz. dark Rum
Juice of half a lime
Cola to fill**

**Stir and garnish with
lime shell.**

Daiquiri

**Fill a short glass with ice.
In a shaker combine:**

**1-1/2 oz. white Rum
1 oz. lime juice
1 tablespoon white sugar
Ice to fill**

**Shake and strain
into the glass.**

Planter's Punch

**Fill a tall glass with ice.
In a shaker combine:**

**1-1/2 oz. dark Rum
1/2 oz. lime juice
1/2 oz. lemon juice
3 oz. orange juice
1 teaspoon white sugar
Dash of grenadine syrup
Ice to fill**

**Shake and strain
into the glass.**

❧

West Indies Distillery (Barbados)
West Indies Distillery 9 Year Old Barbados Rum 92 proof $45.　　　**89**

Deep gold. Moderately full-bodied. Notes of pine needles, golden apple, nutmeg, smoke. Rich texture. Somewhat pungent, with strong aromatics. Intense style as a quick crescendo of flavors is poised to attack. Nice spice and smoky notes add to a deep finish.

Westerhall Plantation (Grenada)
Westerhall Plantation Rum 86 proof $19.95.　　　**86**

Unusual pale yellow-copper hue. Generous toffee, butter, and vanilla aromas. A viscous attack leads to a moderately full-bodied palate. Clean through the finish with slightly sweet flavors. A delicate, aromatic Rum.

Whaler's (USA)
Whaler's Original Dark Rum 80 proof $10.49.　　　**NR**

C.J. Wray (Jamaica)
C.J. Wray Light Dry Rum 80 proof $11.99.　　　**86**

Clear. Moderately light-bodied. Hint of sweetness. Notes of pineapple, almond, nougat. Light, fragrant, candy-flavored entry. Softness is key. Great as a mixer.

Ypióca (Brazil)
Ypióca Cachaca Rum, Ceará 80 proof $19.95/L.　　　**88**

Hot peppers, cooked squash, dried herbs. Tight, smooth texture. Very elegant and complex palate. Only a hint of sweetness is discerned. Exceptionally balanced with a broad spectrum of (exotic) aromatics and flavors.

Ron Zacapa (Guatemala)
Ron Zacapa Centenario Grand Reserve Barrel Aged Rum 80 proof $30.　　　**95**

Very deep mahogany hue. Forward, inviting coconut, toasted wood, and brown sugar aromas. A smooth, viscous attack leads to a full-bodied and flavorful palate. Sweet woody notes show a range of complexity. Finish is a mile long. A hedonistic spirit that screams TROPICS.

Scale: Superlative (96-100), Exceptional (90-95), Highly Recommended (85-89), Recommended (80-84), Not Recommended (Under 80)

Highly Rated Rum

Vintage-Dated Rum

94 • Saint James (Martinique) 1979 Millesime Rhum 86 Proof. $59.99.

90 • J. Bally (Martinique) 1986 Rhum Vieux Agricole Martinique Single Vintage, Plantation Lajus Carbet 90 Proof. $35.

86 • J. Bally (Martinique) 1989 Rhum Vieux Agricole Martinique Single Vintage, Plantation Lajus Carbet 90 Proof. $19.95.

Añejo/Age-Dated Rum

96 • Pampero (Venezuela) Ron Añejo Aniversario 80 Proof. $29.99.

95 • Ron Zacapa (Guatemala) Centenario Grand Reserve Barrel Aged Rum 80 Proof. $30.

94 • Bacardi (Puerto Rico) Casa Bacardi 8 Year Old Limited Edition Rum 80 Proof. $39.99.

93 • Barbancourt (Haiti) 15 Year Old Estate Reserve Rhum 86 Proof. $32.

92 • Ron Botran (Guatemala) Anejo 80 Proof. $12.99.

92 • Mount Gay (Barbados) Extra Old Barbados Rum 80 Proof. $19.99.

92 • Havana Club (Cuba) 7 Year Old Aged Rum 80 Proof. $22.

92 • Cockspur (Barbados) 8 Year Old VSOR Rum 80 Proof. $23.99.

92 • Barbancourt (Haiti) 8 Year Old Reserve Speciale Rhum 86 Proof. $20.

92 • Appleton Estate (Jamaica) 12 Year Old Jamaican Rum 86 Proof. $24.99.

91 • Saint James (Martinique) Hors d'Age Rhum 86 Proof. $39.99.

91 • Cadenhead (Guyana) 25 Year Old Green Label Demerara Rum 92 Proof. $132.

90 • Ron Matusalem (West Indies) Gran Reserva Rum, West Indies 80 Proof. $19.99.

90 • Cruzan (Virgin Islands) Estate Diamond Rum, 4 Year Old 80 Proof. $15.99.

90 • Chauvet (France) 10 Year Old Rhum Martinique 90 Proof. $45/L.

89 • West Indies Distillery (Barbados) 9 Year Old Barbados Rum 92 Proof. $45.

89 • Saint James (Martinique) Extra Old Rhum 84 Proof. $24.99.

89 • Kaniche (Martinique) Rum Martinique 80 Proof. $30.

89 • Kaniche (Guadeloupe) 10 Year Old Rhum Guadeloupe 80 Proof. $25.

89 • Flor de Caña (Nicaragua) 12 Year Old Centenario Rum 80 Proof. $24.99.

89 • Cadenhead (Jamaica) 10 Year Old Green Label Jamaican Rum 92 Proof. $52.

89 • Barbancourt (Haiti) 4 Year Old Rhum 86 Proof. $16.

88 • Brugal (Dominican Republic) Anejo 80 Proof. $12.99.

88 • Appleton Estate (Jamaica) V/X Jamaican Rum 80 Proof. $14.99.

87 • Havana Club (Cuba) Añejo Rum 80 Proof. $16.

86 • Cadenhead (Guyana) 9 Year Old Green Label Guyanan Rum 92 Proof. $46.

85 • Bacardi (Puerto Rico) Bacardi Reserve 80 Proof. $14.99.

Amber/Dark Rum

90 • Ron Matusalem (West Indies) Classic Black Rum, West Indies 80 Proof. $10.99.

90 • Gosling's (Bermuda) Black Seal Rum 80 Proof. $15.

90 • Bacardi (Puerto Rico) Ron Bacardi Select 80 Proof. $11.99.

89 • Rhum des Sargasses (Martinique) Dark Rum 80 Proof. $16.99/L.

88 • Lemon Hart (Guyana) Demerara Rum 80 Proof. $15.99.

88 • Bacardi (Puerto Rico) 1873 Solera Rum 80 Proof. $15.99.

87 • Rhum Baita (France) 80 Proof. $20/L.

87 • Mangoustan's (France) Rhum Carte Gris 84 Proof. $24/L.

86 • Westerhall Plantation (Grenada) Rum 86 Proof. $19.95.

86 • Rhum Chauvet (France) Red Label Rum 88 Proof. $23.
86 • Mount Gay (Barbados) Refined Eclipse Barbados Rum 86 Proof. $14.99.
86 • Cadenhead (Guyana) 9 Year Old Green Label Guyanan Rum 92 Proof. $46.
85 • Mekhong (Thailand) 80 Proof. $14.99.
85 • Cruzan (Virgin Islands) Premium Dark Rum 80 Proof. $9.
85 • Chauffe Coeur (Martinique) Dark Rhum Martinique 94 Proof. $21.99.

Flavored Rum
88 • Cruzan (Virgin Islands) Coconut Rum 55 Proof. $10.
87 • Cruzan (Virgin Islands) Banana Rum 55 Proof. $10.
87 • Bacardi (Puerto Rico) Ron Bacardi Spiced Rum 70 Proof. $10.99.
85 • Cruzan (Virgin Islands) Junkanu Citrus Stash 70 Proof. $17.

White/Silver Rum
88 • Ypióca (Brazil) Cachaca Rum, Ceará 80 Proof. $19.95/L.
86 • C. J. Wray (Jamaica) Light Dry Rum 80 Proof. $11.99.
85 • Cruzan (Virgin Islands) Premium Light Rum 80 Proof. $10.

five

Tequila and Mezcal

"All Tequila is Mezcal, but not all Mezcal is Tequila."

—Tequila marketing mantra

An Overview

The Basis of Tequila and Mezcal

Tequila, and its country cousin Mezcal, are made by distilling the fermented juice of agave plants in Mexico. The agave is a spiky-leafed member of the lily family (it is not a cactus) and is related to the century plant. By Mexican law the agave spirit called Tequila can be made only from one particular type of agave, the blue agave (*Agave Tequiliana Weber*), and can be produced only in specifically designated geographic areas, primarily the state of Jalisco in west-central Mexico.

Mezcal is made from the fermented juice of other species of agave. It is produced throughout most of Mexico.

Both Tequila and Mezcal are prepared for distillation in similar ways. The agave, also know as maguey (pronounced muh-GAY), is cultivated on plantations for eight to 10 years, depending on the type of agave. When the plant reaches sexual maturity it starts to grow a flower stalk. The agave farmer, or *campesino*, cuts off the stalk just as it is starting to grow. This redirects the plant growth into the central stalk, swelling it into a large bulbous shape that contains a sweet juicy pulp. When the swelling is completed, the campesino cuts the plant from its roots and removes the long sword-shaped leaves, using a razor-sharp pike-like tool called a *coa*. The remaining *piña* ("pineapple"—so-called because the cross-thatched denuded bulb resembles a giant green and white pineapple) weighs anywhere from 25 to 100 pounds.

At the distillery the piñas are cut into quarters. For Tequila they are then slowly baked in steam ovens or autoclaves (oversized pressure cookers) until all of the starch has been converted to sugars. For Mezcal they are baked in underground ovens heated with wood charcoal (which gives Mezcal its distinctive smoky taste). They are then crushed (traditionally with a stone wheel drawn around a circular trough by a mule) and shredded to extract the sweet juice, called *aguamiel* (honey water).

The fermentation stage determines whether the final product will be 100% agave or mixed ("*mixto*"). The highest-quality Tequila is made from fermenting and then distilling only agave juice mixed with some water. Mixto is made by fermenting and then distilling a mix of agave juice and other sugars, usually cane sugar with water. Mixtos made and bottled in Mexico can contain up to 40% alcohol derived from other sugars. Mixtos that have been shipped in bulk to other countries for bottling (primarily the United States) may have the agave content further reduced to 51% by the foreign bottler. By Mexican law all 100% agave or aged Tequila must be bottled in Mexico. If a Tequila is 100% agave it will always say so on the bottle label. If it doesn't say 100% it is a mixto, although that term is seldom used on bottle labels.

Tequila and Mezcal at a Glance

Top Scores:

Top Blanco/Silver Tequila

92 • **Don Eduardo (Mexico) Silver Tequila 80 Proof. $32.99.**

Top Gold Tequila

89 • **Sauza (Mexico) Tequila Extra 80 Proof. $11.**

Top Reposado Tequila

93 • **Gusano Real (Mexico) Reposado Tequila 80 Proof. $65.**

Top Anejo Tequila

98 • **Porfidio (Mexico) 100% Blue Agave Single Barrel Anejo, Tequila80 Proof. $72.99.**

Top Flavored Tequila

90 • **Distinqt (Mexico) Orangy, Tequila 80 Proof. $14.99.**

Top Mezcal

97 • **Del Maguey (Mexico) Santo Domingo Albarradas Single Village Mezcal 98.4 Proof. $60.**

Distillation and Aging of Tequila and Mezcal

Traditionally Tequila and Mezcal have been distilled in pot stills to 110° proof (55% ABV). The resulting spirit is clear, but contains a significant amount of congeners and other flavor elements. Some light-colored Tequilas are now being re-distilled in column stills to produce a cleaner, blander spirit.

Color in Tequila and Mezcal comes mostly from the addition of caramel, although barrel aging is a factor in some high-quality brands. Additionally, some distillers add small amounts of natural flavorings such as Sherry, prune concentrate, and coconut to manipulate the product's flavor profile. These added flavors do not stand out themselves, but instead serve to smooth out the often hard-edged palate of agave spirits.

Classifications of Tequila

Beyond the two basic designations of Tequila—agave and mixto—there are four categories:

Silver or **Blanco/White Tequilas** are clear, with little (no more than 60 days in stainless steel tanks) or no aging. They can be either 100% agave or mixto. Silver Tequilas are used primarily for mixing and blend particularly well into fruit-based drinks.

Gold Tequila is unaged silver Tequila that has been colored and flavored with caramel. It is usually a mixto.

Reposado ("rested") **Tequila** is aged in wooden tanks or casks for a legal minimum period of at least two months, with the better-quality brands spending three to nine months in wood. It can be either 100% agave or mixto. Reposado Tequilas are the best-selling Tequilas in Mexico.

Añejo ("old") **Tequila** is aged in wooden barrels (usually old Bourbon barrels) for a minimum of 12 months. The best-quality anejos are aged 18 months to three years for mixtos, and up to four years for 100% agaves. Aging Tequila for more than four years is a matter of controversy. Most Tequila producers oppose doing so because they feel that "excessive" oak aging will overwhelm the distinctive earthy and vegetal agave flavor notes.

Mezcal and the Worm

The rules and regulations that govern the production and packaging of Tequila do not apply to agave spirits produced outside of the designated Tequila areas in Mexico. Some Mezcal distilleries are very primitive and very small. The best known mezcal come from the southern state of Oaxaca (wuh-HA-kuh), although it is produced in a number of other states. Eight varieties of agave are approved for Mezcal production, but the chief variety used is the espadin agave (*agave angustifolia Haw*).

The famous "worm" that is found in some bottles of Mezcal (*con gusano* – "with worm") is actually the larva of one of two moths that live on the agave plant (the red worms are considered higher quality than the white by the way). The reason for adding the worm to the bottle of Mezcal is obscure. But one story, which at least has the appeal of logic to back it up, is that the worm serves as proof of high proof, which is to say that if the worm remains intact in the bottle, the percentage of alcohol in the spirit is high enough to preserve the pickled worm. Consuming the worm, which can be done without harm, has served as a rite of passage for generations of fraternity boys. As a rule, top-quality mezcals do not include a worm in the bottle.

Tequila – History and Origins

Among the pantheon of Aztec gods was Tepoztécal,
the god of alcoholic merriment.

– Pre-Columbian deity tip

Tequila, and Mezcal, trace their origins back at least two thousand years. Around the first century A.D., one or more of the Indian tribes that inhabited what is now central Mexico discovered that the juice of the agave plant, if left exposed to air, would ferment and turn into a milky, mildly alcoholic drink. News of this discovery spread throughout agave-growing areas. The Aztecs called this beverage *octili poliqhui*, which the Spaniards corrupted into *pulque* (POOL-kay).

In Aztec culture pulque drinking had religious significance. Consumption by the masses was limited to specific holidays when large tubs of pulque were set up in public squares. The ruling elite was not subject to the same restrictions, however, and drank pulque throughout the year—a privilege shared by captive warriors just before they were sacrificed to the gods.

When the Spanish arrived in Mexico in the early 16th century, they soon began to make and drink pulque, but the low alcohol content (around 3% ABV) and earthy, vegetal taste made it less popular among the conquistadors than European-style beers and brandies. Early attempts to distill pulque were unsuccessful, as the resulting spirit was harsh and acrid. It was soon discovered, however, that cooking the agave pulp resulted in a sweeter juice, which, when fermented, became known as Mezcal Wine. This "wine" was then distilled into the spirit that we know today as Mezcal.

What Bing Crosby and Jimmy Buffet Have in Common

Modest amounts of Tequila have been exported into U.S. border towns since the late 19th century. The first major boost to Tequila sales in the rest of the United States came in the late 1940s when the Margarita cocktail, a blend of Tequila, lime juice, orange liqueur, and ice was invented. Its origins are uncertain, but Hollywood actors and cocktail parties in California and Mexican resorts seem to be involved in most of the genesis stories. It is known that crooner and actor Bing Crosby was so taken with one particular brand of Tequila, Herradura, that he teamed up with fellow actor Phil Harris to import the brand into the United States. The Margarita, along with the Tequila Sunrise and the Tequila Sour, have become highly popular in the United States; in fact, it is claimed by many in the liquor industry that the Margarita is the single most popular cocktail in the nation. In the 1970s, when balladeer Jimmy Buffet sang of "Wasting away in Margaritaville," the success of the song enticed millions more Americans to sip from the salt-rimmed Margarita glass.

Early Mezcal distilleries in the Spanish colony of Mexico operated in a manner similar to modern-day brewpubs. The distilling plant was usually small, and its production was consumed primarily in the distillery tavern (*taberna*). As the colony grew, the Mezcal wine industry followed apace and soon became an important source of tax revenue for the Crown. Periodic attempts by Spanish brandy producers to shut down the Mezcal industry were about as unsuccessful as similar efforts by English distillers to inhibit rum production in the British colonies of North America.

The Evolution of Tequila

In 1656 the village of Tequila (named for the local Ticuilas Indians) was granted a charter by the governor of New Galicia. Tax records of the time show that Mezcal was already being produced in the area. This Mezcal, made from the local blue agave, established a reputation for having a superior taste, and barrels of the "Mezcal wine from Tequila" were soon being shipped to nearby Guadalajara and more distant cities such as the silver-mining boomtowns of San Luis Potosí and Aguascalientes.

The oldest of the still-existing distilleries in Tequila dates back to 1795, when the Spanish Crown granted a distiller's license to a local padrone by the name of José Cuervo. In 1805 a distillery was established that would ultimately come under the control of the Sauza family. By the mid-1800s there were dozens of distilleries and millions of agave plants under cultivation around Tequila in what had become the state of Jalisco. Gradually, the locally produced Mezcal came to be known as Tequila (just as the grape brandy from the Cognac region in France came to be known simply as Cognac).

Mexico achieved independence from Spain in 1821. But until the 1870s it was a politically unstable country that experienced frequent changes in government, revolutions, and a disastrous war with the United States. Marauding bands of soldiers and guerillas extracted "revolutionary taxes" and "voluntary" contributions in kind from the tabernas and distilleries. In 1876 a general named Porfirio Díaz, who was from the Mezcal-producing state of Oaxaca, came to power and ushered in a 35-year period of relative peace and stability known as the *Porfiriato.*

It was during this period that the Tequila industry became firmly established. Modest exports of Tequila began to the United States and Europe, with Jose Cuervo shipping the first three barrels to El Paso, Texas, in 1873. By 1910 the number of agave distilleries in the state of Jalisco had grown to almost 100.

The collapse of the Díaz regime in 1910 led to a decade-long period of revolution that inhibited the Tequila industry. The return of peace in the 1920s led to the expansion of Tequila production in Jalisco beyond the area around the town of Tequila, with growth being particularly noteworthy in the highlands around the village of Arandas. This period also saw the adoption of modern production techniques from the wine industry such as the use of cultivated yeast and microbiological sanitary practices.

In the 1930s the practice of adding non-agave sugars to the aguamiel, or "honey water," was introduced and quickly adopted by many Tequila producers. These mixto (mixed) Tequilas had a less intense taste than 100% blue agave Tequilas, but this relative blandness also made them more appealing to non-native consumers, particularly those in the United States.

From the 1930s through the 1980s, the bulk of the Tequila being produced was of the blended mixto variety. The original 100% agave Tequilas were reduced to a minor specialty product role in the market. But in the late 1980s the rising popularity of single malt Scotch whiskies and expensive Cognacs in the international marketplace did not go unnoticed among Tequila producers. New brands of 100% blue agave Tequilas were introduced and sales began a steady growth curve that continues to this day. This sales growth has resulted in the opening of new distilleries and the expansion of existing operations. Tequila is on an upswing.

The Worm Turns

The upgrading and upscaling of Tequila has, in turn, inspired Mezcal producers to undertake similar measures. In the past few years an increasing number of high-end Mezcals, including some intriguing "single village" bottlings, have been introduced to the market. Mezcal now seems to be coming into its own as a distinctive, noteworthy spirit.

Reviews

Azabache (Mexico)

Azabache Blanco 100% Blue Agave Tequila 80 proof $34.95.   **90**

Light amber. Medium-bodied. Notes of anise, ginger, pomace, and herbs. Round, soft entry. Highly fragrant on the palate with stony, grappa-like components. Rich, long finish. Exotic style.

Azabache 100% Blue Agave Tequila 80 proof $36.95.   **82**

Yellow. Moderately light-bodied. Notes of white pepper, herbs, and citrus. Very soft texture. Spicy entry with an impression of sweetness. Fragrant, fruity finish.

Azabache Mezcal 80 proof $36.95.   **83**

Clear. Medium-bodied. Notes of violets, herbs, and dried citrus. Smooth, moderately rich texture. Floral fragrance dominates the palate with a touch of fruit. An herbal hint of sweetness in the finish. Elegant style.

Azabache Anejo 100% Blue Agave Tequila 80 proof $38.95.   **89**

Pale yellow. Moderately full-bodied. Notes of sandalwood, jasmine, tangerine, and honey. Soft, smooth texture. Loaded with exotic fragrance and tropical flavors. A sensation of sweetness is an additional embellishment. Rich, long finish.

Beneva (Mexico)

Beneva Gran Reserva Mezcal, 4 Year Old Anejo, Oaxaca 80 proof $69.95.   **93**

Dark gold-amber. Medium-bodied. Vanilla, molasses, dried peach, wet stone, cigar leaf. Moderately full texture. Rich, sweet palate, replete with lush brown spices and firm fruit flavors. Quite refined and an excellent sipper, not unlike a well-aged rum.

Cabrito (Mexico)

Cabrito Tequila Blanco 80 proof $14.99.   **88**

Clear with a metallic gray tint. Medium-bodied. Dried herbs, agave, white pepper. Forward aromas are generous and complex, showing a fine agave character. Lush, supple, and rounded without real cut, but very smooth. Shows very little burn through the finish.

Cabrito Gold Tequila 80 proof $15.99.   **84**

Bright yellow-straw. Medium-bodied. Minerals, dried herbs, wood. Aromatically reserved with a subtle woody quality. Full but drying through the finish, with a touch of heat.

Cabrito Reposado Tequila 80 proof $16.99.   **84**

Very pale straw. Medium-bodied. Dried herbs, minerals, wood. Forward aromas feature a slightly woody, vanilla accent. Rich, oily, and viscous in the mouth with a drying finish that shows a touch of heat. Quite flavorful.

Capitan (Mexico)

Capitan Silver Tequila 80 proof $7.99.   **NR**

Casta Brava (Mexico)

Casta Brava Reposado Tequila 80 proof $26/L.   **89**

Light gold. Moderately full-bodied. Apple, pear, cinnamon, honey. Bold, lush texture. A forceful drink. Intense all the way, with bright, vibrant flavors and woody, spicy nuances. Turns up the heat in the finish.

Casta Oro (Mexico)

Casta Oro Reposado Tequila 80 proof $22.99.   **87**

Gold. Full-bodied. Fig, tea, earth, pine. Bold, rich texture. Big, brawny flavors coat the palate. Nice fruit notes are a bit overshadowed by larger wood tones and an earthy component.

Casta Weber Azul (Mexico)
Casta Weber Azul Añejo Tequila 80 proof $70. **89**

Medium gold. Medium-bodied. Sweet herbs, green olives, lemon, honey. Moderately rich texture. Nice vibrant feel. Well-integrated profile of fragrance, bright flavors with a nice touch of heat at the end.

Cazadores Reposado Tequila (Mexico)
Cazadores 80 proof $29.95. **82**

Pale yellow. Moderately light-bodied. Notes of pine, lemon, and allspice. Soft, light texture. Extreme fragrance from citrus and spice on the palate. Smooth, waxyish finish.

Centinela (Mexico)
Centinela Tequila Blanco 80 proof $24.99. **82**

Clear. Moderately light-bodied. Oil, dried grass, dried citrus peel. Compact texture. Somewhat oily on the palate. Firm, dry, and pungent as tart flavors and crisp spices emerge.

Centinela Añejo Tequila 80 proof $44.99. **88**

Straw with a slightly pale-green cast. Medium-bodied. Green herbs, dried pineapple, clover honey, cedar. Smooth texture. Rounded, somewhat oily palate. Excellent balance of sweet aromatics and plush fruit notes. Quite vibrant into the warming finish.

Chinaco (Mexico)
Chinaco Reposado 100% Blue Agave 80 proof $49. **90**

Medium yellow. Moderately light-bodied. Notes of lemon, pine, grass, and caramel. Deep, smooth, buttery texture. Citrus and herbal components are complemented by a kiss of sweetness. Full, soft finish. Excellent structure.

Cinco de Mayo (Mexico)
Cinco de Mayo Tequila Blanco 40 proof $15.99. **84**

Clear. Medium-bodied. Vibrant agave and citrus aromas. A clean, rounded entry leads to a precise, medium-bodied palate. Snappy, drying finish with a mild burn.

Cuervo (Mexico)
Cuervo 1800 Tequila 80 proof $17.99. **86**

Gold with an orange-copper cast. Moderately full-bodied. Figs, wet stone, dried grasses. Bold, round texture. Smooth, broad feel with deep flavors and a pungent backdrop of earthy nuances. Nice expanding warmth on the rich finish.

Cuervo Cuervo Tradicional 100% Agave Azul 80 proof $17.99. **82**

Pale straw. Moderately light-bodied. Notes of herbs, chili peppers, and grain alcohol. Grainy, light texture. Spicy, almost hot entry. A slight building of fragrance develops and carries into the delicate finish.

Cuervo Reserva Antigua, 1800 Añejo Tequila 80 proof $39.99. **87**

Amber-orange. Medium-bodied. Caramel, vanilla, tangerine, tar. Soft texture. Moderately full palate of deep brown spices with a tart, racy edge. Lean, with hints of bitter flavors emerging on the finish. Has a rumlike profile.

Del Maguey (Mexico)
Del Maguey Chichicapa Single Village Mezcal 95.6 proof $18.99. **89**

Clear. Citrus zest aromas with oily, agave-like accents. Richly textured on the palate with viscosity evident and smooth flavors showing intensity through the chalky finish. Heat is very late in coming on the finish.

Del Maguey Minero, Santa Catarina Minas Single Village Mezcal 98.2 proof $60.   94

Clear. Rich, earthy aromas with an oily, agave-like character showing green herbal qualities. Flavors follow the aromas well, with an oily intensity on the palate and perceptible heat on the finish. Assertively green and olive notes through the finish. Shows outstanding agave character.

Del Maguey San Luis del Rio Single Village Mezcal 96.6 proof $60.   88

Clear. Fairly restrained aromas of mineral oil, agave, and floral notes. The suggestion of grappa. Silky smooth and rich with the flavors following the aromas, though the finish turns hotter and earthier.

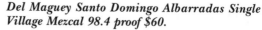

Del Maguey Santo Domingo Albarradas Single Village Mezcal 98.4 proof $60.   97

Clear. Hot, smoky aromas with red berry and spice notes and plenty of agave character. Mouthfeel is rich, smooth, and oily with fine agave flavors and a long, drying finish with a note of spirity heat.

Del Maguey Wild Mountain Mageuy, Tobala, Single Village Mezcal 94.4 proof $120.   92

Clear. Suggestively fruity aromas with floral, agave-like accents and minty, green spice notes. Texture has an oily impression upfront, with a smooth midpalate. The finish is long and drying with a touch of burn.

Distinqt (Mexico)

Distinqt Lemony Tequila 80 proof $14.99.   86

Clear. Moderately light-bodied. Notes of citrus, pomace, and herbs. Soft, smooth texture. On the palate, a stony, grappa-like note overshadows light fruit. Fragrant, elegant finish.

Distinqt Orangy Tequila 80 proof $14.99.   90

Very pale orange. Moderately light-bodied. Notes of orange, anise, and honey. Soft, smooth texture. Strong fruit in a light syrupy sweetness coats the mouth. Very elegant, light finish. A cordial-like style.

Distinqt Platinum Tequila 80 proof $14.99.   82

Clear. Moderately light-bodied. Notes of black pepper, dried peach, and dried herbs. Light, easy texture. Soft, spicy flavors on the palate quickly intensify. Tart, herbal finish.

Don Eduardo (Mexico)

Don Eduardo Silver Tequila 80 proof $32.99.   92

Clear. Medium-bodied. Minerals, slate, bread dough. Subtle aromas lead to a viscous, oily palate feel. Rather neutral in the mouth, but very smooth, with just a touch of heat to the finish.

Don Eduardo Añejo Tequila 80 proof $34.99.   86

Pale yellow-straw cast. Medium-bodied. Agave, dried herbs, sandalwood. Attractive spicy aromas lead to a lighter-styled, well-balanced palate feel. Smooth and clean with a drying edge to the finish. A delicate, restrained style of añejo.

Don Julio (Mexico)

Don Julio Tequila Tres Magueyes Silver 80 proof $38.   88

Clear. Moderately light-bodied. Chalk, wet stone, white pepper, black licorice, pine. Light, zippy texture. Rather vibrant and engaging style. Exhibits complex nature with a wide array of components kept in harmonious balance. Clean and refined in the finish.

Don Julio Reserva Añejo Tequila 80 proof $42. **89**

Light gold. Moderately full-bodied. Vanilla creme, caramel, honey, apple, minerals. Rich texture. Bold yet soft flavors and rich brown spices coat the palate. A deep, plush drink. Noticeable sharpness in the finish.

Dos Gusanos (Mexico)

Dos Gusanos Mezcal 80 proof $13.99. **85**

Medium gold with an orange glow. Moderately full-bodied. Notes of citrus, clove, leather, and herbs. Smooth, silky texture. Almost meaty and gamey on the palate with light fruit following. Deep, fragrant finish.

Dos Reales (Mexico)

Dos Reales Anejo Tequila 80 proof $34.99. **86**

Medium amber. Moderately full-bodied. Notes of dried apricot, flowers, fresh herbs. Lush texture. Fruity entry with abundant floral fragrance. A refreshing note of sea air in the finish.

Reserva del Dueño (Mexico)

Reserva del Dueño Añejo Tequila 83.4 proof $18.99. **87**

Bright straw hue. Generous agave and herb aromas carry a very slight wood accent. A rounded entry leads to a clean, medium-bodied palate, with a subtle drying, woody quality. Precise, snappy finish.

El Conquistador (Mexico)

El Conquistador Reposado Tequila 80 proof $35.95. **91**

Straw. Medium-bodied. Dried apple, honey, hay, wet stone. Rounded texture. Soft, fragrant, and full of lightly sweet flavors. A most engaging style. Could do quite well with a twist and on the rocks.

El Conquistador Añejo Tequila 80 proof $36.95. **87**

Straw with pale gold. Moderately full-bodied. Fig, lemon, clove, minerals. Smooth, slightly rich texture. Almost a chunky sensation with bold flavors and light spicy notes following. Deep, broad palate with noted astringency.

El Mayor Reserve (Mexico)

El Mayor Reserve Anejo Tequila 80 proof $29.99. **82**

Pale old-gold cast. Medium-bodied. Minerals, earth. Shows a subtle fusel quality to the nose. Lean and drying in the mouth. Somewhat lacking in agave character and flavor intensity, but well balanced.

El Rejador (Mexico)

El Rejador Joven Mezcal 76 proof $18.99. **89**

Clear. Aromatically pungent with earth, peat, lavender, and wild herbal character. Flavors follow the aromas with considerable intensity. Texture is oily and smooth showing some viscosity through the finish, with mineral persistence. Finishes with a touch of fruity sweetness. Astonishingly complex.

El Tesoro de Don Felipe (Mexico)

El Tesoro de Don Felipe Silver Tequila 80 proof $25.99. **88**

Clear. Moderately light-bodied. Sweet herbs, dried tropical fruits, anise. Soft texture. Rich palate is loaded with fruit flavors and pronounced aromatics. Intensity is key, as the components keep building together to a deeper, lingering finish.

El Tesoro de Don Felipe Añejo Tequila 80 proof $35.99. **92**

Pale gold, with a slightly pale-green cast. Moderately full-bodied. Fresh flowers, sweet herbs, dried tropical fruits, minerals. Rich, bold texture. Full and bright palate sings of summer garden scents and lovely fruit salad flavors. Deep, vibrant profile is manifested in a long, smooth finish. Classic balance of power and finesse.

El Toro (Mexico)

El Toro Gold Tequila 80 proof $8.99. 88

Gold with a slight orange-amber cast. Medium-bodied. Oil, charcoal, dried pear, honey. Compact texture. A touch rough, with solvent notes prevailing over light fruit flavors. Builds up well into a slightly heated finish. Good mixer.

El Toro White Tequila 80 proof $8.99. NR

Encantado (Mexico)

Encantado Mezcal, Oaxaca 80 proof $40. 90

Clear. Moderately full-bodied. Chalk, lime, anise, dried herbs, burnt wood, leather. Full, bold texture. Quite forceful, with loads of spice and mineral nuances upfront. Lovely fragrant components build as do pungent, richer flavors. A most expansive, weighty finish.

Fernando Romero Blas (Mexico)

Fernando Romero Blas Mezcal Tobala, Oaxaca 80 proof $19.95. NR

Gusano Real (Mexico)

Gusano Real Reposado Tequila 80 proof $65. 93

Medium gold. Medium-bodied. Honey, cinnamon, dried tropical fruits, caraway. Rounded, lush texture. Gorgeous all the way through. Fascinating sweet but not cloying sensations of spice and fruits emerge all wrapped with lovely fragrance. Silky and liqueur-like, this will serve beautifully as an after-dinner sipper.

Gusano Rojo (Mexico)

Gusano Rojo Mezcal 80 proof $13.99. 81

Deep gold with a light amber tint. Moderately full-bodied. Notes of bacon fat, lemon grass, and oak. Rich, oily texture. Very smoky on the palate with a whiff of herbal fragrance. Dry, woody finish.

Hacienda de Chihuahua (Mexico)

Hacienda de Chihuahua Sotol Reposado 76 proof $34.99. 83

Very pale old-gold cast. Moderately full-bodied. Spice cabinet, dill, sweet herbs. Pungent aromas are so forward that this Tequila almost seems to have been spiced. Full and generous in the mouth with a decidedly drying woody edge and a touch of heat.

Herradura (Mexico)

Herradura Silver Tequila 80 proof $19.99. 90

Pale platinum. Medium-bodied. Flowers, dried tropical fruits, sweet herbs, spicy peppers, menthol. Rounded texture. Smooth, rich feel on the palate. Sensuous layers of lush sweet flavors buttressed by heady fragrance. An absolute delight.

Herradura Gold Reposado Tequila 80 proof $22.99. 91

Medium yellow. Medium-bodied. Notes of lemon, honey, grass, and vanilla. Soft, smooth texture. Citrus is key on the palate. Warm brown spice elements add depth. Rich, long finish.

Scale: Superlative (96-100), Exceptional (90-95), Highly Recommended (85-89), Recommended (80-84), Not Recommended (Under 80)

Herradura Añejo Tequila 80 proof $42.99. **92**
Bright yellow-copper cast. Moderately full-bodied. Orange marmalade, wood, vanilla. Intensely aromatic with focused sweet flavors. Full but lean in the mouth with an assertive drying quality. Shows some heat through the finish. Intense.

Herradura Seleccion Suprema, Muy Añejo Tequila 80 proof $260. **97**
Deep bronzed-copper cast. Moderately full-bodied. Honey, Amontillado Sherry, wood. Shows an enticing and outrageously attractive sweet woody quality to the nose. Full and firm in the mouth, with a decidedly drying quality that makes for a clean finish. Powerful and unusual. A brandied style that retains both agave character and Tequila bite.

Hussong's (Mexico)

Hussong's Tequila Reposado 80 proof $23.99. **92**
Light straw with a pale green cast. Medium-bodied. Citrus peel, honey, flowers, sweet herbs, minerals. Rounded, slightly full texture. Lush palate offering rich, tangy sweet flavors. Beautiful floral fragrance adds dimension and pleasure. Nice palate-cleansing astringency on the deep, warm finish.

Juarez (Mexico)

Juarez Gold Tequila 80 proof $6.99. **84**
Gold with an amber glow. Moderately light-bodied. Notes of smoke, almond, and tea. Light texture. Tart, slightly tannic entry. Unusual style combining dryness on the palate with aromas found at a campfire.

Juarez Silver Tequila 80 proof $6.99. **88**
Clear. Medium-bodied. Notes of lime, herbs, and grain alcohol. Smooth, silky texture. Slightly sweet impression, with mineral and grappa-like notes. Dry, clean finish.

La Arandina (Mexico)

La Arandina Dos Amigos Reposado Tequila. $18. **86**
Straw. Medium-bodied. Lime, sea salt, Malabar pepper, dried tropical fruits. Bold texture. A bit intense, both on the nose and palate. Has an interesting burst of spice with salty, tangy sensations and a tart, drying finish.

La Cava de Don Agustin (Mexico)

La Cava de Don Agustin Reposado Reserve Tequila 80 proof $39.99. **90**
Straw, pale gold. Medium-bodied. Pickle barrel, tea, green olives, figs. Soft, smooth texture. Almost lush, with a lovely silky palate. Stronger aromatics give way to light fruity notes. A very elegant, refined style.

Lapiz (Mexico)

Lapiz Añejo Tequila 80 proof $8.99/200 ml. **94**
Bright gold. Moderately full-bodied. Flowers, dill, orange marmalade, vanilla. Moderately rich texture. Soft and delicate with an unctuous palate. Nice buildup of succulent flavors interspersed with lovely sweet floral fragrances. Well knit and pretty.

Pepe Lopez (Mexico)

Pepe Lopez Silver Tequila 80 proof $10.99. **86**
Clear. Moderately light-bodied. Salt, dried herbs, earth, lime. Delicate texture. Light and easy, with refreshing, softer aromatics. Nice fruity note leads into the finish.

Pepe Lopez Gold Tequila 80 proof $12.99. **87**
Deep gold, with an amber cast. Medium-bodied. Dried peach, dried herbs, tar. Moderately creamy texture. Slightly rough palate but packs a lot of flavor upfront. Carries a nice impression of sweetness from the middle into the finish.

≈

Tequila Cocktails

Classic Margarita

**Take a short glass. Wet the rim with lime juice. Put the glass upside down in coarse salt so salt clings to the rim.
In a cocktail shaker combine:**

**1-1/2 oz. silver Tequila
3/4 oz. triple sec
3/4 oz. lime juice
Ice to fill**

Shake and strain into the salt-rimmed glass and garnish with the lime slice.

Frozen Fruit Margarita

**Take a short glass. Wet the rim with lime juice and put the glass upside down in coarse salt so salt clings to the rim
(this step is optional).
Combine the ingredients for the Classic Margarita in a blender with very ripe fruit
(6-7 oz. fresh or 4 oz. frozen).
Add 3/4 cup ice.**

Blend until smooth and pour into the glass.

Tequila Sunrise

Fill a tall glass with ice. Add:

**1-1/2 oz. silver Tequila
Orange juice almost to fill
Slowly pour 1/2 oz. grenadine syrup over the top.
(As it trickles down it creates the "sunrise" effect.)**

≈

Los Arango (Mexico)

Los Arango Blue Agave Reposado Tequila 80 proof $35.99.   **84**

Pale yellow-straw cast. Moderately light-bodied. Lime, dried herbs, pepper. Clean citrus aromas are bright and forward. Generous and oily in the mouth with an exceptionally smooth mouthfeel. Not overly flavorful but eminently drinkable.

Los Camichines Distillery (Mexico)

Los Camichines Distillery Gran Centenario Añejo Tequila 80 proof $19.99.   **94**

Dark gold with an amber cast. Moderately full-bodied. Marmalade, minerals, nut oil, black pepper, butterscotch. Bold, rich texture. Prominent Grand Marnier-like flavors with ample sweet citrus notes. Carries a lovely layer of deep, woody spices. Opens up and settles nicely on the palate with a velvety mouthfeel. Quite fragrant throughout the lasting, warming finish.

Mezcal del Maestro (Mexico)

Mezcal del Maestro Añejo Reserva Mezcal 80 proof $39.   **84**

Gold. Moderately full-bodied. Sea air, salt, peat, tar. Bold, oily texture. Quite deep and powerful with a strong earthy profile. A most unusual libation with all the components of an Islay malt. A touch of spring water will release some wonderful aromatics.

Monte Alban (Mexico)

Monte Alban Mezcal con Gusano 80 proof $17.99.   **91**

Pale straw hue. Pungent spice, wood, and mineral aromas. A rounded, supple attack leads to a smooth, medium-bodied, exotically peppery finish. Shows very little burn. Drying, persistent finish. Great complexity, with an earthy array of flavors.

Montezuma (Mexico)

Montezuma Gold Tequila 80 proof $7.99. **81**

Light gold. Moderately light-bodied. Dried herbs, dried apple, pine. Moderately light texture. A bit muted on the palate. A restrained but pleasant style, with an easy sensation of softer flavors and light aromatics.

Montezuma White Tequila 80 proof $7.99.   **83**

Clear. Medium-bodied. Grain, fresh herbs, cotton candy. Soft texture. Nice and smooth on the palate with a zippy backnote. Slightly sweet sensation follows into the finish.

Scale: Superlative (96-100), Exceptional (90-95), Highly Recommended (85-89), Recommended (80-84), Not Recommended (Under 80)

Patron (Mexico)

Patron Silver Tequila 80 proof $29.99. **89**

Clear. Moderately light-bodied. Fennel, chicory, lime, wet clay. Light yet firm texture. Easy, silky presence on the palate. Lovely soft fragrant notes blend with mineral and backdrops of tart fruit flavors. Splendid integration throughout.

Patron Añejo Tequila 80 proof $34.99. **90**

Deep gold. Medium-bodied. Sweet herbs, chalk, earth, lemon. Soft, moderately rich texture. Nice integration of components and fine balance of earthy, mineral characteristics. Rich and inviting with a warm expanding finish.

Porfidio (Mexico)

Porfidio Silver Tequila 80 proof $24.99. **85**

Clear. Medium-bodied. Citrus, anise, dried flowers, sauna stone. Moderately full texture. Rounded, rich palate. Maintains a lush feel, with complements of floral aromatics and lightly sweet/tart flavors. A pretty style with a warm finish.

Porfidio Añejo Tequila 80 proof $34.99. **90**

Pale straw. Moderately full-bodied. Citrus, honey, anise, minerals. Lush texture. Rounded, oily palate is most inviting. Pretty, fresh aromatics are harmonized by rich, zesty citrus notes and spicy components. Quite elegant, this is not unlike a sambuca, and will serve well with after-dinner espressos.

Porfidio 100% Blue Agave Single Barrel Anejo Tequila 80 proof $72.99. **98**

Medium gold with a copper glow. Full-bodied. Notes of tropical fruits, butterscotch, cedar, and fresh flowers. Rich, plush texture. A sensual and flavorful delight. Rich fruit, floral and wood elements are superbly blended. Soft and creamy in the middle with sweet impression and heady fragrance. Sip slowly, as with any great spirit.

Pueblo Viejo (Mexico)

Pueblo Viejo Reposado Tequila Aged 12 Months 80 proof $27. **85**

Straw. Medium-bodied. Hay, herbs, wet stone, vanilla bean. Compact texture. Somewhat pungent aromatics Portend a bold, abrasive style with some light nutty notes.

Real Hacienda (Mexico)

Real Hacienda Anejo 100% Blue Agave 2 Year Old 80 proof $39. **86**

Deep gold with a copper tint. Moderately full-bodied. Notes of almonds, vanilla, leather, and pine. Rich, silky texture. Creamy feel with an exotic combination of nutty flavors. Woody finish.

Royale Aguila (Mexico)

Royale Aguila Añejo Tequila 80 proof $18.99. **80**

Pale straw hue. Subtle woody aromas. A lean entry leads to a crisp, medium-bodied palate. Drying, slightly herbal finish. A very light style of añejo.

Sauza (Mexico)

Sauza Tequila Blanco 80 proof $10. **84**

Clear. Moderately light-bodied. Grains, charcoal, citrus, wet stone. Smooth texture. Offers a soft palate with stony nuances and light fruit notes. Vibrancy in the long finish.

Sauza Tequila Extra 80 proof $11. **89**

Silver with a slightly pale-gray cast. Medium-bodied. Roasted hazelnut, toasted grain, caramel. Silky texture. Gives a very pleasant, smooth feel on the palate. Interesting aromatics mix with light oil nuances. Quite soft in the finish.

Sauza Hornitos Reposado Tequila 80 proof $18. **86**

Silver-straw. Moderately light-bodied. Grass, grain, lime, minerals. Delicate texture. At first, somewhat restrained with lighter aromatics and a tight, woody palate feel. Vibrant, tart flavors build up and lead into a more developed finish.

Sauza Conmemorativo Añejo Tequila 80 proof $20. **83**

Straw. Medium-bodied. Stone, dried herbs, dried citrus peel. Compact texture in the mouth. Bold and drying, with a pungent feel. Lean and angular on the palate with a hot finish.

Sauza Galardon Gran Reposado Tequila 80 proof $28. **88**

Pale gold. Medium-bodied. Apple, lemon, honey, stone, minerals. Soft, slightly rich texture. Bright, lovely fruit notes upfront. Nicely balanced with light brown spice and a vibrant mineral edge.

Sauza Tres Generaciones Añejo Tequila 80 proof $35. **88**

Straw with a pale golden cast. Medium-bodied. Golden raisins, white pepper, sweet herbs. Rounded texture. Delivers a nice, somewhat lush feel. Ample flavors are well balanced by spice and light fragrance in an oily, smooth format that continues through the finish.

Sierra Brava (Mexico)

Sierra Brava Reposado Tequila 80 proof $29.95/L. **84**

Straw with a light gold, slightly copper cast. Medium-bodied. Peppers, fresh herbs, green olives. Moderately rich texture. Unusual, with intense aromatics. Strong herbal and spice notes attack the palate with a briny feel. Not for everyone, but if you are searching for something different, you've found it.

T.Q. Hot (Mexico)

T.Q. Hot Gold Tequila with Mexican Spice and Citrus Flavor 70 proof $17.99. **88**

Deep yellow with a gold tint. Moderately full-bodied. Notes of citrus, chili peppers, dried flowers. Smooth, rich texture. Intense attack of spice and lush fruit on the palate. Syrupy, liqueur-like, fragrant finish.

Tarantula (Italy)

Tarantula Azul Citrus Tequila 80 proof $18.99. **82**

Bizarre, neon robin's egg blue hue. Forward candied-citrus aromas. A mildly sweet entry leads to a moderately full-bodied palate with a touch of viscosity. Saccharine, citrus finish.

Tehuana (Mexico)

Tehuana Mezcal con Chilli 80 proof $19.95. **89**

Medium gold. Medium-bodied. Dried citrus peels, red pepper, cedar, cigar leaf. Moderately rich texture. Nearly pungent on the palate. Quite an intense style as heat sneaks up fast. Sweet woody notes provide a curious touch to the tart fruit and spices. A good match with well-flavored Latin fare.

Tehuana Mezcal con Gusano, Oaxaca 80 proof $19.95. **88**

Pale gold. Moderately light-bodied. Green tomato, black pepper, dried herbs, caramel. Vibrant texture. Quite sharp on the palate. Racy, with a sting upfront. Vegetal notes are presented with a sweet backdrop of lighter wood spice.

Tehuana Añejo Mezcal 80 proof $33.95. **90**

Deep gold. Medium-bodied. Brown sugar, marmalade, oil, cocoa. Rounded texture. Sweet aromatics and flavors hold forth over some resinous notes. Very elegant, with a fine presence into the finish.

Viuda de Romero (Mexico)

Viuda de Romero 2 Year Old Anejo 80 proof $19. **92**

Gold with a copper tint. Moderately full-bodied. Notes of papaya, herbs, lime, and vanilla. Deep, lush texture. Fabulous combination of succulent tropical flavors with a touch of brown spice. Long, rich, creamy finish.

Scale: Superlative (96-100), Exceptional (90-95), Highly Recommended (85-89), Recommended (80-84), Not Recommended (Under 80)

Xalixco (Mexico)

Xalixco Reposado Tequila 80 proof $15.99.   **84**

Silver with a yellow tint. Moderately light-bodied. Notes of sage, hay, and honey. Delicate, soft texture. Herbs dominate over a touch of sweetness. Grainy notes in the finish.

Highly Rated Tequila and Mezcal

Añejo Tequila

98 • Porfidio (Mexico) 100% Blue Agave Single Barrel Anejo, Tequila 80 Proof. $72.99.

97 • Herradura (Mexico) Seleccion Suprema, Muy Añejo Tequila 80 Proof. $260.

94 • Los Camichines Distillery (Mexico) Gran Centenario Añejo Tequila 80 Proof. $19.99.

94 • Lapiz (Mexico) Añejo Tequila 80 Proof. $8.99/200 ml.

92 • Viuda de Romero (Mexico) 2 Year Old Anejo, Tequila Inmemorial 80 Proof. $19.

92 • Herradura (Mexico) Añejo Tequila 80 Proof. $42.99.

92 • El Tesoro de Don Felipe (Mexico) Añejo Tequila 80 Proof. $35.99.

90 • Porfidio (Mexico) Añejo Tequila 80 Proof. $34.99.

90 • Patron (Mexico) Añejo Tequila 80 Proof. $34.99.

89 • Don Julio (Mexico) Reserva Añejo Tequila 80 Proof. $42.

89 • Casta Weber Azul (Mexico) Añejo Tequila 80 Proof. $70.

89 • Azabache (Mexico) Anejo 100% Blue Agave, Tequila 80 Proof. $38.95.

88 • Sauza (Mexico) Tres Generaciones Añejo Tequila 80 Proof. $35.

88 • Centinela (Mexico) Añejo Tequila 80 Proof. $44.99.

87 • Reserva del Dueño (Mexico) Añejo Tequila 83.4 Proof. $18.99.

87 • El Conquistador (Mexico) Añejo Tequila 80 Proof. $36.95.

87 • Cuervo (Mexico) Reserva Antigua, 1800 Añejo Tequila 80 Proof. $39.99.

86 • Real Hacienda (Mexico) Anejo 100% Blue Agave 2 Year Old, Tequila 80 Proof. $39.

86 • Dos Reales (Mexico) Anejo, Tequila 80 Proof. $34.99.

86 • Don Eduardo (Mexico) Añejo Tequila 80 Proof. $34.99.

Reposado Tequila

93 • Gusano Real (Mexico) Reposado Tequila 80 Proof. $65.

92 • Hussong's (Mexico) Tequila Reposado 80 Proof. $23.99.

91 • Herradura (Mexico) Gold 100% Blue Agave, Reposado Tequila 80 Proof. $22.99.

91 • El Conquistador (Mexico) Reposado Tequila 80 Proof. $35.95.

90 • La Cava de Don Agustin (Mexico) Reposado Reserve Tequila 80 Proof. $39.99.

90 • Chinaco (Mexico) Reposado 100% Blue Agave, Tequila 80 Proof. $49.

89 • Casta Brava (Mexico) Reposado Tequila 80 Proof. $26/L.

88 • Sauza (Mexico) Galardon Gran Reposado Tequila 80 Proof. $28.

87 • Casta Oro (Mexico) Reposado Tequila 80 Proof. $22.99.

86 • Sauza (Mexico) Hornitos Reposado Tequila 80 Proof. $18.

86 • La Arandina (Mexico) Dos Amigos Reposado Tequila $18.

85 • Pueblo Viejo (Mexico) Reposado Tequila Aged 12 Months 80 Proof. $27.

Silver Tequila

92 • Don Eduardo (Mexico) Silver Tequila 80 Proof. $32.99.

90 • Herradura (Mexico) Silver Tequila 80 Proof. $19.99.

90 • Azabache (Mexico) Blanco 100% Blue Agave, Tequila 80 Proof. $34.95.

89 • Patron (Mexico) Silver Tequila 80 Proof. $29.99.

88 • Juarez (Mexico) Silver, Tequila 80 Proof. $6.99.

88 • El Tesoro de Don Felipe (Mexico) Silver Tequila 80 Proof. $25.99.
88 • Don Julio (Mexico) Tequila Tres Magueyes Silver 80 Proof. $38.
88 • Cabrito (Mexico) Cabrito Tequila Blanco 80 Proof. $14.99.
86 • Pepe Lopez (Mexico) Silver Tequila 80 Proof. $10.99.
85 • Porfidio (Mexico) Silver Tequila 80 Proof. $24.99.

Gold Tequila

89 • Sauza (Mexico) Tequila Extra 80 Proof. $11.
88 • El Toro (Mexico) Gold Tequila 80 Proof. $8.99.
87 • Pepe Lopez (Mexico) Gold Tequila 80 Proof. $12.99.
86 • Cuervo (Mexico) 1800 Tequila 80 Proof. $17.99.

Flavored Tequila

90 • Distinqt (Mexico) Orangy, Tequila 80 Proof. $14.99.
89 • Tehuana (Mexico) Mezcal con Chilli 80 Proof. $19.95.
88 • T.Q. Hot (Mexico) Gold Tequila with Mexican Spice and Citrus Flavor
70 Proof. $17.99.
86 • Distinqt (Mexico) Lemony, Tequila 80 Proof. $14.99.

Mezcal

97 • Del Maguey (Mexico) Santo Domingo Albarradas Single Village Mezcal
98.4 Proof. $60.
94 • Del Maguey (Mexico) Minero, Santa Catarina Minas Single Village Mezcal
98.2 Proof. $60.
93 • Beneva (Mexico) Gran Reserva Mezcal, 4 Year Old Anejo, Oaxaca 80 Proof. $69.95.
92 • Del Maguey (Mexico) Wild Mountain Mageuy, Tobala, Single Village Mezcal
94.4 Proof. $120.
91 • Monte Alban (Mexico) Mezcal con Gusano 80 Proof. $17.99.
90 • Tehuana (Mexico) Añejo Mezcal 80 Proof. $33.95.
90 • Encantado (Mexico) Mezcal, Oaxaca 80 Proof. $40.
89 • El Rejador (Mexico) Joven Mezcal 76 Proof. $18.99.
89 • Del Maguey (Mexico) Chichicapa Single Village Mezcal 95.6 Proof. $60.
88 • Tehuana (Mexico) Mezcal con Gusano, Oaxaca 80 Proof. $19.95.
88 • Del Maguey (Mexico) San Luis del Rio Single Village Mezcal 96.6 Proof. $60.
85 • Dos Gusanos Mezcal (Mexico) Mezcal 80 Proof. $13.99.

six

Vodka

"A Vodka martini please. Polish, not Russian.
Shaken, not stirred."

– James Bond, Agent 007, plunging a
stake into the heart of Gin sales.

An Overview

The Basis of Vodka

Vodka is the dominant spirit of eastern Europe. It is made by fermenting and then distilling the simple sugars from a mash of pale grain or vegetal matter. Vodka is produced from grain, potatoes, molasses, beets, and a variety of other plants. Rye and wheat are the classic grains for Vodka, with most of the best Russian Vodkas being made from wheat while in Poland they are mostly made from a rye mash. Swedish and Baltic distillers are partial to wheat mashes. Potatoes are looked down on by Russian distillers, but are held in high esteem by some of their Polish counterparts. Molasses, a sticky, sweet residue from sugar production, is widely used for inexpensive, mass-produced brands of Vodka. American distillers use the full range of base ingredients.

Distillation of Vodka

Vodka is distilled in the manner described in the introductory chapter of this book. The choice of pot or column still does, however, have a fundamental effect on the final character of the Vodka. All Vodka comes out of the still as a clear, colorless spirit, but Vodka from a pot still (the same sort used for Cognac and Scotch whisky) will contain some of the delicate aromatics, congeners, and flavor elements of the crop from which it was produced. Pot stills are relatively "inefficient," and the resulting spirit from the first distillation is usually redistilled (rectified) to increase the proof of the spirit. Vodka from a more "efficient" column still is usually a neutral, characterless spirit.

Except for a few minor styles, Vodka is not put in wooden casks or aged for an extensive period of time. It can, however, be flavored or colored with a wide variety of fruits, herbs, and spices.

Classifications of Vodka

There are no uniform classifications of Vodka. In Poland, Vodkas are graded according to their degree of purity: standard (*zwykly*), premium (*wyborowy*), and deluxe (*luksusowy*). In Russia Vodka that is labeled *osobaya* (special) usually is a superior-quality product that can be exported, while *krepkaya* (strong) denotes an overproof Vodka of at least 56% ABV.

In the United States, domestic Vodkas are defined by U.S. government regulation as "neutral spirits, so distilled, or so treated after distillation with charcoal or other materials, as to be without distinctive character, aroma, taste or color." Because American Vodka is, by law, neutral in taste, there are only very subtle distinctions between brands. Many drinkers feel that the only real way of differentiating between them is by alcohol content and price.

Vodka at a Glance

Top Scores:

Top Vodka

96 • Grey Goose (France) Vodka 80 Proof. $27.

Top Flavored Vodka

92 • Stolichnaya (Russia) Persik, Peach Flavored Vodka 70 Proof. $16.99.

92 • Soomskaya (Ukraine) Riabinovaya, Ashberry Flavored Vodka 80 Proof. $16.

Types of Vodka

Since Vodka tends to be a neutral spirit, it lends itself to blending with flavors and fortifying other beverages. In the 19th century, high-proof "Russian spirit" was held in high esteem by Sherry producers in Spain, who imported it to fortify their wines.

Neutral spirits are still used to fortify Port, Sherry, and other types of fortified wines, although the source of alcohol for such purposes these days tends to be the vast "wine lake" that has been created by European Union agricultural practices.

Flavored Vodkas have been produced from the start, originally to mask the flavor of the first primitive Vodkas, but later as a mark of the distiller's skill. The Russians and Poles in particular still market dozens of flavors. Some of the better known types are:

Kubanskaya – Vodka flavored with an infusion of dried lemon and orange peels.

Limonnaya – Lemon-flavored Vodka, usually with a touch of sugar added.

Okhotnichya – "Hunter's" Vodka is flavored with a mix of ginger, cloves, lemon peel, coffee, anise and other herbs and spices. It is then blended with sugar and a touch of a wine similar to white port. A most unusual Vodka.

Pertsovka – Pepper-flavored Vodka, made with both black peppercorns and red chili peppers.

Starka – "Old" Vodka, a holdover from the early centuries of Vodka production, that can be infused with everything from fruit tree leaves to brandy, Port, Malaga wine, and dried fruit. Some brands are aged in oak casks.

Zubrovka – *Zubrowka* in Polish; Vodka flavored with buffalo (or more properly "bison") grass, an aromatic grass favored by the herds of the rare European bison.

In recent years numerous other flavored Vodkas have been launched on the world market. The most successful of these have been fruit flavors such as currant and orange.

Vodka Regions

Eastern Europe is the homeland of Vodka production. Every country produces Vodka, and most also have local flavored specialties.

Russia, **Ukraine** and **Belarus** produce the full range of Vodka types, and are generally acknowledged to be the leaders in Vodka production. Only the better brands, all of which are distilled from rye and wheat, are exported to the West.

Poland produces and exports both grain- and potato-based Vodkas. Most of the high- quality brands are produced in pot stills.

Finland, and the Baltic States of **Estonia**, **Latvia,** and **Lithuania** produce primarily grain-based Vodkas, mostly from wheat.

Sweden has, in recent decades, developed a substantial export market for its straight and flavored wheat-based Vodkas.

Western Europe has local brands of Vodka wherever there are distilleries. The base for these Vodkas can vary from grains in northern countries such as the **United Kingdom**, **Holland** and **Germany**, to grapes and other fruits in the winemaking regions of France and Italy.

The United States and **Canada** produce nonflavored Vodkas, both from various grains (including corn) and from molasses. American Vodkas are, by law, neutral spirits, so the distinction between brands is more a matter of price and perception than taste.

The Caribbean produces a surprising amount of Vodka, all of it from molasses. Most of it is exported for blending and bottling in other countries.

Australia produces molasses-based Vodkas, but few are exported.

Asia has a smattering of local Vodkas, with the best coming from **Japan**.

> *"Vodka shall be taxed at a rate of two kopecks per bucketful."*
>
> **– 18th-century Czarist government excise tax regulation.**

Vodka: Its History and Significance

The story is told that in A.D. 988 the Grand Prince of Kiev in what is now Ukraine decided that it was time for his people to convert from their pagan ways to one of the monotheistic religions that held sway in the civilized countries to the south. First came the Jewish rabbis. He listened to their arguments, was impressed, but ultimately sent them away after remarking that the followers of Judaism did not control any land. Next came the Moslem mullahs. Again he was impressed, both with their intellectual arguments and the success of Islam as a political and military force, but when he was told that Islam proscribed alcohol he was dismayed and sent them away. Finally came the Christian priests who informed him that not only could good Christians drink alcohol, but that wine was actually required for church rituals such as communion. That was good enough for the Grand Prince, and on his command his subjects converted en masse to Christianity.

The point of this historical anecdote is that the Slavic peoples of the north and their Scandinavian neighbors took alcoholic drinks very seriously. The extreme cold temperatures of winter inhibited the shipment of wines and beers, as these relatively low-proof beverages could freeze during transit. Until the introduction of distilling into Eastern Europe in the 1400s, strong drink was made by fermenting strong wines, meads, and beers, freezing them, and then drawing off the alcoholic slush from the frozen water.

The earliest distilled spirit in eastern Europe was distilled from mead (honey wine) or beer and was called *perevara*. Vodka (from the Russian word *voda*, meaning water) was originally used to describe grain distillates that were used for medicinal purposes. As distilling techniques improved Vodka (*Wodka* in Polish) gradually came to be the accepted term for beverage spirit, regardless of its origin.

Vodka in Russia

Russians firmly believe that Vodka was created in their land. Commercial production was established by the 14th century. In 1540 Czar Ivan the Terrible took a break from beheading his enemies and established the first government Vodka monopoly. Distilling licenses were handled out to the *boyars* (the nobility) and all other distilleries were banned. Needless to say, moonshining became endemic.

Vodka production became an integral part of Russian society. Aristocratic landowners operated stills on their estates and produced high-quality Vodkas, which were frequently flavored with everything from acorns to horseradish to mint. The Czars maintained test distilleries at their country palaces where the first experiments in multiple redistillations were made. In 1780 a scientist at one such distillery invented the use of charcoal filtration to purify Vodka.

By the 18th and well into the 19th century the Russian Vodka industry was probably the most technologically advanced industry in the nation. New types of stills and production techniques from Western Europe were eagerly imported and utilized. State funding and control of Vodka research continued. Under a 1902 law, "Moscow Vodka," a clear 40% ABV rye Vodka made with soft "living" (undistilled) water and without added flavorings was established as the benchmark for Russian Vodka.

The Soviet Union continued government control of Vodka production. All distilleries became government-owned, and while the Communist Party apparatchiks continued to enjoy high-quality rye Vodka, the proletariat masses had to make do with cheap spirits. The societal attitude toward such products could be best summed up by the curious fact that mass-produced Vodka was sold in liter bottles with a non-screw cap. Once you opened the bottle it couldn't be resealed. You had to drink it all in one session.

Vodka production in the current Russian Federation has returned to the pre-revolutionary pattern. High-quality brands are once again being produced for the new social elite and export, while the popularly priced brands are still being consumed, well, like *voda*.

Vodka in Poland

The earliest written records of Vodka production in Poland date from the 1400s, though some Polish historians claim that it was being produced around the southern city of Krakow at least a century earlier. Originally known as *okowita* (from the Latin *aqua vita* — water of life), it was used for a variety of purposes besides beverages. A 1534 medical text defined an aftershave lotion as being "Vodka for washing the chin after shaving." Herbal-infused Vodkas were particularly popular as liniments for the aches and pains of life.

In 1546 King Jan Olbracht of Poland granted the right to distill and sell spirits to every adult citizen. The Polish aristocracy, taking a cue from their Russian peers, soon lobbied to have this privilege revoked and replaced by a royal decree that reserved the right to make Vodka exclusively to them.

Commercial Vodka distilleries were well established by the 18th century. By the mid-19th century a thriving export trade had developed, with Polish Vodkas, particularly those infused with small quantities of fruit spirit, being shipped throughout northern Europe and even into Russia.

With the fall of Communism in the late 1980s, the Vodka distilleries soon returned to private ownership. Nowadays high-quality Polish Vodkas are exported throughout the world.

Vodka in Sweden

Vodka production in Sweden, which dates from the 15th century, has its origins in the local gunpowder industry where high-proof spirit (originally called *brännvin*) was used as a component of black powder for muskets. When distilleries were licensed to produce beverage alcohol (primarily spice-flavored Aquavit, but also Vodka), it was with the understanding that gunpowder makers had first priority over beverage consumers.

Home distilling was long a part of Swedish society. In 1830 there were over 175,000 registered stills in a country of less than three million people. This tradition, in a much diminished and illegal form, still continues to this day. Modern Swedish Vodka is produced by the Vin & Sprit state monopoly.

Vodka in the United States

Vodka was first imported into the United States in commercial quantities around the turn of the 20th century. Its primary market was immigrants from Eastern Europe. After the repeal of National Prohibition in 1933, the Heublein Company bought the rights to the Smirnoff brand of Vodka from its White Russian émigré owners and relaunched Vodka into the U.S. market. Sales languished until an enterprising liquor salesman in South Carolina started promoting it as "Smirnoff White Whisky — No taste. No smell." Sales started to increase and American Vodka, after marking time during World War II, was on its way to marketing success. The first popular Vodka-based cocktail was a combination of Vodka and ginger ale called the Moscow Mule. It was marketed with its own special copper mug, examples of which can still be found on the back shelves of liquor cabinets and in the flea markets of America.

Today Vodka is the dominant white spirit in the United States, helped along by its versatility as a mixer and some very clever advertising campaigns from the various producers. One of the most famous of these was the classic double entendre tag line: "Smirnoff — It leaves you breathless."

Reviews

Absolut (Sweden)
Absolut Kurant Flavored Vodka 80 proof $14.99.   82

Clear. Medium-bodied. Notes of red berries, herbs, wet stone. Moderately rich texture. Pleasant interplay of tart flavors, light spice and mineral notes. Clean fruit dominates finish.

Absolut Citron, Citrus Flavored Vodka 80 proof $14.99.   86

Clear. Medium-bodied. Lemon, salt, minerals. Compact texture. Dry and zesty mouth-feel. Displays a curious sweet/tart interplay of lively citrus. Develops a interesting salty tang in the finish.

Absolut Vodka 80 proof $14.99.   80

Clear. Medium-bodied. Charcoal, wet stone, anise. Soft, smooth texture. Mildly fragrant, with a light, spice-flavored palate and presented in a well- structured format. Delicate, dry finish.

Alps (France)
Alps French Vodka 80 proof $28.   86

Clear. Medium-bodied. Plum, perfume, marzipan. Smooth, soft texture. Most refined and elegant. Lovely fragrance emerges and continues to build alongside fruit and confectionary components. Very seductive style.

Amazon (Brazil)
Amazon Vodka 80 proof $17.70.   NR

Argent (USA)
Argent Vodka 80 proof $12.99.   NR

Attakiska (USA)
Attakiska Vodka 80 proof $12.99.   87

Clear. Medium- to full-bodied. Notes of licorice, stone, dried flowers. Silky, moderately rich texture. Grappa-like fragrance emerges over delicate flavors and a mineral sensation. Long, creamy finish.

Bäälta (Lithuania)
Bäälta Lithuanian Vodka 80 proof $14.95.   87

Clear. Full-bodied. Minerals, hay, citrus. Very subtle citrus flavors lead to a rich and viscous palate feel. Oily through the finish with very little burn. Exceptionally smooth.

Baik (Russia)
Baik Vodka 80 proof $12.99.   91

Clear. Medium-bodied. Notes of citrus, anise, wet stone, flowers. Smooth, elegant texture. The dry mouthfeel, loaded with fragrance and subtle flavors, is reminiscent of grappa. Long, soft finish.

Banff (Canada)
Banff ICE Vodka 80 proof $21.   89

Clear. Medium-bodied. Minerals. Muted aromatics lead to a lighter-styled, oily mouthfeel. Smooth through the finish with a crisp edge.

Barclay's (USA)
Barclay's Vodka 80 proof $5.99.   NR

Scale: Superlative (96-100), Exceptional (90-95), Highly Recommended (85-89), Recommended (80-84), Not Recommended (Under 80)

Barton (USA)
Barton Vodka 80 proof $4.99.   **82**
Clear. Medium-bodied. Minerals, flint. Shows a slightly hot fusel quality to the nose. Lighter in the mouth with a neutral viscous quality. A sound, straightforward mixer.

Belvedere (Poland)
Belvedere Vodka 80 proof $29.99.   **90**
Clear. Full-bodied. Citrus, sweet herbs. Forward aromatics are exceptionally zesty and vibrant. Full and viscous in the mouth with a flavorful citric palate. Smooth through the finish.

Black Death (Belgium)
Black Death Vodka 80 proof $11.99.   **88**
Clear. Medium- to light-bodied. Notes of citrus, minerals, herbs. Soft, delicate texture. Elegant character, in contrast to the name. Very refined with a silky, smooth finish.

Boru (Ireland)
Boru Citrus Flavored Vodka 80 proof $22.99.   **NR**

Boru Orange Flavored Vodka 80 proof $22.99.   **81**
Clear. Intense candied-orange aromas. A smooth attack leads to a rich and viscous palate feel with very little heat. No burn on the clean finish. A tad artificial in flavor, but decent.
Boru Vodka 80 proof $22.99.   **81**
Clear. Warming mineral aromas show a touch of heat. An oily, viscous entry leads to a rounded and smooth mouthfeel. Finishes with very little burn.

Canadian Iceberg (Canada)
Canadian Iceberg Vodka 80 proof $15.99.   **94**
Clear. Moderately full-bodied. Anise, wet stone, dried herbs. Bold, viscous texture. Big, brawny style with ample weight and depth. Loaded with spice, this has a profile not unlike sambuca or pastis and certainly has merit as an after-dinner libation.

Cardinal (Holland)
Cardinal Vodka 80 proof $15.   **NR**

Carmel (Israel)
Carmel Vodka 80 proof $10.99.   **85**
Clear. Medium-bodied. Notes of licorice, grain, wet stone. Soft, delicate texture. A slightly oily feel enhances the mineral and light flavors. Easy, clean finish.
Carmel Citron Vodka 80 proof $10.99.   **91**
Clear. Medium-bodied. Notes of citrus, honey, flowers. Rich, pungent feel. An initial sorbet-like coolness builds up to a smooth, oily, and fragrant finish.

Chopin (Poland)
Chopin Vodka 80 proof $29.99.   **87**
Clear. Moderately full-bodied. Herbs, minerals, medicinal. Pronounced aromas carry an unusual pungent quality. Fairly full in the mouth with very little burn.

CK Vodka (Poland)
CK Polish Vodka 80 proof $16/700ml.   **86**
Clear. Full-bodied. Citrus, flowers. A very subtle nose has slight citric overtones. Thick and viscous in the mouth with a neutral palate and an oily finish.

Crystal Palace (USA)
Crystal Palace Vodka 80 proof $5.99.   NR

Denaka (Denmark)
Denaka Vodka 80 proof $9.99.   90

Clear. Medium- to light-bodied. Notes of white pepper, potato, charcoal. Smooth, delicate texture. Very refined, with a soft, easy entry. Spicy, lively finish.

Elduris (Iceland)
Elduris Icelandic Vodka 80 proof $12.99.   89

Clear. Medium-bodied. Notes of tropical fruits, smoke, herbs. Smooth, almost buttery, rich entry. Subtle fruit notes are combined with strong fragrances. Assertive, deep finish.

Everclear (USA)
Everclear Vodka 84 proof $11.50.   86

Clear. Medium-bodied. Notes of licorice, charcoal, flowers. Moderately rich, deep texture. Soft and highly fragrant, displaying a grappa-like character aided by an impression of sweetness. Long, smooth finish.

Finlandia (Finland)
Finlandia Cranberry Vodka 80 proof $13.99.   84

Bright cherry red. Medium-bodied. Notes of cranberry, grenadine, herbs. Easy, soft texture. Slightly tart with pleasant viscosity. The finish combines sweet and sour impressions.

Finlandia, Vodka of Finland 80 proof $15.   86

Clear. Medium-bodied. Grains, minerals, dried herbs, citrus. Slightly oily texture and an attractive silky sensation. Has pronounced flavors and a refreshing accent from spices and light aromatics.

Fleischmann's (USA)
Fleischmann's Royal Vodka 80 proof $7.99.   82

Clear. Medium-bodied. Grass, green herbs. Compact texture. Rather austere and full on the nose. Somewhat grainy, with a tight feel on the palate. Nice spicy accents. Finishes with a touch of heat.

Fris (Denmark)
Fris Vodka Skandia 80 proof $15.99.   89

Clear. Medium- to full-bodied. Notes of licorice, herbs, flowers. Rich, succulent texture. Dramatic interplay of strong fragrances and subtle flavors is reminiscent of grappa. Elegant finish.

Georgievskaya (Russia)
Georgievskaya Russian Vodka 80 proof $29.99/L.   90

Clear. Moderately full-bodied. Fusel oils, minerals, flint. Exceptionally clean and interesting aromatics lead to a smooth and viscous mouthfeel. Very smooth through the clean finish.

Glenmore (USA)
Glenmore Special Reserve Vodka 80 proof $5.99.   82

Clear. Medium-bodied. Perfume, wet stone, dried flowers. Soft, delicate texture. Easy on the palate, with attractive notes of light aromatics. Will serve quite well as a mixer.

Scale: Superlative (96-100), Exceptional (90-95), Highly Recommended (85-89), Recommended (80-84), Not Recommended (Under 80)

Goldenbärr (Ukraine)
Goldenbärr Chocolate Vodka 80 proof $13.99.　　　　　　83

Colorless. Medium-bodied. Chocolate. Generous aromas carry a definitive candied cocoa quality through the palate. Light and smooth in the mouth with very little heat. Not as flavorful as the nose might suggest. Rather neutral through the finish.

Grey Goose (France)
Grey Goose Vodka 80 proof $27.　　　　　　96

Clear. Medium-bodied. Anise, citrus peel, herbs, minerals. Soft, rounded texture. Plush palate with a delicate edge. Shows off rich fruit elements surrounded by beautiful aromatics. Lovely fragrance holds forth as backnotes of lighter spice and stone come forth. A sensational, elegant drink that will do well with a twist and a good chill.

Hooghoudt (Holland)
Hooghoudt Vodka 80 proof $12.99.　　　　　　86

Clear. Medium- to light-bodied. Notes of anise, grain, wet stone. Light, crisp texture. Dry and assertive on the palate with a burst of minerals and a delicate impression of sweetness.

Icy (Iceland)
Icy Vodka 80 proof $9.99.　　　　　　86

Clear. Medium-bodied. Notes of licorice, herbs, wet stone. Smooth, delicate texture. Soft flavors with light fragrance showcase the elegant and refined style. Easy, clean finish.

Inferno (Canada)
Inferno Pepper Flavored Vodka 78.6 proof $18.99.　　　　　　81

Clear with a very slight straw cast. Medium-bodied. Green pepper, jalapeno. A pungent chili-dominated nose shows an unusual green edge. Smooth on the entry, but rapidly shows an intense spicy quality of the "burns your lips" variety. Interesting for spicy Bloody Marys perhaps, but on the masochistic side without a mixer.

Ketel One (Holland)
Ketel One Vodka 80 proof $16.99.　　　　　　89

Clear. Medium-bodied. Charcoal, minerals, licorice, flowers. Compact texture. Quite intense mineral nose. Smoky accents blend well with light floral notes. A rough and powerful style.

Kremlyovskaya (Russia)
Kremlyovskaya Vodka 80 proof $12.99.　　　　　　87

Clear. Moderately full-bodied. Sweet potato, beet, flowers. Rich texture. Full and brash on the palate. Nice, sweet impressions of light floral aromatics are coupled with vegetable root flavors.

Kristall Dzidrais (Latvia)
Kristall Dzidrais Vodka 80 proof $14.95.　　　　　　85

Clear. Neutral aromas. A soft attack leads to a rounded, oily palate. Smooth, supple finish without heat.

Luksusowa (Poland)
Luksusowa Triple Distilled Potato Vodka
80 proof $14.95.　　　　　　88

Clear. Medium- to full-bodied. Notes of wet stone, citrus, smoke. Rich, heavy texture. Strong notes of stone and light, tart fruit are joined to excellent structure.

Minsk Distillery (Belarus)
Minsk Distillery Charodei Vodka 80 proof $24.99/700ml.   **94**
Clear. Moderately full-bodied. Citrus, flint. Clean high-toned aromas
feature a note of steely citric brightness. Rich and viscous in the mouth with a flavorful
quality through the finish and a slight hint of heat.
Shows complexity.

Moscow Cristall Distillery (Russia)
Moscow Cristall Distillery, Cristall Vodka 80 proof $19.99.   **82**
Clear. Moderately full-bodied. Minerals. Exceptionally clean aromatics lead to a big
viscous mouthfeel. Downright hot through the finish.

Mr. Boston (USA)
Mr. Boston Vodka 80 proof $5.99.   **81**
Clear. Medium-bodied. Citrus, grain alcohol, dried herbs. Soft texture. Mild sensations
throughout. Light touch of fruit and even lighter pinch of spice.

Nord (Poland)
Nord Biata Zimna Vodka 80 proof $26.   **95**
Clear. Minerals, citrus. Bright and clean aromatics lead to a very smooth mouthfeel.
Finishes with complex herbal, citrus flavors and is devoid of heat.

Old Kiev (Ukraine)
Old Kiev Ukranian Vodka 80 proof $14.49.   **86**
Clear. Moderately full-bodied. Licorice, citrus. Aggressive high-toned aromas have
a pronounced anise quality. Viscous and flavorful with an oily mouthfeel. Alcohol is
much more pronounced on the nose than in the mouth. Unusual but interesting.

Original (Poland)
Original Polish Vodka 80 proof $11.66.   **85**
Clear. Subdued mineral aromas carry a slight sweet note and a touch of heat. A viscous
attack leads to an exceptionally smooth palate. No burn whatsoever. Supple, neutral
finish. Shows viscosity and richness with very little heat.

Pole Star (Poland)
Pole Star Vodka 80 proof $9.99.   **80**
Clear. Medium-bodied. Potatoes, toasted grain, minerals. Rounded, smooth texture. Offers
an attractive mouthfeel with soft sensations on the palate. Picks up some heat in the finish.

Polmos (Poland)
Polmos Jazz Jamboree Vodka 80 proof $10.99.   **85**
Clear. Medium- to light-bodied. Notes of citrus, herbs, grain, minerals. Soft, delicate
texture. Light, elegant feel with tart grain flavors and a mineral note that add a touch of
complexity.
Polmos Polonaise Vodka 80 proof $10.99.   **88**
Clear. Medium- to full-bodied. Notes of licorice, lavender, violets. Soft, deep texture.
Intense, perfume-like fragrance is dominant. A superb style matching elegance with
strength.

Scale: Superlative (96-100), Exceptional (90-95), Highly Recommended (85-89),
Recommended (80-84), Not Recommended (Under 80)

Polmos Extra Zytnia Vodka 80 proof $10.99.   **93**

Clear. Medium- to full-bodied. Notes of citrus, pine, anise. An impression of sweetness is found in the soft, rich texture. Bold, distinctive flavors are united by great structure. Deep, lingering finish.

Polmos Koszerna, Prawdziwa Zytnia (Cherry Flavored) 80 proof $10.99.   **86**

Pale ruby. Medium-bodied. Notes of currants, herbs, wet stone. Tart, light texture. Delicate flavors and fragrance blend with an impression of sweetness. Clean finish with a note of minerals.

Pszeniczna (Poland)

Pszeniczna Vodka 80 proof $18/500 ml.   **84**

Clear. Moderately full-bodied. Dried herbs, minerals. Clean aromatics lurk behind a touch of heat. Neutral and viscous in the mouth but finishes with decided burn.

Rain (USA)

Rain 1995 Harvest Vodka 80 proof $17.   **90**

Clear. Moderately full-bodied. Lavender, sweet herbs, orange peel, sesame. Moderately rich, silky texture. Somewhat lush and full on the palate. A very pretty style with engaging fragrance and nice fruit accents and a grainy touch. Quite well rounded into the finish.

Rain 1996 Harvest Vodka 80 proof $17.   **86**

Clear. Medium-bodied. Honey, vegetables. Aggressively aromatic with a wave of unusual but complex flavors. Relatively light in the mouth with a clean and edgy palate. Finishes with a touch of heat. Interesting, but a specialized taste.

Riva (USA)

Riva Vodka 80 proof $5.99.   **NR**

Schenley (USA)

Schenley Superior Vodka 80 proof $6.49.   **NR**

Skol (USA)

Skol Vodka 80 proof $4.99.   **81**

Clear. Medium-bodied. Minerals. A slightly hot and neutral nose leads to a viscous neutral palate. Finishes with a slight burn.

Skyy (USA)

Skyy Vodka 80 proof $13.99.   **85**

Clear. Medium-bodied. Charcoal, minerals, licorice, marshmallow. Tight, oily texture. Somewhat of a toasted-grain mouthfeel. Picks up a touch of heat quickly, yet has a lively, briny sensation.

Smirnoff (Russia)

Smirnoff Vodka (Black Label) 80 proof $17.99.   **90**

Clear. Medium- to full-bodied. Notes of lemon, white pepper, charcoal. Full, bold texture. Smoky sensation on the palate is followed by a burst of rich flavor and spice. Impeccable structure is evidenced by the long, silky finish.

Smirnoff (USA)

Smirnoff Vodka (Red Label) 80 proof $7.99.   **NR**

Smirnoff Vodka (Black Label) 100 proof $10.99.   **88**

Clear. Medium- to full-bodied. Notes of mint, wet stone. Rich, mellow texture. On the palate there is a fascinating hot/cold sensation, aided by strong herbal components. A deep, strong finish indicates the high proof.

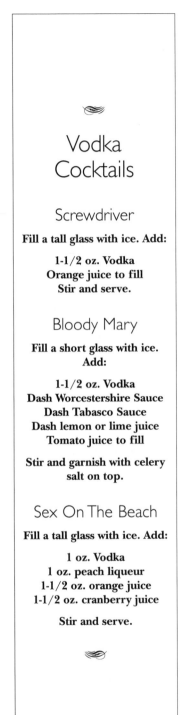

Vodka Cocktails

Screwdriver

Fill a tall glass with ice. Add:

**1-1/2 oz. Vodka
Orange juice to fill
Stir and serve.**

Bloody Mary

**Fill a short glass with ice.
Add:**

**1-1/2 oz. Vodka
Dash Worcestershire Sauce
Dash Tabasco Sauce
Dash lemon or lime juice
Tomato juice to fill**

**Stir and garnish with celery
salt on top.**

Sex On The Beach

Fill a tall glass with ice. Add:

**1 oz. Vodka
1 oz. peach liqueur
1-1/2 oz. orange juice
1-1/2 oz. cranberry juice**

Stir and serve.

Sobieski (Poland)
*Sobieski Pure Rye Vodka
80 proof $18/700ml.*　　**84**
Colorless. Medium-bodied. Flint, herbs. Forward flinty aromas show a decided touch of heat. Clean but fiery in the mouth with a decided burn to the finish.

Soomskaya (Ukraine)
*Soomskaya Horilka
Prehodko, Herb Flavored
Vodka 80 proof $15.*　　**89**
Clear. Moderately full-bodied. Lemon sorbet, wild herbs, flowers. Rich, lush texture. Fruity and spicy, with a sweet/tart entry. Has subtle hints of exotic flora, with good presence and depth. Expansive, somewhat soft finish.

*Soomskaya Riabinovaya, Ashberry
Flavored Vodka 80 proof $16.*　　**92**
Salmon with a copper-dark pink cast. Moderately full-bodied. Wildflowers, honey, dried cranberries, minerals. Bold yet soft texture. Superb integration of decadent spicy, wild aromatics and rich, succulent flavors. Has an elegant, refined presence with strong weight on the finish. An exotic drink.

St. Petersburg (Russia)
*St. Petersburg Russian Vodka
80 proof $14.99/L.*　　**87**
Clear. Medium-bodied. Minerals, anise. Muted aromatics carry a slightly mineral quality. Lighter in the mouth with a slight burn to the finish.

Star of Russia Vodka (Russia)
Star of Russia Vodka 80 proof $15.99.　　**91**
Clear. Medium- to full-bodied. Notes of citrus, charcoal, minerals. Oily and rich on the palate. A hint of smoke covers delicate flavors. Very assertive with a long, lingering finish.

Staraya Moskva (Russia)
*Staraya Moskva Premium
Russian Vodka 80 proof $14.*　　**92**
Clear. Medium-bodied. Sweet herbs, citrus peel, dried flowers. Smooth texture. Soft yet rich palate. Flavorful and aromatic with plenty of lively fruit and floral nuances. Holds together quite well into an expansive, silky finish.

Scale: Superlative (96-100), Exceptional (90-95), Highly Recommended (85-89), Recommended (80-84), Not Recommended (Under 80)

Stolichnaya (Russia)

Stolichnaya Vodka 80 proof $16. **91**

Clear. Moderately full-bodied. Wet stone, anise, dried herbs, charcoal. Rich, smooth texture. Excellent integration with a great interplay of focused flavors riding on a lush, expansive palate. Quite long and deep in the finish. A classic.

Stolichnaya Ohranj, Orange Flavored Vodka 70 proof $16.99. **90**

Clear. Medium-bodied. Citrus, tangerine, minerals, nut oil. Smooth, luxurious mouthfeel. Lovely fragrant and highly flavored entry. Carries a nice stony backnote to broaden its tropical character. The orange flavors play through to the rich, expansive finish.

Stolichnaya Persik, Peach Flavored Vodka 70 proof $16.99. **92**

Clear. Medium-bodied. Sweet peach, melon, apricot, vanilla. Soft, silky texture almost like a cordial in its sweetness and nearly syrupy mouthfeel. Gorgeous, lush sweet flavors throughout. A perfect after-dinner drink.

Stolichnaya Gold Vodka 80 proof $26.95. **93**

Clear. Full-bodied. Wet stone, pine, dried herbs, coconut. Rich, thick texture. Big, bold palate with a broad feel. Deeply spiced, with lighter flavors dominated by mineral notes. An intense drink ideal with caviar or smoked seafood.

Sweedish (Sweden)

Sweedish Svedka Vodka 80 proof $9.99. **84**

Clear. Medium-bodied. Custard, vanilla. Unusual aromas are attractive and show a measure of complexity. Lighter in the mouth with a decided note of heat through the finish.

Tanqueray (England)

Tanqueray Sterling Citrus Vodka 80 proof $13.99. **89**

Clear. Medium-bodied. Notes of lemon, orange, honey. Soft, silky texture. An impression of sweetness on the palate is followed by a light dose of spice. Tangy, lively finish.

Tanqueray Sterling Vodka 80 proof $16. **90**

Clear. Medium-bodied. Lemon peel, minerals, dried mint. Moderately rich, rounded texture. Smooth, with a nice rush of flavor on the palate. Has a zippy, vibrant feel which carries into the finish.

Van Hoo (Belgium)

Van Hoo Vodka. $16. **91**

Clear. Moderately full-bodied. Juniper, citrus, minerals, exotic peppercorns. Richly textured. Full, yet soft on the palate with beautiful floral aromas and flavors. Similar to a heavy Gin, this one waits for some green olives and smoked fish.

Wyborowa (Poland)

Wyborowa Orange Flavored Vodka 76 proof $12. **86**

Clear. Moderately light-bodied. Citrus, sweet beets, minerals. Compact texture. Well-knit, with light, dried, snappy fruit flavors and a deep, flint-edged palate. Quite dry and crisp in the finish.

Wyborowa Pineapple Flavored Vodka 76 proof $12. **80**

Clear. Medium-bodied. Pineapple, mango, nut oil, mocha. Smooth, delicate texture. Moderately rich and oily on the palate. Contains a high dosage of tropical fruit flavors and nutty brown-spice backnotes. Quite bright in the finish.

Wyborowa Vodka 80 proof $12.   88

Clear. Moderately full-bodied. Sweet potato, sugar snap peas, sweet lemon grass, minerals. Lush, rounded texture. Smooth as clear ice on a pond, this glides across the palate. Soft, elegant measures of light sweetness help round out the profile. Deep, lingering finish.

Youri Dolgoruki (Russia)

Youri Dolgoruki Vodka 80 proof $29/700ml.   91

Clear. Moderately full-bodied. Lemon zest, white pepper. Crisp and clean aromatics carry a bright citrus edge. Exceptionally smooth and viscous in the mouth with no burn. Oily and intense.

Highly Rated Vodka

Vodka

96 • Grey Goose (France) Vodka 80 Proof. $27.
95 • Nord (Poland) Biata Zimna Vodka 80 Proof. $26.
94 • Minsk Distillery (Belarus) Charodei Vodka 80 Proof. $24.99/700ml.
94 • Canadian Iceberg (Canada) Vodka 80 Proof. $15.99.
93 • Stolichnaya (Russia) Gold Vodka 80 Proof. $26.95.
93 • Polmos (Poland) Extra Zytnia Vodka 80 Proof. $10.99.
92 • Staraya Moskva (Russia) Premium Russian Vodka 80 Proof. $14.
91 • Youri Dolgoruki (Russia) Youri Dolgoruki Vodka 80 Proof. $29/700ml.
91 • Van Hoo (Belgium) Vodka $16.
91 • Stolichnaya (Russia) Vodka 80 Proof. $16.
91 • Star of Russia Vodka (Russia) 80 Proof. $15.99.
91 • Baik (Russia) Baikalskaya Vodka 80 Proof. $12.99.
90 • Tanqueray (England) Sterling Vodka 80 Proof. $16.
90 • Smirnoff (Russia) Vodka (Black Label), Black Label Vodka 80 Proof. $17.99.
90 • Rain (USA) 1995 Harvest Vodka 80 Proof. $17.
90 • Georgievskaya (Russia) Russian Vodka 80 Proof. $29.99/L.
90 • Denaka (Denmark) Vodka 80 Proof. $9.99.
90 • Belvedere (Poland) Belvedere Vodka 80 Proof. $29.99.
89 • Ketel One (Holland) Vodka 80 Proof. $16.99.
89 • Fris (Denmark) Vodka Skandia 80 Proof. $15.99.
89 • Elduris (Iceland) Icelandic Vodka 80 Proof. $12.99.
89 • Banff (Canada) Banff ICE Vodka 80 Proof. $21.
88 • Wyborowa (Poland) Vodka 80 Proof. $12.
88 • Smirnoff (USA) Vodka (Black Label) 100 Proof. $10.99.
88 • Polmos (Poland) Polonaise Vodka 80 Proof. $10.99.
88 • Luksusowa (Poland) Triple Distilled Potato Vodka 80 Proof. $14.95.
88 • Black Death (Belgium) Vodka 80 Proof. $11.99.
87 • St. Petersburg (Russia) Russian Vodka 80 Proof. $14.99/L.
87 • Kremlyovskaya (Russia) Vodka 80 Proof. $12.99.
87 • Chopin (Poland) Chopin Vodka 80 Proof. $29.99.
87 • Bäälta (Lithuania) Lithuanian Vodka 80 Proof. $14.95.

Scale: Superlative (96-100), Exceptional (90-95), Highly Recommended (85-89), Recommended (80-84), Not Recommended (Under 80)

87 • Attakiska (USA) Alaskan Vodka 80 Proof. $12.99.

86 • Rain (USA) 1996 Harvest Rain Vodka 80 Proof. $17.

86 • Old Kiev (Ukraine) Ukranian Vodka 80 Proof. $14.49.

86 • Icy (Iceland) Vodka of Iceland 80 Proof. $9.99.

86 • Hooghoudt (Holland) Royalty Vodka 80 Proof. $12.99.

86 • Finlandia (Finland) Vodka of Finland 80 Proof. $15.

86 • Everclear (USA) Vodka 84 Proof. $11.50.

86 • CK Vodka (Poland) Polish Vodka 80 Proof. $16/700ml.

86 • Alps (France) French Vodka 80 Proof. $28.

85 • Skyy (USA) Vodka 80 Proof. $13.99.

85 • Polmos (Poland) Jazz Jamboree Vodka 80 Proof. $10.99.

85 • Original (Poland) Polish Vodka 80 Proof. $11.66.

85 • Kristall Dzidrais (Latvia) Vodka 80 Proof. $14.95.

85 • Carmel (Israel) Vodka 80 Proof. $10.99.

Flavored Vodka

92 • Stolichnaya (Russia) Persik, Peach Flavored Vodka 70 Proof. $16.99.

92 • Soomskaya (Ukraine) Riabinovaya, Ashberry Flavored Vodka 80 Proof. $16.

91 • Carmel (Israel) Citron Vodka 80 Proof. $10.99.

90 • Stolichnaya (Russia) Ohranj, Orange Flavored Vodka 70 Proof. $16.99.

89 • Tanqueray (England) Sterling Citrus Vodka 80 Proof. $13.99.

89 • Soomskaya (Ukraine) Horilka Prehodko, Herb Flavored Vodka 80 Proof. $15.

86 • Wyborowa (Poland) Orange Flavored Vodka 76 Proof. $12.

86 • Polmos (Poland) Koszerna, Prawdziwa Zytnia (Cherry Flavored) 80 Proof. $10.99.

86 • Absolut (Sweden) Citron, Citrus Flavored Vodka 80 Proof. $14.99.

seven

Gin

"Why don't you slip out of those wet clothes and into a dry martini?"

– Robert Benchley

An Overview

The Basis of Gin

Gin and its Lowlands cousin Genever (Jenever in Belgium) are white spirits that are flavored with juniper berries and so-called botanicals (a varied assortment of herbs and spices). The spirit base of Gin is primarily grain (usually wheat or rye), which results in a light-bodied spirit.

Genever is made primarily from "malt wine" (a mixture of malted barley, wheat, corn, and rye), which produces a fuller-bodied spirit similar to raw malt whisky. A small number of genevers in Holland and Belgium are distilled directly from fermented juniper berries, producing a particularly intensely flavored spirit.

The chief flavoring agent in both Gin and Genever is the highly aromatic blue-green berry of the juniper, a low-slung evergreen bush (genus *Juniperus*) that is commercially grown in northern Italy, Croatia, the United States, and Canada. Additional botanicals can include anise, angelica root, cinnamon, orange peel, coriander, and cassia bark. All Gin and Genever makers have their own secret combination of botanicals, the number of which can range from as few as four to as many as 15.

Distillation of Gin

Most Gin is initially distilled in efficient column stills. The resulting spirit is high-proof, light-bodied, and clean with a minimal amount of congeners (flavor compounds) and flavoring agents. Genever is distilled in less-efficient pot stills, which results in a lower-proof, more flavorful spirit.

Low-quality "compound" gins are made by simply mixing the base spirit with juniper and botanical extracts. Mass-market gins are produced by soaking juniper berries and botanicals in the base spirit and then redistilling the mixture.

Top-quality Gins and Genevers are flavored in a unique matter. After one or more distillations the base spirit is redistilled one last time. During this final distillation the alcohol vapor wafts through a chamber in which the dried juniper berries and botanicals are suspended. The vapor gently extracts aromatic and flavoring oils and compounds from the berries and spices as it travels through the chamber on its way to the condenser. The resulting flavored spirit has a noticeable degree of complexity.

Classifications of Gin

London Dry Gin is the dominant English style of Gin. As a style it lends itself particularly well to mixing. London Dry Gin is the dominant Gin style in the United Kingdom, former British colonies, the United States, and Spain.

Plymouth Gin is relatively full-bodied (when compared to London Dry Gin). It is clear, slightly fruity, and very aromatic. Originally the local Gin style of the English Channel port of Plymouth, modern Plymouth Gin is nowadays made only by one distillery in Plymouth, Coates & Co., which also controls the right to the term Plymouth Gin.

Gin
at a Glance

Top Scores:

Genever

**88 • Leyden (Holland)
Dry Gin 80 Proof. $18.99.**

Gin

**98 • Bombay (England)
Sapphire London Dry Gin
94 Proof. $17.99.**

Old Tom Gin is the last remaining example of the original lightly sweetened gins that were so popular in 18th-century England. The name comes from what may be the first example of a beverage vending machine. In the 1700s some pubs in England would have a wooden plaque shaped like a black cat (an "Old Tom") mounted on the outside wall. Thirsty passersby would deposit a penny in the cat's mouth and place their lips around a small tube between the cat's paws. The bartender inside would then pour a shot of Gin through the tube and into the customer's waiting mouth. Until fairly recently limited quantities of Old Tom-style Gin were still being made by a few British distillers, but they were, at best, curiosity items.

Genever or **Hollands** is the Dutch style of Gin. Genever is distilled from a malted grain mash similar to that used for whisky. *Oude* ("old") Genever is the original style. It is straw-hued, relatively sweet and aromatic. *Jonge* ("young") Genever has a drier palate and lighter body. Some genevers are aged for one to three years in oak casks. Genevers tend to be lower proof than English gins (72-80% ABV is typical). They are usually served straight up and chilled. The classic accompaniment to a shot of Genever is a dried green herring. Genever is traditionally sold in a cylindrical stoneware crock. Genever-style Gins are produced in Holland, Belgium, and Germany.

Gin Regions

The United Kingdom produces mostly dry Gin, primarily from column stills. British Gins tend to be high proof (90° or 45% ABV) and citrus-accented from the use of dried lemon and Seville orange peels in the mix of botanicals. British gins are usually combined into mixed drinks.

Holland and **Belgium** produce Genever, mostly from pot stills. Genevers are distilled at lower proof levels than English gins and are generally fuller in body. Many of these gins are aged for one to three years in oak casks. Some Genever producers now market fruit-flavored genevers, the best known being black currant. Dutch and Belgian Genevers are usually chilled and served neat.

Germany produces a Genever-style Gin called *Dornkaat* in the North Sea coast region of Frisia. This spirit is lighter in body and more delicate in flavor than both Dutch Genever and English dry Gin. German Gin is usually served straight up and cold.

Spain produces a substantial amount of Gin, all of it in the London Dry style from column stills. Most of it is sold for mixing with cola.

The United States is the world's largest Gin market. London Dry Gin accounts for the bulk of domestic Gin production, with most of it being produced in column stills. American Dry Gins (often termed "soft" Gins) tend to be lower proof (80° or 40% ABV) and less flavorful than their English counterparts ("hard" Gins). This rule applies even to brands such as Gordon's and Gilbey's, which originated in England. America's best-selling Gin, Seagram's Extra Dry, is a rare cask-aged Dry Gin. Three months of aging in charred oak barrels gives the Gin a pale straw color and a smooth palate.

Gin – Origins and History

Gin is a juniper berry-flavored grain spirit. The word is an English shortening of Genever, the Dutch word for juniper. The origins of Gin are rather murky. In the late 1580s a juniper-flavored spirit of some sort was found in Holland by British troops who were fighting against the occupying Spanish in the Dutch War of Independence. They gratefully drank it to give them what they soon came to call "Dutch courage" in battle. The Dutch themselves were encouraged by their government to favor such grain spirits over imported wine and brandy by lack of excise taxes on such local drinks.

A clearer beginning was a few decades later in the 1600s when a Dr. Franciscus de la Boë in the university town of Leiden created a juniper and spice-flavored medicinal spirit that he promoted as a diuretic. Genever soon found favor across the English Channel; first as a medicine (Samuel Pepys wrote in 1660 of curing a case of "colic" with a dose of "strong water made with juniper") and then as a beverage.

When the Dutch Protestant William of Orange and his English wife Mary became co-rulers of England after the "Glorious Revolution" drove James II from the throne, he moved to discourage the importation of brandy from the Catholic wine-making countries by setting high tariffs. As a replacement he promoted the production of grain spirits ("corn brandy" as it was known at the time) by abolishing taxes and licensing fees for the manufacture of such local products as Gin. History has shown that prohibition never works, but unfettered production of alcohol has its problems, too. By the 1720s it was estimated that a quarter of the households in London were used for the production or sale of Gin. Mass drunkenness became a serious problem. The cartoonist Hogarth's famous depiction of such behavior in "Gin Lane" shows a sign above a Gin shop that states, "Drunk for a penny/Dead drunk for twopence/Clean straw for Nothing." Panicky attempts by the government to prohibit Gin production, such as the Gin Act of 1736, resulted in massive illicit distilling and the cynical marketing of "medicinal" spirits with such fanciful names as Cuckold's Comfort and My Lady's Eye Water.

The Martini and the Meaning of Life

The best known of hundreds of Gin-based mixed drinks is the Gin and white vermouth combination called the Martini. As is usually the case with most popular mixed drinks, the origins of the martini are disputed. One school of thought holds that it evolved from the late-19th-century Martinez cocktail, a rather cloying mixture of Old Tom-style Gin and sweet vermouth. A dissenting sect holds that it was created in the bar of the Knickerbocker Hotel in New York City in the early 20th century. The ratio of Gin to vermouth started out at about 2 to 1, and it has been getting drier ever since. The great British statesman Winston Churchill, who devoted a great deal of thought and time to drinking, was of the opinion that passing the cork from the vermouth bottle over the glass of Gin was sufficient. The martini has frequently served as a metaphor for some of the great social and political issues of our times. President Jimmy Carter denounced the "three martini lunch" in a thinly-veiled attempt at class warfare during his election campaign. He was not reelected.

A combination of reimposed government controls, the growth of high-quality commercial Gin distillers, the increasing popularity of imported rum, and a general feeling of public exhaustion gradually brought this mass hysteria under control, although the problems caused by the combination of cheap Gin and extreme poverty extended well into the 19th century. Fagin's irritable comment to a child in the film *Oliver*—"Shut up and drink your Gin!"—had a basis in historical fact.

Starting in the 18th century the British Empire began its worldwide growth; and wherever the Union Jack went, English-style Gins followed. In British North American colonies such celebrated Americans as Paul Revere and George Washington were notably fond of Gin, and the Quakers were well known for their habit of drinking Gin toddies after funerals.

The arrival of the Victorian era in England in the mid-19th century ushered in a low-key rehabilitation of Gin's reputation. The harsh, sweetened "Old Tom" styles of Gin of the early 1700s slowly gave way to a new cleaner style called Dry Gin. This style of Gin became identified with the city of London to the extent that the term "London Dry" Gin became a generic term for the style, regardless of where it was actually produced.

Genteel middle-class ladies sipped their sloe Gin (Gin flavored with sloe berries) while consulting Mrs. Beeton's *Book of Household Management* (a wildly popular Victorian era cross between the *Joy of Cooking* and Martha Stewart lifestyle books) for Gin-based mixed drink recipes. The British military, particularly the officer corps, became a hotbed of Gin consumption. Hundreds of Gin-based mixed drinks were invented and the mastery of their making was considered part of a young officer's training. The best known of these cocktails, the Gin and Tonic, was created as a way for Englishmen in tropical colonies to take their daily dose of quinine, a very bitter medicine used to ward off malaria. Modern tonic water still contains quinine, though as a flavoring rather than a medicine.

In Holland the production of Genever was quickly integrated into the vast Dutch trading system. The port of Rotterdam became the center of Genever distilling, as distilleries opened there to take advantage of the abundance of needed spices that were arriving from the Dutch colonies in the East Indies (present-day Indonesia). Many of today's leading Dutch Genever distillers can trace their origins back to the 16th and 17th centuries. Examples include such firms as Bols (founded 1575) and de Kuyper (1695).

Belgium developed its own juniper-flavored spirit, called *Jenever* (with a "j"), in a manner similar to that in Holland (which controlled Belgium for a time in the early 19th century). The two German invasions of Belgium in World Wars I and II had a particularly hard effect on Jenever producers, as the occupying Germans stripped the distilleries of their copper stills and piping for use in the production of shell casings. The remaining handful of present-day Belgian Jenever distillers produce Jenever primarily for the local domestic market.

Gin may have originated in Holland and developed into its most popular style in England, but its most enthusiastic modern-day consumers are to be found in Spain, which has the highest per capita consumption in the world. Production of London Dry-style Gin began in the 1930s, but serious consumption did not begin until the mix of Gin and Cola became inexplicably popular in the 1960s.

Gin production in the United States dates back to colonial times, but the great boost to Gin production was the advent of National Prohibition in 1920. Moonshining quickly moved in to fill the gap left by the shutdown of commercial distilleries, but the furtive nature of illicit distilling worked against the production of the then-dominant whiskies, all of which required some aging in oak casks. Bootleggers were not in a position to store and age illegal whiskey, and the caramel-colored, prune-juice-dosed grain alcohol substitutes were generally considered to be vile.

Gin, on the other hand, did not require any aging, and was relatively easy to make by mixing raw alcohol with juniper berry extract and other flavorings and spices in a large container such as a bathtub (thus the origin of the term "Bathtub Gin"). These Gins were generally of poor quality and taste, a fact that gave rise to the popularity of cocktails in which the mixers served to disguise the taste of the base Gin. Repeal of Prohibition at the end of 1933 ended the production of bootleg Gin, but Gin remained a part of the American beverage scene. It was the dominant white spirit in the United States until the rise of Vodka in the 1960s. It still remains popular, helped along recently by the revived popularity of the Martini.

Reviews

Barclay's (USA)
Barclay's London Dry Gin 80 proof $6.99.   **81**
Clear. Moderately light-bodied. Light floral aromas lead a soft, light texture with a delicate mouthfeel and a quick finish. Features perceptible juniper flavors throughout.

Barton (USA)
Barton London Extra Dry Gin 80 proof $4.99.   **81**
Clear. Delightfully attractive citrus zest aromas. Smooth and silky on the palate, though it lacks the complexity and cut of London Dry styles. Fine for a martini, this would get lost in tonic.

Beefeater (England)
Beefeater London Distilled Gin 94 proof $14.99.   **92**
Clear. Forcefully aromatic, with extravagant juniper character showing through. A note of viscosity on the palate reinforces the fat, juniper berry impression. The finish is long, rich, and complex. A very stylish, hedonistic Gin.

Bokma (Holland)
Bokma Jonge Graanjenever 70 proof $25.95/L.   **84**
Clear. Heavy, mildly earthy aromas. Rich, viscous, and oily mouthfeel. This will be best appreciated from the freezer. Flavors are quite subdued.

Erven Lucas Bols (Holland)
Erven Lucas Bols Genever Gin 80 proof $14.99.   **86**
Clear. Medium-bodied. Notes of licorice, minerals, dried herbs. Soft texture. Pungent and assertive on the palate. Intense, dry feel with an abundance of tart flavors. Enjoy ice cold with smoked fish.

Bombay (England)
Bombay London Dry Gin 86 proof $13.99.   **92**
Clear. Medium-bodied. Notes of citrus, spice, stone. Soft, delicate texture. All components are superbly balanced in a seamless, captivating fashion.
Bombay Sapphire London Dry Gin 94 proof $17.99.   **98**
Clear. Moderately full-bodied. Aromas of juniper, eucalyptus and spice are powerfully present. The mouthfeel reveals a rich, plush texture. A powerful style, loaded with high-toned, engaging floral aromatics and assertive fruit elements. Quite pungent all the way through the finish.

Boodles (England)
Boodles British Gin 90 proof $12.99.   **96**
Clear. Medium- to full-bodied. Notes of citrus, flowers, spices. Rich, silky texture. Loaded with fragrance, a combination of power and finesse as it lingers with a smooth, oily finish.

Booth's (USA)
Booth's Distilled London Dry Gin 90 proof $7.99.   **80**
Clear. Medium- to light-bodied. Notes of spices, gum, minerals. Silky texture. Soft feel on the palate serving a light dose of fragrance. Easy, delicate style.

Cadenhead (England)
Cadenhead Old Raj Dry Gin 110 proof $55.95.   **89**

Washed out yellow tinge. Oily, tart juniper aromas. Markedly spicy and warm with alcohol heat asserting on the finish. Botanicals seem rather subdued.

Citadelle (France)
Citadelle Gin 88 proof $20.   **85**

Clear. Medium-bodied. Piney, resinous aromas speak of a strong juniper accent. Flavors follow from the aromas, with a silky mouthfeel. Very smooth.

Cork (Ireland)
Cork Dry Gin 80 proof $9.99.   **89**

Clear. Medium- to full-bodied. Notes of dried flowers, fresh herbs, oriental spices. Rich texture. Pungent on the palate, offering a broad spectrum of deep fragrances. Oily, deep finish. A sipper.

Crystal Palace (USA)
Crystal Palace Premium London Dry Gin 80 proof $5.99.   **81**

Clear. Mild citrus zest aromas with subtle botanical notes. Straightforward on the palate with an impression of citrus oil through the finish.

Fleischmann's (USA)
Fleischmann's Extra Dry Gin 80 proof $6.99.   **NR**

W. & A. Gilbey (USA)
W. & A. Gilbey Gilbey's London Dry Gin 80 proof $9.99.   **88**

Clear. Medium- to light-bodied. Notes of spices, minerals, dried herbs. Delicate, creamy texture. Good combination of rich aromatics, packaged in an elegant, refined style. Soft, light finish.

Glenmore (USA)
Glenmore London Dry Gin 80 proof $6.99.   **NR**

Gordon's (USA)
Gordon's London Dry Gin 80 proof $10.20.   **87**

Clear. Medium-bodied. Moderately spicy, floral and minty aromas lead a rounded, smooth mouthfeel with licorice flavors coming through on the deeply flavored finish. Lacks fruity richness on the midpalate.

Greenall's (England)
Greenall's Original London Dry Gin 94 proof $9.99.   **85**

Clear. Medium-bodied. Notes of citrus, stone, fresh herbs. Smooth texture. Bright and assertive on the palate. Richly spiced and well flavored, this would be well suited to ice and a twist of citrus peel.

Leyden (Holland)
Leyden Dry Gin 80 proof $18.99.   **88**

Clear. Moderately light-bodied. Attractive aromas show citrus zest and sweet herbal character. The palate shows an oily, plush texture that reveals softer, more delicate flavors that follow the aromas. A very subtle, fragrant style, less pungent than the best London Dry examples.

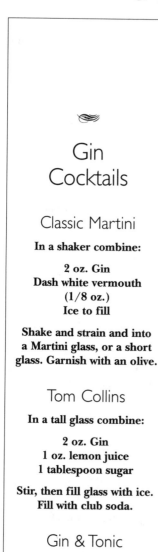

❧

Gin Cocktails

Classic Martini

In a shaker combine:

2 oz. Gin
Dash white vermouth
(1/8 oz.)
Ice to fill

Shake and strain and into a Martini glass, or a short glass. Garnish with an olive.

Tom Collins

In a tall glass combine:

2 oz. Gin
1 oz. lemon juice
1 tablespoon sugar

Stir, then fill glass with ice. Fill with club soda.

Gin & Tonic

Fill a tall glass with ice. Add:

1-1/2 oz. Gin
Tonic water to fill

Garnish with a lime slice.

❧

Mr. Boston (USA)
Mr. Boston English Market Brand Extra Dry Gin 80 proof $6.99.　　**80**
Clear. Medium-bodied. Reserved aromas show a soft herbal and citrus zest character. The palate shows an oily texture with sweet berry flavors and a quick, lightly spicy finish. Though lacking the aromatic intensity of more classic examples, this has pleasant flavors.

Plymouth (England)
Plymouth Original Gin 82.4 proof $24.　　**83**
Clear. Markedly tangy citrus zest and anise aromas, with a hint of licorice. Anise and juniper flavors come through on the palate with a smooth mouthfeel and a warm finish.

Riva (USA)
Riva London Dry Gin 80 proof $6.99.　　**83**
Clear. Moderately light-bodied. The aromas are marked by a fruity, citrus peel character. The texture is quite straightforward, although there are high-toned fruity flavors that will cut through mixers.

Schenley (USA)
Schenley London Dry Gin 80 proof $7.49. **NR**

H.W. Schlichte (Germany)
H.W. Schlichte Steinhaeger Dry Gin 80 proof $15.99.　　**NR**

Seagram's (USA)
Seagram's Extra Dry Gin 80 proof $7.99.　　**86**
Pale straw. Moderately light-bodied. Fat, lush sweet citrus-peel aromas are a standout and a signature of this Gin. Shows a softly textured mouthfeel and flavors that follow from the nose. Finish falls off rather quickly. The aromas are the dominant characteristic. Could eschew mixers and stand on its own merits.

Tanqueray (England)
Tanqueray Special Dry Gin 94.6 proof $16.　　**93**
Clear. Pungent, aggressive citrus and juniper aromas. Very flavorsome with tart cut snappy spice and alcohol heat on the finish. Very persistent.
Tanqueray Original 1839 Recipe Malacca Gin 80 proof $18.　　**92**
Clear. Extraordinarily floral with complex botanicals. The mouthfeel is a standout, rounded and mildly viscous, with juniper notes that linger.

Scale: Superlative (96-100), Exceptional (90-95), Highly Recommended (85-89), Recommended (80-84), Not Recommended (Under 80)

Highly Rated Gin

Genever

88 • Leyden (Holland) Dry Gin 80 Proof. $18.99.

86 • Erven Lucas Bols (Holland) Genever Gin 80 Proof. $14.99.

Gin

98 • Bombay (England) Sapphire London Dry Gin 94 Proof. $17.99.

96 • Cock, Russel, & Co. (England) Boodles British Gin 90 Proof. $12.99.

93 • Tanqueray (England) Special Dry Gin 94.6 Proof. $16.

92 • Tanqueray (England) Original 1839 Recipe Malacca Gin 80 Proof. $18.

92 • Bombay (England) London Dry Gin 86 Proof. $13.99.

92 • Beefeater (England) London Distilled Gin 94 Proof. $14.99.

89 • Cork (Ireland) Dry Gin 80 Proof. $9.99.

89 • Cadenhead (England) Old Raj Dry Gin 110 Proof. $55.95.

88 • W. & A. Gilbey (USA) Gilbey's London Dry Gin 80 Proof. $9.99.

87 • Gordon's (England) London Dry Gin 80 Proof. $10.20.

86 • Seagram's (USA) Extra Dry Gin 80 Proof. $7.99.

85 • Greenall's (England) Original London Dry Gin 94 Proof. $9.99.

85 • Citadelle (France) Gin 88 Proof. $20.

eight

❧

Liqueurs

❧

A History and Overview – Liqueurs, Schnapps, Anise, and Bitters

Liqueurs, Schnapps, Anise, and Bitters are terms that cover a wide variety of types of spirits. What they all share in common is that they are flavored spirits.

Liqueurs (also known as **Cordials**) are sweet, flavor-infused spirits that are categorized according to the flavoring agent (i.e., fruits, nuts, herbal and spice blends, creams and such). The word liqueur comes from the Latin *liquifacere* ("to dissolve") and refers to the dissolving of flavorings in the spirits. Artificial flavorings are strictly regulated in most countries, and where allowed, must be prominently labeled as such.

Top-quality liqueurs are produced by distillation of either the fermented flavor materials or the spirit in which they have been infused. Many liqueurs use finished spirits such as Cognac, Rum, or Whisky as their base. Others macerate fruit or other flavorings in a neutral spirit. Crèmes (crème de menthe, crème de cacao, etc.) are liqueurs with a primary flavor (a single, dominant flavor rather than a mix), while cream liqueurs combine dairy cream and alcohol in a homogenized, shelf-stable blend.

All liqueurs are blends, even those with a primary flavor. A touch of vanilla is added to crème de cacao in order to emphasize the chocolate. Citrus flavor notes sharpen the presentation of anise. Herbal liqueurs may contain dozens of different flavor elements that a master blender manipulates to achieve the desired flavor profile.

Liqueurs are not usually aged for any great length of time (although their base spirit may be), but may undergo resting stages during their production in order to allow the various flavors to "marry" into a harmonious blend.

Liqueurs can be hard to classify, but regardless of flavor they can be broadly divided into two categories. *Generics* are liqueurs of a particular type (Crème de Cacao or Curaçao, for example) that can be made by any producer. *Proprietaries* are liqueurs with trademarked names that are made according to a specific formula. Examples of such liqueurs include Kahlúa, Grand Marnier, and Southern Comfort.

Schnapps is a general term used for an assortment of white and flavored spirits that have originated in northern countries or regions such as Germany or Scandinavia. Schnapps can be made from grain, potatoes, or molasses and be flavored with virtually anything (Watermelon and Root Beer Schnapps from the United States being proof of that). The dividing line between Schnapps and Flavored Vodka is vague and is more cultural than stylistic, although European Schnapps tend to be drier than their American counterparts and liqueurs.

Anise-Flavored Spirits can vary widely in style depending on the country of origin. They can be dry or very sweet, low or high proof, distilled from fermented aniseed or macerated in neutral spirit. In France, *Anis* (as produced by Pernod) is produced by distilling anise and a variety of other botanicals together. *Pastis* is macerated, rather than distilled, and contains fewer botanicals than Anis. In Italy, Sambucca is distilled from anise and botanicals, but is then heavily sweetened to make it a liqueur. Oil of fennel (also known as green anise) is frequently added to boost the aroma of the spirit. Greece has a drier, grappa-like liqueur called Ouzo, which is stylistically close to pastis.

Bitters are the modern-day descendents of medieval medical potions and are marketed as having at least some vaguely therapeutic value as stomach settlers or hangover cures. They tend to be flavored with herbs, roots, and botanicals, contain lower quantities of fruit and sugar than liqueurs, and have astringent notes in the palate.

Reviews

99 Bananas (USA)
99 Bananas Banana Schnapps Liqueur 99 proof $14.99.   NR

After Shock (USA)
After Shock Hot & Cool Cinnamon Liqueur 40 proof $19.   81

Bright, neon cherry-red hue. Pungent hot cinnamon aromas. A thick, syrupy entry leads to a full-bodied palate with marked sweetness offset by a rush of spiciness. Hot, minty finish. Interesting, but rather artificial.

Alizé (France)
Alizé Passion Fruit & Cognac 32 proof $8/375 ml.   82

Hazy, bright yellow-orange hue. Pungent grapefruit aromas. A rounded attack leads to a medium-bodied palate with a touch of viscosity. Citrus flavors expand in the mouth. Rich, pithy finish.

Amaretto di Amore (Italy)
Amaretto di Amore Classico Liqueur 42 proof $11.99.   86

Deep mahogany hue. Generous caramel and almond aromas. A viscous attack leads to a full-bodied, sweet palate. Thick and rich. Syrupy but not cloying, flavorful finish.

Amaretto di Saronno (Italy)
Amaretto di Saronno Originale Liqueur 56 proof $22.   92

Brilliant, bright amber hue. Spirity almond and spice aromas. A lush entrance leads to a moderately full-bodied palate with moderate sweetness. Explodes in flavor on the midpalate. Precise, persistent finish.

Baileys (Ireland)
Baileys Original Irish Cream Liqueur 34 proof $18.   88

Deep milky-brown hue. Interesting spirity, minty aromas. Full-bodied. A thick, viscous attack leads to a full-bodied, rich mouthfeel. Exceptionally rich. Very lengthy, flavorful finish.

Basilica (Italy)
Basilica Amaretto Classico Liqueur 48 proof $17.   81

Deep mahogany hue. Subdued sweet caramel and nut aromas. A viscous entry leads to a full-bodied, spirity palate with moderate sweetness. Quick finish.

Basilica Sambuca Liquore Tradizionale 76 proof $17.   NR

Benedictine (France)

Benedictine Dom B&B Liqueur 80 proof $27.   **95**

Deep amber-orange hue. Pungent spice and herb aromas.
A smooth, mildly sweet attack leads to a medium-bodied, mildly
viscous palate. Complex, lingering finish. Intense, warming,
and unique. A classic.

Blanca de Navarra (Spain)

Blanca de Navarra Blackberry Liqueur 34 proof $15/L.   **89**

Deep, reddish cola-brown hue. Interesting perfumed plum, blackberry, and spice
aromas. A lush attack leads to a medium-bodied palate with marked sweetness. Quick
fade to the finish. Very interesting aromatically.

Blanca de Navarra Green Apple Liqueur 38 proof $15/L.   **84**

Clear. Sweet coconut, apple, and herb aromas show a measure of complexity. A sweet
attack is offset by lean acidity that provides a tart backdrop. Moderately full-bodied.
Fades at the finish. Interesting, particularly aromatically.

Blanca de Navarra Hazelnut Liqueur 38 proof $15/L.   **88**

Bright straw cast. Intense, perfumed, hazelnut aroma. A viscous
entry leads to a moderately full-bodied palate with marked
sweetness. The nutty flavors translate through to the finish,
but lack substantial grip or intensity. Tasty nonetheless.

Blanca de Navarra Lemon Liqueur 38 proof $15/L.   **85**

Hazy, bright yellow-green hue. Aggressive tart citrus aromas. A viscous attack leads to a
thick, full-bodied mouthfeel with moderate sweetness. Smooth, lingering, citrus finish.
An assertive, if slightly syrupy, rendition.

Blanca de Navarra Melon Liqueur 38 proof $15/L.   **81**

Very pale yellow-straw hue. Opulent and explosive honeydew melon aromas. A syrupy
attack leads to a moderately full-bodied palate with marked sweetness. Melon flavors
translate to the finish, but wind up rather cloying.

Blanca de Navarra Peach Liqueur 38 proof $15/L.   **88**

Clear. Pungent aromas of fresh peach smell not the least bit artificial. A sweet entry leads
to a medium-bodied palate with clean and precise flavors. Lengthy, persistent finish. An
admirable effort with a fruit that is usually very difficult to translate.

Blanca de Navarra Pear Liqueur 38 proof $15/L.   **83**

Clear. Subdued, perfumed, floral pear aromas. A sweet attack leads to a medium-bodied
palate. Sugary finish. More sweetness than flavor, but very interesting aromatically.

Blanca de Navarra Raspberry Liqueur 34 proof $15/L.   **88**

Brilliant, pale brick-red hue. Generous ripe raspberry aromas. A sweet entry leads
to a medium-bodied palate. Sweetness is offset by a hint of astringency in the mouth.
Flavorful, ripe finish.

Edmond Briottet (France)

Edmond Briottet Creme de Framboise 36 proof $24.50.   **84**

Pale violet hue. Candied raspberry aromas. Sweet and juicy with an artificial fruit flavor
resonating through the finish. Not a fantastically concentrated or faithful rendition.

Edmond Briottet Creme de Mûre 36 proof $25.   **88**

Deep ruby red hue. Fruit pulp aromas are suggestive of plum skins. Thick, medicinal,
hugely cloying, sweet plummy flavors have a marzipan-like finish. Distinctive, unusual.

Liqueurs at a Glance

Top Scores:

Anise

94 • Opal Nera (Italy)
Sambuca Liquore Alla
80 Proof. $22.

Bitters

91 • Fernet Branca (Italy)
Bitters Liqueur 80 Proof. $27.

Chocolate Liqueur

92 • Mozart (Austria) Original
Salzburger Chocolate Liqueur
34 Proof. $22.

Coffee Liqueur

93 • Tia Maria (Jamaica)
Coffee Liqueur 53 Proof. $22.

Cream Liqueur

93 • McCormick's (Ireland)
Irish Cream Liqueur
34 Proof. $10.99.

Edmond Briottet Creme de Cassis
de Dijon 40 proof $26.95. **90**
Deep ruby hue. Fantastically pure black currant aromas. Very sweet and thick on the palate, also showing a rich cassis character with fruit acids seeming to linger in the sweet finish. Outstandingly concentrated, just a drop will make a kir.

Campari (Italy)
Campari Bitter Liqueur 48 proof $15. **89**
Bright pale cherry-pink color. Piercingly herbal with a blast of bitterness and fruity notes. Hugely bitter and zesty with a searing, tangy finish. Highly concentrated, this needs a shot of something and ice. Leaves the tastebuds very alive.

Canton (China)
Canton Delicate Ginger Liqueur
40 proof $21. **88**
Pale amber hue. Pungent ginger aromas. A rich entry leads to a medium-bodied palate with intense gingery flavors. Shows a mild honey-like sweetness through the finish. If you like ginger, this is it, pure and unadulterated.

Caravella (Italy)
Caravella Limoncello Originale d'Italia
64 proof $14.99. **84**
Cloudy lime-peel appearance. Fresh citrus zest aromas have a distinctly lemony quality. Syrupy and sweet, with a strong zest character that none of the tart lemon flavors in the bouquet would lead you to expect. This will add a zesty tang to any cocktail.

Carolans (Ireland)
Carolans Finest Irish Cream Liqueur
34 proof $9.99. **84**
Deep milky brown hue. Forward, spirity, whiskey-accented lactic flavors. A rich, milky attack leads to a moderately full-bodied palate with a touch of sweetness. Subtle finish.

Chambord (France)
Chambord Royale Deluxe Liqueur
33 proof $14/375 ml. **92**
Rich ruby red hue. Sweet raspberry jam aromas follow faithfully on the thick, sweet, somewhat syrupy palate. The essential ingredient for a Kir Royale. Just add a touch to a glass of Champagne. This would be outstanding over vanilla ice cream, or as a dessert in itself.

Scale: Superlative (96-100), Exceptional (90-95), Highly Recommended (85-89),
Recommended (80-84), Not Recommended (Under 80)

Chartreuse (France)

Chartreuse Liqueur Fabriquée Yellow
80 proof $28. **89**

Pale green-straw appearance. Rather subdued
aromas with a trace of floral and anise. Sweet and
lush on the entry with a distinct anise note and a
mildly cloying floral finish.

Chartreuse Liqueur Fabriquée Green
110 proof $32. **94**

Rich emerald green hue. Fiery aromas show anise
and pepper notes. Exotically herbal and complex.
Intensely hot and spicy with spirity warmth and
anise notes upfront. Finishes with extraordinary
flavor complexity and length.

Chartreuse Liqueur Fabriquée V.E.P
108 proof $75/200 ml. **98**

Bright lime-green luster. Extraordinary perfumed
anise, pine, and herb aromas are complex, with a
touch of spirity heat. Very complex, and changing.
Sweet and intensely flavored on the palate with the
sweetness fading to leave a focused piney, spicy
finish that takes on a fiery note.

Chi Chi's (USA)

Chi Chi's Margarita
20 proof $9.99/1750 ml. **NR**

Chi Chi's Mexican Mudslide
25 proof $9.99/1750 ml. **83**

Thick, milky light brown hue. Generous nut and
chocolate aromas. A rich, creamy entry leads to
a full-bodied, flavorful palate with mild sweetness.
Very flavorful and smooth finish. Chocolate-
dominated and rich.

Cointreau (France)

Cointreau Liqueur 80 proof $28. **93**

Clear. Subdued, clean, piercing orange oil aromas.
A viscous attack leads to a spirity, full-bodied palate.
Orange flavors are very natural and focused. Clean,
fiery finish with a hint of sweetness.

Cristal (Colombia)

Cristal Reserva Especial, Aquardiente
Extra Fino 65 proof $14.99. **83**

Clear. Sweet, candied anise. Mildly viscous with a
reasonably dry palate that finishes cleanly.

Cynar (Italy)

Cynar Liqueur 33 proof $15. **88**

Brownish-amber hue. Earthy, bitter herb aromas
have a zesty accent. Tangy and sweet upfront,
turning very herbal and bitter through the finish.
A drier style.

Flavored Brandy Liqueur

100 • Grande Marnier (France)
Cuvée Spéciale 1827-1977 Cent
cinquantenaire Liqueur $180.

Fruit Liqueur

98 • Emil Scheibel (Germany)
Black Forest Marillen-Liqueur,
Cherry Liqueur 64 Proof.
$27.95/375 ml.

Herb/Spice Liqueur

98 • Chartreuse (France)
Liqueur Fabriquée V.E.P 108
Proof. $75/200 ml.

Nut Liqueur

96 • Frangelico (Italy)
Frangelico Hazelnut Liqueur
48 Proof. $18.99.

Schnapps

95 • Rumple Minze (Germany)
Original Peppermint Schnapps
100 Proof. $25.

DeKuyper (USA)

DeKuyper Butter Shots Butterscotch Schnapps 30 proof $9.   87

Clear. Delightful, delicious butterscotch aromas. Flavors follow through from the aromas. Pure, hedonistic butterscotch flavors with a syrupy mouthfeel. This could be poured over a pound cake or even ice cream.

DeKuyper Hot Damn! Hot Cinnamon Schnapps 48 proof $9.   NR

DeKuyper Original Peachtree Schnapps 43 proof $9.   82

Clear. Sweet, candied peach aromas. Although a touch contrived and very sweet, this has undeniable appeal if you have a sweet tooth. Notably syrupy.

DeKuyper Sour Apple Pucker Schnapps 30 proof $9.   83

Shocking discotheque green. Crisp, freshly cut Granny Smith apple aromas with an artificial candied note. Sweet candied apple flavors upfront turn very sharp and juicy through the finish. Rather syrupy in texture.

Dr. McGillicuddy's (Canada)

Dr. McGillicuddy's Mentholmint Schnapps 48 proof $13.   87

Clear. Strikingly pure minty aromas. Fresh, cool minty flavors are not too masked by sugary sweetness, allowing this to have a long, cool finish. Impressive.

Dr. McGillicuddy's Vanilla Schnapps 48 proof $13.   81

Clear. Sweet, sugary aromas with a vanilla accent. Thick, sweet, and syrupy palate. Vanilla flavors do not get going until the finish, where they linger. This will appeal to those with a sweet tooth.

Drambuie (Scotland)

Drambuie Prince Charles Edward's Liqueur 70 proof $25.   92

Bright yellow-amber cast. Generous licorice, mineral, and buckwheat honey aromas. A syrupy, viscous entry leads to a full-bodied palate with marked sweetness and peaty scotch overtones. Rich, spirity, flavorful finish. Intense and unique. A classic.

Durango (USA)

Durango Rockslide Pie 25 proof $10.99/1750 ml.   82

Deep milky-chocolate hue. Pungent nut, truffle, and nougat aromas. A milky entry leads to a rich mouthfeel. Assertively flavorful though somewhat artificial finish.

E & J Distillers (USA)

E & J Distillers Cask & Cream Brandy and Cream Liqueur 34 proof $11.99.   82

Milky, café au lait hue. Unusual herb and cream aromas have a spirity edge. A rich attack leads to a rather viscous, moderately full-bodied palate. Clipped, milky finish.

Extase (France)

Extase Liqueur d'Orange & Cognac XO 80 proof $41.66/L.   86

Brilliant, pale amber-orange hue. Generous, spirity orange aromas. A rounded, fiery entrance leads to a medium-bodied palate with mild sweetness and a touch of viscosity. Warming, spirity finish. Straightforward, but flavorful.

Fernet Branca (Italy)

Fernet Branca Bitters Liqueur 80 proof $27.   91

Dark brown with an orange cast. Fresh peppermint aromas are very distinctive. A huge blast of menthol assaults the palate with a drying, bitter herb finish. Very dry and concentrated.

Scale: Superlative (96-100), Exceptional (90-95), Highly Recommended (85-89), Recommended (80-84), Not Recommended (Under 80)

Domaine des Forges (France)
*Domaine des Forges Poirelle, Liqueur de Poire William au Cognac XO
56 proof $22.*   84
Brilliant pale copper hue. Subtle spirity, flower, pear, and mineral aromas. A smooth
attack leads to a flavorful, mildly sweet, medium-bodied palate. Clipped, rounded finish.

Frangelico (Italy)
*Frangelico Frangelico Hazelnut Liqueur
48 proof $18.99.*   96
Deep yellow-straw hue. Pungent, hedonistic hazelnut and vanilla
aromas. A lush attack leads to a medium-bodied and flavorful palate
with mild sweetness. Very well balanced. Flavorful, lengthy finish.
Exotic, pure, and intense.

Galliano (Italy)
Galliano Liquore L'Autentico 70 proof $14/375 ml.   91
Neon greenish-yellow hue. Pungent anise, herb, and mineral aromas. A syrupy, sweet
entry leads to a rich, full-bodied palate that bursts with anise flavor. Lengthy, intense
finish. Powerful and rich with lingering sweetness.

Godet (Belgium)
Godet Belgian White Chocolate Liqueur 30 proof $13/375 ml.   86
Pale, milky, café au lait hue. Generous, slightly unusual, candied white chocolate aromas.
A viscous, milky entry leads to a full-bodied, thick white chocolate flavored palate. Rich,
thick finish.

Godiva (USA)
Godiva Chocolate Liqueur 34 proof $12/375 ml.   81
Deep mahogany hue. Subdued caramel and milk chocolate aromas. A rich, viscous
attack leads to a moderately full-bodied palate with bright chocolate flavors. Candied
but not cloying through the finish.

Goldschläger (Switzerland)
*Goldschläger Cinnamon Schnapps Liqueur with Gold Flakes
87 proof $12/375 ml.*   91
Clear with gold leaf flakes. Spicy, cinnamon aromas with alcohol vapors. The palate has a
sweet, syrupy quality with very marked hot spicy flavors that linger. Has a hot bite to the finish.

Grand Monarch (USA)
Grand Monarch Orange & Brandy Liqueur 80 proof $13.95/L.   80
Brilliant pale amber hue. Subtle orange aromas are muted by a hot, spirity accent.
A viscous attack leads to a moderately full-bodied palate with a candied-orange
character. Fiery finish.

Grande Marnier (France)
Grande Marnier Triple Orange Liqueur. $30.   94
Deep amber-orange hue. Pronounced, intense orange and chocolate aromas. A viscous,
spirity, mildly sweet attack leads to a moderately full-bodied palate with an explosion
of flavor. Rich, intense, lengthy, exotic finish.

*Grande Marnier Cuvée du Centenaire 1827-1927 Triple Orange
Liqueur. $95.*   98
Very deep amber-orange hue. A mild spirity nose carries mellow orange and spice
aromas. An exceptionally smooth entry leads to a medium-bodied, smooth palate with
a touch of sweetness. Cognac plays an integral part in this mellow and exceedingly
complex nectar. Smooth, generous finish.

Grande Marnier Cuvée Spéciale 1827-1977 Cent cinquantenaire Liqueur. $180. 100

Very deep amber-orange hue. Generous brown spice, orange, and caramel aromas explode from the glass. A viscous, rich attack leads to a full-bodied palate. Exceptionally intense yet well-integrated flavors with a big, old cognac accent. Outrageous, lengthy finish. A gustatory, post-dinner experience.

Granier (France)

Granier Mon Pastis 90 proof $19.95/L. 86

Clear. Heavy, oily sweet aromas. Turns a weak milky tea color when water is added. Mildly sweet with heavy licorice and anise flavors that linger through the finish. Markedly spicy on the finish.

Heering (Denmark)

Heering Original Cherry Liqueur 48 proof $18. 94

Deep ruby red hue. Heavily spiced cherry aromas lead a thick, sweet palate with abundant spiced cocktail-cherry flavors. Intense and markedly sweet.

Hellinger (South Africa)

Hellinger Pflaume Fine German Style Schnapps 86 proof $10/500 ml. 84

Flowers, pear, and cantaloupe. Tight, compact texture. Soft and sweet aromatics. Very crisp and spicy palate. Engaging, with tart flavors and a bit of heat building up.

Hellinger Apfel Fine German Style Schnapps, Oak Matured 86 proof $15/500 ml. 83

Bright, deep yellow. Lemon cream pie, maple sugar, sweet flowers. Tight, compact texture. Lovely aromatics provide an illusion, as the palate differs greatly. Quite dry with a restrained feel. Could use more depth.

Inga (Italy)

Inga Antico Amaro di Serravalle Rare Herbal Liqueur 60 proof $13.99/375 ml. NR

Irish Mist (Ireland)

Irish Mist Liqueur 70 proof $22. 92

Chestnut, with a deep copper cast. Christmas fruit cake, sweet herbs, citrus. Broad, rich texture. Lovely, deep palate replete with rich honeyed flavor. Sweet whisky notes come forth into the long, smooth finish. A great counterpart to its Scottish 'cousin'.

Jägermeister (Germany)

Jägermeister Herbal Liqueur 70 proof $18.99. 90

Dark amber-brown. Sweet medicinal, spice aromas. Notably sweet and thick on the palate with complex herbs and cinnamon lingering. Quite clean through the finish for all the complex flavors present.

Kahlúa (Mexico)

Kahlúa Licor de Café 53 proof $22. 93

Very deep blackish-mahogany hue. Intense coconut, coffee, and chocolate aromas.
A viscous, spirity attack leads to a full-bodied palate with marked sweetness. Explosively flavorful finish.

Kaloyannis (Greece)

Kaloyannis Ouzo No. 12 86 proof $19.95. 88

Clear, but turns a milky white with water. Very pure anise flavors with a dry lingering finish. Delightfully clean.

Scale: Superlative (96-100), Exceptional (90-95), Highly Recommended (85-89), Recommended (80-84), Not Recommended (Under 80)

Laird's Applejack (USA)
Laird's Applejack 4 Years Old 80 proof $9.99.   **80**

Gold with an orange cast. Moderately light-bodied. Notes of apples, toasted oats, honey. Smooth, soft texture. Round and slightly lush on the palate. A nice offering of tart and sweet apple flavors embellished by light spice. Well suited as a mixer. This interesting blend of apple brandy and neutral grain spirits deserves a category of its own, but we have decided to include it here.

Licor 43 (Spain)
Licor 43 Liqueur 62 proof $18.99.   **83**

Pale yellow-amber hue. Subdued orange and spice aromas carry a touch of heat. A sweet, syrupy entry leads to a full-bodied, viscous palate. Rich, straightforward, warming finish.

Liquore Strega (Italy)
Liquore Strega Special Liqueur 80 proof $23.99.   **89**

Optic yellow-green hue. Pungent sweet herb, anise, and fruit peel aromas. A rich, viscous entry leads to a moderately full-bodied palate with a rush of minty herbal flavors and a touch of heat. Flavorful, fairly sweet finish.

Los Camichines Distillery (Mexico)
Los Camichines Distillery Agavero Tequila Liquer 80 proof $39.99.   **89**

Amber. Moderately full-bodied. Maple syrup, mandarin, mocha, tobacco leaf. Silky, viscous texture. Lovely, syrupy sweet palate replete with lush flavors and fragrance. Has a soft, rich, pleasantly expanding finish.

Luxardo (Italy)
Luxardo Sambuca dei Cesari Liqueur 76 proof $9.95/375 ml.   **90**

Clear. Spicy, heavy anise aromas. A touch drier than expected, yet with a viscous, thick mouthfeel and a lingering finish of intense anise. Not excessively cloying.

Luxardo Limoncello Liqueur 48 proof $18.95.   **81**

Brilliant luminescent lime green. Candied citrus aromas have a lemony theme. Tangy, distinctly confected flavors are not unpleasant though not very reminiscent of lemon.

Luxardo Amaro Liqueur Abano 60 proof $19.95.   **93**

Dark brown with an orange rim. Sweetish aromas suggest peppermint, herbs, and brown spice. Markedly sweet on the palate with complex flavors following the aromas. Very viscous. The finish has an assertive citrus zest quality with a drier character.

Luxardo Amaretto di Saschira Liqueur 56 proof $20.50.   **89**

Deep tawny amber hue. Pungent, attractive sweet almond, caramel, and orange aromas. A viscous attack leads to a full-bodied palate with marked sweetness. Enticing, flavorful finish. Sweet, but balanced.

Luxardo Morlacco Cherry Liqueur, Liquore di Marasca 60 proof $20.95.   **86**

Deep ruby hue. Sweet cherry aromas follow through on a lighter palate with sweet red cherry flavors showing a trace of natural tartness.

Luxardo Triplum Triple Sec Orange Liqueur 78 proof $21.95.   **87**

Clear. Subdued nut and orange aromas show a touch of heat. A viscous attack leads to a full-bodied, fiery palate. Hot, sweet finish.

Luxardo Luxardo il Maraschino Originale 64 proof $25.95.   **90**

Clear. Intense mineral, cinnamon, and cherry aromas. A thick, viscous entry leads to a full-bodied palate with marked sweetness. Intense, flavorful finish. Big and rich with a purity of flavor and real complexity.

Luxardo Luxardo Perla Dry Riserva Speciale 80 proof $29.95.   **90**

Clear. Decidedly grappa-like aromas with a dried herbal, mineral accent. Cinnamon, floral. Very sweet and thick on the palate with complex sweet herbal flavors that develop through the midpalate and linger on the finish. Shows a notable alcohol warmth.

Mandarine Napoleon (Belgium)

Mandarine Napoleon Grande Liqueur Impériale 76 proof $38.   **84**

Very deep amber-orange hue. Pungent herb, tangerine, and mint aromas carry a touch of heat. A moderately sweet, viscous attack leads to a fiery, full-bodied palate. Rich, warming, flavorful finish. Interesting, but certainly quite spiry.

Mandarine Napoleon Mandarine Impériale XO Limited Edition Liqueur 80 proof $184.   **90**

Bright, pale pinkish-amber hue. Subdued, warming tangerine and herb aromas. A smooth entry leads to a moderately full-bodied palate with a touch of sweetness. Deeply flavored and intense. Lingering, velvety finish with a touch of heat.

Marie Brizard (France)

Marie Brizard Kiwi Strawberry Liqueur 34 proof $11.99.   **81**

Brilliant "Star Wars cantina" optic green hue. Bright, pungent green apple aromas. A sweet entry leads to a medium-bodied palate. Clean flavors emerge from the sweetness. OK for the disco bar crowd.

Marie Brizard Orange Banana Liqueur 34 proof $11.99.   **80**

Slightly hazy, deep golden-yellow. Bright, clean lemon citrus aromas. A smooth attack leads to a sweet, light-bodied palate. Sugary, watery finish. Aromatic, but straightforward and cloying in the mouth.

Marie Brizard Watermelon Liqueur 34 proof $11.99.   **80**

Bizarre optic pink hue. Pronounced bubble gum and watermelon aromas. A very syrupy attack leads to a full-bodied, viscous mouthfeel. Flavorful but cloying finish.

Marie Brizard Banana Strawberry Liqueur 34 proof $12.99.   **NR**

Marie Brizard Pineapple Coconut Liqueur 34 proof $12.99.   **NR**

Marie Brizard Cassis de Bordeaux Liqueur 30 proof $18.99.   **81**

Ruby-brown hue. Sweet, lush berry-fruit-cordial aromas follow through. Syrupy, nectarous texture with very sweet fruit-centered flavors. Finishes in a very sweet cloying manner.

Marie Brizard Anisette Liqueur 50 proof $19.99.   **90**

Clear. Rather unusual aromas of herbs and anise. Thick, very sweet and syrupy with an herbal, oily quality, as well as anise flavors that linger through the finish.

G.E. Massenez (France)

G.E. Massenez Crème de Framboise 40 proof $18/375 ml.   **81**

Pale cherry red. Perfumed sweet raspberry aromas. Very sweet, cooked raspberry flavors are quite subtle. Hugely sweet and cloying. Subtly flavored, this will also lend a pale blush to cocktails.

Mazzetti d'Altavilla (Italy)

Mazzetti d'Altavilla Mazzetti Frutti e Grappa Peach 32 proof $12.99.   **83**

Hazy pale peach hue. Pungent candied peach aromas. A sweet, rounded attack leads to a moderately full-bodied palate. Marked sweetness defines the thick finish. A straightforward candied fruit liqueur.

McCormick's (Ireland)

McCormick's Irish Cream Liqueur 34 proof $10.99. **93**

Milky, deep taupe hue. Pleasant, rich cocoa aromas. A thick entry leads to a very rich and flavorful palate. Lengthy finish, with a great persistence of flavor.

F. Meyer (France)

F. Meyer Liqueur de Framboise, Raspberry Liqueur
50 proof $14.95/375 ml. **81**

Pale orange hue. Faintly fruity, floral aromas. Markedly sweet, subtle raspberry flavors finish with a touch of heat. Mouthfeel is not overly thick.

F. Meyer Liqueur de Poire William's, Williams Pear Liqueur
50 proof $14.95/375 ml. **83**

Clear with a faint greenish tint. Sweet candied pear aromas. Quite sweet on the palate though not cloying, with fleshy pear flavors quite pronounced. Nice lingering finish.

F. Meyer Liqueur de Fraise, Strawberry Liqueur
40 proof $16.95/375 ml. **85**

Pale strawberry blush. Candied sweet fruit aromas. Thick and syrupy with cloying strawberry flavors. Very sweet indeed, though this does convey some fruit ripeness.

Midori (Mexico)

Midori Melon Liqueur 42 proof $17. **81**

Bright, neon Kelly green color. Generous, candied melon and apple aromas. A sweet, syrupy attack leads to a full-bodied palate. Flavorful, sugary finish. Interesting, but on the artificial side.

Millwood (Holland)

Millwood Amaretto Cream Liqueur 34 proof $16. **89**

Pale milky-taupe hue. Pungent amaretto-like aromas. A thick, viscous attack leads to a rich and dense mouthfeel. Quite flavorful and lengthy through the well-balanced finish.

Millwood Whiskey Cream Liqueur 34 proof $16. **80**

Deep milky, café au lait hue. Spoiled-milk aromas. Lighter viscous palate. Subtle finish.

Monarch (USA)

Monarch Coffee Liqueur 53 proof $7.95/L. **NR**

Monarch Hazelnut Liqueur 48 proof $8.40/L. **83**

Pale straw hue. Forward, candied-nut aromas. A light, viscous attack leads to a medium-bodied palate with mild sweetness. Fades on the spirity finish.

Mozart (Austria)

Mozart Original Salzburger Chocolate Liqueur 34 proof $22. **92**

Deep milky-brown hue. Intense, unusual nougat, truffle, and milk chocolate aromas. A very thick entry leads to a rich, viscous mouthfeel with intense bittersweet chocolate flavor. Only mildly sweet. Thick, creamy finish.

Mr. Boston (USA)

Mr. Boston Peppermint Schnapps Liqueur 30 proof $4.99. **83**

Colorless. Sweet, minty aromas. The palate shows a note of syrupy thickness with strong mint flavors coming through, though not persisting.

Mr. Boston Blackberry Flavored Brandy 70 proof $6.99. **82**

Very dark reddish-amber hue. Artificial, candied blackberry aromas with a spirity edge. A sweet, rounded entry leads to a medium-bodied palate. Warming, viscous finish.

Mr. Boston Creamy Egg Nog 30 proof $6.99/1750 ml.   **89**

Thick, creamy taupe hue. Very full-bodied. Generous eggnog aromas feature a rich brandy and nutmeg accent. A thick, rich attack leads to a full-bodied palate. Flavorful, generous finish. An excellent bottled eggnog.

Opal Nera (Italy)

Opal Nera Sambuca Liquore Alla 80 proof $22.   **94**

Dark purple-red hue. Sweet cordial and licorice aromas. Very hot and spicy on the palate with a heavy note of black licorice that lingers on the finish. Thick, sweet, and syrupy. Quite complex.

Pernod (France)

Pernod Spiritueux Anise 80 proof $19.95.   **93**

Brilliant lime green. Pungent citrus zest and anise aromas. Turns a milky lime green with water. Dry, marked anise and bergamot flavors with a dry finish. Quite complex.

Pimm's (England)

Pimm's Original No. 1 Cup 50 proof $15.   **86**

Orange-brown hue. Displays very attractive sweet orange peel aromas. Sweet on the palate, but not cloying. Tangy, subtle herbal bittters with brown spice develop on the finish.

Prado (France)

Prado Pastis de Marseille 90 proof $19.95/L.   **91**

Orange-brown hue. Turns a light tan color with water. Spicy anise aromas. Intense anise flavors with a hot, spicy, tongue-numbing quality and a long spicy finish. Dried fruit notes.

Ramazzotti (Italy)

Ramazzotti Sambuca Liqueur 76 proof $15.99.   **83**

Clear. Muted aromas show a touch of anise. Rather sweet and syrupy with a lingering finish showing alcohol heat and sweet anise.

Ramazzotti Amaro Felsina Ramazzotti 60 proof $16.99.   **87**

Deep orange-brown. Sweet citrus peel, herb, peppermint, and spice aromas. Markedly sweet and minty with caramelized flavors and sweetness that takes over through the finish.

RMS Distillery (USA)

RMS Distillery Pear de Pear Liqueur 60 proof $22/375 ml.   **92**

Deep orange hue. Exotically spiced aromas. Not overly sweet, with a spiced, cooked-pear quality that finishes in a caramelized manner. Quite complex and very appealing.

Romana Black (Italy)

Romana Black Sambuca Classica Liqueur 80 proof $11/375 ml.   **88**

Dark purple-red. Peppery licorice aromas. Very syrupy and thick, with a sweet anise- and licorice-laden finish. Not overly sweet.

Roncoco (USA)

Roncoco The Original Coconut Rum Liqueur 48 proof $8.99/.   **NR**

Rumple Minze (Germany)

Rumple Minze Original Peppermint Schnapps 100 proof $25.   **95**

Clear. Assertive peppermint aroma. Medium-bodied. Distinctive minty character with the alcohol heat highlighted by full menthol notes. Hot finish.

Scale: Superlative (96-100), Exceptional (90-95), Highly Recommended (85-89), Recommended (80-84), Not Recommended (Under 80)

Sabra (Israel)
Sabra Chocolate Orange Liqueur 60 proof $18.   88

Deep orange-amber hue. Forward chocolate, orange, and nut aromas. A rounded, spirity attack leads to a medium-bodied palate with mild sweetness. Intense bittersweet chocolate flavors guide the warming finish.

Sabroso (Mexico)
Sabroso Licor de Café 48 proof $8.99.   84

Deep mahogany hue. Powerful, highly roasted coffee aromas. A viscous attack leads to a full-bodied palate with marked sweetness. Flavorful, but straightforward and very sweet finish.

Sambuca di Amore (Italy)
Sambuca di Amore Classico Liqueur 84 proof $12.99.   89

Clear. Fusel oil, licorice aromas. Alcohol heat comes through on the midpalate and warms the finish. Decidedly sweet, with a syrupy mouthfeel and lingering sweetness.

Sambuca Romana (Italy)
Sambuca Romana Liquore Classico 84 proof $22.   89

Clear. Oily, fusel oil, sweet anise aromas. Thick, sweet, and viscous with a distinctly oily note through the finish.

Emil Scheibel (Germany)
Emil Scheibel Black Forest Marillen-Liqueur, Cherry Liqueur
64 proof $27.95/375 ml.   98

Orange-brown hue. Pungent spice and marzipan aromas with some spirity heat. Searing and intense with a concentrated cherry note and some heat and spice on the finish. Outstandingly faithful.

Emil Scheibel Black Forest Quitten-Liqueur, Quince Liqueur
70 proof $27.95/375 ml.   86

Pale yellow-gold. Exotic aromas of spiced fruits are very quince-like. On the palate not overly thick or sweet, with candied fruit flavors that give way to a lingering sweet finish.

Emil Scheibel Black Forest Wald-Himbeer-Liqueur,
Wild Raspberry Liqueur 70 proof $27.95/375 ml.   86

Pale cherry hue. Sweet cooked raspberry aromas. Sweet on the entry though the finish is rather spirity and metallic.

Emil Scheibel Black Forest Kirsch-Liqueur Cherry Liqueur 70 proof
$29.95/375 ml.   90

Pale ruby hue. Spicy, medicinal cherry aromas lead a thick, very sweet palate with a syrupy quality and a touch of alcohol warmth. Intense, faithful black cherry flavors explode on the palate and persist through the finish.

Silvia (Italy)
Silvia Crema di Limoncello Liqueur 31 proof $19.99.   80

Cloudy, pearl-hued. Milky, lemon zest aromas are somewhat alarming. Creamy caramel-like flavors show a citrus undertone, particularly on the finish.

St. Brendan's (Ireland)
St. Brendan's Superior Irish Cream Liqueur 34 proof $12.99.   81

Milky, café au lait hue. Pungent milky, lactic, toasted coconut aromas. A creamy attack leads to a viscous, creamy palate. Rich, mildly sweet finish. Carries an unusual note to the nose, but tasty on the palate.

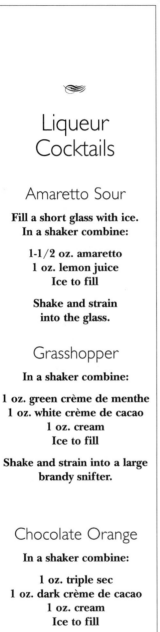

Liqueur Cocktails

Amaretto Sour

**Fill a short glass with ice.
In a shaker combine:**

**1-1/2 oz. amaretto
1 oz. lemon juice
Ice to fill**

**Shake and strain
into the glass.**

Grasshopper

In a shaker combine:

**1 oz. green crème de menthe
1 oz. white crème de cacao
1 oz. cream
Ice to fill**

**Shake and strain into a large
brandy snifter.**

Chocolate Orange

In a shaker combine:

**1 oz. triple sec
1 oz. dark crème de cacao
1 oz. cream
Ice to fill**

**Shake and strain into a
large brandy snifter.**

Tequila Rose (USA)
*Tequila Rose Strawberry Flavored Cream
Liqueur & Tequila 34 proof $15.99.*   **81**
Milky-pink Pepto Bismol hue. Confected strawberry
aromas. A rich, viscous attack leads to a milky, full-
bodied palate. Lingering strawberry flavored finish.

Tia Maria (Jamaica)
Tia Maria Coffee Liqueur 53 proof $22.   **93**
Deep tawny amber hue. Pungent caramel, sugarcane, and coffee aromas. A rounded attack leads
to a medium-bodied palate with an explosion of
flavor. Well balanced and lengthy.

Trimbach (France)
*Trimbach Liqueur de Framboise,
Raspberry Liqueur 50 proof $25.*   **93**
Fading ruby hue. Spicy, complex raspberry aromas.
Apparent oak aging. Warm spicy flavors are very
attractive and complex with a lingering aftertaste
of raspberry fruit.
*Trimbach Liqueur de Poire, Pear Liqueur 70
proof $36/375 ml.*   **86**
Yellow-golden hue. Powerful aromas of spicy pears.
Sweet and syrupy texture on the palate, though just
the right side of cloying, with a lingering persistence
of pear and spice.

Villa Massa (Italy)
*Villa Massa
Liquore di Limoni
60 proof $19.99.* **86**
Brilliant, luminous
lime green. Scented
lemon candy aromas
with zesty peel notes.
Flavors are strikingly
lemony on entry,
picking up a candied
note through the
finish.

Wild Sint Maarten (Saint Maarten)
*Wild Sint Maarten Guavaberry
Island Folk Liqueur 50 proof $18.*   **84**
Deep reddish-mahogany hue. Unusual berry,
cinnamon, and ginger aromas. A rounded attack
leads to a medium-bodied palate with a touch of
sweetness. Flavorful and well balanced through
the finish. Unique and well done.

Highly Rated Liqueurs

Anise

94 • Opal Nera (Italy) Sambuca Liquore Alla 80 Proof. $22.

93 • Pernod (France) Spiritueux Anise 80 Proof. $19.95.

91 • Prado (France) Pastis de Marseille 90 Proof. $19.95/L.

90 • Marie Brizard (France) Anisette Liqueur 50 Proof. $19.99.

90 • Luxardo (Italy) Sambuca dei Cesari Liqueur 76 Proof. $9.95/375 ml.

89 • Sambuca Romana (Italy) Liquore Classico 84 Proof. $22.

89 • Sambuca di Amore (Italy) Classico Liqueur 84 Proof. $12.99.

88 • Romana Black (Italy) Sambuca Classica Liqueur 80 Proof. $11/375 ml.

88 • Kaloyannis (Greece) Ouzo No. 12 86 Proof. $19.95.

86 • Granier (France) Mon Pastis 90 Proof. $19.95/L.

Bitters

91 • Fernet Branca (Italy) Bitters Liqueur 80 Proof. $27.

89 • Campari (Italy) Bitter Liqueur 48 Proof. $15.

Chocolate Liqueur

92 • Mozart (Austria) Original Salzburger Chocolate Liqueur 34 Proof. $22.

88 • Sabra (Israel) Chocolate Orange Liqueur 60 Proof. $18.

86 • Godet (Belgium) Belgian White Chocolate Liqueur 30 Proof. $13/375 ml.

Coffee Liqueur

93 • Tia Maria (Jamaica) Coffee Liqueur 53 Proof. $22.

93 • Kahlúa (Mexico) Licor de Café 53 Proof. $22.

Cream Liqueur

93 • McCormick's (Ireland) Irish Cream Liqueur 34 Proof. $10.99.

89 • Mr. Boston (USA) Creamy Egg Nog 30 Proof. $6.99/1750 ml.

89 • Millwood (Holland) Amaretto Cream Liqueur 34 Proof. $16.

88 • Baileys (Ireland) Original Irish Cream Liqueur 34 Proof. $18.

Flavored Brandy Liqueur

100 • Grande Marnier (France) Cuvée Spéciale 1827-1977 Cent cinquantenaire Liqueur $180.

98 • Grande Marnier (France) Cuvée du Centenaire 1827-1927 Triple Orange Liqueur $95.

95 • Benedictine (France) Dom B&B Liqueur 80 Proof. $27.

94 • Grande Marnier (France) Triple Orange Liqueur $30.

90 • Mandarine Napoleon (Belgium) Mandarine Impériale XO Limited Edition Liqueur 80 Proof. $184.

86 • Extase (France) Liqueur d'Orange & Cognac XO 80 Proof. $41.66/L. Fruit Liqueur

Fruit Liqueur

98 • Emil Scheibel (Germany) Black Forest Marillen-Liqueur, Cherry Liqueur 64 Proof. $27.95/375 ml.

94 • Heering (Denmark) Original Cherry Liqueur 48 Proof. $18.

93 • Trimbach (France) Liqueur de Framboise, Raspberry Liqueur 50 Proof. $25.

93 • Cointreau (France) Liqueur 80 Proof. $28.

92 • RMS Distillery (CA) Pear de Pear Liqueur 60 Proof. $22/375 ml.

92 • Chambord (France) Royale Deluxe Liqueur 33 Proof. $14/375 ml.

90 • Luxardo (Italy) Luxardo il Maraschino Originale 64 Proof. $25.95.

90 • Emil Scheibel (Germany) Black Forest Kirsch-Liqueur Cherry Liquer 70 Proof. $29.95/375 ml.

90 • Edmond Briottet (France) Creme de Cassis de Dijon 40 Proof. $26.95.

89 • Blanca de Navarra (Spain) Blackberry Liqueur 34 Proof. $15/L.

88 • Edmond Briottet (France) Creme de Mûre 36 Proof. $25.

88 • Blanca de Navarra (Spain) Raspberry Liqueur 34 Proof. $15/L.

88 • Blanca de Navarra (Spain) Peach Liqueur 38 Proof. $15/L.

87 • Luxardo (Italy) Triplum Triple Sec Orange Liqueur 78 Proof. $21.95.

86 • Villa Massa (Italy) Liquore di Limoni 60 Proof. $19.99.

86 • Trimbach (France) Liqueur de Poire, Pear Liqueur 70 Proof. $36/375 ml.

86 • Luxardo (Italy) Morlacco Cherry Liqueur, Liquore di Marasca 60 Proof. $20.95.

86 • Emil Scheibel (Germany) Black Forest Wald-Himbeer-Liqueur, Wild Raspberry Liqueur 70 Proof. $27.95/375 ml.

86 • Emil Scheibel (Germany) Black Forest Quitten-Liqueur, Quince Liqueur 70 Proof. $27.95/375 ml.

85 • F. Meyer (France) Liqueur de Fraise, Strawberry Liqueur 40 Proof. $16.95/375 ml.

85 • Blanca de Navarra (Spain) Lemon Liqueur 38 Proof. $15/L.

Herb/Spice Liqueur

98 • Chartreuse (France) Liqueur Fabriquée V.E.P 108 Proof. $75/200 ml.

94 • Chartreuse (France) Liqueur Fabriquée Green 110 Proof. $32.

93 • Luxardo (Italy) Amaro Liqueur Abano 60 Proof. $19.95.

92 • Irish Mist (Ireland) Liqueur 70 Proof. $22.

92 • Drambuie (Scotland) Prince Charles Edward's Liqueur 70 Proof. $25.

91 • Galliano (Italy) Liquore L'Autentico 70 Proof. $14/375 ml.

90 • Luxardo (Italy) Luxardo Perla Dry Riserva Speciale 80 Proof. $29.95.

90 • Jägermeister (Germany) Herbal Liqueur 70 Proof. $18.99.

89 • Los Camichines Distillery (Mexico) Agavero Tequila Liquer 80 Proof. $39.99.

89 • Liquore Strega (Italy) Special Liqueur 80 Proof. $23.99.

89 • Chartreuse (France) Liqueur Fabriquée Yellow 80 Proof. $28.

88 • Cynar (Italy) Liqueur 33 Proof. $15.

88 • Canton (China) Delicate Ginger Liqueur 40 Proof. $21.

87 • Ramazzotti (Italy) Amaro Felsina Ramazzotti 60 Proof. $16.99.

86 • Pimm's (England) Original No. 1 Cup 50 Proof. $15.

Nut Liqueur

96 • Frangelico (Italy) Frangelico Hazelnut Liqueur 48 Proof. $18.99.

92 • Amaretto di Saronno (Italy) Originale Liqueur 56 Proof. $22.

89 • Luxardo (Italy) Amaretto di Saschira Liqueur 56 Proof. $20.50.

88 • Blanca de Navarra (Spain) Hazelnut Liqueur 38 Proof. $15/L.

86 • Amaretto di Amore (Italy) Classico Liqueur 42 Proof. $11.99.

Schnapps

95 • Rumple Minze (Germany) Original Peppermint Schnapps 100 Proof. $25.

91 • Goldschläger (Switzerland) Cinnamon Schnapps Liqueur with Gold Flakes 87 Proof. $12/375 ml.

87 • Dr. McGillicuddy's (Canada) Mentholmint Schnapps 48 Proof. $13.

87 • DeKuyper (USA) Butter Shots Butterscotch Schnapps 30 Proof. $9.

nine

❧

Fortified Wines: Madeira, Port, and Sherry

❧

Any time not spent drinking Port is a waste of time.
- Percy Croft

An Overview and History

The Basis of Port

Port wine in Portugal is made from a blend of up to 48 different grape varieties (28 red and 20 white). This large number of "authorized" grapes reflects the ancient history and fragmented regional nature of local viniculture. The dominant red grape varieties are the *Touriga Nacional, Tinto Cao* ("*Red Dog*"), and *Tinto Francisca* (*red French*—probably the *Pinot Noir*). The major White Port grapes include the *Malvazia Fina, Verdelho, Boal,* and *Sercial,* all of which are also the classic grape types of Madeira wines.

Port-style wines made in other (non-European Union) countries tend to be made from whatever hearty red grape is available. A few American Port producers have planted some of the classic Portuguese Port grapes, but they are the exception rather than the rule. The dominant American Port grape is probably *Zinfandel*.

The Production of Port

Port grapes in Portugal are grown on terraced vineyards in the Upper Douro River Valley, an isolated and wild mountainous region with its own distinctive culture. These vineyards, all of which are officially classified and rated on a point system, are set on amazingly steep slopes with only a row or two of vines per terrace shelf. The rocky soil is primarily fractured shale on a granite base.

Tending and harvesting of the grapes is still mostly done by hand. The harvested grapes are taken to the *quinta* (wine estate). The treading of grapes by foot has now largely given way to mechanical presses. The grape must (*mosto*) is fermented in huge concrete vats in which the fermenting juice is stirred and pumped back onto the floating cap of grape skins (the *manta*) to extract maximum flavor and color. After two or three days the must is drawn off into large casks (*toneis*) and neutral grapes spirits (unaged brandy) is added to arrest the fermentation and raise the alcohol content to 19% ABV. This spirit (called *aguardente*, literally, "burning water") is made from Portuguese grapes and is supplied by a government agency. The wine is then allowed to "rest" until the following late spring when it is shipped in tanker trucks to shipper warehouses (lodges) in Vila Nova de Gaia, across the Douro River from Oporto. The new wine is stored in 145-gallon casks called pipes and begins its maturation process.

The Classifications of Port

Port is divided into two basic categories, depending on how it is aged:

Wood Ports are aged in wood casks and not bottled until they are ready to drink. Different casks of different ages are blended to achieve a shipper's individual brand profile. Types of wood Port, named for their colors, include:

White Port, which varies from very dry to medium sweet. White Ports tend to be oxidized and are, at best, an acquired taste.

Ruby Port, which is a young wood Port that retains its bright ruby color. Ruby Ports are aged for three to seven years and tend to be sweet and fruity.

Tawny Port, which is tawny in color and made in one of two ways. Inexpensive Tawny Port is produced by blending together Ruby and White Port. Better-quality Tawny Port gains its color by extensive cask aging. These Tawny Ports do not lose their bright red color until they are at least eight years old and do not achieve the classic nutty flavor profile until they are 20 years old. The legal age designations for the minimum age in the Tawny Port blend are 10, 20, 30, and over 40 years old.

Colheita Port, which is a Tawny Port from a single vintage year that has been aged for a minimum of seven years before bottling.

Late Bottled Vintage Port (L.B.V.) is a Port that has been declared a vintage Port after four years of aging and then bottled within two years. L.B.V. Ports are similar to Ruby Ports in that they are generally ready to drink when bottled, but they have some of the complexity and character of high-quality vintage Ports.

Vintage-Character Port, formerly known as **Crusted Port**, is a blend of two or three vintages of high-quality Ruby Port. It is similar in style to L.B.V. Port.

Bottle Ports improve with age in the bottle, and are meant to be aged in the bottle before serving.

Vintage Port is a shipper's finest Port from a given year. Each shipper makes an individual decision on whether or not to make a vintage declaration on selected casks from a particular harvest. The wine from these casks is bottled after two years of wood aging. Each vintage matures at a different rate with different wines taking anywhere from 20 to 50 years to reach full maturity. They then begin to slowly break down.

Single Quinta Port is a vintage Port from a single wine estate, or *quinta.*

≈

Porto and Madeira at a Glance

Top Scores:

Porto

98 • Quinta do Noval (Portugal) 1991 Nacional Vintage Porto, Oporto. $250. Cellar Selection.

98 • Dow's (Portugal) 1994 Vintage Porto, Oporto. $38. Cellar Selection.

Madeira

96 • Henriques & Henriques (Portugal) ten year old Sercial, Madeira 5.8% r.s. $29.95

≈

≈

Sherry
at a Glance

Top Score:

**99 • Osborne (Spain)
Rare Palo Cortado,
Solera PΔP, Jerez. $35.**

≈

Port Regions

Portugal is, of course, the home of Port wine, and as a member of the European Union it has compelled other E.U. member states to ban the labeling of any fortified wines from their wineries as "Port." This is not, however, the case elsewhere in the world, and the Portuguese have taken to labeling the Port wines that they ship to such countries as "Porto" to distinguish them from imitators.

The United States produces a substantial amount of fortified wine from a wide variety of grapes that is labeled as Port. Most are only vaguely like a Port in style, but some are quite interesting in their own right. The bulk of American Port is produced in California, but a surprising number are also made in some less well-known wine regions in the Midwest.

Australia has achieved a surprising degree of success with its mostly Shiraz-based Ports from South Australia. The Tawny Ports are the best and are frequently good values for the money.

South Africa has a substantial Port industry in the Cape Province, most of which is consumed domestically. The quality of the Tawny Ports in particular has improved in recent years.

The Basis of Madeira

Madeira wine is classically made from four "noble" grape varieties. In ascending order of sweetness they are *Sercial, Verdelho, Boal/Bual,* and *Malvezia/Malmsey.* In practice these low-yielding and virus-prone grapes have been largely replaced by high-yielding "lesser" grapes such as the *Tinta Negra Mole* in all but the rare vintage Madeiras. All other "noble-grape" designated Madeira wines can contain up to 90% lesser grapes.

The Production of Madeira

Madeira grapes are grown on narrow terraces cut into steep hillsides on the island of Madeira, which is located some 600 miles southwest of Portugal in the Atlantic Ocean. The Madeira grapes grow on tilting *pergolas* and are still harvested by hand. They are then crushed at the vineyards and the fresh must is shipped by truck to lodges in the capital city of

Scale: Superlative (96-100), Exceptional (90-95), Highly Recommended (85-89),
Recommended (80-84), Not Recommended (Under 80)

Funchal for fermentation. This step takes about eight days and the result is a highly acidic dry wine. The fermentation of vintage and higher-quality Madeira wines is arrested before fermentation is complete by the addition of neutral grape spirits in a manner similar to Port production. The percentage of residual sugar determines the type of Madeira. In both cases the wine is then ready to be heated.

Originally heating was achieved by sending casks of Madeira on long ocean voyages as ship's ballast. The heat in the ship's hold combined with the gentle agitation caused by the ship's swaying had a surprisingly positive effect on the taste and quality of the wine. Modern Madeira is heated in more land-bound manners. Vintage Madeiras, and some of the better nonvintage Madeiras, are stored for a year or more in barrels that are stacked in a tin-roofed warehouse called a *canteiro*. The heat of the sun on the metal roof warms the barrels. The casks are then moved to an aging cellar where they are matured for five to 20 years. These casks are topped up periodically, as the rate of evaporation (*ullage*) averages around 2% per year. Less expensive wines are stored in large cement vats with internal steam coils called *estufas* (the word literally means "stove"). The steam coils gradually raise the temperature of the wine to 125° F. and maintain that temperature for three to five months before, over a period of one month, returning the temperature to normal. The wine is then charcoal-filtered and aged for an additional 18 months before a mixture of brandy and sweet concentrated grape juice (*surdo*) is added. The wine is then aged for a minimum of three years (10 years for the better wines) before it is ready for bottling.

Madeiras are the world's longest-living wines, outlasting even vintage Port. Century-old Madeiras show no sign of fading (except perhaps in color). Very old Madeiras tend to lose their sweetness and take on a complex, nutty character.

Classifications of Madeira

The types of Madeira are determined by the noble grape that is used (which also serves as a reference point for the level of sweetness). *Sercial* is dry, *Verdelho* is medium dry, *Boal/Bual* is medium sweet, and *Malvezia/Malmsey* is very sweet. All of these types of Madeira can be made into one of the following varieties:

Vintage Madeira is made solely from one of the four noble grapes and only from one vintage year. It comprises only 5–10% of total production and is becoming increasingly rare. As with Port, each Madeira shipper individually decides on vintage years. A date on the bottle label is not a guarantee that the wine is a vintage Madeira; it can also be a solera Madeira.

Solera Madeira is a blend of vintage Madeiras produced in a manner similar to Sherry. Solera Madeira wines bear the date of when the solera was established, many of which go back well into the 19th century. The minimum age for wines in a solera is five years.

Reserve Madeira is cask aged for a minimum of 20 years and then blended with 10% surdo, and 10% older wine (aged for 20–30 years).

Standard Madeira is aged for a minimum of five years and is a blend of 70% average wine, 10% surdo, and 20% older wine. Most contain a high percentage of non-noble grapes.

Shipper Blends, such as *Rainwater*, are created by shippers to their own specifications. Most contain a high percentage of non-noble grapes.

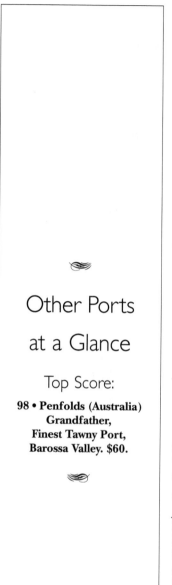

Other Ports at a Glance

Top Score:

**98 • Penfolds (Australia)
Grandfather,
Finest Tawny Port,
Barossa Valley. $60.**

The Basis of Sherry

Sherry is made primarily from the *Palomino Fino*, a white grape that is available in a variety of clones. The *Pedro Ximenez* grape, best known for its intense, raisiny flavor, follows in importance. Other grapes, including the *Moscatel*, are also grown, but are of diminishing importance.

The Production of Sherry

Sherry grapes are grown in vineyards planted in the sunny, softly rolling landscape of the "Sherry Triangle" of Spain, with production primarily centered around the towns of Jerez De La Frontera, Sanlúcar de Barrameda, and Puerto de Santa Maria. The soil can be very sandy and contains a high percentage of chalk that can result in snow-while soil called *albariza*. The grapevines are "head pruned" so that each vine stands independently like a small bush. Most of the grapes are still hand harvested. Once picked, the grapes are shipped to pressing houses where they are gently and repeatedly pressed to extract the juice without crushing the stems or seeds. Primary fermentation in large cement vats lasts up to a week. Secondary fermentation lasts two to three months. The wine is then transferred into casks, which are not totally filled and retain a headspace, classified, and then stored in vast thick-walled warehouses called *bodegas*.

Once in casks a white film of yeast, called the *flor*, can form on the surface of the wine, which leads to the development of Fino Sherry. Non *flor* or arrested *flor* wines become Oloroso Sherries. The flor comes from the same group of yeasts that were used to ferment the wine, but in this form it slowly imparts a nutty flavor that has become a classic characteristic of Sherry.

Sherry is first classified by appearance and aroma. Expert vintners called *catadors* rate and rank each cask. The first-class casks (*Una Raya*) will become Fino Sherry and are fortified with neutral grape spirits to 15.5% ABV. The second- and third-class casks (*Dos Reyas* and *Tres Rayas*) will become Oloroso Sherry and are fortified to 18% ABV. After nine months

Scale: Superlative (96-100), Exceptional (90-95), Highly Recommended (85-89),
Recommended (80-84), Not Recommended (Under 80)

the Sherry is reclassified. Finos that have not continued to develop as proper Finos are reclassified as Olorosos and spiked with more brandy. After an additional nine months to three years of aging, these single-vintage casks (*añada*) are put into the solera system.

The solera system is a way of maturing wine that insures uniformity in taste by minimizing the variability of individual vintages. A series of casks (*criaderas*) are laid out in decending periods of age with each cask containing older wine than the preceding cask. Twice a year, wine (no more than 20% of the volume of the cask) is drawn from the oldest casks. This wine is then replaced with wine drawn from casks on down the line that hold progressively younger wine, with the last cask being topped off with wine from the *añada* casks.

The Classification of Sherry

Fino is generally pale, dry, and delicate. Once bottled it does not improve with age and should be consumed promptly.

Amontillado starts out as a Fino, but with age it develops a deep tawny color and a distinctive nutty bouquet. The best amontillados are aged in casks for a minimum of eight years.

Oloroso is rich, nutty, and complex with a touch of fruitiness. Olorosos can be aged for extensive periods. *Rayas* are lesser-quality Olorosos that are used primarily for blending. *Cream Sherry* and *Brown Sherry* are sweetened Olorosos. *Pedro Ximenez*, named after the grape, is a very dark, very sweet, intensely flavored wine that is used to sweeten Olorosos.

Palo Cortado, which is sometimes classified as an Oloroso, has the dry nutty character of an Amontillado but the deep color and body of an Oloroso. True Palo Cortado is difficult to make and nowadays is rather rare.

History

Fortified wines are wines that have had their alcohol content increased beyond the percentage possible from fermentation by the addition of high-proof spirits (usually, but not always, neutral grape spirits). The major types of fortified wines (Port, Sherry, and Madeira) all share their creation, at least in their modern forms, to the tastes and demands of the British wine market.

Port/Porto

Winemaking in what has become modern Portugal dates back to the second century B.C. when the invading Romans conquered the local Celtic tribe, the mead-drinking Lusitani, and established the province of Lusitania. In northern Lusitania they established the town of Portus at the mouth of the Douro River and planted vineyards along the riverbank.

In A.D. 409 Lusitania was overrun by a series of invading barbarian tribes, including the Vandals, Visigoths, and Swabians. The latter remained, and ruled Lusitania while the Romanized locals continued to tend their vines. In the early 8th century the Moslem Moors swept up from the south and conquered the region, including the town at the mouth of the Douro River, now known as Oporto ("the port" in the newly evolving Portuguese language). Moorish rule was relatively brief in northern Portugal. Within the century Spanish conquistadors drove the Moors from the Douro River region as part of the Christian reconquest of the Iberian Peninsula. In the course of this 500-year drive southward, a Portuguese national identity, separate from the Spanish of Leon and Aragon, evolved, with the Spanish finally acknowledging an independent Portugal in 1143.

While all of this fighting was taking place farther south, the Douro region was left in relative peace. By the 16th century it was producing and exporting wines, some of which, according to chroniclers of the time, were strong, "aromatic" wines that could take several years of aging (unusual at a time when most wines were unstable and soured quickly).

In the mid-1600s England and France were involved in a series of wars that disrupted the substantial wine export business from Bordeaux. British merchants turned elsewhere for sources of wine, including the relatively close Douro region in Portugal. The first British merchant house was established in Oporto in 1692. (It still exists as the modern firm of Taylor, Fladgate & Yeatman.) The English taste in wines at the time was for strong wines with high alcohol levels. Almost from the start some of the Douro wines exported to England were "spiked" with brandy, a procedure similar to that of Sherry and Madeira and done both to stabilize the wine for shipping and cater to British tastes. But unlike these two other fortified wines, Port (as the wine exported from Oporto was now called) had the brandy added during fermentation, rather than afterward. Adoption of this procedure was gradual, and not without controversy, but by the mid-19th century it had become the norm.

The English merchants in Oporto established a substantial local community, dominating the Port wine export trade. As this trade grew through the 18th century, demand frequently outstripped supply, and quality suffered as some farmers and merchants adulterated their wine with inferior wines from outside the Douro district, and with additives such as *baga*, the dark red juice of the elderberry. The Portuguese government finally stepped in and established a monopoly in 1756 that set the limits for the growing regions for Port grapes, classified all of the wine, set prices, controlled how much wine could be exported, determined who could export, and controlled the production of brandy to be used for fortifying the Port. This monopoly lasted only into the mid-19th century before dissolving amidst charges of corruption, but its reforms remained and helped to further shape the development of Port.

The Victorian Era was the golden age of Port. The *Phylloxera* blight, beginning in the 1870s, slowed Port production until the use of grafted American rootstock brought the disease under control. By the early 1900s Port was consumed by all segments of English society, with the upper classes making vintage Port part of their basic lifestyle. The French favored Ruby and Tawny Ports as apéritifs, the Germans mixed Ports with herbs as digestifs, and the Americans drank Ports as "tonic restoratives." The Russian aristocracy single-handedly created and maintained the market for sweet White Ports.

World War I, the Great Depression, and changing tastes altered the nature of the Port trade. The Russian market vanished, as did the American market for "tonic" Ports. The English trade has diminished, as the working class inclination for Ruby Port as a mixer (Port and Lemonade being but one example) is but a fraction of what it used to be. Presently the French are the world's leading consumers of Port (accounting for around 40% of total production). Challenges from competing wines, particularly from the market-savvy Sherry shippers, also have challenged Port's share of the wine market.

Still, as some old markets contract, others continue to open. Portugal itself now consumes a third of Port production, and the markets in northern Europe continue to grow. The United States accounts for only about 2% of the total Port market by volume, but most of that is for vintage and the more expensive Tawny Ports.

Madeira

The Madeira Islands are a group of subtropical volcanic islands in the Atlantic Ocean 350 miles off the coast of Morocco. The Portuguese first seriously explored them in 1419 and soon returned to colonize the islands, beginning with the main island of Madeira. The settlers were faced with a thick forest, which they more or less burned down over the course of seven years. The resulting mix of volcanic soil and ash proved to be extremely fertile and the island was replanted in tropical plants and crops, with grapes, sugarcane, and bananas being the dominant crops. By 1460, the first wine had been exported to Europe. Madeira wines, particularly Malmsey (made from the Malvazia grape), soon became a favorite of the royal courts of England and France. Malmsey earned a distinctive place in English royal history in the mid-15th century when King Edward IV is alleged to have had his treasonous brother George, Duke of Clarence, drowned in a *butt* (a large cask) of Malmsey because that was the duke's favorite tipple.

Madeira, as part of Portugal, shared that nation's place in the world wine market. Along with Port, it filled the vacuum in the English market left by the withdrawal of Bordeaux wine during the various wars between Britain and France between the 17th and early 19th centuries. English merchants set up shipping houses on Madeira, which, while it was part of Portugal, was not actually in Europe, a legal technicality that allowed local shippers to avoid British tariffs on foreign goods shipped to British colonies. The American colonies in particular became a major market for Madeira wines. The signers of the Declaration of Independence reportedly celebrated their deed with a toast of Madeira.

The first quarter of the 19th century was Madeira's golden age, with sales in Britain and Western Europe second only to Port. Starting in the 1830s a gradual decline set in, helped along by competition from cheap imitations from southern France and an assortment of vine diseases, particularly *Oïdium* and *Phylloxera*, that wiped out whole vintages and drove numerous shippers out of business.

Today Madeira is the odd man out among the three major groups of fortified wines. Its largest market is in France, but there it is primarily used in cooking (*Sauce Madère* is a major component of *haute cuisine*). Germany imports a fair amount, as still does England, but the great American market, where George Washington was reputed to end his day with a bedside glass of Malmsey, has all but vanished. A faint echo of this distant past can still be heard, though, in Charleston, South Carolina, where once a year the 200-plus-year-old Madeira Society holds its annual banquet to honor the favorite wine of the Founding Fathers.

"This wine of Spain creepeth subtilly."
– Geoffrey Chaucer,

"The Pardoner's Tale" from Canterbury Tales

Sherry

Sherry wine is produced in the far southwest corner of Spain around the town of Jerez in the province of Cádiz, an ancient region whose capital city, also named Cádiz, is reputed to have been founded by Phoenicians almost 3,000 years ago. The Phoenicians, who originally came from Canaan, are credited with bringing the cultivated grape to the Iberian Peninsula.

In the Roman era, the wines of Andalusia, then the Roman province of Baetica, were exported in great quantities to Rome. The Roman city of Xericium, thought by many to be the predecessor of Jerez, was the regional center of the wine export trade. The invasion of the Iberian Peninsula by barbarian tribes in A.D. 409 ended Roman rule. Andalusia (the "land of the Vandals") came under the rule of the Visigoths, who remained in control until the Moorish invasion of the 8th century put the entire region firmly under Moslem control for the next 500 years. The Moors, although they were Moslems, were not immune to the appeal of wine and permitted their Christian subjects to continue to tend their vineyards and make their wine.

The Spanish drive of reconquest reached Jerez in 1264, and the triumphant King Alphonso X divided the local lands and vineyards among his followers and urged them to plant new vineyards. The local wine trade flourished and soon took in the nearby towns of Puerto de Santa Maria and Sanlúcar de Barrameda.

Wine exports to England probably began in the 14th century and grew to a substantial level during the late 15th century. English merchants were firmly established in Sanúlucar by the 16th century, where they remained, despite the constantly changing political climate as England and Spain fought a series of hot and cold wars during the 16th and 17th centuries. Even the sacking of Cádiz by Sir Francis Drake in 1587, during which he hauled off 2,900 butts (around 450,000 gallons) of Sherry, proved to be a blessing in disguise. Drake flooded the English market with the looted wine, introducing Sherry to many new consumers and greatly increasing the long-term demand for the wines.

The English of this time called these wines "*Sack*" after the Spanish world *sacar* (which roughly means to take out—to export). The contemporary Sherry brand Dry Sack is an homage to this archaic term. The word *Sherry*, which slowly replaced *sack*, is an English corruption of *Jerez*. England became the dominant market for Sherry, reaching an amazing 92% of the export trade in 1844.

The *Phylloxera* blight reached Spain in 1875 and Jerez in 1894. The resulting dev-astation and new competition from imitation sherries brought a slump in the Sherry trade, but the 1920s brought a renewed interest, particularly in the light-bodied Fino sherries.

The comfortable, clubby world of Sherry *bodegas* (producers, or houses) began to change in the 1960s when corporate raiders bought up and absorbed many of the old-line Sherry houses. The largest of these holding companies, Ruiz-Mateos Hermanos S.A. (RUMASA for short) grew to control a third of the entire Sherry trade before collapsing in 1983. Multinational giants now dominate the modern Sherry trade, but it is heartening to know that members of the old Sherry house families are still managing many of these enterprises.

Reviews

Sherry

Alvear (Spain)

Alvear Fino, Montilla-Moriles. $8.   **84**

Bright yellow straw cast. Medium-bodied. Full acidity. Blanched almonds, acetone. Intensely fragrant with a clean and edgy palate feel. Rather unusual in flavor, but crisp and linear through the finish.

Alvear Amontillado, Montilla-Moriles. $7.50.   **83**

Amber with light copper-red highlights. Medium-bodied. Notes of toffee, brown spice, almonds. The sweetness stays in the background. Subtle oxidized character perceptible on the nose and lingering through the finish. Straightforward and well balanced.

Alvear Solera Abuelo Diego, Amontillado, Montilla-Moriles. $14.   **87**

Full golden-straw color. Medium-bodied. Notes of brown spice, roasted almonds, smoke. Spicy, subtly oxidized nose. Long dry palate with delicate roasted flavors that linger through a teasingly long finish that does not become too dry.

Alvear Solera Fundacion, Amontillado Muy Viejo, Montilla-Moriles. $50. **93**

Rich amber. Moderately full-bodied. Notes of blanched almond, salt, citrus peel. Hugely concentrated flavors with a thick viscous mouthfeel give this an imposing presence on the palate. Strikes an intriguing balance between richness and dry flavors on the mid palate. The finish, with a salty, spicy quality lingers for minutes.

Alvear Solera Abuelo Diego Oloroso, Montilla-Moriles. $14.   **86**

Bright amber cast. Medium-bodied. Roasted nuts, brown spices, orange peel. Subtle aromatics have pleasant fruit cake type overtones. Lighter in the mouth with good grip and intensity. Drying through the finish.

Alvear Festival Pale Cream, Montilla-Moriles. $7.   **82**

Very pale appearance with a green tint. Medium-bodied. Notes of lavender, sweet citrus, toasted nuts. Floral rancio aromas lead juicy sweet flavors on the palate with a touch of nutty character through the finish.

Alvear Cream, Montilla-Moriles. $7.50.   **88**

Light chestnut-amber. Moderately full-bodied. Notes of raisins, caramel, toasted nuts. Full, rich sweet smoky nose leads a rounded lush palate with a sweet entry. Tapers to a surprisingly dry finish, with plenty of rich flavors on the mid palate. Not the least bit cloying.

Alvear Moscatel, Montilla-Moriles. $7.50.   **87**

Dark chestnut brown appearance. Medium-bodied. Caramelized brown sugar, sweet peach, brown spice. Big caramel aromas with floral nuances that are well expressed on the surprisingly fresh and balanced palate, with a certain lightness to the mouthfeel. Not cloying. Best served with a slight chill.

Alvear Solera Abuelo Diego, Pedro Ximenez, Montilla-Moriles. $14.   **92**

Deep chestnut amber. Full-bodied. Notes of brown sugar, golden raisins, caramel. Sweet heavy caramel aromas lead a thick mouthful of intensely rich flavors with a sweetness that will find any lurking cavities. Long lingering sweet finish. All the concentrated character one expects from a PX, with a very pure expression of flavors.

Alvear Pedro Ximenez 1830, Dulce Muy Viejo, Montilla-Moriles. $80.   **97**

Motor oil black. Full-bodied. Notes of black licorice, rum raisin. Pours like syrup. Inimitable burnt oily aromas. Thick and viscous on the palate with a mouthcoating sweet quality revealing layers of flavors. Too cloying to be drunk in large quantities. Best sipped and savored as a dessert.

Argueso (Spain)

Argueso San Leon Manzanilla, Sanlucar de Barrameda. $14. **NR**

Argueso Pedro Ximenez Cream Sherry, Jerez de la Frontera. $17. **92**
Deep mahogany with a hint of brightness and a golden edge. Full-bodied. Notes of brown spices, dried herbs, caramel, coffee. Brightly flavored with an attractive complexity. Modest acidity actually gives a sense of liveliness to this rich and highly focused elixir. Extraordinary length to the finish.

Antonio Barbadillo (Spain)

Antonio Barbadillo Very Dry Manzanilla Sherry, Sanlucar de Barrameda. $7.99. **84**
Very pale straw. Moderately light-bodied. Notes of salted almonds, brine. Smooth and rounded mouthfeel with a briny note through the finish. Flavors overall are austere but clean in character.

Antonio Barbadillo Fino Dry Sherry, Jerez de la Frontera. $8.99. **84**
Deep straw cast. Moderately light-bodied. Balanced acidity. Yeast, bread, minerals. Fragrant, but lighter in style with a sense of softness to the palate. Tasty but lacking somewhat for grip.

Antonio Barbadillo Medium Dry Amontillado Sherry, Jerez de la Frontera. $7.99. **84**
Brilliant amber cast. Medium-bodied. Full acidity. Roasted nuts, brown spices. Pleasantly fragrant with a lighter styled and zesty palate feel. Shows just a hint of sweetness that serves to round the clean finish.

Antonio Barbadillo Principe, Dry Amontillado Sherry, Jerez de la Frontera. $75. **91**
Amber with orange highlights. Medium-bodied. Notes of brown spice, roasted nuts. Tight, full flavored palate with some richness on the mouthfeel. Distinguished by a long complex finish with developing nutty flavors. Needs some time to open up.

Antonio Barbadillo Palo Cortado del Obispo Gascon Sherry, Jerez de la Frontera. $125. **92**
Deep amber with reddish-copper highlights. Moderately full-bodied. Notes of brown spice, roasted nuts, salt. Full burnt salty nose. Assertive and austere with a dry lengthy finish and real complexity. Very demanding on the palate.

Antonio Barbadillo Dry Oloroso Sherry, Jerez de la Frontera. $7.99. **85**
Deep amber with a subtle copper cast. Moderately full-bodied. Notes of marzipan, toffee, walnuts. Attractively flavored and relatively full in the mouth with well balanced acidity. Maintains an enticingly roasted character throughout with the faintest suggestion of sweetness in the finish.

Antonio Barbadillo Very Old Oloroso Sherry, Jerez de la Frontera. $11.99. **88**
Dark amber with reddish highlights. Moderately full-bodied. Medium sweetness. Notes of dates, brown spice, raisins. Rich caramelized aromas lead an unctuous palate. Relatively viscous in the mouth, the sweetness of the palate is balanced by a touch of acidity. Subtle burnt herbal overtones add complexity to this straightforward wine.

Antonio Barbadillo Pale Cream Sherry, Jerez de la Frontera. $7.99. **82**
Bright pale straw. Moderately light-bodied. Medium sweetness. Notes of dried herbs, green grapes, citrus. Crisply defined aromatics play out on an angular and snappy palate. Lingering sweetness is moderated by a hint of acidity.

Antonio Barbadillo Cream Sherry, Jerez de la Frontera. $7.99. **84**
Bright amber cast. Moderately light-bodied. Balanced acidity. Subtly extracted. Roasted nuts, caramel. Lighter in style with sweet caramel flavors. Clean and straightforward with lingering nutty flavors.

Antonio Barbadillo Pale Sweet Moscatel Sherry,
Jerez de la Frontera. $7.99.   89

Bright yellow-gold. Medium-bodied. Balanced acidity. This curious Sherry delivers the
orange-blossom and ginger aromas of a good muscat, and the sweetness of a cream
Sherry. A little low in acidity, this is more of a contemplative sipper.

Antonio Barbadillo Rich Sweet Pedro Ximenez Sherry,
Jerez de la Frontera. $10.99.   80

Rich opaque mahogany. Medium-bodied. Notes of treacle, raisins, dried flowers. Quite
viscous though not cloying with lighter, fruit oriented flavors. The acidity helps in
maintaining a sense of balance through the lingering finish.

Croft (Spain)

Croft Original Rare Pale Cream Sherry, Jerez de la Frontera. $10.   86

Golden with a bright yellow hue. Medium-bodied. Notes of blanched almonds, dried
herbs, petrol, lacquer. A classic petrol note often associated with Fino sherries from
Puerto de Santa Maria is distinctly evident in the nose. The palate has a well balanced
marriage of sweetness and acidity that results in a refreshing sense of crispness.

Jose de Soto (Spain)

Jose de Soto Tio Soto Fino Sherry, Jerez de la Frontera. $7.99.   80

Medium straw. Medium-bodied. Notes of brown spice, nuts. Heavy, dull aromas. Quite
crisp and flavorsome with nutty qualities and a little heat on the finish.

Jose de Soto Amontillado Sherry, Jerez de la Frontera. $7.99.   NR

Jose de Soto Cream Sherry, Jerez de la Frontera. $7.99.   80

Brown with reddish highlights. Medium-bodied. Notes of apricot, raisin. Unusual aromas
for a cream Sherry. Tart sweet balance of flavors that lingers through the mildly burnt
finish gives this a simple character.

Bodegas del Principe (Spain)

Bodegas del Principe A. Soler Extra Amontillado Sherry,
Jerez de la Frontera. $3.95.   NR

Bodegas del Principe A. Soler Extra Cream Sherry,
Jerez de la Frontera. $3.59.   NR

Pedro Domecq (Spain)

Pedro Domecq La Ina Very Pale Dry Fino Sherry, Jerez. $16.40.   84

Bright greenish straw cast. Medium-bodied. Blanched almonds, lacquer, minerals.
Intensely fragrant with a lean and edgy palate feel. Shows excellent freshness and an
appropriate degree of snap through the finish.

Pedro Domecq Primero Amontillado Sherry, Jerez de la Frontera. $15.   NR

Pedro Domecq "51-1a", Very Rare Amontillado, Jerez de la Frontera. $73.   93

Very deep bronzed tawny hue. Moderately full-bodied. Aromatic with an intriguing
briny quality. Quite viscous, yet comes across the palate with a sense of lightness due
to its vibrant acidity. Snappy, with a clean drying finish and exceptional complexity.

Pedro Domecq Palo Cortado Sherry, Bottled 1986,
Jerez de la Frontera. $35.   82

Deep rich mahogany. Medium-bodied. Notes of coffee grounds, cardamom, burned
rubber. Unusual aromatics, but explodes with complexity on the palate as it takes
on more conventional flavors. Vibrant acidity serves to unite the whole and offer a
brisk finish.

Pedro Domecq "Sibarita", Very Rare Palo Cortado,
Jerez de la Frontera. $73. 98

Deep mahogany color. Moderately full-bodied. Exotic and complex aromas of toasted coconut and salted nuts lead to a forceful and mouth-filling character on the palate. Excellent grip cleanses the palate and makes way for a finish of extravagant length and intensity. A hint of sweetness serves to balance the vibrant acidity.

Pedro Domecq Rio Viejo Rare Dry Oloroso Sherry,
Jerez de la Frontera. $25. 86

Amber with a subtle greenish cast. Medium-bodied. Notes of black tea, yeast, dried flowers. Pungent and fully flavored with unusual aromatics. Features a subtle burnt character. Well-balanced acidity. Should find favor with those who prefer a fairly aggressive style.

Gonzalez Byass (Spain)

Gonzalez Byass Elegante Manzanilla Sherry, Jerez de la Frontera. $5.99. 85

Medium straw. Moderately light-bodied. Full acidity. Notes of lacquer, citrus zest, wheat toast. Fresh and lively with cleansing acidity and an attractive array of flavors. Features a lovely green note throughout.

Gonzalez Byass Tio Pepe Fino Sherry, Jerez de la Frontera. $12.99. 89

Pale straw with traces of green. Medium-bodied. Moderate acidity. Notes of blanched almonds, petrol, beechwood. Attractive aromatics lead to a broad range of flavors on the mildly weighty palate. Well-balanced acidity.

Gonzalez Byass Elegante Medium Dry Amontillado Sherry,
Jerez de la Frontera. $5.99. 83

Deep amber with a subtle green cast. Medium-bodied. Notes of pumpkin, raisins, earth. Unusual but attractive flavors. Clean and straightforward mouthfeel. The mild sweetness gets the best of the very subtle acidity, lending a lingering sweetness to the finish.

Gonzalez Byass Amontillado Del Duque,
Rare Old Solera Amontillado Viejo, Jerez de la Frontera. $40. 94

Rich, brilliant mahogany with a slight green edge. Moderately full-bodied. Notes of salted nuts, toasted coconut, exotic spices. Impressively fragrant, firmly structured, and quite rich with noticeable viscosity. The flavors are deep, warm, and lingering with a very drying finish. Crisp acidity maintains a sense of freshness, despite its forceful character.

Gonzalez Byass Apostoles, Rare Old Solera Oloroso Abocado,
Jerez de la Frontera. $40. 93

Brilliant deep amber with a subtle green cast. Medium-bodied. Notes of smoke, earth, salted pecans. Distinctly aromatic with a pungent character. Zesty acidity downplays the sweetness on the palate and keeps this exotically flavored Sherry from becoming too aggressive. The finish is lengthy and lends itself to fully flavored meats and cheeses.

Gonzalez Byass San Domingo, Pale Cream Sherry,
Jerez de la Frontera. $12.99. 89

Light golden with a subtle green hue. Moderately full-bodied. Notes of minerals, blanched almonds, stone fruits, savory spices. Distinctively aromatic, with a range of classic Fino flavors. Mouth filling, with just a hint of sweetness and an attractive nutty complexity that rides out a lingering finish. Strikes a pleasant balance between richness and lightness. This is an impressive, all purpose sipping Sherry.

Gonzalez Byass Elegante Cream Sherry, Jerez de la Frontera. $5.99. 87

Glossy deep brown with ruby highlights. Medium-bodied. Notes of ginger, molasses, toasted grains. Moderately complex aromatics play out on a well-balanced palate. Crisp acidity reigns in the sweetness for an uplifting finish.

Gonzalez Byass NOE, Rare Old Solera Pedro Ximenez,
Jerez de la Frontera. $40. 97

Opaque black with a tawny rim. Full-bodied. Notes of cocoa, molasses, toasted coconut, saddle leather. Has the consistency of high performance motor oil and literally coats the glass. Absolutely extraordinary aromatics have raced past the line from dried fruits to dark and roasted flavors. It is obviously the product of extreme age. Thick and concentrated, this is a tour de force of winemaking from a solera with few peers in Jerez.

Harvey's (Spain)

Harvey's Dune, Pale Dry Fino Sherry, Jerez de la Frontera. $12.99.   **83**
Pale golden hue with a greenish cast and brilliant clarity. Moderately light-bodied. Forcefully aromatic, showing a hint of acetone character, with a vibrant attack on the palate. Snappy and pleasantly bitter almond finish with good grip.

Harvey's Harvey's Club Classic Medium Dry Sherry, Jerez. $12.99.   **80**
Deep amber cast. Medium-bodied. Caramel, brown spices. Aromatically reserved with straightforward caramel flavors in the mouth. Supple and round in the mouth with a hint of sweetness.

Harvey's Harvey's Isis Pale Cream Sherry, Jerez de la Frontera. $12.99.   **84**
Pale straw cast. Medium-bodied. Blanched almonds, lacquer. Forward aromas carry a Fino-like quality throughout. Shows a touch of viscosity in the mouth with a hint of sweetness through the finish.

Harvey's Harvey's Bristol Cream Sherry, Jerez de la Frontera. $12.99.   **81**
Pale amber cast. Moderately light-bodied. Roasted nuts, caramel. Shows a touch of heat to the nose. Straightforward and flavorful with a lighter styled mouthfeel. Shows sweet caramel flavors through the finish.

Harvey's 1796 Rare Oloroso Sherry, Jerez de la Frontera. $50.   **88**
Deep mahogany with a ruby cast. Moderately full-bodied. Notes of golden raisins, molasses, orange peel. Lushly textured and hedonically flavored with a rich and sweet character that is well balanced and doesn't overwhelm. Not terribly complex, but very attractive on the whole. A very pleasant after-dinner drink.

Hidalgo (Spain)

Hidalgo La Gitana Manzanilla, Sanlucar de Barrameda. $9.99.   **95**
Very pale straw. Medium-bodied. Notes of citrus zest, petrol, brine. Crisp fragrant rancio aromas with petrol hints lead a crisp palate as clean as whistle with a hint of mild astringency and a subtle salty note through the finish.

Hidalgo Manzanilla Pasada, Sanlucar de Barrameda. $15.49.   **90**
Pale gold. Medium-bodied. Notes of salty blanched almonds, brine. Complex rancio aromas lead a full-flavored palate with a subtle oily-salty note and a lengthy finish with some fresh astringency. Steely edge.

Hidalgo Fino Superior "El Cuadrado", Jerez de la Frontera. $15.49.   **90**
Brilliant light gold. Medium-bodied. Notes of blanched almonds, minerals. Full fresh floral nose. Almost juicy, fresh palate with hint of softness and a lengthy juicy finish with briny notes.

Hidalgo Napoleon Amontillado, Sanlucar de Barrameda. $11.99.   **90**
Bright amber with a greenish copper tinge. Moderately light-bodied. Moderate acidity. Notes of sea salt, dried herbs, smoked peat. The maritime influence in the nose of this Sherry belies its years of cellaring in Sanlúcar on the bay of Cádiz as opposed to inland Jerez. It has definite similarities in its crispness and austerity to the Manzanillas of Sanlucar. A product of further aging, it has subtle peaty notes which are not unlike an Islay whiskey yet nonetheless very light and fresh. Not for everyone, but it would make an excellent fully flavored aperitif.

Hidalgo Amontillado Viejo, Jerez de la Frontera. $63.99.   **93**
Deep burnished amber with dark orange highlights. Moderately full-bodied. Notes of salted almonds, leather, brown spice. Rich, thick palate with an almost fruity acidic note up front balanced by expansive brown spicy notes that linger. The finish develops for some time after swallowing with a salty, nutty tang. This needs plenty of time to aerate and reveal its potential aromas.

Hidalgo Jerez Cortado, Sanlucar de Barrameda. $17.99.   **90**

Rich chestnut. Medium-bodied. Moderate acidity. Notes of browned butter, dried limes, raisins. Darkly aromatic with a broad presence on the palate. Somewhat angular through the finish.

Hidalgo Oloroso Especial, Sanlucar de Barrameda. $15.99.   **89**

Brilliant pale copper with a subtle greenish cast. Medium-bodied. Moderate acidity. Notes of salted almonds, peat smoke, citrus zest. Features a pronounced sea salt and peat smoke character, which is evocative of its lengthy aging only steps from the Atlantic. Racy acidity makes for an Oloroso, which is quite unusual in its fresh and lively character. A medicinal tinge to the finish is vaguely suggestive of an Islay whiskey. Brimming with character this would still make an ideal aperitif in addition to being paired with fully seasoned seafoods.

Hidalgo Pedro Ximenez Viejo, Sanlucar de Barrameda. $16.99.   **89**

Deep opaque mahogany with ruby highlights. Full-bodied. Notes of leather, dates, orange peel. Extremely broad and rich with admirable viscosity. The flavors are pure hedonism with a lengthy finish. Just a touch of acidity keeps it from becoming cloying.

Emilio Lustau (Spain)

Emilio Lustau Jarana, Light Fino Sherry, Jerez de la Frontera. $9.95.   **90**

Very pale straw. Moderately light-bodied. Notes of flowers, citrus zest, green olives. Fresh and lively, with a delectable perfumed character. Finishes crisply to round out the package.

Emilio Lustau Puerto Fino, Puerto de Santa Maria. $10.95.   **91**

Pale gold with green highlights. Moderately light-bodied. Notes of petrol, earth, blanched almonds. Complex and flavorful, with a fresh and lively palate feel. Has a fine finish with a lingering faintly roasted note. An ideal table companion.

Emilio Lustau Dry Amontillado Solera Reserva Los Arcos, Jerez de la Frontera. $9.95.   **87**

Tawny amber with bronze highlights. Medium-bodied. Notes of toasted pecans, honey, minerals. A pleasantly perfumed nose leads to a fuller warming mouthfeel, with an attractively roasted character. Crisp acidity makes for a clean drying finish. Would make an excellent companion to the table.

Emilio Lustau Rare Amontillado Solera Reserva Escuadrilla, Jerez de la Frontera. $15.   **90**

Pale amber with a copper green cast. Notes of brown spices, toasted nuts, flowers. Very enticing overall with a well-integrated character. Fully flavored yet quite crisp in the mouth with snappy acidity that lends a fresh green note. Fine lengthy finish. A definite match for rich seafoods and smoked meats.

Emilio Lustau Amontillado del Puerto, Solera Gran Reserva "San Bartolome", Puerto de Santa Maria. $17.99.   **89**

Deep copper hue with brilliant clarity. Moderately light-bodied. Bewitching praline and salted nut aromatics are well translated on the palate and come through in the lingering finish. Dry, clean, and crisp with good bite and fresh character throughout.

Emilio Lustau Palo Cortado Peninsula, Jerez de la Frontera. $14.95.   **85**

Clear and brilliant amber. Moderately light-bodied. Notes of dried fruits, green tea, old leather. Perfumed, with a soft and seamless mouthfeel. Well integrated, with exotic flavors that are offered on an undemanding framework.

Emilio Lustau Solera Reserva, Don Nuño Dry Oloroso, Jerez de la Frontera. $14.95.   **83**

Brilliant amber with greenish copper highlights. Moderately light-bodied. Moderate acidity. Leather, brown spices, citrus peel. Pleasantly aromatic with a tinge of greenness on the palate. Sprightly acidity has a focusing impact on the clean, snappy finish.

Emilio Lustau Very Rare Oloroso Solera, Reserva Emperatriz Eugenia,
Jerez de la Frontera. $23.95. **94**

Deep tawny amber with a golden rim. Moderately full-bodied. Notes of roasted nuts, leather, dried fruits. The concentrated aromas leap from the glass. Well-balanced acidity maintains a sense of liveliness through the lengthy finish. Would make a beautiful accompaniment to blue veined cheeses.

Emilio Lustau Deluxe Cream Solera Reserva Capataz Andres,
Jerez de la Frontera. $10.95. **91**

Deep mahogany with a tawny rim. Moderately full-bodied. Notes of salted pecans, brown spices, chocolate. Aromatic and flavorful with a lovely roasted character. Zesty acidity balances the sweetness and maintains a sense of freshness. Rich in the mouth, but features a delicate warming finish. Pair with cheeses to enjoy after a meal.

Emilio Lustau Rare Cream Solera Reserva Superior,
Jerez de la Frontera. $14.95. **89**

Deep mahogany with ruby highlights and a greenish rim. Moderately full-bodied. Notes of dried fruits, leather, salted nuts. Aromatic and flavorful with a well-balanced marriage of sweetness and acidity. Pleasant and lingering through the finish.

Emilio Lustau East India Solera Sherry, Jerez de la Frontera. $16.95. **89**

Deep mahogany with ruby highlights. Moderately full-bodied. Notes of molasses, orange peel, dried fruits. Classic, smooth, and rich, the mouthfeel is quite viscous. A touch of acidity in the finish keeps the sweetness in check. Enjoy with or as dessert.

Emilio Lustau 1986 Vendimia Cream Sherry, Jerez de la Frontera. $18.99. **84**

Deep amber. Medium-bodied with a viscous, honeyed mouthfeel. Lively balancing acidity. Very sweet but plays well opposite the acidity. Notes of blood orange, dried peach, brown spices, honey. Complex, supple, and integrated.

Emilio Lustau Moscatel Superior Emilin, Jerez de la Frontera. $14.95. **88**

Deep dark mahogany with ruby overtones. Moderately full-bodied. Notes of raisins, molasses, flowers. Aromatic with a full, viscous palate feel. A touch of acidity lightens up the lengthy finish.

Emilio Lustau "Las Cruces", Centenary Selection Moscatel,
Jerez de la Frontera. $19.99. **92**

Very deep mahogany hue. Full-bodied. Aromatic. Viscous quality to the palate with notes of golden raisins, dates, and black tea, offset by a solid level of acidity. Rich, long and flavorful. An exceptional dessert wine.

Emilio Lustau Pedro Ximenez, Solera Reserva San Emilio,
Jerez de la Frontera. $14.95. **90**

Deep mahogany with a tawny rim. Moderately full-bodied. Notes of golden raisins, dates, exotic spices, blackened nuts. Intriguing and complex, with a highly roasted character. Viscous mouthfeel with a zesty note throughout that keeps it from becoming overwhelming. A brilliant after-dinner drink.

Emilio Lustau Almacenista (Spain)

Emilio Lustau Almacenista Jurado Manzanilla Pasada de Sanlucar,
Sanlucar de Barrameda. $18.99. **89**

Pale gold. Medium-light bodied. Well balanced. Crisp and lean acidity. Palate dominated by nutty flavor elements and a subtle ginger note. Complex and lingering.

Emilio Lustau Almacenista Jose Luis Gonzalez Obregon,
Fino del Puerto, Puerto de Santa Maria. $13.95. **86**

Deep straw. Moderately light-bodied. Notes of dried herbs, toast, sake. Distinctively pungent in aromatics with a softer palate feel. Quite a bit richer than most Finos.

Emilio Lustau Almacenista Miguel Fontadez Florido, Amontillado de Jerez, Jerez de la Frontera. $20.
88

Pale copper with greenish highlights and brilliant clarity. Moderately light-bodied. Full acidity. Notes of leather, toast, roasted nuts, flowers. Perfumed and ephemeral in the nose, with a delicate and restrained overall character. Vibrant acidity lends snap to a sharp clean finish.

Emilio Lustau Almacenista Manuel Cuevas Jurado, Manzanilla Amontillada, Sanlucar de Barrameda. $19.95.
93

Golden with faded copper highlights. Moderately light-bodied. Moderate acidity. Notes of sea salt, roasted nuts, toffee. Features a subtle roasted character, which is admirably offset by its crisp and refreshing framework. A marvelous interplay between delicacy and richness of flavor. Quite complex through the finish. Highly recommended as an accompaniment to smoked fish or scallops.

Emilio Lustau Almacenista Alberto Lorento Piaget, Amontillado Fino de Jerez, Jerez de la Frontera. $20.
89

Copper-toned amber with brilliant clarity. Moderately light-bodied. Full acidity. Notes of smoke, roasted almonds, malt. Enticingly aromatic with an elegant slightly roasted character. These elements are admirably shown against a racy framework with vibrant acidity and a snappy finish. A wonderful marriage between complexity of flavor and a refreshing sense of lightness.

Emilio Lustau Almacenista Vides, Palo Cortado de Jerez, Jerez de la Frontera. $20.
92

Brilliant tawny amber. Medium-bodied. Full acidity. Notes of roasted salted nuts, orange peel, brown spices. Invitingly perfumed and complex with an attractive medicinal note. Ample acidity balances the rich flavors in allowing for a refreshing overall character.

Emilio Lustau Almacenista Rosario Farfante, Dos Cortados de Jerez, Jerez de la Frontera. $21.95.
90

Deep amber with brilliant clarity. Medium-bodied. Moderate acidity. Notes of brown spices, leather, salted nuts. Attractively perfumed with an explosion of flavors on the palate. Angular and zesty through the finish with attractive acidity, which maintains a sense of lightness.

Emilio Lustau Almacenista Vides, Single Cask Palo Cortado, Jerez de la Frontera. $35.
87

Bright copper hue with a subtle greenish cast. Medium-bodied. Very subtle aromas delicately open on the palate. Very dry, with a snappy, sea salt note on the finish. Will show best with food, as the complexities will be drawn out.

Emilio Lustau Almacenista Juan Garcia Jarana, Oloroso Pata de Gallina, Jerez de la Frontera. $21.95.
93

Deep and inviting brilliant amber hue with a greenish cast. Medium-bodied. Full acidity. Notes of dates, toffee, roasted walnuts. Assertively flavored with an attractive roasted character. Crisp acidity makes for a lively and fresh mouthfeel. Lengthy through the finish. A powerful wine to be savored, it would be a fitting end to a meal.

Emilio Lustau Almacenista Aranda y Latorre Oloroso Anada 1918, Jerez de la Frontera. $21.99.
94

Bright and glossy deep amber. Medium-bodied. Well-balanced acidity. Relatively dry with a very subtle impression of sweetness in the finish. Palate is a blend of raisins, walnuts, smoke, and orange. Somewhat tight at first, it opens up beautifully with aeration. Complex.

Emilio Lustau Almacenista Dona Pilar Aranda, Single Cask Oloroso, Jerez de la Frontera. $35.
86

Deep, brilliant mahogany color. Medium-bodied. Subtle, deceptively complex aromas. Crisp and dry on the palate with flavors of molasses, dates, and orange peel. Will perform best with food.

Scale: Superlative (96-100), Exceptional (90-95), Highly Recommended (85-89), Recommended (80-84), Not Recommended (Under 80)

Osborne (Spain)

Osborne Manzanilla Sherry, Jerez de la Frontera. $7.99.   **NR**

Osborne Fino Sherry, Jerez de la Frontera. $7.99.   **NR**

*Osborne Rare Sherry, Fino-Amontillado La Honda,
Jerez de la Frontera. $30.*   **90**

Pale amber with greenish highlights. Moderately light-bodied. Full acidity. Notes of lacquer, dried flowers, salted nuts. This Sherry's unmistakable Fino-like aromatics belie its origins in a rare Fino solera with over 50 years of age. The wine itself has an average age of 18 years, thus its having taken on Amontillado-like characteristics. Delicately wrought and lively, yet pungent and fully flavored, it is a very interesting marriage of the two styles. A definite candidate for the dinner table, where it should be able not only to stand up to fully flavored foods but also to refresh the palate as well.

*Osborne Dry Amontillado Solera AOS Rare Sherry,
Jerez de la Frontera. $35.*   **90**

Brilliant pale copper hue. Pungent aromas of rancio, salted nuts, and Christmas spices are intoxicating and exotic. A lush entry leads to a moderately full-bodied palate with a firm structure and outstanding complexity. Bone dry through the lengthy finish. Drink now.

Osborne Rare Palo Cortado, Solera PΔP, Jerez de la Frontera. $35.   **99**

Deep tawny brown. Medium-bodied. Rich and viscous. Perfectly balanced sweetness is almost overlooked because of the incredible complexity of flavors. Pralines, leather, figs, allspice; the adjectives are widely divergent and nonstop as new nuances are revealed with every return to the glass. Takes well to aeration and is very much a moving target. It continues to develop complexity after being open for some time. Though initially stunning, it seems to be at its best on the second or third day.

Osborne Rare Sherry, Oloroso, Solera India, Jerez de la Frontera. $30.   **92**

Opaque dark brown with ruby highlights. Full-bodied. Notes of treacle, black tea, pipe tobacco, spearmint. Pungent, large scaled, and moderately viscous, this is a Sherry to be reckoned with. The flavors are unique and exotic with ample acidity that makes for a drying finish. Not for everyone, but this wine is truly unique and exhilarating. Would stand up to wild game meats or full-bodied cigars, and becomes more accessible after being decanted and left to sit for several days.

*Osborne Rare Oloroso Amoroso, Solera Alonso el Sabio,
Jerez de la Frontera. $30.*   **98**

Deep mahogany with brilliant ruby highlights. Moderately full-bodied. Notes of toasted coconut, dried fruits, salted almonds. Seductive in nature with lushly perfumed aromatics. The sweetness on the palate is perfectly balanced by the wine's acidity. The overall impression is one of seamless harmony and elegance with warming, pleasantly woody overtones that linger on the palate for several minutes. This is a truly remarkable Sherry that deserves to be enjoyed on a cold night while sitting by the fireplace.

*Osborne Dark Mahogany Olorosa Solera BC 200 Rare Sherry,
Jerez de la Frontera. $35.*   **93**

Deep mahogany hue. Intense treacle, pecan, and sandalwood aromas show great complexity. A lush entry leads to a full-bodied, concentrated palate with great structure. The flavors build through the finish, but seem to end on a delicate note. Drink now.

Osborne Cream Sherry, Jerez de la Frontera. $7.99.   **83**

Brilliant deep amber with a greenish cast. Moderately full-bodied. Notes of brown spices, charred wood, roasted nuts. Forceful aromatics with a distinctive burnt character that winds its way to the finish. Moderately viscous, but balanced by crisp acidity.

Osborne Pedro Ximenez, Jerez de la Frontera. $10.99.   **89**

Dark opaque brown with a tawny rim and subtle greenish highlights. Full-bodied. Notes of golden raisins, mocha, dates. Broadly aromatic with deep and attractive flavors. Large scaled but not cloying. Lovely and quite lengthy through the finish.

Osborne Rare Pedro Ximenez Viejo, Jerez de la Frontera. $35.　　**96**

Opaque, nearly black in color. Full-bodied and extraordinarily viscous, it literally paints the side of the glass. Very sweet, but balanced out by the complexity of competing components. Dense chocolate, mocha, and date notes. An unbelievably concentrated Sherry that shows breeding by its ability to maintain balance and avoid becoming clumsy or cloying, given its scale. Long, lingering finish.

Bodegas Robles (Spain)

Bodegas Robles Robles Extra Cream, DO Montilla-Moriles. $7.　　**87**

Deep tawny hue with a bronzed cast. Medium-bodied. Complex and interesting aromatics lead to a well-balanced and vibrant palate. A hint of sweetness is offset by acidity, making for a refreshing and flavorful finish.

**Bodegas Robles Robles Seleccion Pedro Ximenez,
DO Montilla-Moriles. $12.**　　**88**

Very deep mahogany. Full-bodied. Rich and viscous. Features straightforward golden raisin, molasses, and date flavors with an interesting vinous quality. A solid Pedro Ximenez of midterm age.

Sanchez Romate (Spain)

Sanchez Romate Manzanilla, Sanlucar de Barrameda. $8.99.　　**92**

Pale gold. Medium-bodied. Notes of roasted nuts, toast, sweet herbs. Fuller in body and a touch darker than a standard manzanilla, this wine is exhibiting slight oxidative characteristics, perhaps a function of the age of the samples. Nonetheless, the flavors are fully developed and quite attractive, with a thoroughly cleansing brisk finish.

Sanchez Romate Fino Sherry, Jerez de la Frontera. $6.99.　　**86**

Pale straw. Medium-bodied. Balanced acidity. Notes of flowers, citrus, blanched almonds. Light floral aromas. Crisp greenish entrance with a clean character and delicate flavors through a simple finish. Best served well chilled as an aperitif.

Sanchez Romate Amontillado Sherry, Jerez de la Frontera. $6.99.　　**80**

Deep amber color. Medium-bodied. Notes of vanilla, dates, walnuts. Clean and well made with a touch of viscosity and a mild impression of sweetness. Crisp lingering finish.

Sanchez Romate Cream Sherry, Jerez de la Frontera. $5.99.　　**84**

Bright copper cast with a greenish tinge. Medium-bodied. Full acidity. Subtly extracted. Roasted nuts, citrus, toffee. Forward aromas show a candied nutty quality and a touch of heat. Lighter in the mouth with sweetness offset by vibrant acidity. Flavorful and straightforward.

Sandeman (Spain)

Sandeman Don Fino, Superior Dry Fino, Jerez de la Frontera. $11.99.　　**93**

Very pale clear straw. Moderately light-bodied. Full acidity. Notes of citrus, flowers, savory herbs. Should it be possible to describe color with aroma, this wine would serve as green in the aromatic dictionary. Bright, fresh, lively, and crisp, this is a Sherry of superlatives. Exquisite snap with an attractive astringency to the finish. Just the thing to tame the oppressive heat of an Andalusian summer afternoon.

**Sandeman Character, Medium Dry Amontillado,
Jerez de la Frontera. $13.99.**　　**89**

Brilliant pale amber with a subtle bronze cast. Medium-bodied. Notes of citrus peel, vanilla, dried herbs. Fresh and lively with a crisp green note to the nose. Refreshing and elegantly wrought with a touch of sweetness that is met with a dash of acidity in the finish, where it picks up a warming roasted note. Clean, crisp, and complex.

**Sandeman Royal Ambrosante Rare Palo Cortado,
Jerez de la Frontera. $20.**　　**88**

Nut brown. Medium-bodied and viscous. Sweet and quite rich. Brown sugar, mocha, and golden raisin notes. Full flavored and very enticing.

Sandeman Armada, Rich Cream Oloroso, Jerez de la Frontera. $11.99. **92**

Tawny amber with a greenish cast. Medium-bodied. Notes of leather, salted pecans, dried herbs. Full and complex in the nose with a pungent note, the palate is nonetheless fairly delicate. Moderate sweetness is well accented by pleasant acidity. Lengthy through the clean finish. Enjoy after a meal with cheeses and nuts.

Sandeman Royal Corregidor, Very Old Rare Rich Oloroso,
Jerez de la Frontera. $24.99. **88**

Deep and brilliant mahogany with ruby highlights. Moderately full-bodied. Notes of figs, caramel, roasted nuts. Lush and seamless with an elegant overall character. The sense of sweetness on the palate plants this wine into an after dinner category, but subtle acidity keeps it from becoming cloying.

Sandeman Imperial Corregidor Rarest V.V.O. Oloroso,
Jerez de la Frontera. $25. **91**

Deep brown. Medium-bodied. Very sweet and lush. Smoky dried date, chocolate, and caramel flavors are well defined and decadent. Rich, chewy finish. A densely styled dessert Oloroso.

Valdespino (Spain)

Valdespino Inocente Fino Sherry, Jerez de la Frontera. $14. **87**

Light straw. Medium-bodied. Notes of citrus, green apple, smoke. Quite pungent on the attack, with well-balanced acidity and a tangy finish. Forceful in style.

Valdespino Hartley & Gibson's Amontillado, Jerez de la Frontera. $7.99. **89**

Rich and inviting mahogany. Notes of salted pecans, molasses, smoke. A classically roasted Amontillado character is displayed on a moderately viscous and warm palate. Fully flavored, with a hint of sweetness that is admirably offset by fresh acidity. Very lengthy and elegant through the finish. Could go with food but may be best as a more delicate Oloroso-alternative for the fireplace.

Valdespino Amontillado, Jerez de la Frontera. $13.99. **90**

Deep and rich tawny amber. Moderately full-bodied. Notes of sweet malt, caramel, roasted nuts. Attractively perfumed with a viscous and slightly sweet presence on the palate. It is warm and quite complex with a drier finish due to its sprightly acidity. Classically roasted in character.

Valdespino Amontillado Coliseo, Jerez de la Frontera. $40. **92**

Deep tawny brown with ruby highlights. Full-bodied. Notes of peat, charred wood, dried apricots, toasted coconut. This thrilling Sherry emanates from Valdespino's famous old Coliseo solera. Quite pungent and very fully flavored with a highly extracted character, the vibrant acidity keeps it from seeming overly weighty. It features a medicinal character, which is not unlike that found in an Islay whiskey. Best after a meal, possibly accompanied by fine tobacco. Becomes more accessible after being open for one or two days, and should last a week.

Valdespino Palo Cortado Sherry del Carrascal, Jerez de la Frontera. $20. **88**

Deep amber. Moderately full-bodied. Moderate acidity. Mild sweetness. Notes of toffee, charred wood, exotic spices. Darkly flavored, the subtle sense of sweetness marries well with the acidity to lend an overall sense of complex harmony.

Valdespino Cardenal Palo Cortado Sherry, Jerez de la Frontera. $29. **90**

Rich mahogany. Moderately full-bodied. Notes of redwood, burned salted pecans with medicinal backnotes. Very unusual in style, unlike any other Palo Cortado. Exhibits a full-blown heavily roasted character with rich exotic flavors akin to those found in old cognacs or Islay whiskies. It is obviously the product of extreme barrel age, with a very dry palate and lingering finish that begs for a rich cigar. Outstanding, or just too demanding, depending upon your perspective.

Valdespino Solera 1842, Oloroso Viejo Dulce, Jerez de la Frontera. $19. **90**

Deep and brilliant mahogany with a subtle green cast. Full-bodied. Notes of coffee, brown spices, charred wood. Fully flavored and intense with vibrant acidity on the palate and a big warming finish. Attractively woody in overall character. Equally at home with richly flavored meats and cheeses or served as an ideal after-dinner digestif.

Valdespino Don Gonzalo Old Dry Oloroso Sherry,
Jerez de la Frontera. $20.   90

Deep and rich tawny amber with brilliant clarity. Full-bodied. Notes of leather, brown spices, charred wood. Fully flavored and rich with an almost viscous character on the palate. Heavily roasted woody tones are emphasized by vibrant acidity. Full throttle and lengthy, this is a warming sipping Sherry to be savored after a meal.

Valdespino Hartley & Gibson's Cream Sherry,
Jerez de la Frontera. $7.99.   90

Chestnut with a greenish hue. Medium full-bodied. Notes of oriental spices, dried fruits, redwood. Exotically perfumed, the nose is quite enticing. Moderately sweet and very flavorful. Lengthy and lingering finish.

Williams & Humbert (Spain)

Williams & Humbert Dry Sack Superior Medium Dry Sherry,
Jerez de la Frontera. $13.99.   86

Brilliant amber with copper highlights. Moderately full-bodied. Notes of wild mushrooms, toast, honey. Straightforward and well made with an unusual but enticing nose. The mild sweetness is balanced nicely by a touch of acidity, which keeps the finish fresh.

Porto

Barros (Portugal)

Barros Ruby Porto, Oporto. $8.99.   84

Brownish-garnet. Moderately light-bodied. Notes of dark chocolate, cherries. Ripe fruity character on the palate with mild drying components give this a touch of leanness.

Barros Tawny Porto, Oporto. $8.99.   82

Deep reddish-amber. Medium-bodied. Notes of cherries, brown spice, nuts, raisins. Fruity aromas translate well onto the warm and supple palate. Fruit-driven style.

Barros Quinta D. Matilde Tawny Porto, Oporto. $13.99.   86

Pale amber-rosé. Moderately light-bodied. Notes of dried strawberries, vanilla. Fragrant aromatics. A light and delicate style with subtle nuances.

Barros 20 Anos Tawny Porto, Oporto. $33.99.   90

Light brownish-amber color. Moderately full-bodied. Notes of caramel, Grand Marnier, leather. Intense aromatics precede a silky mouthwatering palate kept lively with fine acids to balance the sugars.

Barros 1991 Vintage Porto, Oporto. $20.99.   91

Black-ruby to a purple rim. Moderately full-bodied. Notes of bramble fruits, flowers, vanilla. Intense ripe fruit nose leads into a deep black fruit palate with good viscosity. Well integrated and balanced.

Borges 1992 Late Bottled Vintage Porto, Oporto. $16.   84

Deep blood red. Rustic, earthy aromas. Deep, sweet flavors on entry lead a full-bodied palate with some rustic, dry flavors that grow on the finish.

Borges 1994 Vintage Porto, Oporto. $25.   91

Deep purple-red. Very youthful, with floral, jammy fruit aromas. Sweet and juicy on the entry with fleshy, young flavors and good body. The tannins are soft and plush on the finish. Hedonistic, but it needs some years to mesh together.

Churchill's (Portugal)

Churchill's 1990 Dry White Porto, Oporto. $16.99.   80

Pale bronze color with a slight haze. Medium-bodied. Notes of brown spices, cream. Has a bit of heat to the nose. Quite round and slightly sweet in the mouth with subtle toasty flavors. Quick hot finish.

Churchill's VC Reserve Porto, Oporto. $11.99.　　　**85**

Deep ruby. Medium-bodied. Balanced acidity. Notes of black cherries, herbs, rubber. Distinct aromatics lead into a palate with some depth, richness, and a few edges.

Churchill's 10 Year Old Tawny Porto, Oporto. $26.99.　　　**84**

Deep mahogany with a fade to the rim. Medium-bodied. Cocoa, brown spices. Reserved aromatically, but the flavors expand on the palate. Finishes with mild astringency and heat.

Churchill's 1990 Late Bottled Vintage Porto, Oporto. $19.99.　　　**86**

Blackish-garnet color. Medium-bodied. Moderately extracted. Brown spices, caramel, black fruits. Rich and aromatic with complex flavors that taper off on a lighter-styled palate feel. Drying on the finish.

Churchill's 1990 Quinta da Agua Alta Single Quinta Vintage Porto, Oporto. $26.95.　　　**85**

Deep purple. Medium- to full-bodied. Notes of bramble fruits, plums, vanilla. Fully flavored and straightforward with a concise integrated character.

Churchill's 1992 Quinta da Agua Alta Single Quinta Vintage Porto, Oporto. $24.95.　　　**88**

Deep purple. Full-bodied. Notes of smoke, bramble fruits, tobacco. Straightforward and direct with forward fruit and an ample framework.

Churchill's 1995 Quinta da Agua Alta Single Quinta Vintage Porto, Oporto. $34.99.　　　**89**

Opaque blackish hue with a purple rim. Moderately full-bodied. Shoe polish, lacquer, black fruits. Aromatic and quite complex in flavor, though somewhat lighter in structure for such a youthful Port. Should be an exceptional drink within a decade.

Churchill's 1991 Vintage Porto, Oporto. $51.99.　　　**85**

Deep blackish-purple hue. Medium-bodied. Black fruits, licorice, lacquer. Still quite youthful, with primarily grape flavors to the fore. Lighter in style on the palate with a sense of leanness to the finish. Still a bit unyielding. Try in another five years.

Churchill's 1994 Vintage Porto, Oporto. $39.99.　　　**87**

Black-ruby with a purple rim. Full-bodied. Highly extracted. Notes of flowers, oriental spice, black fruits. Pronounced floral aromatics. Ripe grape character with a strong exotic spicy component. Quite approachable now but will be even better in the short term when components come together.

Cockburn's (Portugal)

Cockburn's Special Reserve, Oporto. $9.99.　　　**85**

Medium purple. Medium-bodied. Notes of tobacco, prunes, dates, brown spices. Soft and lush on the palate with a sweet finish.

Cockburn's 10 Year Old Tawny Porto, Oporto. $25.　　　**86**

Light copper. Medium-bodied. Moderately extracted. Brown spices, caramel. Lighter in style, with a flavorful wood-accented palate feel. Has a sense of delicacy to the well-balanced, sweet finish.

Cockburn's Directors' Reserve, 20 Year Old Tawny Porto, Oporto. $45.　　　**92**

Deep mahogany hue. Moderately full-bodied. Moderately extracted. Caramel, toasted wood. Pleasantly aromatic, with forceful character on the palate. Deeply flavored and rich with fine length and intensity.

Cockburn's 1992 Late Bottled Vintage Porto, Oporto. $20.　　　**87**

Cherry red. Medium-bodied. Notes of sweet dried cherries, sweet berries. Oak-accented aromas lead a spicy rounded palate with a bright fruity entry that expands on the palate. Finish shows some mildly dry astringency.

Cockburn's 1992 Quinta dos Canais, Oporto. $38.　　　**88**
Deep blackish hue with a ruby rim. Moderately full-bodied. Black fruits, lacquer.
Aromatic and flavorful, still dominated by primary fruit flavors. Rich and firmly
structured on the palate with a mouth-filling character. Fine length and grip.
Could use at least a decade to come into its own.

Cockburn's 1995 Quinta dos Canais, Oporto. $38.　　　**91**
Deep, opaque blackish hue with a purple rim. Moderately full-bodied. Shoe polish,
lacquer, black fruits. Aromatic and profoundly complex with a very sturdy structure.
Well balanced and firm. Should be drinking quite well in 10 to 15 years.

Cockburn's 1991 Vintage Porto, Oporto. $30.　　　**87**
Deep purple. Full-bodied. Notes of plums, pomegranate, vanilla. A rich mouthfeel
carries the suggestion of overripe fruits in a firmly structured framework.

Cockburn's 1994 Vintage Porto, Oporto. $40.　　　**89**
Deep ruby with full purple highlights. Moderately full-bodied. Notes of violets,
chocolate, bramble fruits. Violet-scented nose reveals a very solid palate with tightly
wound concentrated fruit flavors on the midpalate. Finish dominated by spirity
heat and spice.

Croft (Portugal)

Croft Distinction, Tawny Reserve, Oporto. $20.　　　**81**
Bright mahogany with a ruby cast. Moderately light-bodied. Moderately extracted.
Black tea, brown spices. Features a touch of heat in the nose. Lighter in style, with
straightforward, simple, attractive flavors.

Croft 1990 Late Bottled Vintage Porto, Oporto. $21.99.　　　**87**
Deep brick red. Moderately full-bodied. Notes of plums, dried fruits, oak spice. Attractive
oak accented aromas reveal a rich, rounded mouthful of sweet plummy flavors.

Croft 1995 Quinta de Roeda Vintage Porto, Oporto. $40.　　　**88**
Deep and opaque blackish hue with a ruby edge. Moderately full-bodied. Black fruits,
licorice, chocolate. Deeply aromatic with a wave of dark flavors on the palate. A youthful
wine, still dominated by its primary flavors. It should develop nicely with at least a decade
of cellaring.

Croft 1994 Vintage Porto, Oporto. $59.99.　　　**92**
Opaque blackish hue with a ruby edge. Full-bodied. Black fruits, licorice, lacquer.
Aromatic, with a rich and flavorful mouthfeel. Dark and powerful flavors have fine
grip and intensity, while the full-throttle character of the wine's other components
bodes well for decades of cellaring.

Delaforce (Portugal)

Delaforce His Eminence's Reserve Tawny Porto, Oporto. $20.　　　**82**
Bright mahogany with a ruby cast. Moderately light-bodied. Subtly extracted. Toasted
wood. Pleasantly aromatic, with a simple straightforward palate feel. Light and lively
with subtle woody notes to the finish.

Delaforce Curious & Ancient 20 Year Old Tawny Porto, Oporto. $40.　　　**94**
Deep copper. Medium-bodied. Moderately extracted. Brown spices, toasted wood, bacon
fat. Deeply aromatic with a hint of rancio and a wave of complex flavors on the palate.
Good length and grip with real intensity.

Delaforce 1991 Late Bottled Vintage Porto, Oporto. $22.99.　　　**84**
Brick red. Moderately light-bodied. Notes of oak spice, mild sweet plums. Full spicy nose
leads a simple palate with some hot spicy notes through the finish. Simple.

Delaforce 1991 Quinta da Corte Vintage Porto, Oporto. $34.99.　　　**87**
Saturated ruby-black color. Medium-bodied. Notes of licorice, earth, oak spice, black
fruits. Spirity, oaky nose hints at dark fruits. Rich sweet fruit flavors on entry give way to
a solid underlay of firm oak spice and earth. This needs three to four more years for its
components to settle.

Delaforce 1995 Quinta da Corte Vintage Porto, Oporto. $40.   **90**

Very deep and opaque blackish hue with a ruby rim. Full-bodied. Black fruits, anise, chocolate. Profoundly aromatic, very deep and lush, with a powerful mouth-filling character. A forceful wine that should require up to 15 or 20 years to come into its own.

Delaforce 1992 Vintage Porto, Oporto. $35.   **85**

Very dark purple. Full-bodied. Notes of pepper, cherries, black fruits. Richly fruity with subtle acidity and a drying finish.

Dow's (Portugal)

Dow's Christmas Porto, Oporto. $13.99.   **80**

Deep ruby with a slight fade to the rim. Moderately light-bodied. Black fruits. Straightforward and lighter in style with a supple, fruit-accented palate feel. Tapers off on the sweet finish.

Dow's Boardroom Tawny Porto, Oporto. $17.   **82**

Bright tawny-chestnut color. Muted aromas show subtle, nutty, spicy overtones and a spirit-like note. A lush entry leads a medium-bodied palate with a hint of sweetness. The finish is lean and drying. Straightforward. Drink now.

Dow's 10 Year Old Tawny Porto, Oporto. $26.   **81**

Bright mahogany with a ruby tinge. Medium-bodied. Toasted wood, brown spices. Hot in the nose and through the finish. Straightforward chunky flavors carry through to a relatively sweet finish.

Dow's 20 Year Old Tawny Porto, Oporto. $44.99.   **94**

Dark ruby-brown. Very rich aromas of brown spice and rancio. Rich on the entry with golden raisin flavors and rich brown spice character that emerges on the finish along with a touch of sea salt.

Dow's 30 Year Old Tawny Porto, Oporto. $75.   **91**

Deep reddish-amber. Medium light-bodied. Mild acid. Notes of roasted nuts, brown spices. Subtle and delicate with a complex layer of wood tinged flavors. Smooth and lingering.

Dow's 1982 Single Year Tawny Reserve, Oporto. $29.   **86**

Brilliant deep amber hue with ruby overtones. Forward red fruit and brown spice aromas show a harmonious wood accent. A rich entry leads a medium-bodied palate with mild sweetness. The finish is lean and flavorful. Drink now.

Dow's 1991 Late Bottled Vintage Porto, Oporto. $17.   **83**

Deep blackish-ruby hue. Medium-bodied. Moderately extracted. Black fruits, lacquer. Reserved aromatically, with a straightforward fruit-accented palate. Finishes with a touch of heat and a slight herbal note.

Dow's 1992 Late Bottled Vintage Porto, Oporto. $16.99.   **81**

Bright ruby hue. Youthful, floral aromas. Bright, sweet plum flavors on entry, with a medium body and lingering sweet flavors. A very attractive ruby style.

Dow's 1992 Quinta do Bomfim Vintage Porto, Oporto. $12/375 ml.   **89**

Dense purple hue. Supple, full-bodied. Bracing layer upon layer of opulent red fruit, raisins, and soft tannins. Lingering finish.

Dow's 1995 Quinta do Bomfim Vintage Porto, Oporto. $38.   **87**

Saturated deep purplish-red. Moderately full-bodied. Highly extracted. Mildly tannic. Notes of elderberry, plums, oak spice. Spicy rich fruity aromas have a distinct floral note. Rich rounded black fruit flavors show a silky quality on the palate. Solid spicy finish.

Dow's 1991 Vintage Porto, Oporto. $45.   **90**

Opaque blackish-purple. Full-bodied. Notes of pepper, black cherries, cassis. Tightly wound and closed in with a daunting structure. Difficult to evaluate now, but all components seem to be in place for serious aging.

Dow's 1994 Vintage Porto, Oporto. $38.   **98**

Opaque blackish-ruby with a purple rim. Full-bodied. Notes of black fruits, spice. Deep and brooding aromatics translate well onto an extracted and concentrated youthful palate with great structure. A Port for long term cellaring — 20 years or more.

Feist (Portugal)

Feist Baronial Fine White Port, Oporto. $12.   **83**

Full orange luster. Moderately full-bodied. Notes of pepper, sweet citrus fruits, glycerin. Mildly spicy sweet aromas lead a sweet silky mouthfeel showing viscosity and richness of mouthfeel with a lingering medicinal, peppery note.

Feist Baronial, Oporto. $12.   **84**

Medium crimson appearance. Medium-bodied. Notes of sweet baked fruits, flowers. Generous floral black fruit aromas lead a rounded palate with bright fruity flavors that conclude softly. Versatile style.

Feist Vintage Character, Oporto. $14.   **80**

Deep ruby. Medium-bodied. Notes of ripe baked fruits, brown spice. Rounded sweet fruity, Port like aromas. Easy and accessible with a spirity feel. A letdown on the finish.

Feist Fine Baronial Tawny Porto, Oporto. $12.   **80**

Very pale cherry red. Medium-bodied. Notes of sweet red berries, brown spice. Rounded fruity aromas are well expressed on the palate with subtle spicy hints on the finish. More vinous fruit flavors than one would expect from a tawny style.

Feist 10 Year Old Tawny Porto, Oporto. $18.   **85**

Pale orange-brick red color. Medium-bodied. Notes of dates, figs, brown spice. Smooth butterscotch palate has richness of mouthfeel and generous spicy oak flavors through the finish.

Feist 20 Year Old Tawny Porto, Oporto. $30.   **87**

Pale amber with rich reddish-gold highlights. Moderately full-bodied. Notes of rancio, toffee, boiled sweets, brown spice. Complex hints of Amontillado Sherry on the nose lead a rich toffee-like palate with suggestively fruity sweetness that expands on the palate. Lingering rancio notes on the finish.

Feist 30 Year Old Tawny Porto, Oporto. $60.   **92**

Full reddish-amber color. Moderately full-bodied. Notes of rancio, Amontillado, caramel, brown spice. Complex aged Sherry-like aromas lead a rich, rounded palate with outstanding spicy flavors and a lingering finish that reminds one of the finest Amontillado sherries. Complex and exotic.

Feist 40 Year Old Tawny Porto, Oporto. $100.   **91**

Dark chestnut brown color. Full-bodied. Notes of dates, brown spice, licorice. Sweet rich aromas show have mature spicy accents. Rich chewy mouthful of spicy sweet flavors has a velvety viscous feel. Impressively aged with a weighty and assertive character through the finish.

Feist 1974 Colheita, Oporto. $38.   **87**

Deep copper color. Medium-bodied. Brown sugar, caramel. Rather reserved aromatically, with a pleasant roasted quality on the palate. Well balanced with good grip on the finish.

Feist 1967 Colheita, Oporto. $63.   **93**

Deep copper color. Moderately full-bodied. Moderately extracted. Roasted nuts, treacle. Fragrant, with a full and rich roasted character on the palate. Concentrated and well integrated through the finish with fine grip and intensity.

Feist 1966 Colheita, Oporto. $70.   **88**

Bright copper. Medium-bodied. Brown spices, toasted wood. Slightly hot in the nose, with a lean, comparatively light palate feel featuring vibrant acidity through the finish.

Feist 1965 Colheita, Oporto. $72.   **90**

Deep copper cast. Moderately full-bodied. Roasted nuts, molasses. Pleasantly aromatic, with a rich and slightly viscous mouthfeel. Flavorful and well balanced through the finish with good grip and intensity.

Scale: Superlative (96-100), Exceptional (90-95), Highly Recommended (85-89), Recommended (80-84), Not Recommended (Under 80)

Feist 1963 Colheita, Oporto. $76. **92**

Deep copper color. Moderately full-bodied. Brown spices, caramel. Reserved aromatically, but quite rich and flavorful on the palate with deep and supple flavors. Fine grip and length with excellent intensity.

Feist 1957 Colheita, Oporto. $106. **89**

Bright copper hue. Medium-bodied. Orange peel and dried wood. Features some heat and a decided note of rancio richness to the nose. Drying on the palate, with a lean personality and mild astringency to the intense finish.

Feist 1991 Late Bottled Vintage Porto, Oporto. $18. **84**

Full brick red. Medium-bodied. Notes of chocolate, cherry, brown sugar. Generous caramelized aromas show maturity. Some richness in flavors and mouthfeel with plenty of spice that lingers through the dry finish.

Feist 1991 Vintage Porto, Oporto. $26. **85**

Dark cherry red. Medium-bodied. Notes of flowers, sweet red fruits, Sweet vinous aromas lead a rounded smooth mouthfeel showing good integration and development. The finish still shows some awkward tannin that a some years of cellaring will resolve.

Fonseca (Portugal)

Fonseca Bin 27 Fine Reserve Porto, Oporto. $17.99. **88**

Deep, saturated ruby-purple hue. Brooding lacquer, black fruit and chocolate aromas are classic and intense. A firm entry leads a moderately full-bodied palate with mild sweetness and a firm structure. The finish is deep and balanced. Drink now.

Fonseca 10 Year Old Tawny Porto, Oporto. $27.99. **86**

Fading brown with a subtle ruby highlight. Muted aromas have a salty, old barrel character. Sweet entry, with a rounded mouthfeel and flavors of caramel and dates, and notes of rancio and sea salt on the finish.

Fonseca 20 Year Old Tawny Porto, Oporto. $48.99. **91**

Medium ruby-brown. Assertively oaky aromas with rancio notes. Sweet and generous on the attack, with complex and harmoniously integrated brown spice flavors carrying through to an impressively long finish.

Fonseca 1990 Late Bottled Vintage Porto, Oporto. $17.49. **87**

Black-ruby color. Moderately full-bodied. Moderately extracted. Notes of raisins, plums, vanilla. Mild dried fruit aromas lead into a smooth and supple palate with a focused fruit core. Lingering fruity finish.

Fonseca 1995 Guimaraens Vintage Porto, Oporto. $38.99. **92**

Very deep blackish hue with a purple rim that paints the side of the glass. Full-bodied. Notes of black fruits, chocolate, lacquer. Somewhat reined in aromatically, with a very backward and powerful personality. Very rich, with great grip and intensity and a lash of tannin. Has decades of life in front of it. Probably needs a minimum of 10 to 15 years to become approachable.

Fonseca 1994 Vintage Porto, Oporto. $50. **96**

Completely saturated blackish-purple. Full-bodied. Notes of violets, blackberry, chocolate. Attractive floral accents on the nose lead a heavyweight palate with solid, tightly wound fruit flavors showing great generosity up front. The finish is dominated by imposing tannins. A long-term keeper that shows great promise. Cellar 20 years or more.

Graham's (Portugal)

Graham's Six Grapes Porto, Oporto. $19. **86**

Deep blackish-ruby hue with a purple cast. Moderately full-bodied. Briar fruits, lacquer. Aromatic, with a pure and concentrated character on the palate. Clean and lengthy finish with good grip and intensity.

Graham's 10 Year Old Tawny Porto, Oporto. $27.99.　　91

Pale ruby with a copper hue. Caramel and date aromas. The generous entry shows sweet fruit with a good follow-through and well-integrated oak-spice complexity. Very harmonious and long, with notable depth.

Graham's 20 Year Old Tawny Porto, Oporto. $45.99.　　96

Ruby-copper hue with brown highlights. Rich, generous aromas and a concentrated attack with golden raisin flavors and a rich mouthfeel. The finish shows complexity and sweet persistence with rancio and brown spice flavors. This is a fatter style, with Amontillado-like complexity.

Graham's 30 Year Old Tawny Porto, Oporto. $81.　　90

Dark reddish-amber. Medium light-bodied. Notes of toast, hazelnuts, dried cherries. Refined and subtle flavors have a definite sense of sweetness through the finish.

Graham's 1990 Late Bottled Vintage Porto, Oporto. $17.　　89

Black-ruby color. Moderately full-bodied. Notes of black fruits, smoke, pine. Pronounced wood aromas lead into a rich, jammy, and generously proportioned style. Long lingering fruity finish.

Graham's 1991 Late Bottled Vintage Porto, Oporto. $18.　　87

Deep blackish-ruby hue. Moderately full-bodied. Moderately extracted. Black fruits, minerals, lacquer. Reserved aromatically, though rich and supple on the palate with a fruit-accented personality. Chunky and flavorful through the finish.

Graham's 1992 Late Bottled Vintage Porto, Oporto. $17.99.　　83

Medium ruby hue. Mildly fruity, candied, spirity aromas. Sweet plum flavors dominate the attack, with a medium-bodied palate and supple finish.

Graham's 1992 Malvedos Vintage Porto, Oporto. $13.50/375 ml.　　90

Deep purple. Full-bodied. A lush, densely layered palate brimming with berries, oak, and herbs. Excellent large structure with a firm tannic grip and solid acidity. Long, buttery finish. A long-term cellar selection.

Graham's 1995 Malvedos Vintage Porto, Oporto. $43.　　86

Saturated deep purplish-red. Moderately full-bodied. Highly extracted. Notes of plums, licorice, brown spice. Rich sweet plummy aromas. Rounded and fleshy on the palate with generous flavors and some earthy dry tannins on the finish. Solidly structured.

Graham's 1991 Vintage Porto, Oporto. $49.　　95

Very dark purple. Full-bodied. Notes of black cherries, vanilla, black pepper. Fully extracted and lengthy with exceptional balance and grip.

Graham's 1994 Vintage Porto, Oporto. $46.　　95

Deep opaque black with a ruby rim. Full-bodied. Notes of sandalwood, black fruit, to ruby rim. Dark brooding aromas lead into a firm extracted palate. Currently quite closed but it shows richness and depth of flavors. For long-term cellaring.

Harvey's (Portugal)

Harvey's Gold Cap Fine Ruby, Oporto. $17.　　NR

Harvey's Fine Tawny, Oporto. $14.99.　　88

Dark garnet. Medium-bodied. Notes of walnuts, raisins, baked cherries. Well balanced with focused flavors. Lingering dried fruit notes on the finish.

Harvey's Hunting Tawny, Oporto. $17.　　82

Bright copper with a ruby cast. Moderately light-bodied. Caramel, brown spices. Light in style, but with a pleasant array of dried fruit and brown spice flavors on the palate. Delicate wood-accented finish.

Harvey's Director's Bin, 20 Year Old Tawny Porto, Oporto. $32.50.　　85

Pale copper cast. Moderately light-bodied. Subtly extracted. Toasted wood. Light in style with a straightforward woody personality. Pleasantly sweet, mildly hot finish.

Scale: Superlative (96-100), Exceptional (90-95), Highly Recommended (85-89), Recommended (80-84), Not Recommended (Under 80)

Martinez Fine Ruby Porto, Oporto. $11.   **80**

Pale cherry red with a slight fade. Lean red fruit and mineral aromas. A lush entry leads
a moderately light-bodied palate with moderate sweetness and a touch of heat. The finish
is straightforward. A lighter style, but competent. Drink now.

Martinez (Portugal)

Martinez Master's Reserve Porto, Oporto. $16.   **83**

Pale cherry red with a slight fade. Muted red fruit and mineral aromas. A lean entry
leads a medium-bodied palate with marked sweetness and a touch of heat.
Straightforward, spicy finish. Drink now.

Martinez Fine Tawny Porto, Oporto. $11.   **81**

Pale cherry-garnet hue. Spirity red fruit and chocolate aromas. A lush entry leads a
medium-bodied palate with straightforward wood-accented flavors that retain a fruity
overtone. Clean, mildly sweet finish. Drink now.

Martinez 10 Year Old Tawny Porto, Oporto. $26.   **83**

Bright ruby-brown. Fruit-forward aromas with subtle oak spice. Sweet and direct on entry,
though the flavors do not persist. Finishes with subtle rancio. A lighter, sweeter style.

Martinez 20 Year Old Tawny Porto, Oporto. $46.   **84**

Pale ruby-brown. Woody aromas with a spirit-like note. A sweet, spicy entry follows
through on the palate but finishes rather quickly. This does not show the depth of
intensity one expects from a 20-year-old tawny.

Martinez 1995 Single Quinta da Chousa Vintage Porto, Oporto. $40.   **86**

Bright ruby hue with a lightening rim. Wonderfully aromatic with full floral, sweet
fruit aromas. Sweet and rich on the entry with medium body and sugar plum flavors.
Well balanced, in a lighter style. Still needs more time.

Martinez 1995 Quinta da Eira Velha Vintage Porto, Oporto. $45.   **84**

Dark ruby with a blood-red rim. Lean, earthy aromas. A sweet entry leads a moderately
full-bodied palate with fruit fading on the midpalate. Turns rather dry and tannic on
the finish. Though it shows some development, this is not promising for the long haul.

Osborne (Portugal)

Osborne Ruby Porto, Oporto. $10.99.   **82**

Dark ruby-purple. Medium- to full-bodied. Notes of black cherry, pipe tobacco, brown
spice. Vibrant on the palate with a refreshing touch of acidity.

Osborne 1992 Vintage Porto, Oporto. $22.50.   **87**

Deep purple. Medium- to full-bodied. Notes of black cherries, cassis, sandalwood.
Relatively restrained in style with a tightly wound core of fruit flavors. Not overly sweet.

Osborne 1994 Vintage Porto, Oporto. $28.   **88**

Dark ruby with a purple cast. Medium-bodied. Notes of dark fruit, currants, minerals.
Floral aromatics reveal a rich core of brooding dark fruit. Finely extracted with good
acidic backbone. Should cellar well, although surprisingly approachable now.

Pitters (Portugal)

Pitters Premium d'Or, Oporto. $19.95.   **NR**

Quinta de Roriz (Portugal)

Quinta de Roriz 1988 Late Bottled Vintage Porto, Oporto. $16.99.   **86**

Ruby with a garnet cast. Moderately light-bodied. Notes of dried fruits, brown spices,
Light perfumed aromas. A mature example in a lighter and more delicate style.

Quinta de Roriz 1991 Vintage Porto, Oporto. $32.49.   **87**

Black-ruby. Moderately full-bodied. Highly extracted. Notes of black fruits, bitter sweet
chocolate. Subdued and somewhat closed nose. Nice rich center with a sweetish finish
with spirity heat. Simple, easy, pleasant style.

Quinta do Noval (Portugal)

Quinta do Noval Old Coronation Ruby Porto, Oporto. $10.99.   **82**

Very deep ruby hue. Moderately full-bodied. Moderately extracted. Notes of chocolate, cherries, herbs. Sweet fruit character on the palate is contrasted by a solid spicy frame and a reasonably lean, dry finish.

Quinta do Noval Porto L.B. House Reserve, Oporto. $14.99.   **84**

Deep tawny with garnet highlights. Medium-bodied. Notes of candied cherries, tobacco, cedar. Restrained and straightforward fruit with a nice spicy component through the finish.

Quinta do Noval Tawny, Oporto. $10.   **80**

Deep reddish-amber. Medium-bodied. Notes of figs, brown sugar. Straightforward and flavorful with a warming finish.

Quinta do Noval 10 Year Old Tawny Porto, Oporto. $25.99.   **87**

Reddish-amber. Medium-bodied. Notes pine, earth, dried red fruits. Wood influenced aromas reveal a firmly structured, slightly lean style with a dryish finish.

Quinta do Noval 20 Year Old Tawny Porto, Oporto. $82.99.   **91**

Reddish-amber. Medium-bodied. Notes of dried fruit, butterscotch. Rich aromas lead into a succulent assertively fruity palate with layers of nutty complexity through to an elegant textured finish.

Quinta do Noval 1984 Colheita Old Tawny Porto, Oporto. $23.75.   **86**

Deep tawny with garnet highlights. Medium-bodied. Balanced acidity. Notes of earth, cherries, raisins. Warm aromas reveal a generous although not over complex palate that finishes with a pleasing tangy note.

Quinta do Noval 1982 Colheita Old Tawny Porto, Oporto. $28.49.   **88**

Deep orangey-amber. Medium-bodied. Notes of dried fruits, nuts, vanilla. Fruity aromas translate well on the palate with a textured, velvety mouthfeel. A little warmth on the finish.

Quinta do Noval 1976 Colheita Old Tawny Porto, Oporto. $50.49.   **93**

Deep amber. Medium-bodied. Notes of dried fruit, earth, nuts. Fragrant mildly earthy nose leads into a generous palate with a nutty, creamy character. Fruit is showing well.

Quinta do Noval 1971 Colheita Old Tawny Porto, Oporto. $74.99.   **95**

Deep amber. Medium-bodied. Notes of raisins, nuts, caramel, leather. Complex and mildly tangy aromas lead into an expansive sweet palate with a hint of structure. 'Woody' character is nicely offset by fruit acidity.

Quinta do Noval 1968 Colheita Old Tawny Porto, Oporto. $83.49.   **92**

Deep amber. Moderately full-bodied. Notes of dried fruits, caramel, brown spice. Complex aromatics lead into an unctuous mouthfeel and warm spicy palate. Lingering sweet nutty finish.

Quinta do Noval 1967 Colheita Old Tawny Porto, Oporto. $88.99.   **94**

Rich tawny amber. Medium-bodied. Notes of dried fruits, almonds, dark chocolate. Complex aromas lead into a rounded palate and mouthfeel with a long roasted finish.

Quinta do Noval 1966 Colheita Old Tawny Porto, Oporto. $98.49.   **93**

Tawny amber. Medium-bodied. Notes of dried apricot, orange peel, nuts. Vibrant in the mouth with a pronounced nutty character backed up by fine acidity. Complex and lengthy with a lingering finish.

Quinta do Noval 1989 Late Bottled Vintage Porto, Oporto. $18.99.   **87**

Ruby with tawny highlights. Medium-bodied. Notes of raisins, plums, brown spice. A more delicate mature style with fragrant aromatics and soft textured mouthfeel. Well-integrated flavors.

Quinta do Noval 1995 Quinta de Silval Vintage Porto, Oporto. $40.   **86**

Opaque blackish hue with a purple cast to the rim. Moderately full-bodied. Black fruits. Reined in aromatically. Quite flavorful in a fruit-driven way. For a youthful vintage Port, it retains a sense of lightness on the palate, and is quite sweet through the finish. A good candidate for midterm cellaring of a decade or so.

Quinta do Noval 1991 Vintage Porto, Oporto. $29.25. **92**

Blackish-purple. Full-bodied. Notes of black fruits, toasty vanilla, cassis. Rich and concentrated with fully extracted classic flavors and a weighty framework.

Quinta do Noval 1991 Nacional Vintage Porto, Oporto. $250. **98**

Very dark purple. Notes of earth, black cherry, spicy plums. Elegant and supple with an unmistakable note of terroir. The structure is subtle and tactfully wrought. Though almost approachable now, it will clearly improve.

Quinta do Noval 1994 Vintage Porto, Oporto. $35. **90**

Opaque black-ruby with a purple rim. Moderately full-bodied. Notes of black fruits, flowers, tar. Floral accented aromas. Dense and finely extracted palate with some ripe opulent fruit. Still very spirity and tight knit. A medium- to long-term cellar wine for more than 10 years.

Quinta do Noval 1995 Vintage Porto, Oporto. $55. **93**

Deep and opaque blackish hue with a purple rim. Full-bodied. Balanced acidity. Black fruits, lacquer. Deep and powerful with a rich and complex palate feel. Currently tightly wound, with all the components to sustain decades of cellaring. Try in 10 to 15 years.

Ramos Pinto (Portugal)

Ramos Pinto Fine Ruby, Oporto. $13.75. **80**

Blackish-ruby with a garnet rim. Moderately light-bodied. Subtly extracted. Dried herbs, raisins. Shows some subtle oxidation in the nose. Lighter in the mouth, with a straightforward herb-accented finish.

Ramos Pinto Quinta da Urtiga, Oporto. $18. **88**

Dark ruby-brick. Medium-bodied. Notes of earth, brown spice, black fruits. Chewy black fruits on entry reveal a full-flavored earthy style with a hint of tannin on the finish. Shows both substance and character.

Ramos Pinto Superior Tawny, Oporto. $13.75. **80**

Mahogany with a ruby cast. Moderately light-bodied. Toasted wood, brown spices. Pleasantly aromatic, with a lighter-styled palate feel. Features well-integrated wood-accented flavors, but could use more grip.

Ramos Pinto Quinta da Ervamoira,
10 Year Old Tawny Porto, Oporto. $30. **86**

Medium ruby-brick red color. Medium-bodied. Notes of subtle red fruits, brown spice, earth. Piquant aromas reveal an assertive, flavorful palate that shows gutsy character with some earthy nuances and a fine spicy finish. Should be a good match for cigars.

Ramos Pinto Quinta do Bom Retiro,
20 Year Old Tawny Porto, Oporto. $56. **94**

Rich golden-orange with red tinges. Full-bodied. Notes of toffee, earth, brown spice, brown sugar. Opulent and thick mouthfeel gives this an hugely generous palate presence with big toffee like flavors showing complexity and nuances. Some subtle earthy notes provide a contrast. Very flavorful through the finish. A blockbuster.

Ramos Pinto 1989 Late Bottled Vintage Porto, Oporto. $19.50. **84**

Deep blackish-garnet hue. Medium-bodied. Caramel, brown spices, black fruits. Slightly hot in the nose with subtle oxidized overtones. Rich and mildly astringent on the palate with a hint of sweetness to the finish.

Ramos Pinto 1994 Quinta da Ervamoira Vintage Porto, Oporto. $44. **86**

Deep, opaque blackish hue with a ruby rim. Moderately full-bodied. Black fruits, lacquer. Ripe and generous with a sense of lushness to the palate. Fruit-centered flavors dominate the palate, and a lighter structure suggests that this will be approachable within a decade.

Ramos Pinto 1991 Vintage Porto, Oporto. $35. **87**

Very dark purple. Full-bodied. Notes of black fruits, pepper, brown spices. Lush and jammy on the palate with a firm character.

Ramos Pinto 1994 Vintage Porto, Oporto. $50. **88**

Opaque blackish hue with a purple rim. Moderately full-bodied. Black fruits, lacquer. Aromatic with a wave of rich, complex flavors on the palate. Deep, but still maintains a sense of lightness to the structure. This wine should be drinking nicely in 10 to 15 years.

Ramos Pinto 1995 Vintage Porto, Oporto. $35. **87**

Saturated bright ruby-purple. Youthful dark fruit aromas show a floral accent. Lean on the entry, with a moderately full body and sugar plum fruit on the midpalate. The finish is short, with mean tannins showing. Rather structured. Age will improve this but not make it elegant. Can be consumed now or put in the cellar for the long haul.

Rozes (Portugal)

Rozes Special Reserve, Oporto. $14.99. **80**

Dark ruby with brownish tinge. Medium-bodied with a silky mouthfeel. Sweet, roasted qualities chocolate and toffee backnotes.

Rozes Infanta Isabel, 10 Year Old Tawny Porto, Oporto. $25. **88**

Deep mahogany color. Moderately full-bodied. Roasted nuts, toasted wood. Flavorful and complex, with a distinctive note of rancio. Deeply flavored with good grip and fine length.

Rozes 20 Year Old Tawny Porto, Oporto. $45. **89**

Deep mahogany with a ruby cast. Medium-bodied. Moderately extracted. Toasted wood. Lean and flavorful in style, with a deep and intense personality. Focused through the lengthy finish.

Rozes Over 40 Years Old, Wood Matured, Oporto. $125. **92**

Deep copper hue with a big fade to the rim. Medium-bodied. Toasted wood, rancio, sea salt. Aromatic with an flavorful and complex palate feel. Well balanced and deep through the lean finish. Excellent grip and intensity.

Rozes 1992 Late Bottled Vintage Porto, Oporto. $23. **80**

Deep blackish-ruby hue with a garnet edge. Moderately light-bodied. Subtly extracted. Caramel, black fruits. Slightly oxidized, with lean wood-tinged notes on the palate. Drying and mildly hot through the finish.

Rozes 1994 Vintage Porto, Oporto. $46. **84**

Deep blackish-purple hue. Medium-bodied. Black fruits, brown spices. Aromatic and flavorful, though light in style on the palate. Could use a bit more grip but should be drinking nicely in five to 10 years.

Sandeman (Portugal)

Sandeman Founders Reserve Porto, Oporto. $15. **80**

Deep blackish-ruby hue. Moderately full-bodied. Low acidity. Black fruits, minerals. Reserved aromatically with a pronounced mineral palate feel. Lean and straightforward with a drying, mildly hot finish.

Sandeman 20 Year Old Tawny Porto, Oporto. $34. **89**

Deep copper hue. Medium-bodied. Moderately extracted. Toasted wood, caramel. Pleasantly aromatic with a sense of richness to the flavorful palate. Long and lively finish with good grip.

Smith Woodhouse (Portugal)

Smith Woodhouse Lodge Reserve Vintage Character Porto, Oporto. $13.99. **84**

Deep ruby hue. Lean mineral, red fruit and flower aromas. A lush entry leads a medium-bodied palate with mild acidity and lean tannins, and a firm, angular finish. Rather spirity fiery, but well flavored. Drink now.

Scale: Superlative (96-100), Exceptional (90-95), Highly Recommended (85-89), Recommended (80-84), Not Recommended (Under 80)

Smith Woodhouse 10 Year Old Tawny Porto, Oporto. $25.99. **82**
Pale ruby-brown. Aromas show oak spice and spirit-like notes. The sweet red fruit flavors on the entry finish quickly, with brief oak spice flavors taking over. Rather short.

Smith Woodhouse 1982 Madalena Vintage Porto, Oporto. $33.99. **88**
Bright ruby-garnet hue. Baked fruit aromas. Sweet and juicy on the attack with a mature note of coffee. Finishes in a dry, somewhat lean manner. A lighter style, this is drinking well now and does not need further cellaring.

Smith Woodhouse 1995 Madalena Vintage Porto, Oporto. $32. **88**
Saturated deep purplish-red color. Moderately full-bodied. Highly extracted. Mildly tannic. Notes of black fruits, plums, brown spice. Assertive spicy nose leads a palate of ripe rounded fruit flavors that are complimented by a solid spiced oak note through the finish. Well balanced, though this will need some time in the cellar.

Smith Woodhouse 1992 Vintage Porto, Oporto. $12/375 ml. **91**
Inky purple hue. Full-bodied. An elegant marriage of toasty oak and rich, dark fruits. Soft tannins in a fine, long finish.

Smith Woodhouse 1994 Vintage Porto, Oporto. $31. **89**
Opaque black-ruby to a purple rim. Medium-bodied. Notes of black fruit, flowers, chocolate. Aromatic, soft, and lush with a surprisingly open-knit structure. Pleasant floral style makes for short-term cellaring.

Symington's (Portugal)

Symington's 1992 Quinta do Vesuvio Vintage Porto, Oporto. $38. **93**
Deep purple. Full-bodied. Notes of black cherries, brown spices, citrus peel. Elegant and refined with a well-integrated character and all components in balance for the long haul.

Symington's 1994 Quinta do Vesuvio Vintage Porto, Oporto. $50. **96**
Deep opaque with a crimson rim. Medium-bodied. Notes of black fruits, tobacco, flowers. Peachy aromas. Stunningly extracted fruit with a waves of complexity. Very accessible, deriving much of its structure from soft tannins. Should drink well in the near term.

Symington's 1995 Quinta do Vesuvio Vintage Porto, Oporto. $61. **90**
Saturated deep purplish-red. Moderately full-bodied. Notes of vanilla, flowers, plums, black tea. Floral vanilla aromas. Sweet and generous on entry but solid extraction and hefty dry tannins on the finish. Tightly wound with impressive structure. Cellar 10 years or more.

Symington's 1996 Quinta do Vesuvio Vintage Porto, Oporto. $60.99. **95**
Brilliant, opaque violet purple. Very aromatic with full floral, violet and ripe fruit character. Explosively fruity on the attack, with a medium body and soft, lush tannins. Notably hedonistic for such youth. Should be drinkable over the medium term (10 years).

Taylor Fladgate (Portugal)

Taylor Fladgate First Estate Reserve Porto, Oporto. $15.49. **83**
Black-ruby. Moderately full-bodied. Notes of black fruit, licorice, pepper. Reasonably rich core of fruit gives this some assertive character through to a spicy finish.

Taylor Fladgate 10 Year Old Tawny Porto, Oporto. $26.99. **86**
Fading pale ruby-brown. Mulled, spiced fruit aromas with a whiff of rancio. Juicy and bright on the entry, with a smooth midpalate and a finish that features oak spice and lingering rancio notes.

Taylor Fladgate 20 Year Old Tawny Porto, Oporto. $46.99. **90**
Pale ruby-copper hue. Aromatically subdued with a salty note. Bright and sweet on entry with light flavors on the palate and a taut frame. Well balanced though not as intense as typical 20-year-old tawny Port.

Taylor Fladgate 1990 Late Bottled Vintage Porto, Oporto. $16.49. **85**
Deep ruby. Moderately full-bodied. Notes of black fruits, currants, licorice. A jammy full-flavored style with a markedly fruity palate. Some spirity notes.

Taylor Fladgate 1991 Late Bottled Vintage Porto, Oporto. $19.99.   **89**

Deep blood red. Rich plummy yet mildly earthy aromas. A rich entry leads a moderately full-bodied palate with well-stuffed flavors and a hint of tannic backbone. A solid style.

Taylor Fladgate 1991 Quinta de Vargellas Vintage Porto, Oporto. $37.49.   **93**

Dark ruby-black. Silky texture accentuates the medium body. Filled with tones of currants, chocolate, and a berry core. Approachable now, this will develop nicely for several years. A more delicate style for the usually macho Taylor.

Taylor Fladgate 1995 Quinta de Vargellas Vintage Porto, Oporto. $38.99.   **90**

Opaque blackish hue with a ruby-purple rim. Moderately full-bodied. Black fruits, licorice, lacquer. Quite aromatic with a flavorful fruit-accented palate feel. Lighter in style, though still quite rich. Should be approachable in 10 years or so.

Taylor Fladgate 1994 Vintage Porto, Oporto. $50.   **92**

Saturated deep reddish-purple color. Moderately full-bodied. Notes of flowers, fleshy black fruits, brown spice. Brooding dark fruity nose has floral accents. Rich, ripe, and very well extracted with generosity up front, though the finish turns very spirity and hot. Very attractive, though youthfully awkward. Cellar 10 years.

Warre's (Portugal)

Warre's Fine Selected Ruby Porto, Oporto. $10.99.   **82**

Deep blackish-ruby with a slight fade to the rim. Moderately full-bodied. Black fruits, lacquer. Sweet, straightforward, and richly fruity with good intensity and length. A trifle hot on the finish.

Warre's Warrior Porto, Oporto. $14.99.   **84**

Deep blackish-ruby hue. Moderately full-bodied. Black fruits, minerals. Aromatic, with a rich and ripe palate feel. Quite deeply flavored and well balanced with a supple finish.

Warre's Sir William, 10 Year Tawny Porto, Oporto. $22.99.   **82**

Bright mahogany with a ruby cast. Moderately light-bodied. Toasted wood. Lighter in style with a decided woody quality. Some mild heat to the finish.

Warre's 1976 Reserve Tawny, Oporto. $46.99.   **86**

Deep mahogany cast. Moderately full-bodied. Dried fruits, brown spices. Still fairly rich and youthful with dried fruit overtones throughout. Flavorful and straightforward with a touch of heat to the finish.

Warre's 1982 Late Bottled Vintage Porto, Oporto. $24.50.   **85**

Medium ruby. Medium-bodied. Balanced acidity. Notes of berry fruits, currants, herbs. Berry fruit aromas lead into a reasonably rich palate with some fine grainy tannins coming through on the finish.

Warre's 1984 Late Bottled Vintage Porto, Oporto. $21.99.   **83**

Bright blackish-garnet hue with a big fade to the rim. Medium-bodied. Moderately extracted. Red fruits, brown spices. Somewhat reserved aromatically with a decided wood accent. Fairly hot on the palate with spicy flavors and a lean finish.

Warre's 1995 Quinta da Cavadinha Vintage Porto, Oporto. $32.99.   **92**

Saturated deep purplish-red. Medium-bodied. Highly extracted. Notes of citrus, plums, oak spice. Youthful, generous fruity aromas. High-toned sweet fruity flavors belie a sense of tightness with some oak spice and spirity feel on the finish. Outstanding acidity runs through this wine. Young and awkward but with great structure and promise for the future.

Warre's 1991 Vintage Porto, Oporto. $35.   **92**

Blackish-purple. Full-bodied. Notes of ripe black fruits, orange peel, pepper. Lush and lengthy, with supple tannins and well-extracted flavors.

Warre's 1994 Vintage Porto, Oporto. $40.   **94**

Opaque, blackish-ruby to the rim. Moderately full-bodied. Notes of flowers, chocolate, black fruit. Lush and layered mouthfeel with complex flavors on the palate. Displaying some rough edges of its infancy, it quite approachable. Warrants medium-term cellaring. 10 years plus.

Madeira

Blandy's (Portugal)

Blandy's Rainwater, Madeira. $13.99.   **82**

Deep orange with reddish-copper highlights. Medium-bodied. Notes of tangerine, citrus peel. Caramelized citrus aromas with a Sherry-like rancio whiff, play out on the palate with some juicy acids giving this mouthwatering appeal.

Blandy's 5 Year Old Sercial, Madeira. $19.   **86**

Bright pale copper hue. Medium-bodied. Caramel, salted pecans. Quite aromatic with a lighter-styled, zesty palate feel. Crisp acidity lends a refreshing note to the clean and flavorful finish. Excellent grip.

Blandy's 5 Year Old Verdelho, Madeira. $19.   **85**

Deep burnt amber. Medium-bodied. Notes of dried flowers and peaches, nuts. Tangy aromas lead into a juicy assertive palate with nutty notes through the finish. Sweetness is well integrated.

Blandy's 5 Year Old Malmsey, Madeira. $17.99.   **84**

Deep chestnut amber. Moderately full-bodied. Notes of peach, dates, pecan, brown spice. Fresh fruity attack reveals a thickly textured mouthfeel. Firm oak spice flavors come through on the finish.

Blandy's 10 Year Old Malmsey, Madeira. $32.99.   **88**

Brilliant copper-amber hue. Complex brown spice, chocolate, and toffee aromas. A rich entry is followed by a moderately full-bodied palate with marked sweetness and vibrant acidic balance. Supple, flavorful finish.

Blandy's 15 Year Old Malmsey, Madeira. $42.99.   **94**

Very deep tawny amber-copper hue. Forceful roasted nut, rancio and treacle aromas. A viscous entry leads a full-bodied palate with marked sweetness offset by vibrant acidity. The finish is exotic and lengthy. A very stylish wine with great complexity and depth.

Cossart Gordon (Portugal)

Cossart Gordon Rainwater, Madeira. $14.   **82**

Deep copper hue with brilliant clarity. Moderately light-bodied. Caramel. Somewhat reined in aromatically with a rather sugary entry on the palate. Acidity pops up in the finish to lend balance, but overall one-dimensional.

Cossart Gordon 5 Year Old Bual, Madeira. $20.   **88**

Very deep copper with a greenish cast. Moderately full-bodied. Roasted nuts, molasses. Aromatic, with a viscous quality to the mouthfeel that is offset nicely by balancing acidity. Rich and lengthy with solid grip through the finish.

Cossart Gordon 10 Year Old Bual, Madeira. $32.99.   **87**

Brilliant amber hue. Intense toffee and salted pecan aromas show a distinctive rancio quality. A lean entry leads a medium-bodied palate with vibrant acidity and mild sweetness. Lean, flavorful finish with good bite. Shows complexity and depth of flavor with admirable balance.

Cossart Gordon 15 Year Old Bual, Madeira. $44.   **92**

Deep amber with brown highlights. Moderately full-bodied. Notes of raisins, toffee, orange peel. Rich aromas lead into a succulent and assertive palate with some fine acidity to keep the finish from cloying. A rich style showing great balance.

Cossart Gordon 5 Year Old Malmsey, Madeira. $20.   **85**

Very deep mahogany hue with a slight greenish cast. Medium-bodied. Molasses. Deeply aromatic, with a surprisingly light texture in the mouth. Well balanced with a sense of sweetness on the finish.

Cossart Gordon 10 Year Old Malmsey, Madeira. $32.   **89**

Blackish-brown. Full-bodied. Notes of raisins, sea salt, molasses. Fragrant and zesty on the palate with solid balance.

Henriques & Henriques (Portugal)

Henriques & Henriques 5 Year Old Sercial, Madeira. $17.49.   **90**

Deep amber. Medium-bodied. Notes of nuts, yeast, citrus. Very pungent with vibrant acidity and a Sherry-like character through the finish.

Henriques & Henriques 10 Year Old Sercial, Madeira. $29.95.   **96**

Very dark reddish-amber. Medium-bodied. Notes of brown spices, nuts, citrus peel. Extraordinarily intense and lengthy with a complex array of flavors and refreshing acidity making for a very clean finish.

Henriques & Henriques 5 Year Old Verdelho, Madeira. $17.49.   **89**

Dark chestnut hue. Medium-bodied. Notes of cinnamon, nuts, tobacco. Light and pleasant with a complex array of flavors and buttery mouthfeel.

Henriques & Henriques 10 Year Old Verdelho, Madeira. $29.95.   **91**

Dark reddish-amber. Medium-bodied. Notes of dried fruits, roasted nuts, caramel. Lengthy and well balanced with a vibrant character.

Henriques & Henriques 5 Year Old Bual, Madeira. $17.49.   **85**

Deep blackish-amber. Medium-bodied. Notes of mandarin oranges, caramel, sea salt. Complex and slightly viscous with a touch of heat in the finish.

Henriques & Henriques 10 Year Old Bual, Madeira. $29.95.   **92**

Dark amber with reddish tinge. Medium-bodied. Notes of caramel, toffee, orange marmalade. Lively and full on the palate with an amazingly lengthy finish.

Henriques & Henriques 5 Year Old Malmsey, Madeira. $17.49.   **83**

Dark russet-brown. Full-bodied. Notes of raisins, pipe tobacco, nuts. Full and rich with a pleasantly soft mouthfeel.

Henriques & Henriques 10 Year Old Malmsey, Madeira. $29.95.   **85**

Dark russet. Full-bodied. Notes of roasted salted nuts, dried fruits, molasses. Racy and intense in style with a full throttle character. Just the right foil for a good cigar.

Leacock's (Portugal)

Leacock's Rainwater, Madeira. $12.   **82**

Deep amber with orange highlights. Medium-bodied. Notes of dried fruit, honey, nuts. Bright fruity aromas reveal a forwardly fruity and flavorsome palate. Undemanding and straightforward in style.

Leacock's 5 Year Old Sercial, Madeira. $17.99.   **86**

Deep amber with subtle copper highlights. Moderately full-bodied. Notes of Amontillado Sherry, brown spice, caramelized fruits. Baked spicy aromas show a touch of rancio. Dry caramel flavors on the palate linger through the finish. Appealing for it richness, though not enormously complex on the palate.

Leacock's 10 Year Old Bual, Madeira. $32.99.   **87**

Very deep tawny amber hue. Generous coffee and date aromas. A rich entry leads a moderately full-bodied palate with solid acidic bite. Lush, zesty finish with a hint of rancio.

Leacock's 5 Year Old Malmsey, Madeira. $17.99.   **90**

Deep blackish-brown. Medium- to full-bodied. Notes of coffee, redwood, malt, dates. Intense and lively, yet still viscous and syrupy with an expansion of flavors on the palate.

Miles (Portugal)

Miles 5 Year Old Malmsey, Madeira. $16.99.   **82**

Dark brownish-ruby. Medium- to full-bodied. Marked by high acidity and viscosity, but balanced with notes of butter and yellow fruits. Warm, short finish.

Scale: Superlative (96-100), Exceptional (90-95), Highly Recommended (85-89), Recommended (80-84), Not Recommended (Under 80)

US Port-Style Wines

Beringer (CA)
Beringer 1994 Port of Cabernet Sauvignon, Napa Valley. $20.　　**88**

Opaque blackish purple cast. Full-bodied. Balanced acidity. Highly extracted. Heavily oaked. Mildly tannic. Vanilla, cassis. Extraordinarily aromatic, with a melange of wood-accented black fruit flavors. Rich and deep in the mouth, with some drying wood tannins through the finish. Tastes like a fortified Napa Valley Cabernet. Interesting.

Cedar Mountain (CA)
Cedar Mountain 1996 Vintage Port, Amador County. $19.50.　　**92**

Opaque blackish ruby cast. Full-bodied. Balanced acidity. Highly extracted. Chocolate, black fruits, flowers. Shows amazing depth of concentration, with a fragrant and immensely flavorful palate feel. Rich and firmly structured, with just a hint of sweetness in the finish. A dead ringer for a high-end Portuguese wine. Intense and impressive.

Chateau Elan (GA)
Chateau Elan Georgian-Style Port, American. $22.　　**83**

Deep blackish garnet cast. Medium-bodied. Balanced acidity. Moderately extracted. Peaches, blackberries, minerals. Extremely fragrant, with an unusual, high-toned fruit quality throughout. Lighter on the palate, with a sense of brightness through the finish. Interesting.

Duck Walk (ME)
Duck Walk 1996, Blueberry Port, Wild Maine, $12.95/375 ml.　　**87**

Bright blackish purple cast. Moderately full-bodied. Balanced acidity. Moderately extracted. Mildly tannic. Black fruits, minerals, licorice. Pleasantly aromatic and fruit-centered, with concentrated flavors on the palate. Comes across with a sense of lightness and balance throughout. Intense and clean, with an uplifting, angular finish.

Fetzer (CA)
Fetzer 1993 Port, Mendocino County. $18.99.　　**82**

Deep magenta. Medium-bodied. Full acidity. Moderately extracted. Sweet. Reminiscent of roses, cherries, herbs. Intense, ripe fruit is couched in a vibrant frame with a warm, candyish finish. A fun dessert choice.

Ficklin (CA)
Ficklin Tinta Port, California. $12.　　**86**

Deep ruby-garnet cast. Medium-bodied. Balanced acidity. Moderately extracted. Brown spices, toast. Pleasantly aromatic, with a gentle woody note and a touch of heat. Ripe and full in the mouth, with a lingering, flavorful finish.

Ficklin 10 Year Old Tawny Port, California. $22.　　**92**

Opaque mahogany cast with a greenish fade to the rim. Full-bodied. Full acidity. Highly extracted. Salted pecans, rancio, treacle. Extraordinarily flavorful, with a well-aged, Oloroso Sherry-type edge to the complex flavors. Thick, rich, and concentrated on the palate, with great intensity and style.

Ficklin 1988 Vintage Port, California. $25.　　**91**

Deep ruby garnet cast. Moderately full-bodied. Balanced acidity. Moderately extracted. Overripe red fruits, tea, minerals. Quite aromatic and complex, with a mature, flavorful palate feel. Full but well structured on the palate, with a sense of leanness through the finish, provided by buoyant acidity.

J. Filippi (CA)

J. Filippi Fondante Ciello, Chocolate Port, California. $18/500 ml.   **80**

Deep ruby garnet cast. Moderately full-bodied. Balanced acidity. Highly extracted. Chocolate candy, malt. Extremely aromatic, with a candied note to the overt chocolate flavors. Rich, thick, and flavorful in the mouth, with a supple, velvety quality. May prove a bit overwhelming in its chocolatey character for some, but the chocaholics can finish off the non-believers' glasses.

Firestone (CA)

Firestone 1995 Port, Santa Ynez Valley. $20.   **82**

Bright berry red color. Medium-bodied. Balanced acidity. Moderately extracted. Moderately oaked. Moderately tannic. Reminiscent of cassis, red currant, brown spice, cedar. Soft, deep texture. Sweet berry flavors open up with a touch of spice and tannins. Has a plush center, which should improve with moderate cellaring.

Geyser Peak (CA)

Geyser Peak 1995 Henry's Reserve Shiraz Port,
Alexander Valley. $15/375 ml.   **87**

Opaque dark cherry red. Medium-bodied. Moderately extracted. Reminiscent of blackberries, plums, black tea. Rich plummy black fruit aromas open up on the mid palate. Finishes with a dry solid layer of tannins that would suggest that this will soften with some age. Good balance.

Goose Watch (NY)

Goose Watch 1997 Finale White Port, Finger Lakes. $16.50/375 ml.   **82**

Deep straw cast. Medium-bodied. Full acidity. Moderately extracted. Dried herbs, citrus. Shows a distinctive herbal edge to the flavors. Quite light on the palate, with zesty acidity and a hint of sweetness. Seems more like a late-harvest table wine.

Guenoc (CA)

Guenoc 1994 Vintage Port, California. $25.   **87**

Dark cherry, with a ruby cast. Medium-bodied. Balanced acidity. Moderately extracted. Moderately oaked. Moderately tannic. Reminiscent of tobacco, lacquer, brown spice, baked raspberry tart. Compact texture. A brawny style, with youthful tannins upfront. Sweet berry notes are nicely accented by soft, plush earthy components. A polished style, if a bit coarse at the present. Should cellar well.

Heitz (CA)

Heitz 1996 Grignlino Port, Napa Valley. $18.   **83**

Deep blackish purple hue. Medium-bodied. Low acidity. Moderately extracted. Black fruits, licorice. Pleasantly aromatic and solidly fruit-centered, with a touch of heat. Ripe, flavorful, and straightforward on the palate, with a decidedly sweet finish.

Horton (CA)

Horton 1995 Vintage Port, Orange County. $20.   **84**

Opaque blackish ruby hue. Full-bodied. Balanced acidity. Highly extracted. Brown spices, licorice, earth. Pungent in style, with complex, if rather unusual aromatics. Rich, round, and full on the palate, with just a hint of sweetness.

Justin (CA)

Justin 1996 Obtuse, Paso Robles. $22.50.   **86**

Opaque blackish purple color. Full-bodied. Balanced acidity. Highly extracted. Mildly tannic. Black fruits, minerals. Quite aromatic, with a full and flavorful palate feel. Round and rich, though well structured through the finish.

Scale: Superlative (96-100), Exceptional (90-95), Highly Recommended (85-89),
Recommended (80-84), Not Recommended (Under 80)

Lonz (OH)

Lonz 3 Islands American Ruby Port. $6.50.   **86**

Deep ruby red with brick rim. Moderately full-bodied. Balanced acidity. Moderately extracted. Heavily oaked. Medium sweetness. Reminiscent of dried orange peel, vanilla, raisins. Richly textured and firmly structured on the palate, and layered with distinctive sweet, woody nuances.

Meier's (OH)

Meier's No. 44 American Ruby Port. $6.95.   **86**

Deep brickish garnet hue. Medium-bodied. Balanced acidity. Moderately extracted. Medium sweetness. Reminiscent of nuts, earth, coffee, cherries. Well focused and firmly textured, with sweet fruit nuances that play into the finish. Surprisingly well integrated for a "port" of this price.

Mount Pleasant (MO)

Mount Pleasant JRL's Barrel Select Port, Augusta, Missouri. $11.95.   **85**

Reddish brick color with a distinctly browning rim. Medium-bodied. Highly extracted. Mildly tannic. Reminiscent of earth, dates, coffee. A caramelized coffeelike note runs through this. Somewhat tawny in style, it still has plenty of stuffing.

Mount Pleasant 1990 Port, Augusta, Missouri. $18.   **86**

Opaque blackish garnet cast. Moderately full-bodied. Low acidity. Highly extracted. Charred yeast, smoke, treacle. Features an odd charred note to the nose that is hard to overlook. Lean and drying through the finish. Strange.

Mount Pleasant 8 Barrel Tawny Port, Augusta, Missouri. $23.42.   **NR**

Mount Pleasant 15 Barrel Tawny Port, Augusta, Missouri. $23.50.   **88**

Bright pale amber. Medium-bodied. Full acidity. Moderately extracted. Medium sweetness. Reminiscent of golden raisins, toffee, pralines. Thick, slightly syrupy textured fruit is countered by a pleasant, acidic snap. Assertive dried fruit notes last well in the finish, accompanied by a pleasant warmth.

Mount Pleasant Tawny Port, Library Vol. V, Augusta, Missouri. $28.   **85**

Bright orangeish copper cast. Medium-bodied. Balanced acidity. Moderately extracted. Roasted nuts, caramel, brown spices. Pleasantly aromatic, with lush wood accents throughout. Rich and harmonious on the palate, with a well-balanced, lengthy finish.

Mount Pleasant 1996 White Port, Augusta, Missouri. $25/375 ml.   **86**

Deep straw cast. Moderately full-bodied. Balanced acidity. Moderately extracted. Blanched almonds, petrol, flowers. Quite aromatic and very traditional, with a touch of heat. Full, flavorful, and well balanced in the mouth, with a rounded, though not heavy, impression. Fresh, stylish, and convincing.

Orfila (CA)

Orfila Tawny Port, California. $14.98/500 ml.   **83**

Deep orangeish copper cast with a definite haze. Medium-bodied. Balanced acidity. Moderately extracted. Caramel, toffee. Pleasantly aromatic, with a gentle woody tone throughout. Lighter on the palate with a straightforward character. Finishes with a touch of heat.

Paul Masson (CA)

Paul Masson Rich Ruby Port, California. $5.99.   **82**

Black ruby hue. Moderately full-bodied. Balanced acidity. Highly extracted. Medium sweetness. Reminiscent of black fruits, tar, cherry, tobacco. Sturdy and straightforward, with well-concentrated flavors and fairly weighty texture.

Pesenti (CA)

Pesenti 1997 Zinfandel Port, Second Estate Reserve,
Paso Robles. $20/500 ml. **84**

Opaque blackish purple hue. Full-bodied. Full acidity. Highly extracted. Moderately tannic. Briar fruits, minerals. Extremely aromatic and wholly fruit-centered, with a ripe, jammy quality throughout. Full-throttled and intense, this wine is really showing its youth. Not for the faint of heart.

Pindar (NY)

Pindar 1995 Port, North Fork of Long Island. $24.99. **89**

Deep ruby red hue with a slight fade. Brooding berry and wood aromas carry a complex medicinal overtone. A firm entry leads to a full-bodied, moderately sweet palate with drying tannins. Full, rich, and ripe. Drink now or later.

Pine Ridge (CA)

Pine Ridge 1993 Black Diamond Port, Napa Valley. $16/375 ml. **80**

Medium body. Medium acid. Medium fruit. Medium oak. Lots of tannin. Medium sweetness. Reminiscent of earth, black fruits, black pepper, cola. Rhone-like, with powerful pepper notes, smoky oak, and firmness. Surprising dryness for a fortified wine.

Prager Winery & Port Works (CA)

Prager Winery & Port Works 1993 Royal Escort LBV Port,
Napa Valley. $38.50. **88**

Deep blackish ruby cast. Moderately full-bodied. Full acidity. Highly extracted. Mildly tannic. Brown spices, black fruits, chocolate. Redolent of oak, with spicy flavors throughout. Full, though drying on the palate, with a deep core of dark fruit flavors. Finishes with a touch of heat.

Prager Winery & Port Works Noble Companion 10 Year Old Tawny Port,
Napa Valley. $45. **89**

Deep mahogany cast. Moderately full-bodied. Full acidity. Highly extracted. Mildly tannic. Salted nuts, treacle, brown spices. Carries a fiery impression on the nose. Full throttled and flavorful on the palate, with some Sherry-like complexities. The lengthy finish is a touch hot.

Pugliese (NY)

Pugliese Rafaello White Port, North Fork of Long Island. $14.99/375 ml. **NR**

Bright greenish straw hue. Bizarre, floral, foxy aromas. Medium-bodied with a hint of sweetness, but simple and foxy. Drink now.

Pugliese Port Bello, North Fork of Long Island. $26.99. **80**

Medium ruby hue with a slight fade. Generous wood and red fruit aromas. A firm entry leads to a full-bodied palate with a hint of sweetness and grainy tannins. Full, rich, and straightforward. Drink now.

Quady (CA)

Quady Batch 88 Starboard, California. $11.50. **89**

Deep ruby-garnet cast. Full-bodied. Balanced acidity. Highly extracted. Chocolate, tea, black fruits. Aromatic and quite complex, with a wide range of flavors throughout. Lush, rounded, and well balanced on the palate, with a lengthy finish.

Quady 1993 LBV Port, Amador County. $12. **91**

Deep blackish garnet cast. Moderately full-bodied. Balanced acidity. Highly extracted. Chocolate, brown spices, black fruits. Carries a generous wood accent throughout, with a deeply flavored, supple palate feel. Shows fine grip and intensity, with excellent length.

Quady 1989 Frank's Vineyard Vintage Starboard, California. $19.   **90**

Deep ruby with brick rim. Moderately full-bodied. Balanced acidity. Moderately extracted. Mild sweetness. Reminiscent of black fruits, earth, dried apricots. Rich earthy aromas introduce this full-flavored port with a firm, woody character. The sweetness is subsumed by well balanced acidity and wood influences. Finishes with complex, sherry-like tones.

Quady 1990 Frank's Vineyard Vintage Starboard, California. $19.   **89**

Black ruby with brickish rim. Moderately full-bodied. Balanced acidity. Highly extracted. Medium sweetness. Reminiscent of black fruits, vanilla, butterscotch. Rich, ripe tasting, and very nicely textured with grainy tannins lingering in a long, flavorful finish. Evolving nicely and destined for further improvement.

Quady 1990 Vintage Starboard, Amador County. $21.50.   **93**

Opaque blackish garnet cast. Moderately full-bodied. Balanced acidity. Moderately extracted. Minerals, black fruits, olives. Quite aromatic, with pleasant, mature nuances throughout. Rich, supple, and velvety in the mouth, with a very lengthy finish. Classic and stylish.

Renwood (CA)

Renwood 1994 Vintage Port, Shenandoah Valley. $21.95/500 ml.   **84**

Deep blackish garnet cast. Moderately full-bodied. Balanced acidity. Moderately extracted. Minerals, earth, black fruits. Fragrant and flavorful, with a deep and brooding array of flavors. Well balanced, with measured sweetness to the finish.

Rosenblum (CA)

Rosenblum 1994 Port, California. $10/375 ml.   **82**

Deep ruby red appearance. Medium-bodied. Moderately extracted. Mildly tannic. Reminiscent of red currants. Raisiny, currant nose is confirmed on the palate with a pleasant mouthfeel. Sense of richness dissipates with the hard tannins on the finish.

St. Amant (CA)

St. Amant 1995 Vintage Port, Amador County. $28.   **85**

Saturated blackish red color. Medium-bodied. Highly extracted. Moderately tannic. Reminiscent of blueberry, chocolate, raspberries. Complex and exotic plummy nose. Deep extracted and flavorsome though somewhat compact on the palate at present with some dry tannins coming through on the finish. Needs some time.

St. Julian (MI)

St. Julian Catherman's Port, Michigan. $12.   **81**

Opaque blackish purple cast. Medium-bodied. Full acidity. Highly extracted. Cassis, flowers. Pleasantly aromatic, with brooding dark fruit flavors. Surprisingly bright on the palate, with tangy acidity and balanced sweetness. Intense, berryish, and flavorful.

Sonora Winery & Port Works (CA)

Sonora Winery & Port Works 1992 Vintage Port,
Sierra Foothills. $15.99/500 ml.   **80**

Black with purple rim. Moderately full-bodied. Full acidity. Highly extracted. Medium sweetness. Reminiscent of flowers, black fruits, chocolate syrup. Very rich and flavorful, with a firm mouthfeel and pronounced wood tones.

Sonora Winery & Port Works 1994 Vintage Port,
Sierra Foothills. $16/500 ml.   **86**

Opaque blackish purple cast. Moderately full-bodied. Low acidity. Highly extracted. Mildly tannic. Minerals, black fruits. Rather reserved aromatically, but opens up on the lush, rounded mouthfeel. Deep, brooding, and intense, with marked sweetness to the finish. Could use a few more years of age.

Stone Hill (MO)
Stone Hill 1994 Estate Bottled Port, Hermann. $23.99.   **83**
Saturated black cherry color. Moderately full-bodied. Highly extracted. Mildly tannic. Reminiscent of black cherries, earth, minerals. Expressive fruity aromas. Rich black fruit entry gives way to a solid minerally finish.

Taylor (NY)
Taylor Tawny Port, New York. $3.99.   **NR**

Taylor Port, New York. $7/500 ml.   **NR**

Trentadue (CA)
Trentadue 1994 Merlot Port, Alexander Valley. $20.   **84**
Bright cherry red. Medium-bodied. Balanced acidity. Moderately extracted. Mildly oaked. Mildly tannic. Reminiscent of plums, mint, mocha. Soft, moderately lush texture. Bright plummy nose leads a racy palate with high-toned fruity flavors, delicate brown spice, and some gentle tannins in the finish.

Trentadue 1994 Petite Sirah Port, Alexander Valley. $20.   **88**
Opaque reddish purple. Moderately full-bodied. Highly extracted. Reminiscent of cherry, apple, black fruits. Sweet plummy entry expands on the midpalate, with the finish showing tannic grip and spicy notes. A bit unapproachable now, but should soften up beautifully with time.

Twin Hills (CA)
Twin Hills Zinfandel Port, Lot XCII, Paso Robles. $25.   **89**
Deep garnet cast. Moderately full-bodied. Full acidity. Highly extracted. Roasted salted nuts, rancio, treacle. Extraordinarily aromatic, with an intense Sherry-like quality to the complex flavors. Rich and intense, with a roasted accent and an angular finish provided by juicy acidity.

Whidbey (WA)
Whidbey 1990 Port, Washington. $12.99.   **90**
Blackish ruby hue with brick rim. Moderately full-bodied. Balanced acidity. Highly extracted. Moderately tannic. Medium sweetness. Reminiscent of mocha, dried plums, grenadine. Intensely concentrated and still quite youthful, with a lengthy palate of sweet-tasting fruit enlivened by tangy spice notes. Shows nice grip in the finish.

Widmer (NY)
Widmer Port, New York. $5.   **NR**

Willamette Valley Vineyards (OR)
Willamette Valley Vineyards 1994 Quinta Reserva, Oregon. $18.   **80**
Deep purple. Moderately light-bodied. Full acidity. Moderately extracted. Mild sweetness. Reminiscent of minerals, dried herbs, red fruits. Overtly perfumed, with lean fruit and a persistent herbal finish.

Windsor (CA)
Windsor Rare Port, California. $13.   **85**
Deep blackish garnet cast. Moderately full-bodied. Balanced acidity. Moderately extracted. Brown spices, raisins. Made in more of a tawny style, with an obvious wood accent to the flavors. Ripe, thick, and lush. Well-balanced finish with a touch of heat.

Yakima River (WA)

Yakima River 1995 Johns Vintage Port, Yakima Valley. $16. **83**

Deep ruby garnet cast. Full-bodied. Full acidity. Highly extracted. Brown spices, black fruits, minerals. Carries a distinctive toasty-oak note throughout. Quite flavorful, though full-throttle and somewhat fierce, with a marked hot quality. Drying through the finish, with very slight sweetness.

Australian Port-Style Wines

Benjamin (Australia)

Benjamin Tawny Port, Australia. $12.99. **85**

Light amber. Medium- to full-bodied. Notes of caramel, brown sugar, dried fruits, nuts. Has very good balance, an impression of high alcohol, and a moderate length. A blend of Cabernet Sauvignon, Shiraz, and Merlot.

Hardys (Australia)

Hardys Tall Ships Tawny Port, South Australia. $12.99. **82**

Light amber. Medium- to full-bodied. Notes of baked apples, prunes, cinnamon, flowers. Subtle and attractive, with a nice balance of fruit and oak.

Hardys Whiskers Blake Tawny Port, Australia. $14. **88**

Pale reddish-amber. Medium-bodied. Notes of caramel, brown spice, baked apple. Baked caramelized aromas. Sweet, juicy rich flavors expand on the palate with a delicate spice on the finish. Well balanced.

Marienberg (Australia)

Marienberg 12 Year Old Tawny Port, Australia. $13. **85**

Bright chestnut. Medium-bodied. Moderately extracted. Apricot, nuts. Sweet and spicy. Fruity aromas lead a caramel and raisin palate with sweetness remaining on the right side of cloying. Very attractive.

Penfolds (Australia)

Penfolds Club Tawny Port, South Australia. $9. **84**

Amber-brown hue. Moderately full-bodied. Caramel, toffee, raisins. Sweet and nectarous with raisin flavors and sweet toffee notes lingering on the finish. Very generous, with the sweeter flavors persisting through the finish.

Penfolds Club Port, Reserve, South Australia. $11. **86**

Chestnut appearance. Moderately full-bodied. Fig, toffee. Heavily spiced aromas lead a toffee, caramel-like entry with sweetness lingering through the finish. Subtle rancio qualities.

Penfolds Grandfather, Finest Tawny Port, Barossa Valley. $60. **98**

Dark chestnut. Full-bodied. Rancio, spice. Powerful aromas of caramel and brown spice lead a very tangy palate with vibrant acids keeping the considerable sugars in check through the finish. Thick, syrupy mouthfeel does not betray any cloying character. Complex salty, rancio notes linger.

Queen Adelaide (Australia)

Queen Adelaide Woodley Tawny Port, South Australia. $8. **89**

Medium reddish-amber. Medium-bodied. Notes of earth, nuts, caramel apples. A balanced, remarkably easy sipping style with attractive caramel undertones. Sweet notes play in the finish, as alcohol provides a pleasing warmth.

Chateau Reynella (Australia)

Chateau Reynella 1992 Vintage Port, McLaren Vale. $12.
86

Deep purple. Medium- to full-bodied. Notes of cherries, blueberries, pepper. Nice length, a viscous mouthfeel and an impression of high alcohol makes this a powerful after-dinner drink.

Chateau Reynella Old Cave Fine Tawny Port, McLaren Vale. $18.99.
93

Dark brown-amber. Full-bodied. Salt, rancio, oak spice lead a powerfully flavored palate with heavy brown spice and sweet caramel flavors upfront and a dry finish. Extraordinarily complex and not overly sweet.

Seppelt (Australia)

Seppelt Trafford Tawny Port, Barossa Valley. $11.
91

Rusty-amber. Medium-bodied. Notes of brown spice, dates, Amontillado Sherry. Subtle mature spicy nose hints at the elegance of age. Sweet and spicy flavors are refined and conclude with a dry Amontillado Sherry-like finish.

Seppelt Para Port Tawny, Australia. $24.99.
93

Deep mahogany hue. Attractive, exotic fig, toffee, and roasted nut aromas show the type of complexity that only comes with extreme age. A rich attack leads to a moderately full-bodied palate with mild sweetness and a wave of roasted flavors. Intense and firm. Develops in the glass with aeration and keeps some time in the bottle. Drink now.

Sheldrake (Australia)

Sheldrake Tawny Port, Australia. $13/500 ml.
82

Dark chestnut color with ruby highlights. Medium-bodied. Wood, brown spices, mulled cherries. Aromatically reserved with a hot quality to the nose. Lean and sturdy in the mouth with an angular finish. A tad rustic.

Yalumba (Australia)

Yalumba Clocktower Tawny Port, Australia. $9.99.
86

Tawny amber. Medium-bodied. Notes of caramel, baked fruits, mild brown spice. Mildly vinous quality on the nose reveals flavors of sweet caramelized fruits that expand on the palate and linger through the finish. Vinous fruit flavors are more apparent than spicy wood.

Yalumba Galway Pipe Tawny Port, Australia. $22.99.
90

Brownish-amber. Medium-bodied. Notes of walnut, ginseng, dried fruits. Sweet exotically spicy nose shows great harmony that is confirmed on the palate of nectarous spicy flavors. Elegant lingering finish has persistent delicate spice flavors.

Highly Rated Sherry

Manzanilla Sherry

95 • Hidalgo (Spain) La Gitana Manzanilla, Sanlucar de Barrameda. $9.99.

92 • Sanchez Romate (Spain) Manzanilla, Sanlucar de Barrameda. $8.99.

90 • Hidalgo (Spain) Manzanilla Pasada, Sanlucar de Barrameda. $15.49.

89 • Emilio Lustau (Spain) Almacenista, Jurado Manzanilla Pasada de Sanlucar, Sanlucar de Barrameda. $18.99.

85 • Gonzalez Byass (Spain) Elegante Manzanilla Sherry, Jerez de la Frontera. $5.99.

Fino Sherry

93 • Sandeman (Spain) Don Fino, Superior Dry Fino, Jerez de la Frontera. $11.99.

91 • Emilio Lustau (Spain) Puerto Fino, Puerto de Santa Maria. $10.95.

90 • Hidalgo (Spain) Fino Superior "El Cuadrado", Jerez de la Frontera. $15.49.

90 • Emilio Lustau (Spain) Jarana, Light Fino Sherry, Jerez de la Frontera. $9.95.

89 • Gonzalez Byass (Spain) Tio Pepe Fino Sherry, Jerez de la Frontera. $12.99.

87 • Valdespino (Spain) Inocente Fino Sherry, Jerez de la Frontera. $14.

86 • Sanchez Romate (Spain) Fino Sherry, Jerez de la Frontera. $6.99.

86 • Emilio Lustau (Spain) Almacenista, Jose Luis Gonzalez Obregon, Fino del Puerto, Puerto de Santa Maria. $13.95.

Amontillado Sherry

94 • Gonzalez Byass (Spain) Amontillado Del Duque, Rare Old Solera Amontillado Viejo, Jerez de la Frontera. $40.

93 • Pedro Domecq (Spain) "51-1a", Very Rare Amontillado , Jerez de la Frontera. $73.

93 • Hidalgo (Spain) Amontillado Viejo, Jerez de la Frontera. $63.99.

93 • Emilio Lustau (Spain) Almacenista, Manuel Cuevas Jurado, Manzanilla Amontillada, Sanlucar de Barrameda. $19.95.

93 • Alvear (Spain) Solera Fundacion, Amontillado Muy Viejo, Montilla-Moriles. $50.

92 • Valdespino (Spain) Amontillado Coliseo, Jerez de la Frontera. $40.

91 • Antonio Barbadillo (Spain) Principe, Dry Amontillado Sherry, Jerez de la Frontera. $75.

90 • Valdespino (Spain) Amontillado, Jerez de la Frontera. $13.99.

90 • Osborne (Spain) Rare Sherry, Fino-Amontillado La Honda, Jerez de la Frontera. $30.

90 • Osborne (Spain) Dry Amontillado Solera AOS Rare Sherry, Jerez de la Frontera. $35.

90 • Hidalgo (Spain) Napoleon Amontillado, Sanlucar de Barrameda. $11.99.

90 • Emilio Lustau (Spain) Rare Amontillado Solera Reserva Escuadrilla, Jerez de la Frontera. $15.

89 • Valdespino (Spain) Hartley & Gibson's Amontillado, Jerez de la Frontera. $7.99.

89 • Sandeman (Spain) Character, Medium Dry Amontillado, Jerez de la Frontera 4.8% rs. $13.99.

89 • Emilio Lustau (Spain) Amontillado del Puerto, Solera Gran Reserva "San Bartolome", Puerto de Santa Maria. $17.99.

89 • Emilio Lustau (Spain) Almacenista, Alberto Lorento Piaget, Amontillado Fino de Jerez, Jerez de la Frontera. $20.

88 • Emilio Lustau (Spain) Almacenista, Miguel Fontadez Florido, Amontillado de Jerez, Jerez de la Frontera. $20.

87 • Emilio Lustau (Spain) Dry Amontillado Solera Reserva Los Arcos, Jerez de la Frontera. $9.95.

87 • Alvear (Spain) Solera Abuelo Diego, Amontillado, Montilla-Moriles. $14.

86 • Williams & Humbert (Spain) Dry Sack Superior Medium Dry Sherry, Jerez de la Frontera. $13.99.

Palo Cortado Sherry

99 • Osborne (Spain) Rare Palo Cortado, Solera PΔP, Jerez de la Frontera. $35.

98 • Pedro Domecq (Spain) "Sibarita", Very Rare Palo Cortado, Jerez de la Frontera. $73.

92 • Emilio Lustau (Spain) Almacenista Vides, Palo Cortado de Jerez,
Jerez de la Frontera. $20.

92 • Antonio Barbadillo (Spain) Palo Cortado del Obispo Gascon Sherry,
Jerez de la Frontera. $125.

90 • Valdespino (Spain) Cardenal Palo Cortado Sherry, Jerez de la Frontera. $29.

90 • Hidalgo (Spain) Jerez Cortado, Sanlucar de Barrameda. $17.99.

90 • Emilio Lustau (Spain) Almacenista, Rosario Farfante, Dos Cortados de Jerez,
Jerez de la Frontera. $21.95.

88 • Valdespino (Spain) Palo Cortado Sherry del Carrascal, Jerez de la Frontera. $20.

88 • Sandeman (Spain) Royal Ambrosante Rare Palo Cortado, Jerez de la Frontera. $20.

87 • Emilio Lustau (Spain) Almacenista, Vides, Single Cask Palo Cortado,
Jerez de la Frontera. $35.

85 • Emilio Lustau (Spain) Palo Cortado Peninsula, Jerez de la Frontera. $14.95.

Oloroso Sherry

98 • Osborne (Spain) Rare Oloroso Amoroso, Solera Alonso el Sabio,
Jerez de la Frontera 5% rs. $30.

94 • Emilio Lustau (Spain) Very Rare Oloroso Solera, Reserva Emperatriz Eugenia,
Jerez de la Frontera. $23.95.

94 • Emilio Lustau (Spain) Almacenista, Aranda y Latorre Oloroso Anada 1918,
Jerez de la Frontera. $21.99.

93 • Osborne (Spain) Dark Mahogany Olorosa Solera BC 200 Rare Sherry,
Jerez de la Frontera. $35.

93 • Gonzalez Byass (Spain) Apostoles, Rare Old Solera Oloroso Abocado,
Jerez de la Frontera. $40.

93 • Emilio Lustau (Spain) Almacenista, Juan Garcia Jarana, Oloroso Pata de Gallina,
Jerez de la Frontera. $21.95.

92 • Osborne (Spain) Rare Sherry, Oloroso, Solera India, Jerez de la Frontera 6% rs. $30.

91 • Sandeman (Spain) Imperial Corregidor Rarest V.V.O. Oloroso,
Jerez de la Frontera. $25.

90 • Valdespino (Spain) Solera 1842, Oloroso Viejo Dulce, Jerez de la Frontera. $19.

90 • Valdespino (Spain) Don Gonzalo Old Dry Oloroso Sherry, Jerez de la Frontera. $20.

89 • Hidalgo (Spain) Oloroso Especial, Sanlucar de Barrameda. $15.99.

88 • Sandeman (Spain) Royal Corregidor, Very Old Rare Rich Oloroso,
Jerez de la Frontera 14% rs. $24.99.

88 • Harvey's (Spain) 1796 Rare Oloroso Sherry, Jerez de la Frontera. $50.

88 • Antonio Barbadillo (Spain) Very Old Oloroso Sherry, Jerez de la Frontera. $11.99.

86 • Pedro Domecq (Spain) Rio Viejo Rare Dry Oloroso Sherry,
Jerez de la Frontera. $25.

86 • Emilio Lustau (Spain) Almacenista, Dona Pilar Aranda, Single Cask Oloroso,
Jerez de la Frontera. $35.

86 • Alvear (Spain) Solera Abuelo Diego Oloroso, Montilla-Moriles. $14.

85 • Antonio Barbadillo (Spain) Dry Oloroso Sherry, Jerez de la Frontera. $7.99.

Cream Sherry

92 • Sandeman (Spain) Armada, Rich Cream Oloroso,
Jerez de la Frontera 13.5% rs. $11.99.

91 • Emilio Lustau (Spain) Deluxe Cream Solera Reserva Capataz Andres,
Jerez de la Frontera 6.5% rs. $10.95.

90 • Valdespino (Spain) Hartley & Gibson's Cream Sherry, Jerez de la Frontera. $7.99.

89 • Gonzalez Byass (Spain) San Domingo, Pale Cream Sherry,
Jerez de la Frontera. $12.99.

Scale: Superlative (96-100), Exceptional (90-95), Highly Recommended (85-89),
Recommended (80-84), Not Recommended (Under 80)

89 • Emilio Lustau (Spain) Rare Cream Solera Reserva Superior,
Jerez de la Frontera. $14.95.

89 • Emilio Lustau (Spain) East India Solera Sherry, Jerez de la Frontera. $16.95.

88 • Alvear (Spain) Cream, Montilla-Moriles. $7.50.

87 • Gonzalez Byass (Spain) Elegante Cream Sherry, Jerez de la Frontera. $5.99.

87 • Bodegas Robles (Spain) Robles Extra Cream, DO Montilla-Moriles. $7.

86 • Croft (Spain) Original Rare Pale Cream Sherry, Jerez de la Frontera. $10.

Moscatel Sherry

92 • Emilio Lustau (Spain) "Las Cruces", Centenary Selection Moscatel,
Jerez de la Frontera. $19.99.

89 • Antonio Barbadillo (Spain) Pale Sweet Moscatel Sherry, Jerez de la Frontera. $7.99.

88 • Emilio Lustau (Spain) Moscatel Superior Emilin, Jerez de la Frontera. $14.95.

87 • Alvear (Spain) Moscatel, Montilla-Moriles. $7.50.

Pedro Ximenez Sherry

97 • Gonzalez Byass (Spain) NOE, Rare Old Solera Pedro Ximenez,
Jerez de la Frontera. $40.

97 • Alvear (Spain) Pedro Ximenez 1830, Dulce Muy Viejo, Montilla-Moriles. $80.

96 • Osborne (Spain) Rare Pedro Ximenez Viejo, Jerez. $35.

92 • Argueso (Spain) Pedro Ximenez Cream Sherry, Jerez de la Frontera. $17.

92 • Alvear (Spain) Solera Abuelo Diego, Pedro Ximenez, Montilla-Moriles. $14.

90 • Emilio Lustau (Spain) Pedro Ximenez, Solera Reserva San Emilio,
Jerez de la Frontera. $14.95.

89 • Osborne (Spain) Pedro Ximenez, Jerez de la Frontera 37.5% rs. $10.99.

89 • Hidalgo (Spain) Pedro Ximenez Viejo, Sanlucar de Barrameda 16% rs. $16.99.

88 • Bodegas Robles (Spain) Robles Seleccion Pedro Ximenez,
DO Montilla-Moriles. $12.

Highly Rated Porto

Ruby/Vintage Character Porto

88 • Ramos Pinto (Portugal) Quinta da Urtiga, Oporto 3.1% rs. $18.

88 • Fonseca (Portugal) Bin 27 Fine Reserve Porto, Oporto 9.5% rs. $17.99.

86 • Graham's (Portugal) Six Grapes Porto, Oporto. $19.

85 • Cockburn's (Portugal) Special Reserve, Oporto. $9.99.

85 • Churchill's (Portugal) VC Reserve Porto, Oporto. $11.99.

Late Bottled Vintage Porto

89 • Taylor Fladgate (Portugal) 1991 Late Bottled Vintage Porto, Oporto 10% rs. $19.99.

89 • Graham's (Portugal) 1990 Late Bottled Vintage Porto, Oporto. $17.

87 • Quinta do Noval (Portugal) 1989 Late Bottled Vintage Porto, Oporto. $18.99.

87 • Graham's (Portugal) 1991 Late Bottled Vintage Porto, Oporto. $18.

87 • Fonseca (Portugal) 1990 Late Bottled Vintage Porto, Oporto. $17.49.

87 • Croft (Portugal) 1990 Late Bottled Vintage Porto, Oporto. $21.99.

87 • Cockburn's (Portugal) 1992 Late Bottled Vintage Porto, Oporto. $20.

86 • Quinta de Roriz (Portugal) 1988 Late Bottled Vintage Porto, Oporto. $16.99.

86 • Churchill's (Portugal) 1990 Late Bottled Vintage Porto, Oporto. $19.99.

85 • Warre's (Portugal) 1982 Late Bottled Vintage Porto, Oporto. $24.50.

85 • Taylor Fladgate (Portugal) 1990 Late Bottled Vintage Porto, Oporto. $16.49.

Single Quinta Vintage Porto

96 • Symington's (Portugal) 1994 Quinta do Vesuvio Vintage Porto, Oporto. $50.

95 • Symington's (Portugal) 1996 Quinta do Vesuvio Vintage Porto, Oporto. $60.99. Cellar Selection.

93 • Taylor Fladgate (Portugal) 1991 Quinta de Vargellas Vintage Porto, Oporto 7.05% rs. $37.49. Cellar Selection.

93 • Symington's (Portugal) 1992 Quinta do Vesuvio Vintage Porto, Oporto. $38. Cellar Selection.

92 • Warre's (Portugal) 1995 Quinta da Cavadinha Vintage Porto, Oporto. $32.99. Cellar Selection.

92 • Fonseca (Portugal) 1995 Guimaraens Vintage Porto, Oporto. $38.99.

91 • Cockburn's (Portugal) 1995 Quinta dos Canais, Oporto. $38.

90 • Taylor Fladgate (Portugal) 1995 Quinta de Vargellas Vintage Porto, Oporto 7% rs. $38.99.

90 • Symington's (Portugal) 1995 Quinta do Vesuvio Vintage Porto, Oporto. $61.

90 • Graham's (Portugal) 1992 Malvedos Vintage Porto, Oporto. $13.50/375 ml. Cellar Selection.

90 • Delaforce (Portugal) 1995 Quinta da Corte Vintage Porto, Oporto. $40.

89 • Dow's (Portugal) 1992 Quinta do Bomfim Vintage Porto, Oporto. $12/375 ml. Cellar Selection.

89 • Churchill's (Portugal) 1995 Quinta da Agua Alta Single Quinta Vintage Porto, Oporto. $34.99.

88 • Smith Woodhouse (Portugal) 1995 Madalena Vintage Porto, Oporto. $32. Cellar Selection.

88 • Smith Woodhouse (Portugal) 1982 Madalena Vintage Porto, Oporto. $33.99.

88 • Croft (Portugal) 1995 Quinta de Roeda Vintage Porto, Oporto. $40.

88 • Cockburn's (Portugal) 1992 Quinta dos Canais, Oporto. $38.

88 • Churchill's (Portugal) 1992 Quinta da Agua Alta Single Quinta Vintage Porto, Oporto. $24.95. Cellar Selection.

87 • Dow's (Portugal) 1995 Quinta do Bomfim Vintage Porto, Oporto. $38. Cellar Selection.

87 • Delaforce (Portugal) 1991 Quinta da Corte Vintage Porto, Oporto. $34.99. Cellar Selection.

86 • Ramos Pinto (Portugal) 1994 Quinta da Ervamoira Vintage Porto, Oporto. $44.

86 • Quinta do Noval (Portugal) 1995 Quinta de Silval Vintage Porto, Oporto. $40.

86 • Martinez (Portugal) 1995 Single Quinta da Chousa Vintage Porto, Oporto 10.4% rs. $40. Cellar Selection.

86 • Graham's (Portugal) 1995 Malvedos Vintage Porto, Oporto. $43. Cellar Selection.

85 • Churchill's (Portugal) 1990 Quinta da Agua Alta Single Quinta Vintage Porto, Oporto. $26.95.

Vintage Porto

98 • Quinta do Noval (Portugal) 1991 Nacional Vintage Porto, Oporto. $250. Cellar Selection.

98 • Dow's (Portugal) 1994 Vintage Porto, Oporto. $38. Cellar Selection.

96 • Fonseca (Portugal) 1994 Vintage Porto, Oporto. $50.

95 • Graham's (Portugal) 1994 Vintage Porto, Oporto. $46. Cellar Selection.

95 • Graham's (Portugal) 1991 Vintage Porto, Oporto. $49. Cellar Selection.

94 • Warre's (Portugal) 1994 Vintage Porto, Oporto. $40. Cellar Selection.

93 • Quinta do Noval (Portugal) 1995 Vintage Porto, Oporto. $55.

92 • Warre's (Portugal) 1991 Vintage Porto, Oporto. $35. Cellar Selection.

92 • Taylor Fladgate (Portugal) 1994 Vintage Porto, Oporto. $50. Cellar Selection.

92 • Quinta do Noval (Portugal) 1991 Vintage Porto, Oporto. $29.25. Cellar Selection.

92 • Croft (Portugal) 1994 Vintage Porto, Oporto. $59.99.

91 • Smith Woodhouse (Portugal) 1992 Vintage Porto,

Scale: Superlative (96-100), Exceptional (90-95), Highly Recommended (85-89), Recommended (80-84), Not Recommended (Under 80)

Oporto. $12/375 ml. Cellar Selection.

91 • Borges (Portugal) 1994 Vintage Porto, Oporto. $25. Cellar Selection.

91 • Barros (Portugal) 1991 Vintage Porto, Oporto. $20.99. Cellar Selection.

90 • Quinta do Noval (Portugal) 1994 Vintage Porto, Oporto. $35. Cellar Selection.

90 • Dow's (Portugal) 1991 Vintage Porto, Oporto. $45. Cellar Selection.

89 • Smith Woodhouse (Portugal) 1994 Vintage Porto, Oporto. $31.

89 • Cockburn's (Portugal) 1994 Vintage Porto, Oporto. $40. Cellar Selection.

88 • Ramos Pinto (Portugal) 1994 Vintage Porto, Oporto. $50.

88 • Osborne (Portugal) 1994 Vintage Porto, Oporto. $28. Cellar Selection.

87 • Ramos Pinto (Portugal) 1995 Vintage Porto, Oporto. $35. Cellar Selection.

87 • Ramos Pinto (Portugal) 1991 Vintage Porto, Oporto. $35.

87 • Quinta de Roriz (Portugal) 1991 Vintage Porto, Oporto. $32.49. Cellar Selection.

87 • Osborne (Portugal) 1992 Vintage Porto, Oporto 10.02% rs. $22.50. Cellar Selection.

87 • Cockburn's (Portugal) 1991 Vintage Porto, Oporto. $30.

87 • Churchill's (Portugal) 1994 Vintage Porto, Oporto. $39.99. Cellar Selection.

85 • Feist (Portugal) 1991 Vintage Porto, Oporto. $26.

85 • Delaforce (Portugal) 1992 Vintage Porto, Oporto. $35.

85 • Churchill's (Portugal) 1991 Vintage Porto, Oporto. $51.99.

Tawny Porto

88 • Harvey's (Portugal) Fine Tawny, Oporto. $14.99.

86 • Barros (Portugal) Quinta D. Matilde Tawny Porto, Oporto. $13.99.

10 Year Tawny Porto

91 • Graham's (Portugal) 10 Year Old Tawny Porto, Oporto. $27.99.

88 • Rozes (Portugal) Infanta Isabel, 10 Year Old Tawny Porto, Oporto. $25.

87 • Quinta do Noval (Portugal) 10 Year Old Tawny Porto, Oporto. $25.99.

86 • Taylor Fladgate (Portugal) 10 Year Old Tawny Porto, Oporto 10.5% rs. $26.99.

86 • Ramos Pinto (Portugal) Quinta da Ervamoira, 10 Year Old Tawny Porto, Oporto 3.5% rs. $30.

86 • Fonseca (Portugal) 10 Year Old Tawny Porto, Oporto 10.5% rs. $27.99.

86 • Cockburn's (Portugal) 10 Year Old Tawny Porto, Oporto. $25.

85 • Feist (Portugal) 10 Year Old Tawny Porto, Oporto. $18.

20 Year Tawny Porto

96 • Graham's (Portugal) 20 Year Old Tawny Porto, Oporto. $45.99.

94 • Ramos Pinto (Portugal) Quinta do Bom Retiro, 20 Year Old Tawny Porto, Oporto 4% rs. $56.

94 • Dow's (Portugal) 20 Year Old Tawny Porto, Oporto. $44.99.

94 • Delaforce (Portugal) Curious & Ancient 20 Year Old Tawny Porto, Oporto. $40.

92 • Cockburn's (Portugal) Directors' Reserve, 20 Year Old Tawny Porto, Oporto. $45.

91 • Quinta do Noval (Portugal) 20 Year Old Tawny Porto, Oporto. $82.99.

91 • Fonseca (Portugal) 20 Year Old Tawny Porto, Oporto 11.5% rs. $48.99.

90 • Taylor Fladgate (Portugal) 20 Year Old Tawny Porto, Oporto 11.5% rs. $46.99.

90 • Barros (Portugal) 20 Anos Tawny Porto, Oporto. $33.99.

89 • Sandeman (Portugal) 20 Year Old Tawny Porto, Oporto. $34.

89 • Rozes (Portugal) 20 Year Old Tawny Porto, Oporto. $45.

87 • Feist (Portugal) 20 Year Old Tawny Porto, Oporto. $30.

85 • Harvey's (Portugal) Director's Bin, 20 Year Old Tawny Porto, Oporto. $32.50.

30/40 Year Tawny Porto

92 • Rozes (Portugal) Over 40 Years Old, Wood Matured, Oporto. $125.

92 • Feist (Portugal) 30 Year Old Tawny Porto, Oporto. $60.

91 • Feist (Portugal) 40 Year Old Tawny Porto, Oporto. $100.
91 • Dow's (Portugal) 30 Year Old Tawny Porto, Oporto. $75.
90 • Graham's (Portugal) 30 Year Old Tawny Porto, Oporto. $81.

Colheita Porto

95 • Quinta do Noval (Portugal) 1971 Colheita Old Tawny Porto, Oporto. $74.99.
94 • Quinta do Noval (Portugal) 1967 Colheita Old Tawny Porto, Oporto. $88.99.
93 • Quinta do Noval (Portugal) 1976 Colheita Old Tawny Porto, Oporto. $50.49.
93 • Quinta do Noval (Portugal) 1966 Colheita Old Tawny Porto, Oporto. $98.49.
93 • Feist (Portugal) 1967 Colheita, Oporto. $63.
92 • Quinta do Noval (Portugal) 1968 Colheita Old Tawny Porto, Oporto. $83.49.
92 • Feist (Portugal) 1963 Colheita, Oporto. $76.
90 • Feist (Portugal) 1965 Colheita, Oporto. $72.
89 • Feist (Portugal) 1957 Colheita, Oporto. $106.
88 • Quinta do Noval (Portugal) 1982 Colheita Old Tawny Porto, Oporto. $28.49.
88 • Feist (Portugal) 1966 Colheita, Oporto. $70.
87 • Feist (Portugal) 1974 Colheita, Oporto. $38.
86 • Warre's (Portugal) 1976 Reserve Tawny, Oporto. $46.99.
86 • Quinta do Noval (Portugal) 1984 Colheita Old Tawny Porto, Oporto. $23.75.
86 • Dow's (Portugal) 1982 Single Year Tawny Reserve, Oporto. $29.

Highly Rated Madeira

Sercial Madeira

96 • Henriques & Henriques (Portugal) 10 Year Old Sercial, Madeira 5.8% rs. $29.95.
90 • Henriques & Henriques (Portugal) 5 Year Old Sercial, Madeira 5.2% rs. $17.49.
86 • Leacock's (Portugal) 5 Year Old Sercial, Madeira. $17.99.
86 • Blandy's (Portugal) 5 Year Old Sercial, Madeira. $19.

Verdelho Madeira

91 • Henriques & Henriques (Portugal) 10 Year Old Verdelho, Madeira 8.2% rs. $29.95.
89 • Henriques & Henriques (Portugal) 5 Year Old Verdelho, Madeira 7.5% rs. $17.49.
85 • Blandy's (Portugal) 5 Year Old Verdelho, Madeira. $19.

Bual Madeira

92 • Henriques & Henriques (Portugal) 10 Year Old Bual, Madeira 9.2% rs. $29.95.
92 • Cossart Gordon (Portugal) 15 Year Old Bual, Madeira. $44.
88 • Cossart Gordon (Portugal) 5 Year Old Bual, Madeira. $20.
87 • Leacock's (Portugal) 10 Year Old Bual , Madeira. $32.99.
87 • Cossart Gordon (Portugal) 10 Year Old Bual, Madeira. $32.99.
85 • Henriques & Henriques (Portugal) 5 Year Old Bual, Madeira 9% rs. $17.49.

Malmsey Madeira

94 • Blandy's (Portugal) 15 Year Old Malmsey, Madeira. $42.99.
90 • Leacock's (Portugal) 5 Year Old Malmsey, Madeira. $17.99.
89 • Cossart Gordon (Portugal) 10 Year Old Malmsey, Madeira. $32.
88 • Blandy's (Portugal) 10 Year Old Malmsey, Madeira. $32.99.
85 • Henriques & Henriques (Portugal) 10 Year Old Malmsey, Madeira 12.4% rs. $29.95.
85 • Cossart Gordon (Portugal) 5 Year Old Malmsey, Madeira. $20.

Highly Rated US Port-Style Wine

Port-Style Wine

93 • Quady (CA) 1990 Vintage Starboard, Amador County 10.6% rs. $21.50.

92 • Cedar Mountain (CA) 1996 Vintage Port, Amador County 10% rs. $19.50.

91 • Quady (CA) 1993 LBV Port, Amador County 8.18% rs. $12. Best Buy.

91 • Ficklin (CA) 1988 Vintage Port, California 9% rs. $25.

90 • Whidbey (WA) 1990 Port, Washington 9.8% rs. $12.99.
Cellar Selection and Best Buy.

90 • Quady (CA) 1989 Frank's Vineyard Vintage Starboard, California 10.4% rs. $19.

89 • Twin Hills (CA) Zinfandel Port, Lot XCII, Paso Robles 5% rs. $25.

89 • Quady (CA) Batch 88 Starboard, California 11.1% rs. $11.50. Best Buy.

89 • Quady (CA) 1990 Frank's Vineyard Vintage Starboard, California 10.2% rs. $19.
Cellar Selection.

89 • Pindar (NY) 1995 Port, North Fork of Long Island. $24.99.

88 • Trentadue (CA) 1994 Petite Sirah Port, Alexander Valley 8.6% rs. $20.
Cellar Selection.

88 • Prager Winery & Port Works (CA) 1993 Royal Escort LBV Port, Petite Sirah,
Napa Valley 5.5% rs. $38.50.

88 • Beringer (CA) 1994 Port of Cabernet Sauvignon, Napa Valley 10.29% rs. $20.

87 • Guenoc (CA) 1994 Vintage Port, California 9.7% rs. $25. Cellar Selection.

87 • Geyser Peak (CA) 1995 Henry's Reserve Shiraz Port, Alexander Valley. $15/375 ml.

87 • Duck Walk (NY) 1996 Blueberry Port 10% rs. $12.95/375 ml.

86 • Sonora Winery & Port Works (CA) 1994 Vintage Port, Sierra Foothills 8.5% rs.
$16/500 ml. Cellar Selection.

86 • Mount Pleasant (MI) 1996 White Port, Augusta Missouri 10.5% rs. $25/375 ml.

86 • Mount Pleasant (MI) 1990 Port, Augusta, Missouri 11.1% rs. $18.

86 • Meier's (OH) No. 44 American Ruby Port 8.3% rs. $6.95. Best Buy.

86 • Lonz (OH) 3 Islands American Ruby Port 9.9% rs. $6.50. Best Buy.

86 • Justin (CA) 1996 Obtuse, Paso Robles 15% rs. $22.50.

86 • Ficklin (CA) Tinta Port, California 8.5% rs. $12. Best Buy.

85 • Windsor (CA) Rare Port, California 11.9% rs. $13.

85 • St. Amant (CA) 1995 Vintage Port, Amador County 7% rs. $28. Cellar Selection.

85 • Mount Pleasant (MO) JRL's Barrel Select Port, Augusta 6.75% rs. $11.95. Best Buy.

84 • Trentadue (CA) 1994 Merlot Port, Alexander Valley 9.7% rs. $20.

84 • Renwood (CA) 1994 Vintage Port, Shenandoah Valley 6.5% rs. $21.95/500 ml.

84 • Pesenti (CA) 1997 Zinfandel Port, Second Estate Reserve, Paso Robles 7% rs.
$20/500 ml.

84 • Horton (VA) 1995 Vintage Port, Orange County 6% rs. $20.

83 • Yakima River (WA) 1995 Johns Vintage Port, Yakima Valley 6% rs. $16.

83 • Stone Hill (MO) 1994 Estate Bottled Port, Hermann 8% rs. $23.99.

83 • Heitz (CA) 1996 Grignlino Port, Napa Valley 12.5% rs. $18.

83 • Chateau Elan (GA) Georgian-Style Port, American 7.9% rs. $22.

82 • Rosenblum (CA) 1994 Port, California 9.35% rs. $10/375 ml.

82 • Paul Masson (CA) Rich Ruby Port, California 10.2% rs. $5.99. Best Buy.

82 • Goose Watch (NY) 1997 Finale White Port, Finger Lakes 5% rs. $16.50/375 ml.

82 • Firestone (CA) 1995 Port, Santa Ynez Valley 9.5% rs. $20. Cellar Selection.

82 • Fetzer (CA) 1993 Port, Mendocino County 9.36% rs. $18.99.

81 • St. Julian (MI) Catherman's Port, Michigan 16% rs. $12.

80 • Willamette Valley Vineyards (OR) 1994 Quinta Reserva, Pinot Noir Port,
Oregon 8% rs. $18.

80 • Sonora Winery & Port Works (CA) 1992 Vintage Port, Sierra Foothills 8.5% rs. $15.99/500 ml.

80 • Pugliese (NY) Port Bello, North Fork of Long Island. $26.99.

80 • Pine Ridge (CA) 1993 Black Diamond Port, Napa Valley 2.78% rs. $16/375 ml.

80 • J. Filippi (CA) Fondante Ciello, Chocolate Port, California 10% rs. $18/500 ml.

NR • Taylor (NY) Port, New York. $7/500 ml.

NR • Pugliese (NY) Rafaello White Port, North Fork of Long Island. $14.99/375 ml.

NR • Widmer (NY) Port, New York. $5.

Tawny Port-Style Wine

92 • Ficklin (CA) 10 Year Old Tawny Port, California 9.5% rs. $22.

89 • Prager Winery & Port Works (CA) Noble Companion 10 Year Old Tawny Port, Napa Valley 8.4% rs. $45.

88 • Mount Pleasant (MO) 15 Barrel Tawny Port, Augusta 8.5% rs. $23.50.

85 • Mount Pleasant (MI) Tawny Port, Library Vol. V, Augusta Missouri 10.9% rs. $28.

83 • Orfila (CA) Tawny Port, California 10% rs. $14.98/500 ml.

NR • Mount Pleasant (MO) 8 Barrel Tawny Port, Augusta 7% rs. $23.42.

NR • Taylor (NY) Tawny Port, New York. $3.99.

Highly Rated Australian Port-Style Wine

Tawny Port-Style Wine

98 • Penfolds (Australia) Grandfather, Finest Tawny Port, Barossa Valley. $60.

93 • Seppelt (Australia) Para Port Tawny, Australia. $24.99.

93 • Chateau Reynella (Australia) Old Cave Fine Tawny Port, McLaren Vale. $18.99.

91 • Seppelt (Australia) Trafford Tawny Port, Barossa Valley. $11.

90 • Yalumba (Australia) Galway Pipe Tawny Port, Australia. $22.99.

89 • Queen Adelaide (Australia) Woodley Tawny Port, South Australia. $8.

88 • Hardys (Australia) Whiskers Blake Tawny Port, Australia. $14.

86 • Yalumba (Australia) Clocktower Tawny Port, Australia. $9.99.

86 • Penfolds (Australia) Club Port, Reserve, South Australia. $11.

85 • Marienberg (Australia) 12 Year Old Tawny Port, Australia. $13.

85 • Benjamin (Australia) Tawny Port, Australia 17% rs. $12.99.

Vintage Port-Style Wine

86 • Chateau Reynella (Australia) 1992 Vintage Port, McLaren Vale. $12. Cellar Selection.

Brand Index and
Bibliography

Brand Index

Bibliography

Amis, Kingsley. 1973. *Kingsley Amis On Drink.* New York: Harcourt Brace Jovanovich.

Begg, Desmond. 1998. *The Vodka Companion.* Philadelphia: Running Press.

Bradford, Sarah. 1978. *The Story of Port.* London: Christie's Wine Publications.

Brown, Gordon. 1990. *The Handbook of Fine Brandies.* New York: Macmillan.

Carr, Jess. 1972. *Second Oldest Profession: An Informal History of Moonshining in America.* Englewood Cliffs, NJ: Prentice-Hall.London: Andre Deutsch.

Cooper, Rosalind. 1982. *Spirits & Liqueurs.* Tucson, AZ: HPBooks.

Cossart, Noel. 1984. *Madeira: The Island Vineyard.* London: Christie's Wine Publications.

Crowgey, Henry G. 1971. *Kentucky Bourbon - The Early Years of Whiskeymaking.* Lexington: University Press of Kentucky.

Dabney, Joseph Earl. 1974. *Mountain Spirits.* Asheville, NC: Bright Mountain Books.

———. 1980. *More Mountain Spirits.* Asheville, NC: Bright Mountain Books.

Emmons, Bob. 1997. *The Book of Tequila.* Chicago: Open Court Publishing.

Faith, Nicholas. 1987. *Cognac.* Boston: David R. Godine.

Ford, Gene. 1983. *Ford's Illustrated Guide to Wines, Brews & Spirits.* Dubuque: Wm. C. Brown Publishers.

Getz, Oscar. 1978. *Whiskey, An American Pictorial History.* New York: David McKay.

Green, Ben A. 1967. *Jack Daniel's Legacy.* Shelbyville, TN: Ben A. Green.

Greenberg, Emanuel and Madeline. 1983. *The Pocket Guide to Spirits & Liqueurs.* New York: Perigee Books.

Gunn, Neil M. 1988. *Whisky & Scotland.* London: Souvenir Press.

Hamilton, Edward. 1997. *The Complete Guide to Rum.* Chicago: Triumph Books.

Jackson, Michael. 1989. *Michael Jackson's Malt Whisky Companion.* London: Dorling Kindersley.

———. 1988. *The World Guide to Whisky.* Topsfield, MA: Salem House.

Jefford, Andrew. 1988. *Port: An Essential Guide to the Classic Drink.* New York: Exeter Books.

Jeffs, Julian. 1992. *Sherry.* London: Faber and Faber.

Lembeck, Harriet. 1983. *Grossman's Guide to Wines, Beers, and Spirits.* New York: Scribner's.

Liddell, Alex. 1998. *Madeira.* Faber and London: Faber.

Lockhart, Sir Robert Bruce. 1970. *Scotch: The Whiskey of Scotland in Fact and Story.* London: Putnam & Co.

MacLean, Charles. 1993. *The Mitchell Beazley Pocket Whisky Book.* London: Reed Consumer Books.

Magee, Malachy. 1980. *Irish Whiskey: A 1000 Year Tradition.* Dublin: O'Brien Press.

McDowall, R. J. S. 1967. *Whiskies of Scotland.* New York: Abelard Schuman.

Milroy, Wallace. 1997. *The Malt Whisky Almanac.* Moffat: Interlink Publishing.

Morrice, Philip. 1979. *The Schwepps Guide to Scotch.* Sherborne: Alphabooks.

Murphy, Brian. 1979. *The World Book of Whiskey.* Chicago: Rand McNally.

Murray, Jim. 1994. *Jim Murray's Irish Whiskey Almanac.* Glasgow: Neil Wilson Publishing.

Pacult, F. Paul. 1997. *Kindred Spirits.* New York: Hyperion.

Pla, Rosa and Tapia, Jesús. 1990. *El Agave Azul de las mieles al tequila.* Ciudad Mexico: CEMCA.

Reed, Jan. 1988. *Sherry and the Sherry Bodegas.* London: Sotheby's Publications.

Regan, Gary and Mardee Haidan. 1995. *The Book of Bourbon.* Shelburne: Vermont Publishing.

Regan, Gary and Mardee Haidin. 1998. *Bourbon Companion: A Connoisseur's Guide.* Philadelphia: Running Press.

Spence, Godfrey. 1997. *Port Companion: A Connoisseur's Guide.* New York: Macmillan General Reference.

Voss, Roger. 1989. *The Simon & Schuster Pocket Guide to Fortified and Dessert Wine.* New York: Simon & Schuster.

Walker, Alice and Larry. 1994. *Tequila: The Book.* San Francisco: Chronicle Books.

Wasserman, Pauline and Sheldon. 1983. *Guide to Fortified Wines.* Morganville, NJ: Marlborough Press.